Modern Actuarial Risk Theory

Modern Actuarial Risk Theory

by

Rob Kaas
University of Amsterdam, The Netherlands

Marc Goovaerts
Catholic University of Leuven, Belgium and University of Amsterdam, The Netherlands

Jan Dhaene
Catholic University of Leuven, Belgium and University of Amsterdam, The Netherlands

and

Michel Denuit
Université Catholique de Louvain, Belgium

KLUWER ACADEMIC PUBLISHERS
BOSTON / DORDRECHT / LONDON

A C.I.P. Catalogue record for this book is available from the Library of Congress.

ISBN 0-7923-7636-6

Published by Kluwer Academic Publishers,
P.O. Box 17, 3300 AA Dordrecht, The Netherlands.

Sold and distributed in North, Central and South America
by Kluwer Academic Publishers,
101 Philip Drive, Norwell, MA 02061, U.S.A.

In all other countries, sold and distributed
by Kluwer Academic Publishers,
P.O. Box 322, 3300 AH Dordrecht, The Netherlands.

Printed on acid-free paper

Printed in the Netherlands

Foreword

Risk Theory has been identified and recognized as an important part of actuarial education; this is for example documented by the Syllabus of the *Society of Actuaries* and by the recommendations of the *Groupe Consultatif.* Hence it is desirable to have a diversity of textbooks in this area.

I welcome the arrival of this new text in risk theory, which is original in several respects. In the language of figure skating or gymnastics, the text has two parts, the compulsory part and the free-style part. The compulsory part includes Chapters 1–4, which are compatible with official material of the Society of Actuaries. This feature makes the text also useful to students who prepare themselves for the actuarial exams. Other chapters are more of a free-style nature, for example Chapter 10 (*Ordering of Risks*, a speciality of the authors). And I would like to mention Chapter 8 in particular: to my knowledge, this is the first text in risk theory with an introduction to *Generalized Linear Models*.

Special pedagogical efforts have been made throughout the book. The clear language and the numerous exercises are an example for this. Thus the book can be highly recommended as a textbook.

I congratulate the authors to their text, and I would like to thank them also in the name of students and teachers that they undertook the effort to translate their text into English. I am sure that the text will be successfully used in many classrooms.

H.U. Gerber Lausanne

Preface

This book gives a comprehensive survey of non-life insurance mathematics. It was originally written for use with the actuarial science programs at the Universities of Amsterdam and Leuven, but its Dutch version has been used at several other universities, as well as by the Dutch Actuarial Society. It provides a link to the further theoretical study of actuarial science. The methods presented can not only be used in non-life insurance, but are also effective in other branches of actuarial science, as well as, of course, in actuarial practice.

Apart from the standard theory, this text contains methods that are directly relevant for actuarial practice, for instance the rating of automobile insurance policies, premium principles and IBNR models. Also, the important actuarial statistical tool of the Generalized Linear Models is presented. These models provide extra features beyond ordinary linear models and regression which are the statistical tools of choice for econometricians. Furthermore, a short introduction is given to credibility theory. Another topic which always has enjoyed the attention of risk theoreticians is the study of ordering of risks.

The book reflects the state of the art in actuarial risk theory. Quite a lot of the results presented were published in the actuarial literature only in the last decade of the previous century.

Models and paradigms studied

An essential element of the models of life insurance is the time aspect. Between paying premiums and collecting the resulting pension, some decennia generally elapse. This time-element is less prominently present in non-life insurance mathematics. Here, however, the statistical models are generally more involved. The topics in the first five chapters of this textbook are basic for non-life actuarial science. The remaining chapters contain short introductions to some other topics traditionally regarded as non-life actuarial science.

1. *The expected utility model*
The very existence of insurers can be explained by way of the expected utility model. In this model, an insured is a risk averse and rational decision maker, who by virtue of Jensen's inequality is ready to pay more than the expected value of his claims just to be in a secure financial position. The mechanism through which decisions are taken under uncertainty is not by direct comparison of the expected payoffs of decisions, but rather of the expected utilities associated with these payoffs.

2. *The individual risk model*
In the individual risk model, as well as in the collective risk model that follows below, the total claims on a portfolio of insurance contracts is the random variable of interest. We want to compute, for instance, the probability that a certain capital will be sufficient to pay these claims, or the value-at-risk at level 95% associated with the portfolio, being the 95% quantile of its cumulative distribution function (cdf). The total claims is modelled as the sum of all claims on the policies, which are assumed independent. Such claims cannot always be modelled as purely discrete random variables, nor as purely continuous ones, and we provide a notation that encompasses both these as special cases. The individual model, though the most realistic possible, is not always very convenient, because the available data is used integrally and not in any way condensed. We study other techniques than convolution to obtain results in this model. Using transforms like the moment generating function helps in some special cases. Also, we present approximations based on fitting moments of the distribution. The Central Limit Theorem, which involves fitting two moments, is not sufficiently accurate in the important right-hand tail of the distribution. Hence, we also look at two more refined methods using three moments: the translated gamma approximation and the normal power approximation.

3. *Collective risk models*
A model that is often used to approximate the individual model is the collective risk model. In this model, an insurance portfolio is viewed as a process that produces claims over time. The sizes of these claims are taken to be independent, identically distributed random variables, independent also of the number of claims generated.

This makes the total claims the sum of a random number of iid individual claim amounts. Usually one assumes additionally that the number of claims is a Poisson variate with the right mean. For the cdf of the individual claims, one takes an average of the cdf's of the individual policies. This leads to a close fitting and computationally tractable model. Several techniques, including Panjer's recursion formula, to compute the cdf of the total claims modelled this way are presented.

4. *The ruin model*
In the ruin model the stability of an insurer is studied. Starting from capital u at time $t = 0$, his capital is assumed to increase linearly in time by fixed annual premiums, but it decreases with a jump whenever a claim occurs. Ruin occurs when the capital is negative at some point in time. The probability that this ever happens, under the assumption that the annual premium as well as the claim generating process remain unchanged, is a good indication of whether the insurer's assets are matched to his liabilities sufficiently well. If not, one may take out more reinsurance, raise the premiums or increase the initial capital.

Analytical methods to compute ruin probabilities exist only for claims distributions that are mixtures and combinations of exponential distributions. Algorithms exist for discrete distributions with not too many mass points. Also, tight upper and lower bounds can be derived. Instead of looking at the ruin probability, often one just considers an upper bound for it with a simple exponential structure (Lundberg).

5. *Premium principles*
Assuming that the cdf of a risk is known, or at least some characteristics of it like mean and variance, a premium principle assigns to the risk a real number used as a financial compensation for the one who takes over this risk. Note that we study only risk premiums, disregarding surcharges for costs incurred by the insurance company. By the law of large numbers, to avoid eventual ruin the total premium should be at least equal to the expected total claims, but additionally, there has to be a loading in the premium to compensate the insurer for being in a less safe position. From this loading, the insurer has to build a reservoir to draw upon in adverse times, so as to avoid getting in ruin. We present a number of premium principles, together with the most important properties that can be attributed to premium principles. The choice of a premium principle depends heavily on the importance attached to such properties. There is no premium principle which is uniformly best.

6. *Bonus-malus systems*
With some types of insurance, notably car insurance, charging a premium based exclusively on factors known a priori is insufficient. To incorporate the effect of risk factors of which the use as rating factors is inappropriate, such as race or quite

often sex of the policy holder, and also of non-observable factors, such as state of health, reflexes and accident proneness, many countries apply an experience rating system. Such systems on the one hand use premiums based on a priori factors such as type of coverage and catalogue price or weight of a car, on the other hand they adjust these premiums by use of some kind of bonus-malus system, where one gets more discount after a claim-free year, but pays a higher premium after filing one or more claims. In this way, premiums are charged that reflect the exact driving capabilities of the driver better. The situation can be modelled as a Markov chain.

7. *Credibility theory*
The claims experience on a policy may vary by two different causes. The first is the quality of the risk, expressed through a risk parameter. This represents the average annual claims in the hypothetical situation that the policy is monitored without change over a very long period of time. The other is the purely random good and bad luck of the policyholder that results in yearly deviations from the risk parameter. Credibility theory assumes that the risk quality is a drawing from a certain structure distribution, and that conditionally given the risk quality, the actual claims experience is a sample from a distribution having the risk quality as its mean value. The predictor for next year's experience that is linear in the claims experience and optimal in the sense of least squares turns out to be a weighted average of the claims experience of the individual contract and the experience for the whole portfolio. The weight factor is the credibility attached to the individual experience, hence it is called the credibility factor, and the resulting premiums are called credibility premiums. As a special case, we study a bonus-malus system for car insurance based on a gamma-Poisson mixture model.

8. *Generalized linear models*
Many problems in actuarial statistics can be written as Generalized Linear Models (GLM). Instead of assuming the error term to be normally distributed, other types of randomness are allowed as well, such as Poisson, gamma and binomial. Moreover, the expected value of the dependent variable is not necessarily linear in the regressors, but it may also be equal to a function of a linear form of the covariates, for instance the logarithm. In this last case, one gets the multiplicative models which are appropriate in most insurance situations.

This way, one can for instance tackle the problem of estimating the reserve to be kept for IBNR claims, see below. But one can also easily estimate the premiums to be charged for drivers from region i in bonus class j with car weight w.

In credibility models, there are random group effects, but in GLM's the effects are fixed, though unknown. For the latter class of problems, software is available that can handle a multitude of models.

9. *IBNR techniques*
An important statistical problem for the practicing actuary is the forecasting of the total of the claims that are Incurred, But Not Reported, hence the acronym IBNR, or not fully settled. Most techniques to determine estimates for this total are based on so-called run-off triangles, in which claim totals are grouped by year of origin and development year. Many traditional actuarial reserving methods turn out to be maximum likelihood estimations in special cases of GLM's.

10. *Ordering of risks*
It is the very essence of the actuary's profession to be able to express preferences between random future gains or losses. Therefore, stochastic ordering is a vital part of his education and of his toolbox. Sometimes it happens that for two losses X and Y, it is known that every sensible decision maker prefers losing X, because Y is in a sense 'larger' than X. It may also happen that only the smaller group of all risk averse decision makers agree about which risk to prefer. In this case, risk Y may be larger than X, or merely more 'spread', which also makes a risk less attractive. When we interpret 'more spread' as having thicker tails of the cumulative distribution function, we get a method of ordering risks that has many appealing properties. For instance, the preferred loss also outdoes the other one as regards zero utility premiums, ruin probabilities, and stop-loss premiums for compound distributions with these risks as individual terms. It can be shown that the collective model of Chapter 3 is more spread than the individual model it approximates, hence using the collective model, as a rule, leads to more conservative decisions regarding premiums to be asked, reserves to be held, and values-at-risk. Also, we can prove that the stop-loss insurance, proven optimal as regards the variance of the retained risk in Chapter 1, is also preferable, other things being equal, in the eyes of all risk averse decision makers.

Sometimes, stop-loss premiums have to be set under incomplete information. We give a method to compute the maximal possible stop-loss premium assuming that the mean, the variance and an upper bound for a risk are known.

In the individual and the collective model, as well as in ruin models, we assume that the claim sizes are stochastically independent non-negative random variables. Sometimes this assumption is not fulfilled, for instance there is an obvious dependence between the mortality risks of a married couple, between the earthquake risks of neighboring houses, and between consecutive payments resulting from a life insurance policy, not only if the payments stop or start in case of death, but also in case of a random force of interest. We give a short introduction to the risk ordering that applies for this case. It turns out that stop-loss premiums for a sum of random variables with an unknown joint distribution but fixed marginals are maximal if these variables are as dependent as the marginal distributions allow, making it impossible that the outcome of one is 'hedged' by another.

Educational aspects

As this text has been in use for more than a decade at the University of Amsterdam and elsewhere, we could draw upon a long series of exams, resulting in long lists of exercises. Also, many examples are given, making this book well-suited as a textbook. Some less elementary exercises have been marked by [♠] , and these might be skipped.

The required mathematical background is on a level such as acquired in the first stage of a bachelors program in quantitative economics (econometrics or actuarial science), or mathematical statistics, making it possible to use the book either in the final year of such a bachelors program, or in a subsequent masters program in either actuarial science proper or in quantitative financial economics with a strong insurance component. To make the book accessible to non-actuaries, notation and jargon from life insurance mathematics is avoided. Therefore also students in applied mathematics or statistics with an interest in the stochastic aspects of insurance will be able to study from this book. To give an idea of the mathematical rigor and statistical sophistication at which we aimed, let us remark that moment generating functions are used routinely, while characteristic functions and measure theory are avoided. Prior experience with regression models is not required, but helpful.

As a service to the student help is offered, in a separate section at the end of the book, with most of the exercises. It takes the form of either a final answer to check one's work, or a useful hint. There is an extensive index, and the tables that might be needed on an exam are printed in the back. The list of references is not a thorough justification with bibliographical data on every result used, but more a list of useful books and papers containing more details on the topics studied, and suggesting further reading.

Ample attention is given to computing techniques, but there is also attention for old fashioned approximation methods like the Central Limit Theorem (CLT). These methods are not only fast, but also often prove to be surprisingly accurate, and moreover they provide solutions of a parametric nature such that one does not have to recalculate everything after a minor change in the data. Also, we want to stress that 'exact' methods are as exact as their input. The order of magnitude of errors resulting from inaccurate input is often much greater than the one caused by using an approximate method.

The notation used in this book conforms to what is usual in mathematical statistics as well as non-life insurance mathematics. See for instance the book by Bowers et al. (1986), the non-life part of which is similar in design to the first part of this book.

About this translation
This book is a translation of the Dutch book that has been in use on several universities in The Netherlands and Belgium for more than ten years. Apart from a few corrections and the addition of a section on convex order and comonotonic risks which have gotten in vogue only in the short period since the second edition of the Dutch version appeared, it has remained largely the same, except that the Dutch and Belgian bonus-malus systems of Chapter 6 were replaced by a generic bonus-malus system.

Acknowledgements
First and most of all, the authors would like to thank David Vyncke for the excellent way he translated this text simultaneously into English and into TeX. He also produced the figures.

In the past, many have helped in making this book as it is. Earlier versions, and this one as well, have been scrutinized by our former students, now colleagues, Angela van Heerwaarden and Dennis Dannenburg. Working on their Ph.D.'s, they co-authored books that were freely used in this text. We also thank Richard Verrall and Klaus Schmidt for their comments. We also acknowledge the numerous comments of the users, students and teachers alike.

In this second printing, we corrected some errors that were found in the first. We thank Bjørn Sundt, Vsevolod Malinovskii as well as Ruud Koning for their contributions.

World wide web support
The authors would like to keep in touch with the users of this text. On the internet page *http://www.fee.uva.nl/ke/act/people/kaas/ModernART.htm* we maintain a list of all typos that have been found so far, and indicate how teachers may obtain solutions to the exercises and other help.

R. Kaas
M.J. Goovaerts
J. Dhaene
M. Denuit

Amsterdam, Leuven, Louvain-la-Neuve
July 9, 2002

Contents

1

Utility theory and insurance

1.1 INTRODUCTION

The insurance industry exists because people are willing to pay a price for being insured which is higher than their expected claims. As a result, an insurer collects a premium that is larger than the expected claim size. In this chapter, we sketch an economic theory that explains why insureds are willing to pay a premium that is larger than the *net premium*, i.e., the mathematical expectation of the insured loss. The theory that explains this phenomenon postulates that a decision maker, generally without being aware of it, attaches a value $u(w)$ to his wealth w instead of just w, where $u(\cdot)$ is called his *utility function*. If the decision maker has to choose between random losses X and Y, then he compares $\mathrm{E}[u(w-X)]$ with $\mathrm{E}[u(w-Y)]$ and chooses the loss with the highest expected utility. With this model, the insured with wealth w is able to determine the maximum premium P^+ he is prepared to pay for a random loss X. This is done by solving the equilibrium equation $\mathrm{E}[u(w-X)] = u(w-P)$. At the equilibrium, he doesn't care, in terms of utility, whether he is insured or not. The model applies to the other party involved as well. The insurer, with his own utility function and perhaps supplementary expenses, will determine a minimum premium P^-. If the insured's maximum premium P^+

is larger than the insurer's minimum premium P^-, both parties involved increase their utility if the premium is between P^- and P^+.

Although it is impossible to determine a person's utility function exactly, we can give some plausible properties of it. For instance, more wealth generally implies a larger utility level, so $u(w)$ should be a non-decreasing function. It is also logical that 'reasonable' decision makers are *risk averse*, which means that they prefer a fixed loss over a random loss that has the same expected value. We will define some classes of utility functions which possess these properties and study their advantages and disadvantages.

Suppose that an insured can choose between an insurance policy with a fixed deductible and another policy with the same expected payment by the insurer and with the same premium. It can be shown that it is better for the insured to choose the former policy. If a reinsurer is insuring the total claim amount of an insurer's portfolio of risks, then the insurance with a fixed maximal own risk is called a *stop-loss* reinsurance. From the theory of ordering of risks, we will see that this type of reinsurance is optimal for risk averse decision makers. In this chapter, we will prove that a stop-loss reinsurance results in the smallest variance of the retained risk. We will also discuss a situation where the insurer prefers a *proportional* reinsurance, with a reinsurance payment proportional to the claim amount.

1.2 THE EXPECTED UTILITY MODEL

Imagine that an individual runs the risk of losing an amount B with probability 0.01. He can insure himself against this loss, and is willing to pay a premium P for this insurance policy. How are B and P related? If B is very small, then P will be hardly larger than $0.01B$. However, if B is somewhat larger, say 500, then P will be a little larger than 5. If B is very large, P will be a lot larger than $0.01B$, since this loss could result in bankruptcy. So clearly, the premium for a risk is not *homogeneous*, i.e., not proportional to the risk.

Example 1.2.1 (St. Petersburg paradox)
For a price P, one may enter the following game. A fair coin is tossed until a head appears. If this takes n trials, the gain is an amount 2^n. Therefore, the expected gain from the game equals $\sum_{n=1}^{\infty} 2^n(\frac{1}{2})^n = \infty$. Still, unless P is small, it turns out that very few are willing to enter the game, which means no one merely looks at expected profits. ∇

In economics, the model developed by Von Neumann & Morgenstern (1947) describes how decision makers choose between uncertain prospects. If a decision maker is able to choose consistently between potential random losses X, then there exists a utility function $u(\cdot)$ to appraise the wealth w such that the decisions he makes are exactly the same as those resulting from comparing the losses X based on the expectation $\mathrm{E}[u(w-X)]$. In this way, a complex decision is reduced to the comparison of real numbers.

For the comparison of X with Y, the utility function $u(x)$ and its linear transform $a\,u(x)+b$ for some $a>0$ are equivalent, since they result in the same decision:

$$\begin{aligned} &\mathrm{E}[u(w-X)] \le \mathrm{E}[u(w-Y)] \qquad \text{if and only if} \\ &\mathrm{E}[a\,u(w-X)+b] \le \mathrm{E}[a\,u(w-Y)+b]. \end{aligned} \tag{1.1}$$

So from each class of equivalent utility functions, we can select one, for instance by requiring that $u(0)=0$ and $u(1)=1$. Assuming $u'(0)>0$, we could also use the utility function $v(\cdot)$ with $v(0)=0$ and $v'(0)=1$:

$$v(x)=\frac{u(x)-u(0)}{u'(0)}. \tag{1.2}$$

It is impossible to determine which utility functions are used 'in practice'. Utility theory merely states the existence of a utility function. We could try to reconstruct a decision maker's utility function from the decisions he takes, by confronting him with a large number of questions like: "Which premium P are you willing to pay to avoid a loss 1 that could occur with probability q"? Then, with $u(0)=0$, $u(-1)=-1$ and initial wealth 0, we find out for which value of P we have

$$u(-P)=(1-q)u(0)+q\,u(-1)=-q. \tag{1.3}$$

In practice, we would soon experience the limitations of utility theory: the decision maker will grow increasingly irritated as the interrogation continues and his decisions will become inconsistent, for instance because he asks a larger premium for a smaller risk or a totally different premium for nearly the same risk. Mistakes of this kind are inevitable, unless the decision maker is explicitly using a utility function.

Example 1.2.2 (Risk loving versus risk averse)
Suppose that a person owns a capital w and that he values his wealth by the utility function $u(\cdot)$. He is given the choice of losing the amount b with probability $\frac{1}{2}$ or

just paying a fixed amount $\frac{1}{2}b$. He chooses the former if $b = 1$, the latter if $b = 4$, and if $b = 2$ he doesn't care. Apparently the person likes a little gamble, but he's afraid of a larger one, like someone with a fire insurance policy who takes part in a lottery. What can be said about the utility function $u(\cdot)$?

The value of w is irrelevant in this case: we can choose $w = 0$ by switching to a utility function shifted over a distance w. Furthermore, we assume that $u(0) = 0$ and $u(-1) = -1$. The decision maker is indifferent between a loss 2 with probability $\frac{1}{2}$ and a fixed loss 1 ($b = 2$). This implies that

$$u(-1) = \frac{1}{2}\{u(0) + u(-2)\}. \tag{1.4}$$

For $b = 1$ and $b = 4$, we have apparently

$$u(-\frac{1}{2}) < \frac{1}{2}\{u(0) + u(-1)\} \quad \text{and} \quad u(-2) > \frac{1}{2}\{u(0) + u(-4)\}. \tag{1.5}$$

Because of these inequalities, the function $u(\cdot)$ is neither convex, nor concave. Note that we use the term convex function for what is currently known as a function which is 'concave up', and concave for 'concave down'.

Since $u(0) = 0$ and $u(-1) = -1$, (1.4) and (1.5) yield

$$u(-2) = -2, \quad u(-\frac{1}{2}) < -\frac{1}{2} \quad \text{and} \quad u(-4) < -4. \tag{1.6}$$

A smooth curve through these five points lies below the diagonal for $-1 < x < 0$ and $x < -2$, and above the diagonal for $x \in (-2, -1)$. ∇

We assume that utility functions are non-decreasing, although the reverse is conceivable, for instance in the event of capital levy. Hence, the *marginal utility* is non-negative: $u'(x) \leq 0$. An important class of decision makers are the *risk averse* ones. They have a *decreasing marginal utility*, so $u''(x) \leq 0$. Note that we will not be very rigorous in distinguishing between the notions increasing and non-decreasing. If needed, we will use the phrase 'strictly increasing'. To explain why such decision makers are called risk averse, we use the following fundamental theorem (for a proof, see Exercises 1.2.1 and 1.2.2):

Theorem 1.2.3 (Jensen's inequality)
If $v(x)$ is a convex function and Y is a random variable, then

$$\mathrm{E}[v(Y)] \geq v(\mathrm{E}[Y]), \tag{1.7}$$

with equality if and only if $v(\cdot)$ is linear on the support of Y or $\text{Var}[Y] = 0$. ∇

From this inequality, it follows that for a concave utility function

$$\text{E}[u(w - X)] \leq u(\text{E}[w - X]) = u(w - \text{E}[X]). \tag{1.8}$$

So this particular decision maker is rightly called risk averse: he prefers to pay a fixed amount $\text{E}[X]$ instead of a risky amount X.

Now, suppose that a risk averse insured with capital w uses the utility function $u(\cdot)$. Assuming he is insured against a loss X for a premium P, his expected utility will increase if

$$\text{E}[u(w - X)] \leq u(w - P). \tag{1.9}$$

Since $u(\cdot)$ is a non-decreasing continuous function, this is equivalent to $P \leq P^+$, where P^+ denotes the maximum premium to be paid. It is the solution to the following utility equilibrium equation

$$\text{E}[u(w - X)] = u(w - P^+). \tag{1.10}$$

The insurer, with utility function $U(\cdot)$ and capital W, will insure the loss X for a premium P if $\text{E}[U(W + P - X)] \geq U(W)$, hence $P \geq P^-$ where P^- denotes the minimum premium to be asked. This premium follows from solving the utility equilibrium equation reflecting the insurer's position:

$$U(W) = \text{E}[U(W + P^- - X)]. \tag{1.11}$$

A deal improving the expected utility for both sides will be possible if $P^+ \geq P^-$.

From a theoretical point of view, insurers are often considered to be virtually risk neutral. So for any risk X, disregarding additional costs, a premium $\text{E}[X]$ is sufficient. Therefore,

$$\text{E}[U(W + \text{E}[X] - X)] = U(W) \text{ for any risk } X. \tag{1.12}$$

In Exercise 1.2.3 it is proven that this entails that the utility function $U(x)$ must be linear.

Example 1.2.4 (Risk aversion coefficient)
Given the utility function $u(x)$, how can we approximate the maximum premium P^+ for a risk X?

Let μ and σ^2 denote the mean and variance of X. Using the first terms in the series expansion of $u(\cdot)$ in $w - \mu$, we obtain

$$u(w - P^+) \approx u(w - \mu) + (\mu - P^+)u'(w - \mu);$$
$$u(w - X) \approx u(w - \mu) + (\mu - X)u'(w - \mu) + \frac{1}{2}(\mu - X)^2 u''(w - \mu). \tag{1.13}$$

Taking expectations on both sides of the latter approximation yields

$$\mathrm{E}[u(w - X)] \approx u(w - \mu) + \frac{1}{2}\sigma^2 u''(w - \mu). \tag{1.14}$$

Substituting (1.10) into (1.14), it follows from (1.13) that

$$\frac{1}{2}\sigma^2 u''(w - \mu) \approx (\mu - P^+)u'(w - \mu). \tag{1.15}$$

Therefore, the maximum premium P^+ for a risk X is approximately

$$P^+ \approx \mu - \frac{1}{2}\sigma^2 \frac{u''(w - \mu)}{u'(w - \mu)}. \tag{1.16}$$

This suggests the following definition: the (absolute) *risk aversion coefficient* $r(w)$ of the utility function $u(\cdot)$ at a wealth w is given by

$$r(w) = -\frac{u''(w)}{u'(w)}. \tag{1.17}$$

Then the maximum premium P^+ to be paid for a risk X is approximately

$$P^+ \approx \mu + \frac{1}{2}r(w - \mu)\sigma^2. \tag{1.18}$$

Note that $r(w)$ does not change when $u(x)$ is replaced by $a\,u(x) + b$. From (1.18), we see that the risk aversion coefficient indeed reflects the degree of risk aversion: the more risk averse one is, the larger the premium one is prepared to pay. ∇

1.3 CLASSES OF UTILITY FUNCTIONS

Besides the linear functions, other families of suitable utility functions exist which have interesting properties:

$$\begin{array}{llll} \textit{linear utility:} & u(w) = w & & \\ \textit{quadratic utility:} & u(w) = -(\alpha - w)^2 & (w \leq \alpha) & \\ \textit{logarithmic utility:} & u(w) = \log(\alpha + w) & (w > -\alpha) & \quad (1.19) \\ \textit{exponential utility:} & u(w) = -\alpha e^{-\alpha w} & (\alpha > 0) & \\ \textit{power utility:} & u(w) = w^c & (w > 0,\ 0 < c \leq 1) & \end{array}$$

These utility functions, and of course their linear transforms as well, have a non-negative and non-decreasing marginal utility; for the quadratic utility function, we set $u(w) = 0$ if $w \geq \alpha$. The risk aversion coefficient for the linear utility function is 0, while for the exponential utility function, it equals α. For the other utility functions, it can be written as $(\gamma + \beta w)^{-1}$ for some γ and β, see Exercise 1.3.1.

Example 1.3.1 (Exponential premium)
Suppose that an insurer has an exponential utility function with parameter α. What is the minimum premium P^- to be asked for a risk X?

Solving the equilibrium equation (1.11) with $U(x) = -\alpha e^{-\alpha x}$ yields

$$P^- = \frac{1}{\alpha}\log(m_X(\alpha)), \tag{1.20}$$

where $m_X(\alpha) = \mathrm{E}[e^{\alpha x}]$ is the moment generating function of X at argument α. We observe that this *exponential premium* is independent of the insurer's current wealth W, in line with the risk aversion coefficient being a constant.

The expression for the maximum premium P^+ is the same as (1.20), see Exercise 1.3.3, but now of course α represents the risk aversion of the insured. Assume that the loss X is exponentially distributed with parameter β. Taking $\beta = 0.01$ yields $\mathrm{E}[X] = \frac{1}{\beta} = 100$. If the insured's utility function is exponential with parameter $\alpha = 0.005$, then

$$P^+ = \frac{1}{\alpha}\log(m_X(\alpha)) = 200\log\left(\frac{\beta}{\beta - \alpha}\right) = 200\log(2) \approx 138.6, \tag{1.21}$$

so the insured is willing to accept a sizable loading on the net premium $\mathrm{E}[X]$.

The approximation (1.18) from Example 1.2.4 yields

$$P^+ \approx \mathrm{E}[X] + \frac{1}{2}\alpha \mathrm{Var}[X] = 125. \tag{1.22}$$

Obviously, the approximation (1.22) is decreasing with α, but also the premium (1.20) is decreasing if X is a non-negative random variable with finite variance, as we will prove next. Let

$$v(x) = x^{\alpha/\gamma} \tag{1.23}$$

with $0 < \alpha < \gamma$. Then, $v(\cdot)$ is a strictly concave function. From Jensen's inequality, it follows that

$$v(\mathrm{E}[Y]) > \mathrm{E}[v(Y)] \tag{1.24}$$

for any random variable Y with $\mathrm{Var}[Y] > 0$. Choosing $Y = \exp(\gamma X)$ yields $v(Y) = \exp(\alpha X)$, and

$$\{\mathrm{E}[e^{\gamma X}]\}^{\alpha} = \left\{(\mathrm{E}[Y])^{\alpha/\gamma}\right\}^{\gamma} = \{v(\mathrm{E}[Y])\}^{\gamma} > \{\mathrm{E}[v(Y)]\}^{\gamma} = \left\{\mathrm{E}[e^{\alpha X}]\right\}^{\gamma}. \tag{1.25}$$

Therefore,

$$\{m_X(\alpha)\}^{\gamma} < \{m_X(\gamma)\}^{\alpha}, \tag{1.26}$$

which implies that, for any $\gamma > \alpha$,

$$\frac{1}{\alpha}\log(m_X(\alpha)) < \frac{1}{\gamma}\log(m_X(\gamma)). \tag{1.27}$$

Just as for the approximation (1.18), the limit of (1.20) as $\alpha \downarrow 0$ is the net premium. This follows immediately from the series expansion of $\log(m_X(t))$, see also Exercise 1.3.4. ∇

Example 1.3.2 (Quadratic utility)
Suppose that for $w < 5$, the insured's utility function is $u(w) = 10w - w^2$. What is the maximum premium P^+ as a function of w, $w \in [0,5]$, for an insurance policy against a loss 1 with probability $\frac{1}{2}$? What happens to this premium if w increases?

Again, we solve the equilibrium equation (1.10). The expected utility after a loss X equals

$$\mathrm{E}[u(w - X)] = 11w - \frac{11}{2} - w^2, \tag{1.28}$$

and the utility after paying a premium P equals

$$u(w-P) = 10(w-P) - (w-P)^2. \tag{1.29}$$

By the equilibrium equation (1.10), the right hand sides of (1.28) and (1.29) should be equal, and after some calculations we find the maximum premium as

$$P = P(w) = \sqrt{\left(\frac{11}{2} - w\right)^2 + \frac{1}{4}} - (5-w), \quad w \in [0,5]. \tag{1.30}$$

One may verify that $P'(w) > 0$, see also Exercise 1.3.2. We observe that a decision maker with quadratic utility is willing to pay larger premiums as his wealth increases towards the saturation point 5. Because of this property, the quadratic utility is considered to be less appropriate to model the behavior of risk averse decision makers. The quadratic utility function still has its uses, of course, since knowing only the expected value and the variance of the risk suffices to do the calculations. ∇

Example 1.3.3 (Uninsurable risk)
A decision maker with an exponential utility function with risk aversion $\alpha > 0$ wants to insure a gamma(n,1) distributed risk. Determine P^+ and prove that $P^+ > n$. When is $P^+ = \infty$ and what does that mean?

From formula (1.20), it follows that

$$P^+ = \frac{1}{\alpha}\log(m_X(\alpha)) = \begin{cases} -\frac{n}{\alpha}\log(1-\alpha) & \text{for } 0 < \alpha < 1 \\ \infty & \text{for } \alpha \geq 1. \end{cases} \tag{1.31}$$

Since $\log(1+x) < x$ for all $x > -1$, $x \neq 0$, we have also $\log(1-\alpha) < -\alpha$ and consequently $P^+ > \mathrm{E}[X] = n$. So, the resulting premium is larger than the net premium. If $\alpha \geq 1$, then $P^+ = \infty$, which means that the decision maker is willing to pay any finite premium. An insurer with risk aversion $\alpha \geq 1$ insuring the risk will suffer a loss, in terms of utility, for any finite premium P, since also $P^- = \infty$. For such insurers, the risk is *uninsurable*. ∇

Remark 1.3.4 (Allais paradox (1953), Yaari's dual theory (1987))
Consider the following possible capital gains:

$$X = \quad 1\,000\,000 \quad \text{with probability } 1$$

$$Y = \begin{cases} 5\,000\,000 & \text{with probability } 0.10 \\ 1\,000\,000 & \text{with probability } 0.89 \\ 0 & \text{with probability } 0.01 \end{cases}$$

$$V = \begin{cases} 1\,000\,000 & \text{with probability } 0.11 \\ 0 & \text{with probability } 0.89 \end{cases}$$

$$W = \begin{cases} 5\,000\,000 & \text{with probability } 0.10 \\ 0 & \text{with probability } 0.90 \end{cases}$$

Experimental economy has revealed that, having a choice between X and Y, many people choose X, but at the same time they prefer W over V. This result violates the expected utility hypothesis, since, assuming an initial wealth of 0, the latter preference $\mathrm{E}[u(W)] > \mathrm{E}[u(V)]$ is equivalent to $0.11\,u(1\,000\,000) < 0.1\,u(5\,000\,000) + 0.01\,u(0)$, but the former leads to exactly the opposite inequality. Apparently, expected utility does not always describe the behavior of decision makers adequately. Judging from this example, it would seem that the attraction of being in a completely safe situation is stronger than expected utility indicates, and induces people to make irrational decisions.

Yaari (1987) has proposed an alternative theory of decision making under risk that has a very similar axiomatic foundation. Instead of using a utility function, Yaari's dual theory computes 'certainty equivalents' not as expected values of transformed wealth levels (utilities), but with distorted probabilities of large gains and losses. It turns out that this theory leads to paradoxes that are very similar to the ones vexing utility theory. ∇

1.4 OPTIMALITY OF STOP-LOSS REINSURANCE

Reinsurance treaties usually cover only part of the risk. *Stop-loss (re)insurance* covers the top part. It is defined as follows: if the loss is X (we assume $X \geq 0$), the payment equals

$$(X-d)_+ := \max\{X-d, 0\} = \begin{cases} X-d & \text{if } X > d \\ 0 & \text{if } X \leq d. \end{cases} \tag{1.32}$$

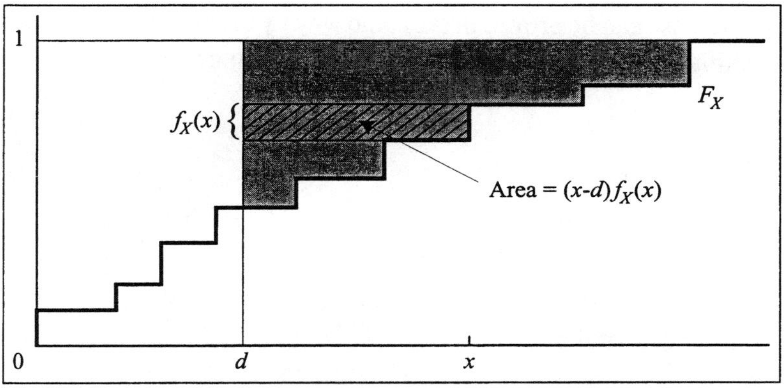

Fig. 1.1 Graphical derivation of (1.34) for a discrete cdf.

The insurer retains a risk d (his *retention*) and lets the reinsurer pay for the remainder. In the reinsurance practice, the retention equals the maximum amount to be paid out for every single claim and d is called the priority. Why this type of coverage is called 'stop-loss' is obvious: from the insurer's point of view, the loss stops at d. We will prove that, regarding the variance of the insurer's retained loss, a stop-loss reinsurance is optimal. The other side of the coin is that reinsurers don't offer stop-loss insurance under the same conditions as other types of reinsurance.

By a *stop-loss premium*, we mean the net premium $\mathrm{E}[(X-d)_+]$ for a stop-loss contract. We write

$$\pi_X(d) := \mathrm{E}[(X-d)_+]. \tag{1.33}$$

In the discrete case, where $F_X(x)$ is a step function with a step $f_X(x)$ in x, as well as in the continuous case, where $F_X(x)$ has $f_X(x)$ as its derivative, it can be shown that the stop-loss premium is given by

$$\pi_X(d) = \left\{ \begin{array}{ll} \sum_{x>d}(x-d)f_X(x) & \text{(discrete)} \\ \int_d^\infty (x-d)f_X(x)dx & \text{(continuous)} \end{array} \right\} = \int_d^\infty [1-F_X(x)]dx. \tag{1.34}$$

A graphical 'proof' for the discrete case is given in Figure 1.1. The right hand side of the equation (1.34), i.e., the total shaded area enclosed by the graph of $F_X(x)$, the horizontal line at 1 and the vertical line at d, is divided into small bars with a height $f_X(x)$ and a width $x-d$. We see that the total area equals the left hand side of (1.34).

The continuous case can be proven in the same way by taking limits, considering bars with an infinitesimal height. To prove it by partial integration, write

$$\begin{aligned} \mathrm{E}[(X-d)_+] &= \int_d^\infty (x-d) f_X(x) dx \\ &= -(x-d)[1-F_X(x)]\Big|_d^\infty + \int_d^\infty [1-F_X(x)] dx. \end{aligned} \tag{1.35}$$

The only choice $F_X(x) + C$ for an antiderivative of $f_X(x)$ that might produce finite terms on the right hand side is $F_X(x) - 1$. That the integrated term vanishes for $x \to \infty$ is proven as follows: since $\mathrm{E}[X] < \infty$, the integral $\int_0^\infty x f_X(x) dx$ is convergent, and hence the 'tails' tend to zero, so

$$x[1-F_X(x)] = x \int_x^\infty f_X(t) dt \leq \int_x^\infty t f_X(t) dt \downarrow 0 \text{ for } x \to \infty. \tag{1.36}$$

From (1.34), it follows that:

$$\pi_X'(d) = F_X(d) - 1. \tag{1.37}$$

Since $F_X(x) = \Pr[X \leq x]$, each cdf F_X is continuous from the right. Accordingly, the derivative in (1.37) is a right hand derivative. From (1.37), we see that $\pi_X(d)$ is a continuous function which is strictly decreasing as long as $F_X(d) < 1$. Indeed, it is evident that a stop-loss premium decreases when the retention increases. If X is non-negative, then $\pi_X(0) = \mathrm{E}[X]$, while always $\pi_X(\infty) = 0$. These properties are illustrated in Figure 1.2.

In the next theorem, we prove that a stop-loss insurance minimizes the variance of the retained risk.

Theorem 1.4.1 (Optimality of stop-loss reinsurance)
Let $I(X)$ be the payment on some reinsurance contract if the loss is X, with $X \geq 0$. Assume that $0 \leq I(x) \leq x$ holds for all $x \geq 0$. Then,

$$\mathrm{E}[I(X)] = \mathrm{E}[(X-d)_+] \Rightarrow \mathrm{Var}[X - I(X)] \geq \mathrm{Var}[X - (X-d)_+]. \tag{1.38}$$

Proof. Note that because of the above remarks, for every $I(\cdot)$ we can find a retention d such that the expectations are equal. We write the retained risks as follows:

$$V(X) = X - I(X) \quad \text{and} \quad W(X) = X - (X-d)_+. \tag{1.39}$$

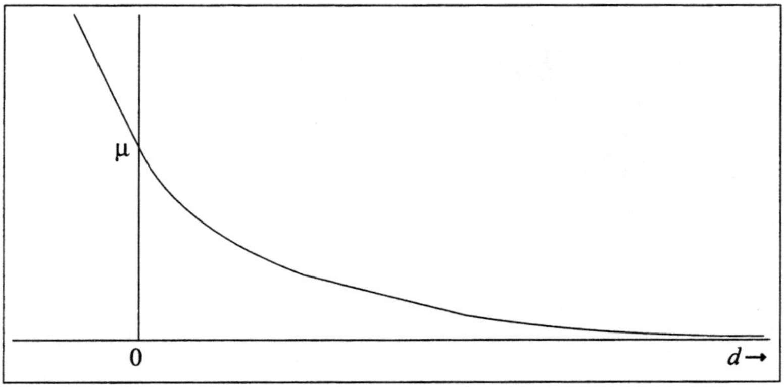

Fig. 1.2 A stop-loss premium $\pi_X(d)$ as a function of d.

Since $\mathrm{E}[V(X)] = \mathrm{E}[W(X)]$, it suffices to prove that

$$\mathrm{E}[\{V(X) - d\}^2] \geq \mathrm{E}[\{W(X) - d\}^2]. \tag{1.40}$$

A sufficient condition for this to hold is that $|V(X) - d| \geq |W(X) - d|$ with probability one. This is trivial in the event $X \geq d$, since then $W(X) \equiv d$ holds. For $X < d$, we have $W(X) \equiv X$, and hence

$$V(X) - d = X - d - I(X) \leq X - d = W(X) - d < 0. \tag{1.41}$$

This completes the proof. ∇

As stated before, this theorem can be extended: using the theory of ordering of risks, one can prove that stop-loss insurance not only minimizes the variance of the retained risk, but also maximizes the insured's expected utility, see Chapter 10.

In the above theorem, it is crucial that the premium for a stop-loss coverage is the same as the premium for another type of coverage with the same expected payment. Since the variance of the reinsurer's capital will be larger for a stop-loss coverage than for another coverage, the reinsurer, who is without exception at least slightly risk averse, in practice will charge a higher premium for a stop-loss insurance.

Example 1.4.2 ([♠] Optimality of proportional reinsurance)
To illustrate the importance of the requirement that the premium does not depend

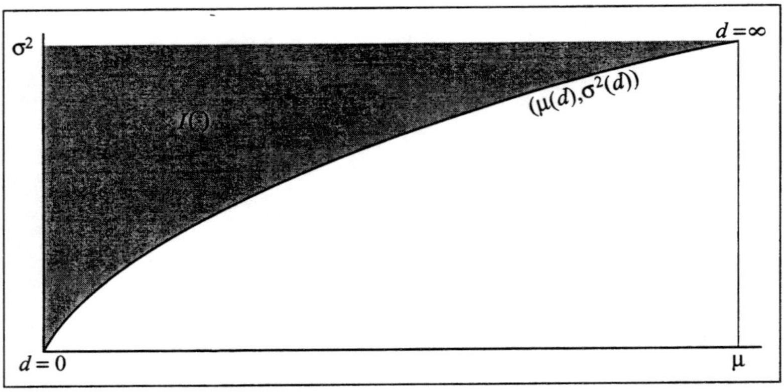

Fig. 1.3 Expected value and variance of the retained risk for different reinsurance contracts. The boundary line constitutes the stop-loss contracts with $d \in [0, \infty)$. The shaded area contains other feasible reinsurance contracts.

on the type of reinsurance, we consider a related problem: suppose that the insurer collects a premium $(1+\theta)\mathrm{E}[X]$ and that he is looking for the most profitable reinsurance $I(X)$ with $0 \leq I(X) \leq X$ and given variance

$$\mathrm{Var}[X - I(X)] = V. \tag{1.42}$$

The insurer wants to maximize his expected profit, under the assumption that the instability of his own financial situation is fixed in advance. We consider two methods for the reinsurer to calculate his premium for $I(X)$. In the first scenario (A), the reinsurer collects a premium just like the insurer's (*original terms*). So, the premium equals $(1+\lambda)\mathrm{E}[I(X)]$. In the second scenario (B), the reinsurer determines the premium according to the *variance principle*, which means that he asks a premium which equals the expected value plus a loading equal to a constant, say α, times the variance of $I(X)$. Then, the insurer can determine his expected profit, which equals the collected premium minus the expected value of the retained risk minus the reinsurance premium, as follows:

$$\begin{aligned}
\mathrm{A}: \quad & (1+\theta)\mathrm{E}[X] - \mathrm{E}[X - I(X)] - (1+\lambda)\mathrm{E}[I(X)] \\
& = \theta\mathrm{E}[X] - \lambda\mathrm{E}[I(X)]; \\
\mathrm{B}: \quad & (1+\theta)\mathrm{E}[X] - \mathrm{E}[X - I(X)] - (\mathrm{E}[I(X)] + \alpha\mathrm{Var}[I(X)]) \\
& = \theta\mathrm{E}[X] - \alpha\mathrm{Var}[I(X)].
\end{aligned} \tag{1.43}$$

As one sees, in both scenarios the expected profit equals the original expected profit $\theta\mathrm{E}[X]$ reduced by the expected profit of the reinsurer. Clearly, we have to minimize the expected profit of the reinsurer, hence the following minimization problems arise:

$$\begin{aligned} \text{A}: \quad & \text{Min } \mathrm{E}[I(X)] & \text{and} \quad \text{B}: \quad & \text{Min } \mathrm{Var}[I(X)] \\ & \text{s.t. } \mathrm{Var}[X - I(X)] = V & & \text{s.t. } \mathrm{Var}[X - I(X)] = V \end{aligned} \tag{1.44}$$

Problem B is the easier one to solve. We can write

$$\mathrm{Var}[I(X)] = \mathrm{Var}[X] + \mathrm{Var}[I(X) - X] - 2\mathrm{Cov}[X, X - I(X)]. \tag{1.45}$$

Since the first two terms on the right hand side are fixed, the left hand side is minimal if the covariance term is maximized. Because the variances are given, this can be accomplished by taking X and $X - I(X)$ linearly dependent, choosing $I(x) = \gamma + \beta x$. From $0 \leq I(x) \leq x$, we find $\gamma = 0$ and $0 \leq \beta \leq 1$; from (1.42), it follows that $(1-\beta)^2 = V/\mathrm{Var}[X]$. So, if the variance of the retained risk is given and the reinsurer uses the variance principle, then *proportional reinsurance* $I(X) = \beta X$ with $\beta = 1 - \sqrt{V/\mathrm{Var}[X]}$ is optimal.

For the solution of problem A, we use Theorem 1.4.1. By calculating the derivatives with respect to d, see Exercise 1.4.3, we can prove that $\mu(d) = \mathrm{E}[X - (X-d)_+]$ as well as $\sigma^2(d) = \mathrm{Var}[X - (X-d)_+]$ are continuously increasing in d. Notice that $\mu(0) = \sigma^2(0) = 0$ and $\mu(\infty) = \mathrm{E}[X]$, $\sigma^2(\infty) = \mathrm{Var}[X]$.

In Figure 1.3, we plot the points $(\mu(d), \sigma^2(d))$ for $d \in [0, \infty)$ for some loss random variable X. Because of Theorem 1.4.1, other reinsurance contracts $I(\cdot)$ can only have an expected value and a variance of the retained risk above the curve in the μ, σ^2-plane, since the variance is at least as large as for the stop-loss reinsurance with the same expected value. This also implies that such a point can only be located to the left of the curve. From this we conclude that, just as in Theorem 1.4.1, the non-proportional stop-loss solution is optimal for problem A. The stop-loss contracts in this case are Pareto-optimal: there are no other solutions with both a smaller variance and a higher expected profit. ∇

1.5 EXERCISES

Section 1.2

1. Prove Jensen's inequality: if $v(x)$ is convex, then $\mathrm{E}[v(X)] \geq v(\mathrm{E}[X])$. Use the following definition of convexity: a function $v(x)$ is convex if, and only if, for every x_0 a line $l_0(x) =$

$a_0x + b_0$ exists, such that $l_0(x_0) = v(x_0)$ and moreover $l_0(x) \le v(x)$ for all x [usually, $l_0(\cdot)$ is a tangent line of $v(\cdot)$]. Pay special attention to the case $v(x) = x^2$.

2. Also prove the reverse of Jensen's inequality: if $\mathrm{E}[v(X)] \ge v(\mathrm{E}[X])$ for every random variable X, then v is convex.
3. Prove: if $\mathrm{E}[v(X)] = v(\mathrm{E}[X])$ for every random variable X, then v is linear.
4. A decision maker has utility function $u(x) = \sqrt{x}$, $x \ge 0$. He is given the choice between two random amounts X and Y, in exchange for his entire present capital w. The probability distributions of X and Y are given by

x	$\Pr[X = x]$
400	0.5
900	0.5

and

y	$\Pr[Y = y]$
100	0.6
1600	0.4

Show that he prefers X to Y. Determine for which values of w he should decline the offer. Can you think of utility functions with which he would prefer Y to X?

5. Prove that $P^- \ge \mathrm{E}[X]$ for risk averse insurers.
6. An insurer undertakes a risk X and after collecting the premium, he owns a capital $w = 100$. What is the maximum premium the insurer is willing to pay to a reinsurer to take over the complete risk, if his utility function is $u(w) = \log(w)$ and $\Pr[X = 0] = \Pr[X = 36] = 0.5$? Determine not only the exact value, but also the approximation (1.18) of Example 1.2.4.
7. Assume that the reinsurer's minimum premium to take over the risk of the previous exercise equals 19 and that the reinsurer has the same utility function. Determine his capital W.
8. Describe the utility function of a person with the following risk behavior: after winning an amount 1, he answers 'yes' to the question 'double or quits?'; after winning again, he agrees only after a long huddle; the third time he says 'no'.

Section 1.3

1. Prove that the utility functions in (1.19) have a non-negative and non-increasing marginal utility. Show how the risk aversion coefficient of all these utility functions can be written as $r(w) = (\gamma + \beta w)^{-1}$.
2. Show that, for quadratic utility, the risk aversion increases with the capital. Check (1.28)–(1.30) and verify that $P'(w) > 0$ in (1.30).
3. Prove the formula (1.20) for P^- for the case of exponential utility. Also show that (1.10) yields the same solution for P^+.
4. Prove that the exponential premium P^- in (1.20) decreases to the net premium if the risk aversion α tends to zero.
5. Show that the approximation in Example 1.2.4 is exact if $X \sim N(\mu, \sigma^2)$ and $u(\cdot)$ is exponential.
6. Using the exponential utility function with $\alpha = 0.001$, determine which premium is higher: the one for $X \sim N(400, 25\,000)$ or the one for $Y \sim N(420, 20\,000)$. Determine for which values of α the former premium is higher.

7. Assume that the marginal utility of $u(w)$ is proportional to $1/w$, i.e., $u'(w) = k/w$ for some $k > 0$ and all $w > 0$. What is $u(w)$? With this utility function, which prices P in the St. Petersburg paradox of Example 1.2.1 make entering the game worthwhile?
8. For the premium P an insurer with exponential utility function asks for a $N(1000, 100^2)$ distributed risk it is known that $P \geq 1250$. What can be said about his risk aversion α? If the risk X has *dimension* 'money', then what is the dimension of α?
9. For a random variable X with mean $\mathrm{E}[X] = \mu$ and variance $\mathrm{Var}[X] = \sigma^2$ it is known that for every possible $\alpha > 0$, the zero utility premium with exponential utility with risk aversion α contains a relative safety loading $\frac{1}{2}\sigma^2\alpha/\mu$. What distribution can X have?
10. Which utility function results if in the class of power utility functions we let $c \downarrow 0$? [Look at the linear transformation $(w^c - 1)/c$.]

Section 1.4

1. Sketch the stop-loss transform corresponding to the following cdf:

$$F(x) = \begin{cases} 0 & \text{for } x < 2 \\ x/4 & \text{for } 2 \leq x < 4 \\ 1 & \text{for } 4 \leq x \end{cases}$$

2. Determine the distribution of S if $\mathrm{E}[(S-d)_+] = \frac{1}{3}(1-d)^3$ for $0 \leq d \leq 1$.
3. [♠] Prove that, for the optimization of problem A,

$$\mu'(d) = 1 - F_X(d) \quad \text{and} \quad (\sigma^2)'(d) = 2[1 - F_X(d)][d - \mu(d)].$$

Verify that both are non-negative.

4. [♠] What happens if we replace '=' by '≤' in (1.42), taking V to be an upper bound for the variance of the retained risk in the scenarios A and B?
5. Define the coefficient of variation $V[\cdot]$ for a risk X with an expected value μ and a variance σ^2 as σ/μ. By comparing the variance of the retained risk $W(X) = X - (X-d)_+$ resulting from a stop-loss reinsurance with the one obtained from a suitable proportional reinsurance, show that $V[W] \leq V[X]$. Also show that $V[\min\{X, d\}]$ is decreasing in *d*, by using the following equality: if $d < t$, then $\min\{X, d\} = \min\{\min\{X, t\}, d\}$.
6. Suppose for the random loss $X \sim N(0,1)$ an insurance of *franchise* type is in operation: the amount $I(x)$ paid in case the damage is x equals x when $x \geq d$ for some $d > 0$, and zero otherwise. Show that the net premium for this type of insurance is $\phi(x)$, where $\phi(\cdot)$ is the standard normal density. Compare this with the net stop-loss premium with a retention *d*.

2

The individual risk model

2.1 INTRODUCTION

In this chapter we focus on the distribution function of the total claim amount S for the portfolio of an insurer. We intend to determine not only the expected value and the variance of the insurer's random capital, but also the probability that the amounts paid exceed a fixed threshold. A model for the total claim amount S is also needed to be able to apply the theory of the previous chapter. To determine the value-at-risk at, say, the 99.9% level, we need also good approximations for the inverse of the cdf, especially in the far tail. In this chapter we deal with models which still recognize the individual, usually different, policies. As is done often in non-life insurance mathematics, the 'time' aspect will be ignored. This aspect is nevertheless important in disability and long term care insurance. For this reason, these types of insurance are sometimes counted as life insurances.

In the insurance practice, risks usually can't be modelled by purely discrete random variables, nor by purely continuous random variables. For instance, in liability insurance a whole range of positive amounts can be paid out, each of them with a very small probability. There are two exceptions: the probability of having no claim, i.e., claim size 0, is quite large, and the probability of a claim size which equals the maximum sum insured, i.e., a loss exceeding that threshold, is also not negligible. For the expected value of such mixed random variables, we use the Riemann-Stieltjes integral, without going too deeply into its mathematical aspects. A simple and flexible model that produces random variables of this type is a mixture model. Depending on the outcome of one event ('no claim or maximum claim' or 'other claim'), a second drawing is done from either a discrete distribution, producing zero or the maximal claim amount, or a continuous distribution. In the sequel, we present some examples of mixed models for the claim amount per policy.

Assuming that the risks in a portfolio are independent random variables, the distribution of their sum can be calculated by making use of convolution. It turns out that this technique is quite laborious, so there is a need for other methods. One of the alternative methods is to make use of moment generating functions (mgf) or of related transforms like characteristic functions, probability generating functions (pgf) and cumulant generating functions (cgf). Sometimes it is possible to recognize the mgf of a convolution and consequently identify the distribution function.

A totally different approach is to approximate the distribution of S. If we consider S as the sum of a 'large' number of random variables, we could, by virtue of the Central Limit Theorem, approximate its distribution by a normal distribution with the same mean and variance as S. We will show that this approximation usually is not satisfactory for the insurance practice, where especially in the tails, there is a need for more refined approximations which explicitly recognize the substantial probability of large claims. More technically, the third central moment of S is usually greater than 0, while for the normal distribution it equals 0. We present an approximation based on a translated gamma random variable, as well as the normal power (NP) approximation. The quality of these approximations is comparable. The latter can be calculated directly by means of a $\mathrm{N}(0,1)$ table, the former can be calculated numerically using a computer or, if desired, it can be approximated by the same $\mathrm{N}(0,1)$ table.

Another way to approximate the individual risk model is to use the collective risk models described in the next chapter.

2.2 MIXED DISTRIBUTIONS AND RISKS

In this section, we discuss some examples of insurance risks, i.e., the claims on an insurance policy. First, we have to slightly extend our set of distribution functions, because purely discrete random variables and purely continuous random variables both turn out to be inadequate for modelling the risks.

From the theory of probability, we know that every function $F(\cdot)$ which satisfies

$$\begin{aligned} &F(-\infty) = 0; F(+\infty) = 1 \\ &F(\cdot) \text{ is non-decreasing} \\ &F(\cdot) \text{ is right-continuous} \end{aligned} \tag{2.1}$$

is a cumulative distribution function (cdf). If $F(\cdot)$ is a step function, i.e., a function with constant parts and a denumerable set of discontinuities (steps), then $F(\cdot)$ and any random variable X with $F(x) = \Pr[X \leq x]$ are called *discrete*. The associated probability density function (pdf) represents the height of the step at x, so

$$f(x) = F(x) - F(x-0) = \Pr[X = x] \quad \text{for all } x \in (-\infty, \infty). \tag{2.2}$$

For all x, we have $f(x) \geq 0$, and $\sum_x f(x) = 1$ where the sum is taken over all x satisfying $f(x) > 0$.

Another special case is when $F(\cdot)$ is *absolutely continuous*. This means that if $f(x) = F'(x)$, then

$$F(x) = \int_{-\infty}^{x} f(t)dt. \tag{2.3}$$

In this case $f(\cdot)$ is called the probability density function, too. Again, $f(x) \geq 0$ while now $\int f(x)dx = 1$. Note that, just as is customary in mathematical statistics, this notation without integration limits represents the *definite* integral of $f(x)$ over the interval $(-\infty, \infty)$, and not just an arbitrary antiderivative, i.e., any function having $f(x)$ as its derivative.

In statistics, almost without exception random variables are either discrete or continuous, but this is definitely not the case in insurance. Many distribution functions that are employed to model insurance payments have continuously increasing parts, but also some positive steps. Let Z represent the payment on some contract. Then, as a rule, there are three possibilities:

1. The contract is claim-free, hence $Z = 0$.

2. The contract generates a claim which is larger than the maximum sum insured, say M. Then, $Z = M$.

3. The contract generates a 'normal' claim, hence $0 < Z < M$.

Apparently, the cdf of Z has steps in 0 and in M. For the part in-between we could use a discrete distribution, since the payment will be some entire multiple of the monetary unit. This would produce a very large set of possible values, each of them with a very small probability, so using a continuous cdf seems more convenient. In this way, a cdf arises which is neither purely discrete, nor purely continuous. In Figure 2.2 a diagram of a mixed continuous/discrete cdf is given, see also Exercise 1.4.1.

The following two-staged model allows us to construct a random variable with a distribution that is a mixture of a discrete and a continuous distribution. Let I be an *indicator random variable*, with values $I = 1$ or $I = 0$, where $I = 1$ indicates that some event has occurred. Suppose that the probability of the event is $q = \Pr[I = 1]$, $0 \leq q \leq 1$. If $I = 1$, the claim Z is drawn from the distribution of X, if $I = 0$, then from Y. This means that

$$Z = IX + (1 - I)Y. \tag{2.4}$$

If $I = 1$ then Z can be replaced by X, if $I = 0$ it can be replaced by Y. Note that we can consider X and Y to be stochastically independent of I, since given $I = 0$ the value of X is irrelevant, so we can take $\Pr[X \leq x | I = 0] = \Pr[X \leq x | I = 1]$ just as well. Hence, the cdf of Z can be written as

$$\begin{aligned} F(z) &= \Pr[Z \leq z] \\ &= \Pr[Z \leq z \;\&\; I = 1] + \Pr[Z \leq z \;\&\; I = 0] \\ &= \Pr[X \leq z \;\&\; I = 1] + \Pr[Y \leq z \;\&\; I = 0] \\ &= q \Pr[X \leq z] + (1 - q) \Pr[Y \leq z]. \end{aligned} \tag{2.5}$$

Now, let X be a discrete random variable and Y a continuous random variable. From (2.5) we get

$$\begin{aligned} &F(z) - F(z - 0) = q \Pr[X = z] \quad \text{and} \\ &F'(z) = (1 - q) \frac{d}{dz} \Pr[Y \leq z]. \end{aligned} \tag{2.6}$$

This construction yields a cdf $F(z)$ with steps where $\Pr[X = z] > 0$, but it is not a step function, since $F'(z) > 0$ on the range of Y.

To calculate the moments of Z, the moment generating function $\mathrm{E}[e^{tZ}]$ and the stop-loss premiums $\mathrm{E}[(Z - d)_+]$, we have to calculate the expectations of functions of Z. For that purpose, we use the iterative formula of conditional expectations:

$$\mathrm{E}[W] = \mathrm{E}[\mathrm{E}[W | V]]. \tag{2.7}$$

We apply this formula with $W = g(Z)$ for an appropriate function $g(\cdot)$ and replace V by I. Then, introducing $h(i) = \mathrm{E}[g(Z)|I = i]$, we get

$$\begin{aligned}\mathrm{E}[g(Z)] &= \mathrm{E}[\mathrm{E}[g(Z)|I]] = \mathrm{E}[h(I)] = qh(1) + (1-q)h(0)\\ &= q\mathrm{E}[g(Z)|I=1] + (1-q)\mathrm{E}[g(Z)|I=0]\\ &= q\mathrm{E}[g(X)|I=1] + (1-q)\mathrm{E}[g(Y)|I=0]\\ &= q\mathrm{E}[g(X)] + (1-q)\mathrm{E}[g(Y)]\\ &= q\sum_z g(z)\Pr[X=z] + (1-q)\int_{-\infty}^{\infty} g(z)\frac{d}{dz}\Pr[Y \le z]dz\\ &= \sum_z g(z)[F(z) - F(z-0)] + \int_{-\infty}^{\infty} g(z)F'(z)dz.\end{aligned} \tag{2.8}$$

By $F(z-0)$, we mean the limit from the left; we have $F(z+0) = F(z)$ because cdf's are continuous from the right.

Remark 2.2.1 (Riemann-Stieltjes integrals)
Note that the result in (2.8), consisting of a sum and an ordinary Riemann integral, can be written as a right hand Riemann-Stieltjes integral:

$$\mathrm{E}[g(Z)] = \int_{-\infty}^{\infty} g(z)dF(z). \tag{2.9}$$

The differential $dF(z) = F_Z(z) - F_Z(z-dz)$ replaces the probability of z, i.e., the height of the step at z if there is one, or $F'(z)dz$ if there is no step at z. Here, dz denotes a positive infinitesimal number. This a 'number' that can be regarded as what is left of an $\varepsilon \downarrow 0$, just before it actually vanishes. Its main properties are that it is positive, but smaller than any other positive number. Note that the cdf $F(z) = \Pr[Z \le z]$ is continuous from the right. In life insurance mathematics, Riemann-Stieltjes integrals, also known as generalized Riemann integrals, give rise to the problem of determining which value of the integrand should be used: the limit from the right, the limit from the left, or the actual function value. We avoid this problem by considering continuous integrands only. ∇

Remark 2.2.2 (Mixed random variables and distributions)
We can summarize the above as follows: a mixed continuous/discrete cdf $F_Z(z) = \Pr[Z \le z]$ arises when a mixture of random variables

$$Z = IX + (1-I)Y \tag{2.10}$$

is used, where X is a discrete random variable, Y is a continuous random variable and I is a Bernoulli(q) random variable independent of X and Y. The cdf of Z is again a mixture, in the sense of convex combinations, of the cdf's of X and Y, see (2.5):

$$F_Z(z) = qF_X(z) + (1-q)F_Y(z) \tag{2.11}$$

For expectations of functions $g(\cdot)$ of Z we get the same mixture of expectations of $\mathrm{E}[g(X)]$ and $\mathrm{E}[g(Y)]$, see (2.8):

$$\mathrm{E}[g(Z)] = q\mathrm{E}[g(X)] + (1-q)\mathrm{E}[g(Y)]. \tag{2.12}$$

It is important to note that the convex combination $T = qX + (1-q)Y$ does not have (2.11) as its cdf, although (2.12) is valid for $g(z) = z$. See also Exercises 2.2.8 and 2.2.9. ∇

Example 2.2.3 (Insurance against bicycle theft)
We consider an insurance policy against bicycle theft which pays b in case the bicycle is stolen, upon which event the policy ends. Obviously, the number of payments is 0 or 1 and the amount is known in advance, just like in most life insurance policies. Assume that the probability of theft is q and let $X = Ib$ denote the claim payment, where I is a Bernoulli(q) distributed indicator random variable. Then $I = 1$ if the bicycle is stolen, $I = 0$ if not. In analogy to (2.4), we can rewrite X as $X = Ib + (1-I)0$. The distribution and the moments of X can be obtained from those of I:

$$\begin{aligned} &\Pr[X=b] = \Pr[I=1] = q; && \Pr[X=0] = \Pr[I=0] = 1-q; \\ &\mathrm{E}[X] = b\mathrm{E}[I] = bq; && \mathrm{Var}[X] = b^2\mathrm{Var}[I] = b^2q(1-q). \end{aligned} \tag{2.13}$$

Now, suppose that only half the amount is paid out in case the bicycle was not locked. In the Netherlands, many bicycle theft insurance policies incorporate a distinction like this. Insurers check this by requiring that all the original keys have to be handed over in the event of a claim. Then, $X = IB$, where B represents the stochastic payment. Assuming that the probabilities of a claim $X = 400$ and $X = 200$ are 0.05 and 0.15, we get

$$\Pr[I=1 \,\&\, B=400] = 0.05; \quad \Pr[I=1 \,\&\, B=200] = 0.15. \tag{2.14}$$

Hence, $\Pr[I=1] = 0.2$ and consequently $\Pr[I=0] = 0.8$. Also,

$$\Pr[B=400|I=1] = \frac{\Pr[B=400 \,\&\, I=1]}{\Pr[I=1]} = 0.25. \tag{2.15}$$

This represents the conditional probability that the bicycle was locked given the fact that it was stolen. ∇

Example 2.2.4 (Exponential claim size, if there is a claim)
Suppose that risk X is distributed as follows:

1. $\Pr[X = 0] = \frac{1}{2}$;
2. $\Pr[X \in [x, x + dx)] = \frac{1}{2}\beta e^{-\beta x}dx \quad \text{for } \beta = 0.1, x > 0,$

where dx denotes a positive infinitesimal number. What is the expected value of X, and what is the maximum premium for X that someone with an exponential utility function with risk aversion $\alpha = 0.01$ is willing to pay?

The random variable X is not continuous, because the cdf of X has a step in 0. It is also not a discrete random variable, since the cdf is not a step function, as the derivative, which can be written as $\Pr[x \leq X < x + dx]/dx$, using infinitesimal numbers, is positive for $x > 0$. We can calculate the expectations of functions of X by dealing with the steps in the cdf separately, see (2.9). This leads to

$$\begin{aligned} \mathrm{E}[X] &= \int_{-\infty}^{\infty} x dF_X(x) = 0\, dF_X(0) + \int_0^{\infty} x F_X'(x) dx \\ &= \frac{1}{2}\int_0^{\infty} x\beta e^{-\beta x} dx = 5. \end{aligned} \tag{2.16}$$

If the utility function of the insured is exponential with parameter $\alpha = 0.01$, then (1.21) yields for the maximum premium P^+:

$$\begin{aligned} P^+ &= \frac{1}{\alpha}\log(m_X(\alpha)) = \frac{1}{\alpha}\log\left(e^0 dF_X(0) + \frac{1}{2}\int_0^{\infty} e^{\alpha x}\beta e^{-\beta x} dx\right) \\ &= \frac{1}{\alpha}\log\left(\frac{1}{2} + \frac{1}{2}\frac{\beta}{\beta - \alpha}\right) = 100\log\left(\frac{19}{18}\right) \approx 5.4. \end{aligned} \tag{2.17}$$

This same result can of course be obtained by writing X as in (2.10). ∇

Example 2.2.5 (Liability insurance with a maximum coverage)
Consider an insurance policy against a liability loss S. We want to determine the expected value, the variance and the distribution function of the payment X on this policy, when there is a deductible of 100 and a maximum payment of 1000. In other words, if $S \leq 100$ then $X = 0$, if $S \geq 1100$ then $X = 1000$, otherwise $X = S - 100$. The probability of a positive claim ($S > 100$) is 10% and the

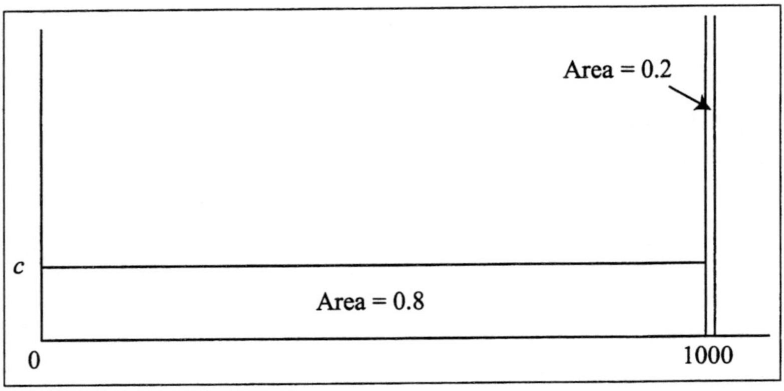

Fig. 2.1 'Probability density function' corresponding to B given $I = 1$.

probability of a large loss ($S \geq 1100$) is 2%. Given $100 < S < 1100$, S has a uniform$(100, 1100)$ distribution. Again, we write $X = IB$ where I denotes the number of payments, 0 or 1, and B represents the amount paid, if any. Hence,

$$\begin{aligned} &\Pr[B = 1000|I = 1] = 0.2; \\ &\Pr[B \in (x, x + dx)|I = 1] = c\,dx \quad \text{for } 0 < x < 1000. \end{aligned} \tag{2.18}$$

Integrating the latter probability over $x \in (0, 1000)$ yields 0.8, so $c = 0.0008$.

The conditional distribution function of B, given $I = 1$, is neither discrete, nor continuous. In Figure 2.1 we attempt to depict a pdf by representing the probability mass at 1000 by a bar with infinitesimal width and infinite height such that the area equals 0.2. In actual fact we have plotted $f(\cdot)$, where $f(x) = 0.0008$ on $(0, 1000)$ and $f(x) = 0.2/\varepsilon$ on $(1000, 1000 + \varepsilon)$ with ε very small and positive.

For the cdf F of X we have

$$\begin{aligned} F(x) &= \Pr[X \leq x] = \Pr[IB \leq x] \\ &= \Pr[IB \leq x \& I = 0] + \Pr[IB \leq x \& I = 1] \\ &= \Pr[IB \leq x|I = 0]\Pr[I = 0] + \Pr[IB \leq x|I = 1]\Pr[I = 1] \end{aligned} \tag{2.19}$$

which yields

$$F(x) = \begin{cases} 0 \times 0.9 + 0 \times 0.1 = 0 & \text{for } x < 0 \\ 1 \times 0.9 + 1 \times 0.1 = 1 & \text{for } x \geq 1000 \\ 1 \times 0.9 + c\,x \times 0.1 & \text{for } 0 \leq x < 1000. \end{cases} \tag{2.20}$$

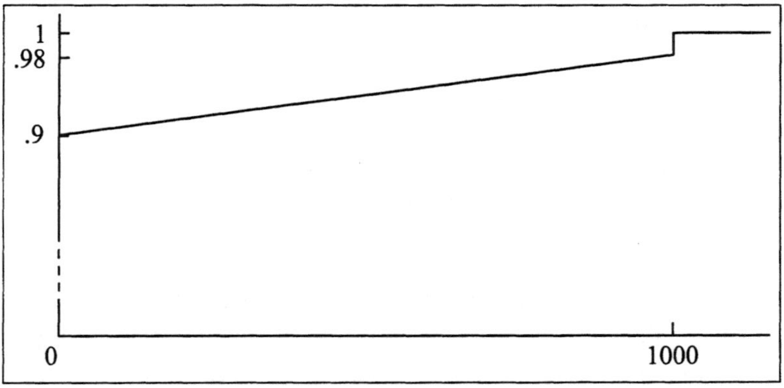

Fig. 2.2 Cumulative distribution function F of X in Example 2.2.5.

A graph of the cdf F is shown in Figure 2.2. For the differential ('density') of F, we have

$$dF(x) = \begin{cases} 0.9 & \text{for } x = 0 \\ 0.02 & \text{for } x = 1000 \\ 0 & \text{for } x < 0 \text{ or } x > 1000 \\ 0.00008\,dx & \text{for } 0 < x < 1000. \end{cases} \tag{2.21}$$

The moments of X can be calculated by using this differential. ∇

The variance of risks of the form IB can be calculated through the conditional distribution of B, given I, by use of the well-known variance decomposition rule, cf. (2.7):

$$\text{Var}[W] = \text{Var}[\text{E}[W|V]] + \text{E}[\text{Var}[W|V]]. \tag{2.22}$$

Note that the conditional distribution of B given $I = 0$ is irrelevant. For convenience, let it be equal to the one of B, given $I = 1$, meaning that we take I and B to be independent. Then, letting $q = \Pr[I = 1]$, $\mu = \text{E}[B]$ and $\sigma^2 = \text{Var}[B]$, we have $\text{E}[X|I = 1] = \mu$ and $\text{E}[X|I = 0] = 0$. Therefore, $\text{E}[X|I = i] = \mu i$, $i = 0, 1$, and analogously, $\text{Var}[X|I = i] = \sigma^2 i$. Hence,

$$\text{E}[X|I] \equiv \mu I \quad \text{and} \quad \text{Var}[X|I] \equiv \sigma^2 I, \tag{2.23}$$

from which it follows that

$$\begin{aligned} \text{E}[X] &= \text{E}[\text{E}[X|I]] = \text{E}[\mu I] = \mu q; \\ \text{Var}[X] &= \text{Var}[\text{E}[X|I]] + \text{E}[\text{Var}[X|I]] = \text{Var}[\mu I] + \text{E}[\sigma^2 I] \\ &= \mu^2 q(1-q) + \sigma^2 q. \end{aligned} \tag{2.24}$$

2.3 CONVOLUTION

In the individual risk model we are interested in the distribution of the total S of the claims on a number of policies, with

$$S = X_1 + X_2 + \cdots + X_n, \tag{2.25}$$

where X_i, $i = 1, 2, \ldots, n$, denotes the payment on policy i. The risks X_i are assumed to be independent random variables. If this assumption is violated for some risks, for instance in case of fire insurance policies on different floors of the same building, then these risks should be combined into one term in (2.25).

The operation 'convolution' calculates the distribution function of $X + Y$ from those of two independent random variables X and Y, as follows:

$$\begin{aligned} F_{X+Y}(s) &= \Pr[X + Y \leq s] \\ &= \int_{-\infty}^{\infty} \Pr[X + Y \leq s | X = x] dF_X(x) \\ &= \int_{-\infty}^{\infty} \Pr[Y \leq s - x | X = x] dF_X(x) \\ &= \int_{-\infty}^{\infty} \Pr[Y \leq s - x] dF_X(x) \\ &= \int_{-\infty}^{\infty} F_Y(s - x) dF_X(x) =: F_X * F_Y(s). \end{aligned} \tag{2.26}$$

The cdf $F_X * F_Y(\cdot)$ is called the convolution of the cdf's $F_X(\cdot)$ and $F_Y(\cdot)$. For the density function we use the same notation. If X and Y are discrete random variables, we find

$$\begin{aligned} F_X * F_Y(s) &= \sum_x F_Y(s - x) f_X(x) \quad \text{and} \\ f_X * f_Y(s) &= \sum_x f_Y(s - x) f_X(x), \end{aligned} \tag{2.27}$$

where the sum is taken over all x with $f_X(x) > 0$. If X and Y are continuous random variables, then

$$F_X * F_Y(s) = \int_{-\infty}^{\infty} F_Y(s - x) f_X(x) dx \tag{2.28}$$

and, taking the derivative under the integral sign,

$$f_X * f_Y(s) = \int_{-\infty}^{\infty} f_Y(s-x) f_X(x) dx. \tag{2.29}$$

Note that convolution is not restricted to two cdf's. For the cdf of $X+Y+Z$, it does not matter in which order we do the convolutions, hence we have

$$(F_X * F_Y) * F_Z \equiv F_X * (F_Y * F_Z) \equiv F_X * F_Y * F_Z. \tag{2.30}$$

For the sum of n independent and identically distributed random variables with marginal cdf F, the cdf is the n-fold convolution power of F, which we write as

$$F * F * \cdots * F =: F^{*n}. \tag{2.31}$$

Example 2.3.1 (Convolution of two uniform distributions)
Suppose that $X \sim$ uniform(0,1) and $Y \sim$ uniform(0,2) are independent. What is the cdf of $X+Y$?

To facilitate notation, we introduce the concept 'indicator function'. The indicator function of a set A is defined as follows:

$$I_A(x) = \begin{cases} 1 & \text{if } x \in A \\ 0 & \text{if } x \notin A. \end{cases} \tag{2.32}$$

Indicator functions provide us with a concise notation for functions that are defined differently on some intervals. For all x, the cdf of X can be written as

$$F_X(x) = x I_{[0,1)}(x) + I_{[1,\infty)}(x), \tag{2.33}$$

while $F_Y'(y) = \frac{1}{2} I_{[0,2)}(y)$ for all y, which leads to the differential

$$dF_Y(y) = \frac{1}{2} I_{[0,2)}(y) dy. \tag{2.34}$$

The convolution formula (2.26), applied to $Y+X$ rather than $X+Y$, then yields

$$F_{Y+X}(s) = \int_{-\infty}^{\infty} F_X(s-y) dF_Y(y) = \int_0^2 F_X(s-y) \frac{1}{2} dy, \; s \geq 0. \tag{2.35}$$

The interval of interest is $0 \le s < 3$. Subdividing it into $[0,1)$, $[1,2)$ and $[2,3)$ yields

$$\begin{aligned} F_{X+Y}(s) = & \left\{\int_0^s (s-y)\frac{1}{2}dy\right\} I_{[0,1)}(s) \\ & +\left\{\int_0^{s-1} \frac{1}{2}dy + \int_{s-1}^{s} (s-y)\frac{1}{2}dy\right\} I_{[1,2)}(s) \\ & +\left\{\int_0^{s-1} \frac{1}{2}dy + \int_{s-1}^{2} (s-y)\frac{1}{2}dy\right\} I_{[2,3)}(s) \\ = & \frac{1}{4}s^2 I_{[0,1)}(s) + \frac{1}{4}(2s-1)I_{[1,2)}(s) + [1-\frac{1}{4}(3-s)^2]I_{[2,3)}(s). \end{aligned} \tag{2.36}$$

Notice that $X+Y$ is symmetric around $s = 1.5$. Although this problem could be solved in a more elegant way graphically by calculating the probabilities by means of areas, see Exercise 2.3.5, the above derivation provides an excellent illustration that convolution can be a laborious process, even in simple cases. ∇

Example 2.3.2 (Convolution of discrete distributions)
Let $f_1(x) = \frac{1}{4}, \frac{1}{2}, \frac{1}{4}$ for $x = 0, 1, 2$, $f_2(x) = \frac{1}{2}, \frac{1}{2}$ for $x = 0, 2$ and $f_3(x) = \frac{1}{4}, \frac{1}{2}, \frac{1}{4}$ for $x = 0, 2, 4$. Let f_{1+2} denote the convolution of f_1 and f_2 and let f_{1+2+3} denote the convolution of f_1, f_2 and f_3. To calculate F_{1+2+3}, we need to compute the values as shown in Table 2.1. In the discrete case, too, convolution is clearly a laborious exercise. Note that the more often we have $f_i(x) \neq 0$, the more calculations need to be done. ∇

Example 2.3.3 (Convolution of iid uniform distributions)
Let X_i, $i = 1, 2, \ldots, n$, be independent and identically uniform$(0,1)$ distributed. By using the convolution formula and induction, it can be shown that for all $x > 0$, the pdf of $S = X_1 + \cdots + X_n$ equals

$$f_S(x) = \frac{1}{(n-1)!}\sum_{h=0}^{[x]} \binom{n}{h}(-1)^h (x-h)^{n-1} \tag{2.37}$$

where $[x]$ denotes the integer part of x. See also Exercise 2.3.4. ∇

Example 2.3.4 (Convolution of Poisson distributions)
Let $X \sim$ Poisson(λ) and $Y \sim$ Poisson(μ) be independent random variables. From

x	$f_1(x)$	$*$	$f_2(x)$	$=$	$f_{1+2}(x)$	$*$	$f_3(x)$	$=$	$f_{1+2+3}(x)$	$\Rightarrow$	$F_{1+2+3}(x)$
0	1/4		1/2		1/8		1/4		1/32		1/32
1	1/2		0		2/8		0		2/32		3/32
2	1/4		1/2		2/8		1/2		4/32		7/32
3	0		0		2/8		0		6/32		13/32
4	0		0		1/8		1/4		6/32		19/32
5	0		0		0		0		6/32		25/32
6	0		0		0		0		4/32		29/32
7	0		0		0		0		2/32		31/32
8	0		0		0		0		1/32		32/32

Table 2.1 Convolution computations for Example 2.3.2

(2.27) we have, for $s = 0, 1, 2, \ldots$,

$$f_{X+Y}(s) = \sum_{x=0}^{s} f_Y(s-x) f_X(x) = \frac{e^{-\mu-\lambda}}{s!} \sum_{x=0}^{s} \binom{s}{x} \mu^{s-x} \lambda^x \\ = e^{-(\lambda+\mu)} \frac{(\lambda+\mu)^s}{s!} \tag{2.38}$$

where the last equality is the binomial theorem. Hence, $X+Y$ is Poisson$(\lambda+\mu)$ distributed. For a different proof, see Exercise 2.4.2. ∇

2.4 TRANSFORMS

Determining the distribution of the sum of independent random variables can often be made easier by using transforms of the cdf. The moment generating function (mgf) suits our purposes best. For a non-negative random variable X, it is defined as

$$m_X(t) = \mathrm{E}\left[e^{tX}\right], \quad -\infty < t < h, \tag{2.39}$$

for some h. Since the mgf is going to be used especially in an interval around 0, we require $h > 0$. If X and Y are independent, then

$$m_{X+Y}(t) = \mathrm{E}\left[e^{t(X+Y)}\right] = \mathrm{E}\left[e^{tX}\right] \mathrm{E}\left[e^{tY}\right] = m_X(t) m_Y(t). \tag{2.40}$$

So, the convolution of cdf's corresponds to simply multiplying the mgf's. Note that the mgf-transform is one-to-one, so every cdf has exactly one mgf, and continuous, so the mgf of the limit of a series of cdf's is the limit of the mgf's. See Exercises 2.4.12 and 2.4.13.

For random variables with a heavy tail, such as the Cauchy distribution, the mgf does not exist. The characteristic function, however, always exists. It is defined as follows:

$$\phi_X(t) = \mathrm{E}\left[e^{itX}\right], \quad -\infty < t < \infty. \tag{2.41}$$

A possible disadvantage of the characteristic function is the need to work with complex numbers, although experience tells us that applying the same function formula derived for real t to imaginary t as well produces the correct results most of the time, resulting for instance in $e^{(it)^2} = e^{-t^2}$ as the characteristic function of the $\mathrm{N}(0, 2)$ distribution which has mgf e^{t^2}.

As their name indicates, moment generating functions can be used to generate moments of random variables. The usual series expansion of e^x yields

$$m_X(t) = \sum_{k=0}^{\infty} \frac{\mathrm{E}\left[X^k\right] t^k}{k!}, \tag{2.42}$$

so the k-th moment of X equals

$$\mathrm{E}\left[X^k\right] = \frac{d^k}{dt^k} m_X(t)\bigg|_{t=0}. \tag{2.43}$$

A similar technique can be used for the characteristic function.

The probability generating function (pgf) is used exclusively for random variables with natural numbers as values:

$$g_X(t) = \mathrm{E}\left[t^X\right] = \sum_{k=0}^{\infty} t^k \Pr[X = k]. \tag{2.44}$$

So, the probabilities $\Pr[X = k]$ in (2.44) serve as coefficients in the series expansion of the pgf. The series (2.44) always converges if $|t| \leq 1$.

The cumulant generating function (cgf) is convenient for calculating the third central moment; it is defined as:

$$\kappa_X(t) = \log m_X(t). \tag{2.45}$$

Differentiating (2.45) three times and setting $t = 0$, one sees that the coefficients of $\frac{t^k}{k!}$ for $k = 1, 2, 3$ are $\mathrm{E}[X]$, $\mathrm{Var}[X]$ and $\mathrm{E}[(X - \mathrm{E}[X])^3]$. The quantities generated this way are the cumulants of X, and they are denoted by κ_k, $k = 1, 2, \ldots$. An alternative derivation goes as follows: let μ_k denote $\mathrm{E}\left[X^k\right]$ and let $O(t^k)$ denote 'terms of order t to the power k or higher'. Then,

$$m_X(t) = 1 + \mu_1 t + \frac{1}{2}\mu_2 t^2 + \frac{1}{6}\mu_3 t^3 + O(t^4), \tag{2.46}$$

which, using $\log(1+z) = z - \frac{1}{2}z^2 + \frac{1}{3}z^3 + O(z^4)$, yields

$$\begin{aligned}
\log m_X(t) = & \log\left(1 + \mu_1 t + \frac{1}{2}\mu_2 t^2 + \frac{1}{6}\mu_3 t^3 + O(t^4)\right) \\
= & \mu_1 t + \frac{1}{2}\mu_2 t^2 + \frac{1}{6}\mu_3 t^3 + O(t^4) \\
& - \frac{1}{2}\left\{\mu_1^2 t^2 + \mu_1\mu_2 t^3 + O(t^4)\right\} \\
& + \frac{1}{3}\left\{\mu_1^3 t^3 + O(t^4)\right\} + O(t^4) \\
= & \mu_1 t + \frac{1}{2}(\mu_2 - \mu_1^2)t^2 + \frac{1}{6}(\mu_3 - 3\mu_1\mu_2 + 2\mu_1^3)t^3 + O(t^4) \\
= & \mathrm{E}[X]t + \mathrm{Var}[X]\frac{1}{2}t^2 + \mathrm{E}[(X - \mathrm{E}[X])^3]\frac{1}{6}t^3 + O(t^4).
\end{aligned} \tag{2.47}$$

The *skewness* of a random variable X is defined as the following dimension-free quantity:

$$\gamma_X = \frac{\kappa_3}{\sigma^3} = \frac{\mathrm{E}[(X-\mu)^3]}{\sigma^3}, \tag{2.48}$$

with $\mu = \mathrm{E}[X]$ and $\sigma^2 = \mathrm{Var}[X]$. If $\gamma_X > 0$, large values of $X - \mu$ are likely to occur, hence the (right) tail of the cdf is *heavy*. A negative skewness $\gamma_X < 0$ indicates a heavy left tail. If X is symmetrical then $\gamma_X = 0$, but having zero skewness is not sufficient for symmetry. For some counterexamples, see the exercises.

The cumulant generating function, the probability generating function, the characteristic function and the moment generating function are related to each other through the formal relationships

$$\kappa_X(t) = \log m_X(t); \quad g_X(t) = m_X(\log t); \quad \phi_X(t) = m_X(it). \tag{2.49}$$

2.5 APPROXIMATIONS

A well-known method to approximate a cdf using the standard normal cdf Φ is the Central Limit Theorem (CLT). Its simplest form is

Theorem 2.5.1 (Central Limit Theorem)
If $X_1, X_2, \ldots, X_n$ are independent and identically distributed random variables with mean μ and variance $\sigma^2 < \infty$, then

$$\lim_{n\to\infty} \Pr\left[\sum_{i=1}^{n} X_i \leq n\mu + x\sigma\sqrt{n}\right] = \Phi(x). \tag{2.50}$$

Proof. We restrict ourselves to proving the convergence of the cgf. Let $S^* = (X_1 + \cdots + X_n - n\mu)/\sigma\sqrt{n}$, then for $n \to \infty$:

$$\begin{aligned} \log m_{S^*}(t) &= -\frac{\sqrt{n}\mu t}{\sigma} + n\left\{\log m_X(\frac{t}{\sigma\sqrt{n}})\right\} \\ &= -\frac{\sqrt{n}\mu t}{\sigma} + n\left\{\mu(\frac{t}{\sigma\sqrt{n}}) + \frac{1}{2}\sigma^2(\frac{t}{\sigma\sqrt{n}})^2 + O((\frac{1}{\sqrt{n}})^3)\right\} \\ &= \frac{1}{2}t^2 + O(\frac{1}{\sqrt{n}}), \end{aligned} \tag{2.51}$$

which converges to the cgf of the $\mathrm{N}(0,1)$ distribution, with mgf $\exp(\frac{1}{2}t^2)$. ∇

As a result, we can approximate the cdf of $S = X_1 + \cdots + X_n$ by

$$F_S(s) \approx \Phi\left(s; \sum_{i=1}^{n} \mathrm{E}[X_i], \sum_{i=1}^{n} \mathrm{Var}[X_i]\right). \tag{2.52}$$

This approximation can safely be used if n is 'large'. It is difficult to define 'large' formally, as is shown in the following classical examples.

Example 2.5.2 (Generating normal random deviates)
A fast and easy way of generating $\mathrm{N}(0,1)$ distributed numbers, without the time-consuming calculation of logarithms or the inversion of the normal cdf, is to add up twelve uniform$(0,1)$ numbers and to subtract 6 from this sum. This technique is based on the CLT with $n = 12$. Comparing this cdf with the normal cdf, for instance by using (2.37), yields a maximum difference of 0.002. Hence, the CLT performs quite well in this case. See also Exercise 2.4.5. ∇

Example 2.5.3 (Illustrating the various approximations)
Suppose that a thousand young men take out a life insurance policy for a period of 1 year. The probability of dying within this year is 0.001 for every man and the payment for every death is 1. We want to calculate the probability that the total payment is at least 4. This total payment is binomial$(1000, 0.001)$ distributed and since $n = 1000$ is quite large and $p = 0.001$ is quite small, we will approximate this probability by a Poisson(np) distribution. Calculating the probability at $3 + \frac{1}{2}$ instead of at 4, applying a continuity correction needed later on, we find

$$\Pr[S \geq 3.5] = 1 - e^{-1} - e^{-1} - \frac{1}{2}e^{-1} - \frac{1}{6}e^{-1} = 0.01899. \tag{2.53}$$

Note that the exact binomial probability is 0.01893. Although n is much larger than in the previous example, the CLT gives a poor approximation: with $\mu = \mathrm{E}[S] = 1$ and $\sigma^2 = \mathrm{Var}[S] = 1$, we find

$$\begin{aligned} \Pr[S \geq 3.5] &= \Pr\left[\frac{S-\mu}{\sigma} \geq \frac{3.5-\mu}{\sigma}\right] \\ &\approx 1 - \Phi(2.5) = 0.0062. \end{aligned} \tag{2.54}$$

The CLT approximation is so bad because of the extreme skewness of the terms X_i and the resulting skewness of S, which is $\gamma_S = 1$. In the previous example, we started from symmetrical terms, leading to a higher order of convergence, as can be seen from derivation (2.51). ∇

As an alternative for the CLT, we give two more refined approximations: the translated gamma approximation and the normal power approximation (NP). In numerical examples, these approximations turn out to be much more accurate than the CLT approximation, while their respective inaccuracies are comparable, and are minor compared with the errors that result from the lack of precision in the estimates of the first three moments that are involved.

Translated gamma approximation
Most total claim distributions have roughly the same shape as the gamma distribution: skewed to the right ($\gamma > 0$), a non-negative range and unimodal. Besides the usual parameters α and β, we add a third degree of freedom by allowing a shift over a distance x_0. Hence, we approximate the cdf of S by the cdf of $Z + x_0$, where $Z \sim$ gamma(α, β). We choose α, β and x_0 in such a way that the approximating random variable has the same first three moments as S.

The translated gamma approximation can then be formulated as follows:

$$F_S(s) \approx G(s - x_0; \alpha, \beta), \text{ where}$$
$$G(x; \alpha, \beta) = \frac{1}{\Gamma(\alpha)} \int_0^x y^{\alpha-1} \beta^\alpha e^{-\beta y} dy, \quad x \geq 0. \tag{2.55}$$

Here $G(x; \alpha, \beta)$ is the gamma cdf. To ensure that α, β and x_0 are chosen such that the first three moments agree, hence $\mu = x_0 + \frac{\alpha}{\beta}$, $\sigma^2 = \frac{\alpha}{\beta^2}$ and $\gamma = \frac{2}{\sqrt{\alpha}}$, they must satisfy

$$\alpha = \frac{4}{\gamma^2}, \quad \beta = \frac{2}{\gamma\sigma} \quad \text{and} \quad x_0 = \mu - \frac{2\sigma}{\gamma}. \tag{2.56}$$

For this approximation to work, the skewness γ has to be strictly positive. In the limit $\gamma \downarrow 0$, the normal approximation appears. Note that if the first three moments of the cdf $F(\cdot)$ are the same as those of $G(\cdot)$, by partial integration it can be shown that the same holds for $\int_0^\infty x^j [1 - F(x)] dx$, $j = 0, 1, 2$. This leaves little room for these cdf's to be very different from each other.

Example 2.5.4 (Illustrating the various approximations, continued)
If $S \sim$ Poisson(1), we have $\mu = \sigma = \gamma = 1$, and (2.56) yields $\alpha = 4$, $\beta = 2$ and $x_0 = -1$. Hence, $\Pr[S \geq 3.5] \approx 1 - G(3.5 - (-1); 4, 2) = 0.0212$. This value is much closer to the exact value than the CLT approximation. ∇

The translated gamma approximation leads to quite simple formulas to approximate the moments of a stop-loss claim $(S-d)_+$ or of the retained loss $S-(S-d)_+$. A potential disadvantage may be the need of a numerical algorithm to evaluate the gamma cdf, but in most spreadsheet programs the gamma distribution is included, although the accuracy often leaves much to be desired. Note that in many applications, notably MS Excel, the parameter β should be replaced by $\frac{1}{\beta}$.

In the unlikely event that only tables are available, the evaluation problem can also be solved by using a χ^2-table and the fact that, if $Y \sim$ gamma(α, β), then $2\beta Y \sim \chi^2_{2\alpha}$. It generally will be necessary to interpolate in the χ^2-table to obtain the desired values. Another way of dealing with the evaluation problem is to use the relation that exists between the gamma(α, β) distribution, with α integer-valued, and the Poisson distribution, see the exercises.

Example 2.5.5 (Translated gamma approximation)
A total claim amount S has expected value 10000, standard deviation 1000 and

skewness 1. From (2.56) we have $\alpha = 4$, $\beta = 0.002$ and $x_0 = 8000$. Hence,

$$\begin{aligned}\Pr[S > 13000] &\approx 1 - G(13000 - 8000; 4, 0.002) \\ &= 1 - G(20; 4, 0.5) \\ &= \Pr[\chi^2_8 > 20].\end{aligned} \tag{2.57}$$

The exact value is 0.010, which agrees with the 99% critical value (= 20.1) of the χ^2_8 distribution. The regular CLT approximation is much smaller: 0.0013.

From the same χ^2_8 table of critical values we find that $\Pr[\chi^2_8 > 15.5] = 0.95$; hence, the value-at-risk on a 95% level is found by reversing the computation (2.57), resulting in 11875. ∇

Remark 2.5.6 (Normal approximation to the translated gamma cdf)
For large values of α, we could approximate the gamma(α, β) distribution by a normal distribution, using the CLT and the fact that, for integer α, a gamma(α, β) random variable is the convolution of α exponential(β) distributions. Of course, in this context this would be pointless since this simply leads to the CLT-approximation again, and we are looking for more accuracy. A better way is to use the following approximation: if $Y \sim$ gamma(α, β) with $\alpha \geq \frac{1}{4}$, thus $\gamma_Y \leq 4$, then roughly $\sqrt{4\beta Y} - \sqrt{4\alpha - 1} \sim \mathrm{N}(0, 1)$, see also Exercise 2.5.14. For the translated gamma approximation for S with parameters α, β and x_0, this yields

$$\Pr[S \leq s] \approx \Phi\left(\sqrt{4\beta(s - x_0)} - \sqrt{4\alpha - 1}\right). \tag{2.58}$$

The corresponding inverse, i.e., the $1 - \varepsilon$ quantile which is needed to approximate values-at-risk, follows from

$$\Pr\left[S \leq x_0 + \frac{1}{4\beta}(y + \sqrt{4\alpha - 1})^2\right] \approx 1 - \varepsilon \tag{2.59}$$

where y is such that $\Phi(y) = 1 - \varepsilon$.

When we substitute α, β and x_0 as found in (2.56) into (2.59), we find

$$\Pr\left[\frac{S - \mu}{\sigma} \leq y + \frac{\gamma}{8}(y^2 - 1) - y\left(1 - \sqrt{1 - \frac{\gamma^2}{16}}\right)\right] \approx 1 - \varepsilon. \tag{2.60}$$

The right hand side of the inequality is written as y plus a correction to compensate for the skewness of S. The inverse (2.58) leads to

$$\Pr\left[\frac{S - \mu}{\sigma} \leq z\right] \approx \Phi\left(\sqrt{\frac{16}{\gamma^2} + \frac{8z}{\gamma}} - \sqrt{\frac{16}{\gamma^2} - 1}\right). \tag{2.61}$$

If the skewness tends to zero, both correction terms in (2.60) vanish, while (2.61) can be shown to tend to $\Phi(z)$. ∇

NP approximation

The following approximation is very similar to (2.60). The correction term has a simpler form, and it is slightly larger. It can be obtained by the use of certain expansions for the cdf, but we will not reproduce that derivation here.

If $\mathrm{E}[S] = \mu$, $\mathrm{Var}[S] = \sigma^2$ and $\gamma_S = \gamma$, then, for $s \geq 1$,

$$\Pr\left[\frac{S-\mu}{\sigma} \leq s + \frac{\gamma}{6}(s^2-1)\right] \approx \Phi(s) \tag{2.62}$$

or, equivalently, for $x \geq 1$,

$$\Pr\left[\frac{S-\mu}{\sigma} \leq x\right] \approx \Phi\left(\sqrt{\frac{9}{\gamma^2} + \frac{6x}{\gamma} + 1} - \frac{3}{\gamma}\right). \tag{2.63}$$

The latter formula can be used to approximate the cdf of S, the former produces approximate quantiles. If $s < 1$ (or $x < 1$), the correction term is negative, which implies that the CLT gives more conservative results.

Example 2.5.7 (Illustrating the various approximations, continued)

If $S \sim \text{Poisson}(1)$, then the NP approximation yields $\Pr[S \geq 3.5] \approx 1 - \Phi(2) = 0.0228$. Again, this is a better result than the CLT approximation. ∇

Example 2.5.8 (Recalculating Example 2.5.5 by the NP approximation)

We apply (2.62) to determine the capital that covers S with probability 95%:

$$\Pr\left[\frac{S-\mu}{\sigma} \leq s + \frac{\gamma}{6}(s^2-1)\right] \approx \Phi(s) = 0.95 \quad \text{if } s = 1.645, \tag{2.64}$$

hence for the desired 95% quantile of S we find

$$\mathrm{E}[S] + \sigma_S\left(1.645 + \frac{\gamma}{6}(1.645^2 - 1)\right) = \mathrm{E}[S] + 1.929\sigma_S = 11929. \tag{2.65}$$

To determine the probability that capital 13000 will be insufficient to cover the losses S, we apply (2.63) with $\mu = 10000$, $\sigma = 1000$ and $\gamma = 1$:

$$\begin{aligned}\Pr[S > 13000] = \Pr\left[\frac{S-\mu}{\sigma} > 3\right] &\approx 1 - \Phi(\sqrt{9 + 6 \times 3 + 1} - 3) \\ &= 1 - \Phi(2.29) = 0.011.\end{aligned} \tag{2.66}$$

Note that the translated gamma approximation gave 0.010, while the approximations (2.58) or (2.61) yield 0.007, against only 0.0013 for the CLT. ∇

2.6 APPLICATION: OPTIMAL REINSURANCE

An insurer is looking for an optimal reinsurance for a portfolio consisting of 20000 one-year life insurance policies which are grouped as follows:

Insured amount b_k	Number of policies n_k
1	10000
2	5000
3	5000

The probability of dying within one year is $q_k = 0.01$ for each insured, and the policies are independent. The insurer wants to optimize the probability of being able to meet his financial obligations by choosing the best retention, which is the maximum payment per policy. The remaining part of a claim is paid by the reinsurer. For instance, if the retention is 1.6 and someone with insured amount 2 dies, then the insurer pays 1.6, the reinsurer pays 0.4. After collecting the premiums, the insurer holds a capital B from which he has to pay the claims and the reinsurance premium. This premium is assumed to be 120% of the net premium.

First, we set the retention equal to 2. From the point of view of the insurer, the policies are then distributed as follows:

Insured amount b_k	Number of policies n_k
1	10000
2	10000

The expected value and the variance of the insurer's total claim amount S are equal to

$$\begin{aligned} \mathrm{E}[S] &= n_1 b_1 q_1 + n_2 b_2 q_2 \\ &= 10000 \times 1 \times 0.01 + 10000 \times 2 \times 0.01 = 300, \\ \mathrm{Var}[S] &= n_1 b_1^2 q_1 (1 - q_1) + n_2 b_2^2 q_2 (1 - q_2) \\ &= 10000 \times 1 \times 0.01 \times 0.99 + 10000 \times 4 \times 0.01 \times 0.99 \\ &= 495. \end{aligned} \tag{2.67}$$

By applying the CLT, we get for the probability that the costs S plus the reinsurance premium $1.2 \times 0.01 \times 5000 \times 1 = 60$ exceed the available capital B:

$$\begin{aligned}\Pr[S + 60 > B] &= \Pr\left[\frac{S - \mathrm{E}[S]}{\sigma_S} > \frac{B - 360}{\sqrt{495}}\right] \\ &\approx 1 - \Phi\left(\frac{B - 360}{\sqrt{495}}\right).\end{aligned} \tag{2.68}$$

We leave it to the reader to determine this same probability for retentions between 2 and 3, as well as to determine which retention for a given B leads to the largest probability of survival. See the exercises with this section.

2.7 EXERCISES

Section 2.2

1. Determine the expected value and the variance of $X = IB$ if the claim probability equals 0.1. First, assume that B equals 5 with probability 1. Then, let $B \sim$ uniform$(0, 10)$.
2. Throw a true die and let X denote the outcome. Then, toss a coin X times. Let Y denote the number of heads obtained. What are the expected value and the variance of Y?
3. In Example 2.2.4, plot the cdf of X. Also determine, with the help of the obtained differential, the premium the insured is willing to pay for being insured against an inflated loss $1.1X$. Do the same by writing $X = IB$. Has the zero utility premium followed inflation exactly?
4. Calculate $\mathrm{E}[X]$, $\mathrm{Var}[X]$ and the moment generating function $m_X(t)$ in Example 2.2.5 with the help of the differential. Also plot the 'density'.
5. If $X = IB$, what is $m_X(t)$?
6. Consider the following cdf F:

$$F(x) = \begin{cases} 0 & \text{for } x < 2 \\ \frac{x}{4} & \text{for } 2 \leq x < 4 \\ 1 & \text{for } 4 \leq x \end{cases}$$

   Determine independent random variables I, X and Y such that $Z = IX + (1 - I)Y$ has cdf F, $I \sim$ Bernoulli, X is a discrete and Y a continuous random variable.
7. Consider the following differential of cdf F:

$$dF(x) = \begin{cases} dx/3 & \text{for } 0 < x < 1 \text{ and } 2 < x < 3 \\ \frac{1}{6} & \text{for } x \in \{1, 2\} \\ 0 & \text{elsewhere} \end{cases}$$

   Find a discrete cdf G, a continuous cdf H and a real constant c with the property that $F(x) = cG(x) + (1 - c)H(x)$ for all x.

8. Suppose that $T = qX + (1-q)Y$ and $Z = IX + (1-I)Y$ with $I \sim$ Bernoulli(q). Compare $\mathrm{E}[T^k]$ with $\mathrm{E}[Z^k]$, $k = 1, 2$.
9. In the previous exercise, assume additionally that X and Y are independent $\mathrm{N}(0,1)$. What distributions do T and Z have?

Section 2.3

1. Calculate $\Pr[S = s]$ for $s = 0, 1, \ldots, 6$ when $S = X_1 + 2X_2 + 3X_3$ and $X_j \sim$ Poisson(j).
2. Determine the number of multiplications of non-zero numbers that are needed for the calculation of all probabilities $f_{1+2+3}(x)$ in Example 2.3.2. How many multiplications are needed to calculate $F_{1+\cdots+n}(x)$, $x = 0, \ldots, 4n-4$ if $f_k = f_3$ for $k = 4, \ldots, n$?
3. Prove by convolution that the sum of two independent normal distributions has a normal distribution.
4. [♠] Verify the expression (2.37) in Example 2.3.3 for $n = 1, 2, 3$ by using convolution. Determine $F_S(x)$ for these values of n. Using induction, verify (2.37) for arbitrary n.
5. Assume that $X \sim \mathrm{uniform}(0,3)$ and $Y \sim \mathrm{uniform}(-1,1)$. Calculate $F_{X+Y}(z)$ graphically by using the area of the sets $\{(x,y) | x + y \leq z, x \in (0,3) \text{ and } y \in (-1,1)\}$.

Section 2.4

1. Determine the cdf of $S = X_1 + X_2$ where the X_k are independent and exponential(k) distributed. Do this both by convolution and by calculating the mgf and identifying the corresponding density using the method of partial fractions.
2. Same as Example 2.3.4, but now by making use of the mgf's.
3. What is the fourth cumulant κ_4 in terms of the central moments?
4. Determine the cgf and the cumulants of the following distributions: Poisson, binomial, normal and gamma.
5. Prove that the sum of twelve independent uniform(0,1) random variables has variance 1 and expected value 6. Determine κ_3 and κ_4.
6. Determine the skewness of a Poisson(μ) distribution.
7. Determine the skewness of a gamma(α, β) distribution.
8. If X is symmetrical, then $\gamma_X = 0$. Prove this, but also, for $S = X_1 + X_2 + X_3$ with $X_1 \sim$ Bernoulli(0.4), $X_2 \sim$ Bernoulli(0.7) and $X_3 \sim$ Bernoulli(p), all independent, calculate the value of p such that S has skewness $\gamma_S = 0$, and verify that S is not symmetrical.
9. Determine the skewness of a risk of the form Ib where $I \sim$ Bernoulli(q) and b is a fixed amount. For which values of q and b is the skewness equal to zero, and for which of these values is I actually symmetrical?
10. Determine the pgf of the binomial, the Poisson and the negative binomial distribution.
11. Prove that cumulants actually cumulate in the following sense: if X and Y are independent, then the kth cumulant of $X + Y$ equals the sum of the kth cumulants of X and Y.

12. Show that X and Y are equal in distribution if they have the same range $\{0, 1, \ldots, n\}$ and the same pgf. If $X_1, X_2, \ldots$ are risks, again with range $\{0, 1, \ldots, n\}$, such that the pgf's of X_i converge to the pgf of Y for each argument t when $i \to \infty$, verify that also $\Pr[X_i = x] \to \Pr[Y = x]$ for all x.
13. Show that X and Y are equal in distribution if they have the same range $\{0, \delta, 2\delta, \ldots, n\delta\}$ for some $\delta > 0$ and moreover, they have the same mgf.
14. Examine the equality $\phi_X(t) = m_X(it)$ from (2.49), for the special case that $X \sim$ exponential(1). Show that the characteristic function is real-valued if X is symmetrical around 0.
15. Show that the skewness of $Z = X + 2Y$ is 0 if $X \sim$ binomial$(8, p)$ and $Y \sim$ Bernoulli$(1-p)$. For which values of p is Z symmetrical?
16. For which values of δ is the skewness of $X - \delta Y$ equal to 0, if $X \sim$ gamma$(2, 1)$ and $Y \sim$ exponential(1)?
17. Can the pgf of a random variable be used to generate moments? Can the mgf of an integer-valued random variable be used to generate probabilities?

Section 2.5

1. What happens if we replace the argument 3.5 in Example 2.5.3 by $3-0, 3+0, 4-0$ and $4+0$? Is a correction for continuity needed here?
2. Prove that both versions of the NP approximation are equivalent.
3. Derive (2.60) and (2.61).
4. Show that the translated gamma approximation as well as the NP approximation result in the normal approximation (CLT) if μ and σ^2 are fixed and $\gamma \downarrow 0$.
5. Approximate the critical values of a χ^2_{18} distribution for $\varepsilon = 0.05, 0.1, 0.5, 0.9, 0.95$ with the NP approximation and compare the results with the exact values to be found in any χ^2-table. What is the result if the translated gamma approximation is used?
6. Approximate $G(4.5; 4, 2)$ by using the methods proposed after Example 2.5.4.
7. Use the identity 'having to wait longer than x for the nth event' $\equiv$ 'at most $n-1$ events occur in $(0, x)$' in a Poisson process to prove that $\Pr[Z > x] = \Pr[N < n]$ if $Z \sim$ gamma$(n,1)$ and $N \sim$ Poisson(x). How can this fact be used to calculate the translated gamma approximation?
8. Compare the exact critical values of a χ^2_{18} distribution for $\varepsilon = 0.05, 0.1, 0.5, 0.9, 0.95$ with the approximations obtained from (2.59).
9. An insurer's portfolio contains 2000 one-year life insurance policies. Half of them are characterized by a payment $b_1 = 1$ and a probability of dying within 1 year of $q_1 = 1\%$. For the other half, we have $b_2 = 2$ and $q_2 = 5\%$. Use the CLT to determine the minimum safety loading, as a percentage, to be added to the net premium to ensure that the probability that the total payment exceeds the total premium income is at most 5%.
10. As the previous exercise, but now using the NP approximation. Employ the fact that the third cumulant of the total payment equals the sum of the third cumulants of the risks.
11. Show that the right hand side of (2.63) is well-defined for all $x \geq -1$. What are the minimum and the maximum values? Is the function increasing? What happens if $x = 1$?

12. Suppose that X has expected value $\mu = 1000$ and standard deviation $\sigma = 2000$. Determine the skewness γ if (i) $X \sim$ gamma(α, β), (ii) $X \sim$ inverse Gaussian(α, β) or (iii) $X \sim$ lognormal(ν, τ^2). Show that the skewness is infinite if (iv) $X \sim$ Pareto.
13. A portfolio consists of two types of contracts. For type k, $k = 1, 2$, the claim probability is q_k and the number of policies is n_k. If there is a claim, then its size is x with probability $p_k(x)$:

	n_k	q_k	$p_k(1)$	$p_k(2)$	$p_k(3)$
Type 1	1000	0.01	0.5	0	0.5
Type 2	2000	0.02	0.5	0.5	0

Assume that the contracts are independent. Let S_k denote the total claim amount of the contracts of type k and let $S = S_1 + S_2$. Calculate the expected value and the variance of a contract of type k, $k = 1, 2$. Then, calculate the expected value and the variance of S. Use the CLT to determine the minimum capital that covers all claims with probability 95%.
14. [♠] Let $Y \sim N(\sqrt{4\alpha - 1}, 1)$, $U \sim$ gamma(α, β) and $T = \sqrt{4\beta U}$. Show that $\mathrm{E}[T] \approx \mathrm{E}[Y]$ and $\mathrm{E}[T^2] = \mathrm{E}[Y^2]$, so $\mathrm{Var}[T] \approx 1$. Also compare the third and fourth moments of T with those of Y.
15. [♠] A justification for the 'correction for continuity', see Example 2.5.3, used to approximate cdf's of integer valued random variables by continuous ones, goes as follows. Let G be the continuous cdf of some non-negative random variable, and construct cdf H by $H(k + \varepsilon) = G(k + 0.5), k = 0, 1, 2, \ldots, 0 \leq \varepsilon < 1$. Using the *midpoint rule* with intervals of length 1 to approximate the rhs of (1.34) at $d = 0$, show that the means of G and H are about equal. Conclude that if G is a continuous cdf that is a plausible candidate for approximating the discrete cdf F and has the same mean as F, by taking $F(x) := G(x + 0.5)$ one gets an approximation with the proper mean value. [Taking $F(x) = G(x)$ instead, one gets a mean that is about $\mu + 0.5$ instead of μ. Thus very roughly speaking, each tail probability of the sum approximating (1.34) will be too big by a factor $\frac{1}{2\mu}$.]
16. To get a feel for the approximation error as opposed to the error caused by errors in the estimates of μ, σ and γ needed for the NP approximation and the gamma approximation, recalculate Example 2.5.5 if the following parameters are changed: (i) $\mu = 10100$ (ii) $\sigma = 1020$ (iii) $\mu = 10100$ and $\sigma = 1020$ (iv) $\gamma = 1.03$. Assume that the remaining parameters are as they were in Example 2.5.5.

Section 2.6

1. In the situation of Section 2.6, calculate the probability that B will be insufficient for retentions $d \in [2, 3]$. Give numerical results for $d = 2$ and $d = 3$ if $B = 405$.
2. Determine the retention $d \in [2, 3]$ which minimizes this probability for $B = 405$. Which retention is optimal if $B = 404$?
3. Calculate the probability that B will be insufficient if $d = 2$ by using the NP approximation.

3

Collective risk models

3.1 INTRODUCTION

In this chapter, we introduce collective risk models. Just as in Chapter 2, we calculate the distribution of the total claim amount in a certain time period, but now we regard the portfolio as a collective that produces a claim at random points in time. We write

$$S = X_1 + X_2 + \cdots + X_N, \tag{3.1}$$

where N denotes the number of claims and X_i is the ith claim, and by convention, we take $S = 0$ if $N = 0$. So, the terms of S in (3.1) correspond to actual claims; in (2.25), there are many terms equal to zero, corresponding to the policies which do not produce a claim. The number of claims N is a random variable, and we assume that the individual claims X_i are independent and identically distributed. We also assume that N and X_i are independent. In the special case that N is Poisson distributed, S has a *compound Poisson distribution.* If N is (negative) binomial distributed, then S has a *compound (negative) binomial distribution.*

In collective models, some policy information is ignored. If a portfolio contains only one policy that could generate a high claim, this term will appear at most once in the individual model (2.25). In the collective model (3.1), however, it could occur several times. Moreover, in collective models we require the claim number N and the claim amounts X_i to be independent. This makes it somewhat less appropriate to model a car insurance portfolio, since for instance bad weather conditions will cause a lot of small claim amounts. In practice, however, the influence of these phenomena appears to be small.

The main advantage of a collective risk model is that it is a computationally efficient model, which is also rather close to reality. We give some algorithms to calculate the distribution of (3.1). An obvious but quite laborious method is convolution. We also discuss the sparse vector algorithm (usable if $N \sim$ Poisson), which is based on the fact that the frequencies of the claim amounts are independent Poisson random variables. Finally, for a larger class of distributions, we can use Panjer's recursion, which expresses the probability of $S = s$ recursively in terms of the probabilities of $S = k$, $k = 0, 1, \ldots, s-1$. We can also express the moments of S in terms of those of N and X_i. With this information we can again approximate the distribution of S with the CLT if $\mathrm{E}[N]$ is large, as well as with the more refined approximations from the previous chapter.

Next, we look for appropriate distributions for N and X_i such that the collective model fits closely to a given individual model. It will turn out that the Poisson distribution and the negative binomial distribution are often appropriate choices for N. We will show some relevant relations between these distributions. We will also discuss some special properties of the compound Poisson distributions.

In the last few years, stop-loss insurance policies have become more widespread, for instance for insuring absence due to illness. We give a number of techniques to calculate stop-loss premiums for discrete distributions, but also for several continuous distributions. With the help of the approximations for distribution functions introduced in Chapter 2, we can also approximate stop-loss premiums.

3.2 COMPOUND DISTRIBUTIONS

Assume that S is a compound distribution as in (3.1), and that the terms X_i are distributed as X. Further use the following notation:

$$\mu_k = \mathrm{E}[X^k], \qquad P(x) = \Pr[X \leq x], \qquad F(s) = \Pr[S \leq s]. \tag{3.2}$$

We can then calculate the expected value of S by using the conditional distribution of S, given N. First, we use the condition $N = n$ to substitute outcome n for the random variable N on the left of the conditioning bar below. Next, we use the independence of X_i and N to get rid of the condition $N = n$. This gives the following computation:

$$\begin{aligned} \mathrm{E}[S] = \mathrm{E}[\mathrm{E}[S|N]] &= \sum_{n=0}^{\infty} \mathrm{E}[X_1 + \cdots + X_N | N = n] \Pr[N = n] \\ &= \sum_{n=0}^{\infty} \mathrm{E}[X_1 + \cdots + X_n | N = n] \Pr[N = n] \\ &= \sum_{n=0}^{\infty} \mathrm{E}[X_1 + \cdots + X_n] \Pr[N = n] \\ &= \sum_{n=0}^{\infty} n\mu_1 \Pr[N = n] = \mu_1 \mathrm{E}[N]. \end{aligned} \tag{3.3}$$

Note that the expected claim total equals expected claim number times expected claim size.

The variance can be determined with the formula of the conditional variance, see (2.7):

$$\begin{aligned} \mathrm{Var}[S] &= \mathrm{E}[\mathrm{Var}[S|N]] + \mathrm{Var}[\mathrm{E}[S|N]] \\ &= \mathrm{E}[N\mathrm{Var}[X]] + \mathrm{Var}[N\mu_1] \\ &= \mathrm{E}[N]\mathrm{Var}[X] + \mu_1^2 \mathrm{Var}[N]. \end{aligned} \tag{3.4}$$

The same technique as used in (3.3) yields for the mgf:

$$\begin{aligned} m_S(t) &= \mathrm{E}[\mathrm{E}[e^{tS}|N]] \\ &= \sum_{n=0}^{\infty} \mathrm{E}[e^{t(X_1+\cdots+X_N)}|N = n] \Pr[N = n] \\ &= \sum_{n=0}^{\infty} \mathrm{E}[e^{t(X_1+\cdots+X_n)}] \Pr[N = n] \\ &= \sum_{n=0}^{\infty} \{m_X(t)\}^n \Pr[N = n] = \mathrm{E}[(e^{\log m_X(t)})^N] \\ &= m_N(\log m_X(t)). \end{aligned} \tag{3.5}$$

Example 3.2.1 (Compound distribution with closed form cdf)
Let $N \sim$ geometric(p), $0 < p < 1$, and $X \sim$ exponential(1). What is the cdf of S?

Write $q = 1 - p$. First, we compute the mgf of S, and then we try to identify it. For $qe^t < 1$, which means $t < -\log q$, we have

$$m_N(t) = \sum_{n=0}^{\infty} e^{nt} pq^n = \frac{p}{1 - qe^t}. \tag{3.6}$$

Since $X \sim$ exponential(1), i.e. $m_X(t) = (1-t)^{-1}$, (3.5) yields

$$m_S(t) = m_N(\log m_X(t)) = \frac{p}{1 - qm_X(t)} = p + q\frac{p}{p-t}, \tag{3.7}$$

so the mgf of S is a mixture of the mgf's of the constant 0 and of the exponential(p) distribution. Because of the one-to-one correspondence of cdf's and mgf's, we may conclude that the cdf of S is the same mixture:

$$F(x) = p + q(1 - e^{-px}) = 1 - qe^{-px} \quad \text{for } x \geq 0. \tag{3.8}$$

This is a distribution function which has a jump of size p in 0 and is exponential otherwise. ∇

Convolution formula for a compound cdf
The conditional distribution of S, given $N = n$, allows us to calculate F:

$$\begin{aligned} F(x) &= \Pr[S \leq x] \\ &= \sum_{n=0}^{\infty} \Pr[X_1 + \cdots + X_N \leq x | N = n] \Pr[N = n], \end{aligned} \tag{3.9}$$

so

$$F(x) = \sum_{n=0}^{\infty} P^{*n}(x) \Pr[N = n], \;\; f(x) = \sum_{n=0}^{\infty} p^{*n}(x) \Pr[N = n]. \tag{3.10}$$

These expressions are called the *convolution formulae* for a compound cdf.

Example 3.2.2 (Application of the convolution formula)
Let $\Pr[N = j - 1] = 0.1j$ for $j = 1, 2, 3, 4$, and let $p(1) = 0.4$, $p(2) = 0.6$. By

using (3.10), $F(x)$ can be calculated as follows:

x	$p^{*0}(x)$	$p^{*1}(x)$	$p^{*2}(x)$	$p^{*3}(x)$		$f(x)$		$F(x)$
0	1					0.1000		0.1000
1		0.4				0.0800		0.1800
2		0.6	0.16			0.1680		0.3480
3			0.48	0.064		0.1696		0.5176
4			0.36	0.288		$\vdots$		$\vdots$
5				0.432		$\vdots$		$\vdots$
$\vdots$				$\vdots$		$\vdots$		$\vdots$
	$\updownarrow\times$	$+\updownarrow\times$	$+\updownarrow\times$	$+\updownarrow\times$	$=$	$\uparrow$	$\Rightarrow$	$\uparrow$
$\Pr[N=n]$	0.1	0.2	0.3	0.4				

The probabilities $\Pr[N=n]$ in the bottom row are multiplied by the numbers in a higher row. Then, the sum of these results is put in the corresponding row in the column $f(x)$. For instance: $0.2 \times 0.6 + 0.3 \times 0.16 = 0.168$. ∇

Example 3.2.3 (Compound distributions, exponential claim amounts)
From expression (3.10) for $F(x)$, we see that it is convenient to choose the distribution of X in such a way that the n-fold convolution is easy to calculate. This is the case for the normal and the gamma distribution: the sum of n independent $\mathrm{N}(\mu,\sigma^2)$ random variables is $\mathrm{N}(n\mu, n\sigma^2)$, while the sum of n gamma(α,β) random variables is a gamma$(n\alpha,\beta)$ random variable.

Suppose the claim amounts have an exponential(1) distribution, which is the same as gamma(α,β) with $\alpha=\beta=1$. From queueing theory, see also Exercise 2.5.7, we know that the probability of waiting at least a time x for the n-th event, which is at the same time the probability that at most $n-1$ events have occurred at time x, is a Poisson(x) probability. Hence we have

$$1 - P^{*n}(x) = \int_x^\infty y^{n-1}\frac{e^{-y}}{(n-1)!}dy = e^{-x}\sum_{i=0}^{n-1}\frac{x^i}{i!}. \tag{3.11}$$

This can also be proven with partial integration, or by comparing the derivatives, see Exercise 3.2.7. So, for $x > 0$,

$$1 - F(x) = \sum_{n=1}^{\infty}\Pr[N=n]e^{-x}\sum_{i=0}^{n-1}\frac{x^i}{i!}. \tag{3.12}$$

This gives an efficient algorithm, since we can stop the outer summation as soon as $\Pr[N \geq n]$ is smaller than the required precision; also, two successive inner sums differ by the final term only, which implies that a single summation suffices.

It will turn out that computing the distribution of the sum is much easier if the terms are discrete, so we will often approximate X by a discrete random variable. ∇

3.3 DISTRIBUTIONS FOR THE NUMBER OF CLAIMS

In practice, we will not have a lot of relevant data at our disposal to choose a distribution for N. Consequently, we should resort to a model for it, preferably with only a few parameters. To describe 'rare events', the Poisson distribution which has only one parameter is always the first choice. It is well-known that the expected value and the variance of a Poisson(λ) distribution are both equal to λ. If the model for the number of claims exhibits a larger spread around the mean value, one may use the negative binomial distribution instead. We consider two models in which the latter distribution is derived as a generalization of a Poisson distribution.

Example 3.3.1 (Poisson distribution, uncertainty about the parameter)
Assume that some car driver causes a Poisson(λ) distributed number of accidents in one year. The parameter λ is unknown and different for every driver. We assume that λ is the outcome of a random variable Λ. The conditional distribution of N, the number of accidents in one year, given $\Lambda = \lambda$, is Poisson(λ). What is the marginal distribution of N?

Let $U(\lambda) = \Pr[\Lambda \leq \lambda]$ denote the distribution function of Λ. Then we can write the marginal distribution of N as

$$\Pr[N = n] = \int_0^\infty \Pr[N = n | \Lambda = \lambda] dU(\lambda) = \int_0^\infty e^{-\lambda} \frac{\lambda^n}{n!} dU(\lambda), \tag{3.13}$$

while for the mean and variance of N we have

$$\begin{aligned} \mathrm{E}[N] &= \mathrm{E}[\mathrm{E}[N|\Lambda]] = \mathrm{E}[\Lambda]; \\ \mathrm{Var}[N] &= \mathrm{E}[\mathrm{Var}[N|\Lambda]] + \mathrm{Var}[\mathrm{E}[N|\Lambda]] = \mathrm{E}[\Lambda] + \mathrm{Var}[\Lambda] \geq \mathrm{E}[N]. \end{aligned} \tag{3.14}$$

Now assume additionally that $\Lambda \sim \text{gamma}(\alpha, \beta)$, then

$$\begin{aligned} m_N(t) &= \mathrm{E}[\mathrm{E}[e^{tN}|\Lambda]] = \mathrm{E}[\exp\{\Lambda(e^t - 1)\}] = m_\Lambda(e^t - 1) \\ &= \left(\frac{\beta}{\beta - (e^t - 1)}\right)^\alpha = \left(\frac{p}{1 - (1-p)e^t}\right)^\alpha \end{aligned} \tag{3.15}$$

where $p = \beta/(\beta+1)$, so N has a negative binomial$(\alpha, \beta/(\beta+1))$ distribution.

Obviously, the value of Λ for a particular driver is a non-observable random variable. It is the 'long run claim frequency', the value to which the observed average number of accidents in a year would converge if the driver could be observed for a very long time, during which his claims pattern doesn't change. The distribution of Λ is called the structure distribution, see also Chapter 7. ∇

Example 3.3.2 (Compound negative binomial is also compound Poisson)
At some intersection there are N fatal traffic accidents in a year. The number of casualties in the ith accident is L_i, so the total number of casualties is $S = L_1 + L_2 + \cdots + L_N$. Now, assume $N \sim$ Poisson(λ) and $L_i \sim$ logarithmic(c), hence

$$\Pr[L_i = k] = \frac{c^k}{k\,h(c)}, \qquad k = 1, 2, \ldots \quad \text{and} \quad 0 < c < 1. \tag{3.16}$$

The division by the function $h(\cdot)$ serves to make the sum of the probabilities equal to 1. From the usual series expansion of $\log(1+x)$, it is clear that this function is equal to $h(c) = -\log(1-c)$, hence the name logarithmic distribution. What is the distribution of S?

The mgf of the terms L_i is given by

$$m_L(t) = \sum_{k=1}^{\infty} \frac{e^{tk} c^k}{k\,h(c)} = \frac{h(ce^t)}{h(c)}. \tag{3.17}$$

Then, for the mgf of S, we get

$$\begin{aligned} m_S(t) &= m_N(\log m_L(t)) = \exp \lambda(m_L(t) - 1) \\ &= \left(\exp\{h(ce^t) - h(c)\}\right)^{\lambda/h(c)} = \left(\frac{1-c}{1-ce^t}\right)^{\lambda/h(c)}, \end{aligned} \tag{3.18}$$

which we recognize as the mgf of a negative binomial distribution with parameters $\lambda/h(c) = -\lambda/\log(1-c)$ and $1-c$.

On the one hand, the total payment Z for the casualties has a compound Poisson distribution since it is the sum of a Poisson(λ) number of payments per fatal accident. On the other hand, summing over the casualties leads to a compound negative binomial distribution. It can be shown that if S_2 is compound negative binomial with parameters r and $p = 1 - q$ and claims distribution $P_2(\cdot)$, then S_2

has the same distribution as S_1, where S_1 is compound Poisson distributed with parameter λ and claims distribution $P_1(\cdot)$ given by:

$$\lambda = rh(q) \quad \text{and} \quad P_1(x) = \sum_{k=1}^{\infty} \frac{q^k}{kh(q)} P_2^{*k}(x). \tag{3.19}$$

In this way, any compound negative binomial distribution can be written as a compound Poisson distribution. ∇

Remark 3.3.3 (Compound Poisson distributions in probability theory)
The compound Poisson distributions are also object of study in probability theory. If we extend this class with its limits, to which the gamma and the normal distribution belong, then we have just the class of infinitely divisible distributions, which consists of the random variables X with the property that for each n, a sequence of iid random variables $X_1, X_2, \ldots, X_n$ exists with $X \sim X_1 + X_2 + \cdots + X_n$.

3.4 COMPOUND POISSON DISTRIBUTIONS

In this section we prove some important theorems on compound Poisson distributions and use them to construct a better algorithm to calculate $F(\cdot)$. First, we show that the class of compound Poisson distributions is closed under convolution.

Theorem 3.4.1 (Sum of compound Poisson is compound Poisson)
If $S_1, S_2, \ldots, S_m$ are independent compound Poisson random variables with Poisson parameter λ_i and claims distribution P_i, $i = 1, 2, \ldots, m$, then $S = S_1 + S_2 + \cdots + S_m$ is compound Poisson distributed with parameters

$$\lambda = \sum_{i=1}^{m} \lambda_i \quad \text{and} \quad P(x) = \sum_{i=1}^{m} \frac{\lambda_i}{\lambda} P_i(x). \tag{3.20}$$

Proof. Let m_i be the mgf of P_i. Then S has the following mgf:

$$m_S(t) = \prod_{i=1}^{m} \exp\{\lambda_i [m_i(t) - 1]\} = \exp \lambda \left\{ \sum_{i=1}^{m} \frac{\lambda_i}{\lambda} m_i(t) - 1 \right\}. \tag{3.21}$$

So S is a compound Poisson mgf with parameters (3.20). ∇

Consequently, a combination of m independent compound Poisson portfolios, or the same portfolio considered in m years, assuming that the annual results are independent, is again compound Poisson distributed.

A special case is when the S_i have fixed claims x_i, hence $S_i = x_i N_i$ with $N_i \sim$ Poisson(λ_i). The random variable

$$S = x_1 N_1 + x_2 N_2 + \cdots + x_m N_m \tag{3.22}$$

is compound Poisson with parameters, assuming the x_i to be all different:

$$\lambda = \lambda_1 + \cdots + \lambda_m \quad \text{and} \quad p(x_i) = \frac{\lambda_i}{\lambda}, i = 1, \ldots, m. \tag{3.23}$$

We can also prove the reverse statement, as follows:

Theorem 3.4.2 (Frequencies of claim sizes are independent Poisson)
Assume that S is compound Poisson distributed with parameter λ and with discrete claims distribution

$$\pi_i = p(x_i) = \Pr[X = x_i], \quad i = 1, 2, \ldots, m. \tag{3.24}$$

If S is written as (3.22), where N_i denotes the frequency of the claim amount x_i, i.e., the number of terms in S with value x_i, then $N_1, \ldots, N_m$ are independent and Poisson($\lambda\pi_i$), $i = 1, \ldots, m$, distributed random variables.

Proof. Let $N = N_1 + \cdots + N_m$ and $n = n_1 + \cdots + n_m$. Conditionally on $N = n$, we have $N_1, \ldots, N_m \sim$ Multinomial($n, \pi_1, \ldots, \pi_m$). Hence,

$$\begin{aligned}
&\Pr[N_1 = n_1, \ldots, N_m = n_m] \\
&\quad = \Pr[N_1 = n_1, \ldots, N_m = n_m | N = n] \Pr[N = n] \\
&\quad = \frac{n!}{n_1! n_2! \ldots n_m!} \pi_1^{n_1} \pi_2^{n_2} \ldots \pi_m^{n_m} e^{-\lambda} \frac{\lambda^n}{n!} \\
&\quad = \prod_{i=1}^{m} e^{-\lambda\pi_i} \frac{(\lambda\pi_i)^{n_i}}{n_i!}.
\end{aligned} \tag{3.25}$$

By summing over all n_i, $i \neq k$, we see that N_k is marginally Poisson($\lambda\pi_k$) distributed. The N_i are independent since $\Pr[N_1 = n_1, \ldots, N_m = n_m]$ is the product of the marginal probabilities of $N_i = n_i$. ∇

Example 3.4.3 (Application: sparse vector algorithm)
If the claims X are integer-valued and non-negative, we can calculate the compound Poisson cdf F in an efficient way. We explain this by the following example: let $\lambda = 4$ and $\Pr[X = 1, 2, 3] = \frac{1}{4}, \frac{1}{2}, \frac{1}{4}$. Then, gathering together terms as we did

in (3.22), we can write S as $S = 1N_1 + 2N_2 + 3N_3$ and calculate the distribution of S by convolution. We can compute $f(x) = \Pr[S = x]$ as follows:

x	$\Pr[N_1 = x]$ $(e^{-1}\times)$	$\times \Pr[2N_2 = x]$ $(e^{-2}\times)$	$= \Pr[N_1 + 2N_2 = x]$ $(e^{-3}\times)$	$\times \Pr[3N_3 = x]$ $(e^{-1}\times)$	$= \Pr[S = x]$ $(e^{-4}\times)$
0	1	1	1	1	1
1	1	–	1	–	1
2	1/2	2	5/2	–	5/2
3	1/6	–	13/6	1	19/6
4	1/24	2	⋮	–	⋮
⋮	⋮	⋮	⋮	⋮	⋮
	↑	↑		↑	
	$1/x!$	$2^{x/2}/(x/2)!$		$1/(x/3)!$	

The total amount of the claims of size $1, 2, \ldots, j-1$ is convoluted with jN_j. In the column with probabilities of jN_j, only the rows $0, j, 2j, \ldots$ are filled, which is why this algorithm is called a 'sparse vector' algorithm. These probabilities are Poisson($\lambda\pi_j$) probabilities. ∇

3.5 PANJER'S RECURSION

Although the sparse vector algorithm was a lot better than the convolution formula, there was still some room for improvement. In 1981, Panjer described a method to calculate the probabilities $f(x)$ recursively. Similar relations were already derived in the queueing theory. As a result of Panjer's publication, a lot of other articles have appeared in the actuarial literature covering similar recursion relations. The recursion relation described by Panjer is as follows:

Theorem 3.5.1 (Panjer's recursion)
Consider a compound distribution with integer-valued non-negative claims with pdf $p(x)$, $x = 0, 1, 2, \ldots$, for which the probability q_n of having n claims satisfies the following recursion relation

$$q_n = (a + \frac{b}{n})q_{n-1}, \quad n = 1, 2, \ldots \tag{3.26}$$

for some real a and b. Then, the following relations for the probability of a total claim equal to s hold:

$$
\begin{aligned}
f(0) &= \begin{cases} \Pr[N=0] & \text{if } p(0)=0; \\ m_N(\log p(0)) & \text{if } p(0)>0; \end{cases} \\
f(s) &= \frac{1}{1-ap(0)} \sum_{h=1}^{s} (a+\frac{bh}{s}) p(h) f(s-h), \quad s=1,2,\ldots
\end{aligned}
\tag{3.27}
$$

Proof. $\Pr[S=0] = \sum_{n=0}^{\infty} \Pr[N=n] p^n(0)$ gives us the starting value $f(0)$. Write $T_k = X_1 + \cdots + X_k$. First, note that because of symmetry:

$$
\mathrm{E}[a + \frac{bX_1}{s} | T_k = s] = a + \frac{b}{k}. \tag{3.28}
$$

This expectation can also be determined in the following way:

$$
\begin{aligned}
\mathrm{E}[a + \frac{bX_1}{s} | T_k = s] &= \sum_{h=0}^{s} (a + \frac{bh}{s}) \Pr[X_1 = h | T_k = s] \\
&= \sum_{h=0}^{s} (a + \frac{bh}{s}) \frac{\Pr[X_1 = h] \Pr[T_k - X_1 = s-h]}{\Pr[T_k = s]}.
\end{aligned}
\tag{3.29}
$$

Because of (3.26) and the previous two equalities, we have, for $s = 1, 2, \ldots$,

$$
\begin{aligned}
f(s) &= \sum_{k=1}^{\infty} q_k \Pr[T_k = s] = \sum_{k=1}^{\infty} q_{k-1} (a + \frac{b}{k}) \Pr[T_k = s] \\
&= \sum_{k=1}^{\infty} q_{k-1} \sum_{h=0}^{s} (a + \frac{bh}{s}) \Pr[X_1 = h] \Pr[T_k - X_1 = s-h] \\
&= \sum_{h=0}^{s} (a + \frac{bh}{s}) \Pr[X_1 = h] \sum_{k=1}^{\infty} q_{k-1} \Pr[T_k - X_1 = s-h] \\
&= \sum_{h=0}^{s} (a + \frac{bh}{s}) p(h) f(s-h) \\
&= ap(0) f(s) + \sum_{h=1}^{s} (a + \frac{bh}{s}) p(h) f(s-h),
\end{aligned}
\tag{3.30}
$$

from which the second relation of (3.27) follows immediately. ∇

Example 3.5.2 (Distributions suitable for Panjer's recursion)
Only the following distributions satisfy relation (3.26):

1. Poisson(λ) with $a = 0$ and $b = \lambda \geq 0$; in this case, (3.27) simplifies to:

$$f(0) = e^{-\lambda(1-p(0))};$$
$$f(s) = \frac{1}{s}\sum_{h=1}^{s} \lambda h p(h) f(s-h); \tag{3.31}$$

2. Negative binomial(r, p) with $p = 1 - a$ and $r = 1 + \frac{b}{a}$; so $0 < a < 1$ and $a + b > 0$;

3. Binomial(k, p) with $p = \frac{a}{a-1}$ and $k = -\frac{b+a}{a}$; so $a < 0$, $b = -a(k+1)$.

If $a + b = 0$, then $q_0 = 1$ and $q_j = 0$ for $j = 1, 2, \ldots$, so we get a Poisson(0) distribution. For other values of a and b than the ones used above, (3.26) doesn't produce a probability distribution: if $q_0 > 0$, then $a + b < 0$ results in negative probabilities, and the same happens if $a < 0$ and $b \neq -a(n+1)$ for all n; if $a \geq 1$ and $a + b > 0$, (3.26) implies $(n+1)q_{n+1} \geq nq_n$, hence $q_n \geq \frac{q_1}{n}$, $n = 1, 2, \ldots$ and consequently $\sum_n q_n = \infty$. Note that by allowing (3.26) to hold only for $n \geq 2$, hence with an arbitrary probability of no claims, it is possible to find similar recursions for a larger class of counting distributions. ∇

Example 3.5.3 (Panjer's recursion)
Consider again, see also Example 3.4.3, a compound Poisson distribution with $\lambda = 4$ and $\Pr[X = 1, 2, 3] = \frac{1}{4}, \frac{1}{2}, \frac{1}{4}$. Then (3.31) yields, with $\lambda = 4$, $p(2) = \frac{1}{2}$ and $p(1) = p(3) = \frac{1}{4}$,

$$f(s) = \frac{1}{s}[f(s-1) + 4f(s-2) + 3f(s-3)], \quad s = 1, 2, \ldots, \tag{3.32}$$

and the starting value is $f(0) = e^{-4} \approx 0.0183$. We have

$$f(1) = f(0) = e^{-4}$$
$$f(2) = \frac{1}{2}[f(1) + 4f(0)] = \frac{5}{2}e^{-4} \tag{3.33}$$
$$f(3) = \frac{1}{3}[f(2) + 4f(1) + 3f(0)] = \frac{19}{6}e^{-4}$$

and so on. ∇

Example 3.5.4 (Panjer's recursion and stop-loss premiums)
For an integer-valued S, we can write the stop-loss premium in an integer retention d as follows, see Section 1.4:

$$E[(S-d)_+] = \sum_{x=d}^{\infty}(x-d)f(x) = \sum_{x=d}^{\infty}[1-F(x)]. \tag{3.34}$$

The stop-loss premium is piecewise linear in the retention on the intervals where the cdf remains constant, since for the right hand derivative we have

$$\frac{d}{dt}E[(S-t)_+] = F(t) - 1. \tag{3.35}$$

The stop-loss premiums for non-integer d follow by interpolation.

With Panjer's recursion the stop-loss premiums can be calculated recursively, too, since from the last relation in (3.34), we have for integer d

$$\pi(d) := E[(S-d)_+] = \pi(d-1) - [1 - F(d-1)]. \tag{3.36}$$

As an example, take $S \sim$ compound Poisson(1) with $p(1) = p(2) = \frac{1}{2}$. Then, Panjer's recursion relation (3.31) simplifies to

$$f(x) = \frac{1}{x}\left[\frac{1}{2}f(x-1) + f(x-2)\right], \quad x = 1, 2, \ldots \tag{3.37}$$

with starting values

$$f(0) = e^{-1} \approx 0.368, \quad F(0) = f(0), \quad \pi(0) = E[S] = \lambda\mu_1 = \frac{3}{2}. \tag{3.38}$$

This leads to the following calculations:

x	$f(x) = (3.37)$	$F(x) = F(x-1) + f(x)$	$\pi(x) = \pi(x-1) - 1 + F(x-1)$
0	0.368	0.368	1.500
1	0.184	0.552	0.868
2	0.230	0.782	0.420
3	0.100	0.881	0.201
4	0.070	0.951	0.083
5	0.027	0.978	0.034

∇

Remark 3.5.5 (Proof of Panjer's recursion through pgf's)
Panjer's recursion can also be proven by using probability generating functions. For the compound Poisson distribution, this goes as follows. First write

$$\frac{dg_S(t)}{dt} = \frac{d}{dt}\sum_{s=0}^{\infty} t^s \Pr[S=s] = \sum_{s=1}^{\infty} st^{s-1}\Pr[S=s]. \tag{3.39}$$

Because of

$$g_S(t) = g_N(g_X(t)) = \exp\lambda(g_X(t)-1), \tag{3.40}$$

the derivative also equals $g'_S(t) = \lambda g_S(t) g'_X(t)$. For other distributions, similar expressions can be derived, using (3.26). Now for $g_S(\cdot)$ and $g'_X(\cdot)$, substitute their series expansions:

$$\begin{aligned}
\lambda g_S(t) g'_X(t) &= \lambda\left(\sum_{s=0}^{\infty} t^s \Pr[S=s]\right)\left(\sum_{x=1}^{\infty} xt^{x-1}\Pr[X=x]\right)\\
&= \sum_{x=1}^{\infty}\sum_{s=0}^{\infty} \lambda x t^{s+x-1}\Pr[S=s]\Pr[X=x]\\
&= \sum_{x=1}^{\infty}\sum_{v=x}^{\infty} \lambda x t^{v-1}\Pr[S=v-x]\Pr[X=x]\\
&= \sum_{v=1}^{\infty}\sum_{x=1}^{v} \lambda x t^{v-1}\Pr[S=v-x]\Pr[X=x].
\end{aligned} \tag{3.41}$$

Comparing the coefficients of t^{s-1} in (3.39) and (3.41) yields

$$s\Pr[S=s] = \sum_{x=1}^{s} \lambda x \Pr[S=s-x]\Pr[X=x]. \tag{3.42}$$

which is equivalent with Panjer's recursion relation (3.31) for the Poisson case. ∇

Remark 3.5.6 (Convolution using Panjer's recursion)
How can we calculate the n-fold convolution of a distribution on $0, 1, 2, \ldots$ with Panjer's recursion?

Assume that $p(0) > 0$. If we replace X_i by $I_i Y_i$ where $\Pr[I_i = 1] = \Pr[X_i > 0] =: p$ and $Y_i \sim X_i | X_i > 0$, then $\sum_i X_i$ has the same distribution as $\sum_i I_i Y_i$, which gives us a compound binomial distribution with $p < 1$ as required in Example 3.5.2. Another method is to take limits for $p \uparrow 1$ in (3.27) for those values of a and b that produce a binomial(n, p) distribution. ∇

3.6 APPROXIMATIONS FOR COMPOUND DISTRIBUTIONS

In the previous chapter approximations were given that were refinements of the CLT in which the distribution of a sum of a large number of random variables is approximated by a normal distribution. These approximations can also be used if the number of terms in a sum is a random variable with large values. For instance, for the compound Poisson distribution with large λ we have the following counterpart of the CLT; similar results can be derived for the compound (negative) binomial distributions.

Theorem 3.6.1 (CLT for compound Poisson distributions)
Let S be compound Poisson distributed with parameter λ and general claims cdf $P(\cdot)$ with finite variance. Then, with $\mu = \text{E}[S]$ and $\sigma^2 = \text{Var}[S]$,

$$\lim_{\lambda\to\infty} \Pr\left[\frac{S-\mu}{\sigma} \leq x\right] = \Phi(x). \tag{3.43}$$

Proof. If $N_1, N_2, \ldots$ is a series of independent Poisson(1) random variables and if X_{ij}, $i = 1, 2, \ldots, j = 1, 2, \ldots$ are independent random variables with cdf $P(\cdot)$, then for integer-valued λ, we have

$$S \sim \sum_{j=1}^{\lambda}\sum_{i=1}^{N_j} X_{ij}, \quad \text{since} \sum_{j=1}^{\lambda} N_j \sim N. \tag{3.44}$$

As S in (3.44) is the sum of λ independent and identically distributed random variables, the CLT can be applied directly. Note that taking λ to be an integer presents no loss of generality, since the influence of the fractional part vanishes for large λ. ∇

To use the approximations, one needs the cumulants of S. Again, let μ_k denote the kth moment of the claims distribution. Then, for the compound Poisson distribution, we have

$$\kappa_S(t) = \lambda(m_X(t) - 1) = \lambda \sum_{k=1}^{\infty} \mu_k \frac{t^k}{k!}. \tag{3.45}$$

From (2.45) we know that the coefficients of $\frac{t^k}{k!}$ are the cumulants. Hence

$$\text{E}[S] = \lambda\mu_1, \quad \text{Var}[S] = \lambda\mu_2 \quad \text{and} \quad \text{E}[(S - \text{E}[S])^3] = \lambda\mu_3. \tag{3.46}$$

The skewness is proportional to $\lambda^{-1/2}$:

$$\gamma_S = \frac{\mu_3}{\mu_2^{3/2}\sqrt{\lambda}}. \tag{3.47}$$

Remark 3.6.2 (Asymptotics and underflow)
There are certain situations where one would have to resort to approximations. First of all, if the calculation time is too long: for the calculation of $f(s)$ in (3.31) for large s, we need a lot of multiplications, see Exercise 3.5.4. Second, the recursion might not 'get off the ground': if $f(0)$ is extremely small and consequently numerically undistinguishable from 0 (underflow), then all probabilities $f(s)$ in (3.31) are zero too. For instance, if we use a 6-byte real data type as it was used in some programming languages, then the underflow already occurs if $\lambda(1-p(0)) \geq 88$. So for a portfolio of n life insurance policies with probabilities of claim equal to 0.5%, the calculation of $\Pr[S=0]$ already experiences underflow for $n = 17600$. The present generation of processors allow real arithmetic with a much larger precision, and can easily cope with portfolios having $\lambda \approx 11340$, i.e. $\Pr[S=0] \approx 10^{-5000}$.

Fortunately, the approximations improve with increasing λ; they are asymptotically exact, since in the limit they coincide with the usual normal approximation based on the CLT. ∇

3.7 INDIVIDUAL AND COLLECTIVE RISK MODEL

In the preceding sections we have shown that replacing the individual model by the collective risk model has distinct computational advantages. In this section we focus on the question which collective model should be chosen. We consider a situation from life insurance, but it can also be applied to non-life insurance, for instance when fines are imposed (malus) if an employee gets disabled.

Consider n one-year life insurance policies. The claim on policy i has two possible values: at death, which happens with probability q_i, the claim amount is b_i, assumed positive, otherwise it is 0. We want to approximate the total amount of the losses and profits over all policies with a collective model. For that purpose, we replace the I_i payments of size b_i for policy i, where $I_i \sim$ Bernoulli(q_i), by a Poisson(λ_i) distributed number of payments b_i. Instead of the cdf of the total payment in the individual model, i.e.,

$$\widetilde{S} = \sum_{i=1}^{n} I_i b_i, \quad \text{with } \Pr[I_i = 1] = q_i = 1 - \Pr[I_i = 0], \tag{3.48}$$

we consider the cdf of the following approximating random variable:

$$S = \sum_{i=1}^{n} Y_i, \quad \text{with } Y_i = N_i b_i = \sum_{j=1}^{N_i} b_i \quad \text{and} \quad N_i \sim \text{Poisson}(\lambda_i). \tag{3.49}$$

If we choose $\lambda_i = q_i$, the expected number of payments for policy i is equal in both models. To stay on the safe side, we could also choose $\lambda_i = -\log(1 - q_i) > q_i$. With this choice, the probability of 0 claims on policy i is equal in both the collective and the individual model. This way, we incorporate implicit margins by using a larger total claim size than the original one. See also Example 10.4.1.

Although (3.49) still has the form of an individual model, S is a compound Poisson distributed random variable, because of Theorem 3.4.1, so it is indeed a collective model as in (3.1). The parameters are:

$$\lambda = \sum_{i=1}^{n} \lambda_i \quad \text{and} \quad P(x) = \sum_{i=1}^{n} \frac{\lambda_i}{\lambda} I_{[b_i,\infty)}(x), \tag{3.50}$$

with the indicator function $I_A(x) = 1$ if $x \in A$ and 0 otherwise. From this it is clear that the expected numbers of payments are equal if $\lambda_i = q_i$ is taken:

$$\lambda = \sum_{i=1}^{n} \lambda_i = \sum_{i=1}^{n} q_i. \tag{3.51}$$

Also, by (3.48) and (3.49), the expectations of $\widetilde{S}$ and S are then equal:

$$\mathrm{E}[\widetilde{S}] = \sum_{i=1}^{n} q_i b_i = \mathrm{E}[S]. \tag{3.52}$$

For the variances of S and $\widetilde{S}$ we have

$$\begin{aligned} \mathrm{Var}[S] &= \sum_{i=1}^{n} q_i b_i^2; \\ \mathrm{Var}[\widetilde{S}] &= \sum_{i=1}^{n} q_i(1 - q_i) b_i^2 = \mathrm{Var}[S] - \sum_{i=1}^{n} (q_i b_i)^2. \end{aligned} \tag{3.53}$$

We see that S has a larger variance. If $\lambda_i = q_i$ then using a collective model will result in risk averse decision makers tending to take more conservative decisions, see further Chapter 10. Also notice that the smaller $\sum_{i=1}^{n}(q_i b_i)^2$, the less the collective model will differ from the individual model.

Remark 3.7.1 (*The* collective model)
By *the* collective model for a portfolio, we mean a compound Poisson distribution as in (3.50) with $\lambda_i = q_i$. We also call it the *canonical* collective approximation.

In Exercise 3.7.3 we show that in the situation (3.48), *the* collective model can be obtained as well by replacing each claim X_i by a Poisson(1) number of independent claims with the same distribution as X_i. We can also do this if the random variables X_i are more general than those in (3.48). For instance, assume that contract i can take values $b_0 = 0, b_1, b_2, \ldots, b_n$ with probabilities $p_0, p_1, \ldots, p_n$. Then we can write

$$X_i \equiv I_0 b_0 + I_1 b_1 + \cdots + I_n b_n, \tag{3.54}$$

where for the marginal distributions of I_j, we have $\Pr[I_j = 1] = p_j = 1 - \Pr[I_j = 0]$, and for their joint distribution we have $I_0 + I_1 + \cdots + I_n \equiv 1$, since X_i equals exactly one of the possible claim sizes. One can show that if we choose the canonical collective model, we actually replace X_i by the compound Poisson distributed random variable Y_i, with

$$Y_i = N_0 b_0 + N_1 b_1 + \cdots + N_n b_n, \tag{3.55}$$

where the N_j are independent Poisson(p_j) random variables. In this way, the expected frequencies of all claim sizes remain unchanged. ∇

Remark 3.7.2 (Model for an *open* portfolio)
The second proposed model with $\lambda_i = -\log(1 - q_i)$ can be used to model an open portfolio, with entries and exits not on renewal times. Assume that in a certain policy the waiting time W until death has an exponential(β) distribution. To make the probability of no claims equal to the desired value $1 - q$, $\Pr[W > 1] = 1 - q$ has to hold, i.e. $\beta = -\log(1 - q)$. Now assume that, at the moment of death, each time we replace this policy by an identical one. Thus, we have indeed an open model for our portfolio. The waiting times until death are always exponentially(β) distributed. But from the theory of the Poisson process, see also Exercise 2.5.7, we know that the number of deaths before time 1 is Poisson(β) distributed. In this model, replacing for each i the payment on the ith policy by a Poisson($-\log(1-q_i)$) distributed number of copies, we end up with the safer *open* collective model as an approximation for the individual model, see also Example 10.4.1. ∇

Remark 3.7.3 (Negative risk amounts)
If we assume that the b_i are positive integers, then we can quickly calculate the probabilities for S, and consequently quickly approximate those for $\widetilde{S}$, with Panjer's recursion. However, if the b_i can be negative as well as positive, we can't use this recursion. In that case, we can split up S in two parts $S = S^+ - S^-$ where S^+ is precisely the sum of the terms Y_i in (3.49) with $b_i \geq 0$. As can be seen from Theorem 3.4.2, S^+ and S^- are independent compound Poisson random variables with non-negative terms. The cdf of S can then be calculated by convolution of those of S^+ and S^-.

If one wants to calculate the stop-loss premium $\mathrm{E}[(S-d)_+]$ for only one value of d, then the time consuming convolution of S^+ and S^- can easily be avoided. Conditioning on the total S^- of the negative claims, we can rewrite the stop-loss premium as follows:

$$\mathrm{E}[(S-d)_+] = \sum_{x \geq 0} \mathrm{E}[(S^+ - (x+d))_+] \Pr[S^- = x]. \tag{3.56}$$

To calculate this we only need the stop-loss premiums of S^+, which follow as a by-product of Panjer's recursion, see Example 3.5.4. Then the desired stop-loss premium can be calculated with a simple summation. For the convolution, a double summation is necessary. ∇

3.8 SOME PARAMETRIC CLAIM SIZE DISTRIBUTIONS

For a motor insurance portfolio, we could use a collective model with Poisson parameter equal to the average number of claims in the preceding years, adjusted for the trend in the number of policies. The cdf for the individual claim size could be estimated from the observed distribution of the past, and adjusted for inflation.

For some purposes, for instance to compute premium reductions in case of a deductible, it is convenient to use a parametric distribution that fits the observed claims distribution well. The following well-known distributions of positive random variables are suitable:

1. gamma(α, β) distribution: in particular, this distribution is used if the tail of the cdf is not too 'heavy', such as in motor insurance for damage to the own vehicle;

2. lognormal(μ, σ^2) distribution: for branches with somewhat heavier tails, like fire insurance;

3. Pareto(α, x_0): for branches with a considerable probability of large claims, notably liability insurance.

In the exercises we derive some useful properties of these distributions. Besides these distributions there are a lot more possibilities, including the inverse Gaussian and mixtures/combinations of exponential distributions.

Inverse Gaussian distributions[♠]
A distribution that sometimes pops up in the actuarial literature, for several purposes, is the inverse Gaussian. Its properties resemble those of the above-mentioned distributions. Various parametrizations are in use. We will use the one with a shape parameter α and a scale parameter β, just like the gamma distribution. The inverse Gaussian distribution has never gained much popularity because it is hard to manage mathematically. For instance, it is already hard to prove that the probability density function integrates to 1. The most convenient way is to start by defining the cdf, on $x \in (0, \infty)$, as

$$F(x;\alpha,\beta) = \Phi\left(\frac{-\alpha}{\sqrt{\beta x}} + \sqrt{\beta x}\right) + e^{2\alpha}\Phi\left(\frac{-\alpha}{\sqrt{\beta x}} - \sqrt{\beta x}\right). \tag{3.57}$$

Note that the limit for $x \downarrow 0$ is zero; for $x \to \infty$ it is one. Its derivative is the following function, positive on $(0, \infty)$:

$$f(x;\alpha,\beta) = \frac{\alpha}{\sqrt{2\pi\beta}} x^{-\frac{3}{2}} e^{-\frac{(\alpha-\beta x)^2}{2\beta x}}, \quad x > 0. \tag{3.58}$$

So (3.57) is indeed a cdf. Using the fact that (3.58) is actually a density, we can prove that the mgf equals

$$m(t;\alpha,\beta) = \exp\left\{\alpha\left[1 - \sqrt{1 - \frac{2t}{\beta}}\right]\right\}, \quad t \leq \frac{\beta}{2}. \tag{3.59}$$

Notice that the mgf is finite for $t = \frac{\beta}{2}$, but not for $t > \frac{\beta}{2}$. The name inverse Gaussian derives from the fact that the cumulant generating function is the inverse of the one of normal distribution.

The special case with $\alpha = \beta$ is also known as the Wald distribution. By using the mgf, it is easy to prove that β is indeed a scale parameter, since βX is inverse

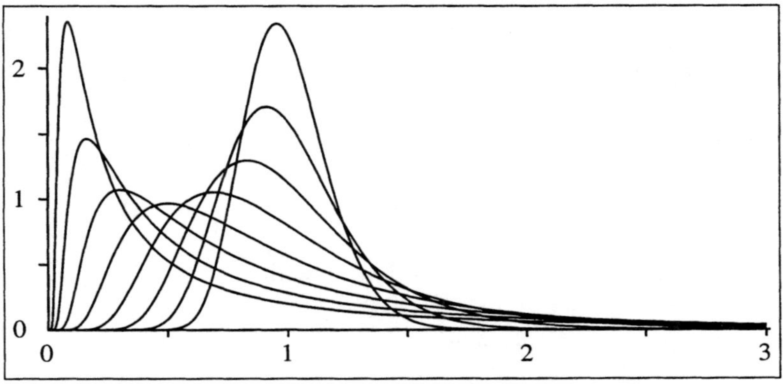

Fig. 3.1 Inverse Gaussians for $\alpha=\beta=\frac{1}{4},\frac{1}{2},1,2,4,8,16,32$ (from left to right).

Gaussian$(\alpha, 1)$ distributed if $X \sim$ inverse Gaussian(α, β). We also see that adding two independent inverse Gaussian distributed random variables, with parameters α_1, β and α_2, β, yields an inverse Gaussian random variable with parameters $\alpha_1 + \alpha_2, \beta$. The expected value and the variance are α/β and α/β^2 respectively, just as in the gamma distribution; the skewness is $3/\sqrt{\alpha}$, hence somewhat larger than for a gamma distribution with the same mean and variance. The flexibility of the inverse Gaussian distributions, from very skew to almost normal, is illustrated in Figure 3.1. Note that all depicted distributions have the same expected value 1.

Mixtures/combinations of exponential distributions

Other useful parametric distributions are the mixtures/combinations of exponential distributions, sometimes also referred to as Coxian distributions. A *mixture* arises if the parameter of an exponential distribution is a random variable which equals α with probability q and β with probability $1 - q$. The density is then given by

$$p(x) = q\alpha e^{-\alpha x} + (1 - q)\beta e^{-\beta x}, \quad x > 0. \tag{3.60}$$

For each q with $0 \leq q \leq 1$, the function $p(\cdot)$ is a probability density function. But also for $q < 0$ or $q > 1$, $p(\cdot)$ in (3.60) is sometimes a pdf. In that case $p(x) \geq 0$ for all x must hold. From Exercise 3.8.4, we learn that it suffices if $p(0) \geq 0$. If we assume that $\alpha < \beta$, then $p(0) \geq 0$ is equivalent with $1 < q \leq \beta/(\beta - \alpha)$, and in this case (3.60) is called a *combination* of exponential distributions.

An example of a proper combination of exponential distributions is given by

$$p(x) = 2(e^{-x} - e^{-2x}) = 2 \times 1e^{-1x} - 1 \times 2e^{-2x}, \tag{3.61}$$

i.e. $q = 2$, $\alpha = 1$ and $\beta = 2$. A second example is the function

$$p(x) = \frac{4}{3}(e^{-x} - \frac{1}{2}e^{-2x}) = \frac{4}{3} \times 1e^{-1x} - \frac{1}{3} \times 2e^{-2x}. \tag{3.62}$$

If $X \sim$ exponential(α) and $Y \sim$ exponential(β), with $\alpha \neq \beta$, then

$$m_{X+Y}(t) = \frac{\alpha\beta}{(\alpha - t)(\beta - t)} = \frac{\beta}{\beta - \alpha}\frac{\alpha}{\alpha - t} - \frac{\alpha}{\beta - \alpha}\frac{\beta}{\beta - t}, \tag{3.63}$$

so a sum of independent exponential random variables has a combination of exponential distributions as its density. The reverse is not always true: (3.61) is the pdf of the convolution of an exponential(1) and an exponential(2) distribution, since $q = \beta/(\beta - \alpha) = 2$, but the pdf (3.62) can't be written as such a convolution.

If $\alpha \uparrow \beta$, then $\beta/(\beta - \alpha) \to \infty$, and $X + Y$ tends to a gamma(2,β) distribution. Hence, the gamma distributions with $r = 2$ are limits of densities that are combinations of exponential distributions, and the same holds for all gamma distributions with an integer scale parameter.

There is a two-stage model which produces *all* random variables with pdf (3.60). Let X, Y and I be independent with X and $Y \sim$ exponential(1) and $I \sim$ Bernoulli(γ) with $0 \leq \gamma \leq 1$, and let $0 < \alpha < \beta$. Then

$$Z = I\frac{X}{\alpha} + \frac{Y}{\beta} \tag{3.64}$$

has the following mgf

$$m_Z(t) = \left(1 - \gamma + \gamma\frac{\alpha}{\alpha - t}\right)\frac{\beta}{\beta - t} = \frac{\alpha\beta - t\beta(1 - \gamma)}{(\alpha - t)(\beta - t)}. \tag{3.65}$$

To show that this is the mgf of a combination or a mixture of exponential distributions, it suffices to find q, using partial fractions, such that (3.65) equals the mgf of (3.60), which is

$$q\frac{\alpha}{\alpha - t} + (1 - q)\frac{\beta}{\beta - t}. \tag{3.66}$$

Comparing (3.65) and (3.66) we see that

$$q\alpha + (1 - q)\beta = \beta(1 - \gamma), \quad \text{hence} \quad q = \frac{\beta\gamma}{\beta - \alpha}. \tag{3.67}$$

Since $0 < \alpha < \beta$, we have that $0 \le q \le 1$ if $0 \le \gamma \le 1 - \alpha/\beta$, and then Z is mixture of exponential distributions. If $1 - \alpha/\beta < \gamma \le 1$, then $q > 1$, and Z is a combination of exponential distributions. The loss Z in (3.64) can be viewed as the result of an experiment where one suffers a loss Y/β in any case and where it is decided by tossing a coin with probability γ of success whether one loses an additional amount X/α. Another interpretation is that the loss is drawn from either Y/β or $X/\alpha + Y/\beta$, since $Z = I(X/\alpha + Y/\beta) + (1 - I)Y/\beta$. If $\gamma = 1$, then again a sum of two exponential distributions arises.

3.9 STOP-LOSS INSURANCE AND APPROXIMATIONS

The payment by a reinsurer in case of a stop-loss reinsurance with retention d for a loss S is equal to $(S - d)_+$. In this section we look for analytical expressions for the net stop-loss premium for several distributions. Note that expressions for stop-loss premiums can also be used to calculate net excess of loss premiums.

If $\pi(d)$ denotes the stop-loss premium for a loss with cdf $F(\cdot)$ as a function of d, then $\pi'(d + 0) = F(d) - 1$. This fact can be used to verify the expressions for stop-loss premiums. For the necessary integrations, we often use partial integration.

Example 3.9.1 (Stop-loss premiums for the normal distribution)
If $X \sim N(\mu, \sigma^2)$, what is the stop-loss premium for X if the retention is d?

As always for non-standard normal distributions, it is advisable to consider the case $\mu = 0$ and $\sigma^2 = 1$ first, and then use the fact that if $U \sim N(0, 1)$, then $X = \sigma U + \mu \sim N(\mu, \sigma^2)$. The required stop-loss premium follows from

$$\mathrm{E}[(X - d)_+] = \mathrm{E}[(\sigma U + \mu - d)_+] = \sigma \mathrm{E}\left[\left(U - \frac{d - \mu}{\sigma}\right)_+\right]. \tag{3.68}$$

Since $\phi'(u) = -u\phi(u)$, we have the following relation

$$\int_t^\infty u\phi(u)du = \int_t^\infty [-\phi'(u)]du = \phi(t). \tag{3.69}$$

It immediately follows that

$$\pi(t) = \mathrm{E}[(U - t)_+] = \phi(t) - t[1 - \Phi(t)], \tag{3.70}$$

and hence

$$\mathrm{E}[(X - d)_+] = \sigma\phi\left(\frac{d - \mu}{\sigma}\right) - (d - \mu)\left[1 - \Phi\left(\frac{d - \mu}{\sigma}\right)\right]. \tag{3.71}$$

For a table with a number of stop-loss premiums for the standard normal distribution, we refer to Example 3.9.5 below. See also Table C at the end of this book. ∇

Example 3.9.2 (Gamma distribution)
Another distribution which has a rather simple expression for the stop-loss premium is the gamma distribution. If $S \sim \text{gamma}(\alpha, \beta)$ and $G(\cdot; \alpha, \beta)$ denotes the cdf of S, then

$$\mathrm{E}[(S-d)_+] = \frac{\alpha}{\beta}[1 - G(d; \alpha+1, \beta)] - d[1 - G(d; \alpha, \beta)]. \tag{3.72}$$

We can also derive expressions for the higher moments of the stop-loss payment $\mathrm{E}[(S-d)_+^k]$, $k = 2, 3, \ldots$. Even the mgf can be calculated analogously, and consequently also exponential premiums for the stop-loss payment. ∇

Remark 3.9.3 (Moments of the retained loss)
Since either $S \leq d$, so $(S-d)_+ = 0$, or $S > d$, so $(S-d)_+ = S - d$, the following equivalence holds in general:

$$[(S-d) - (S-d)_+][(S-d)_+] \equiv 0. \tag{3.73}$$

With this, we can derive the moments of the retained loss $S - (S-d)_+$ from those of the stop-loss payment, using the equivalence

$$\begin{aligned} \{S-d\}^k &\equiv \{[S-d-(S-d)_+] + (S-d)_+\}^k \\ &\equiv \{S-d-(S-d)_+\}^k + \{(S-d)_+\}^k. \end{aligned} \tag{3.74}$$

This holds since, due to (3.73), the remaining terms in the binomial expansion vanish. ∇

In this way, if the loss approximately follows a translated gamma distribution, one can approximate the expected value, the variance and the skewness of the retained loss. See Exercise 3.9.4.

Example 3.9.4 (Stop-loss premiums approximated by NP)
The probabilities of $X > y$ for some random variable can be approximated quite well with the NP approximation. Is it possible to derive an approximation for the stop-loss premium for X too?

Define the following auxiliary functions for $u \geq 1$ and $y \geq 1$:

$$q(u) = u + \frac{\gamma}{6}(u^2 - 1) \quad \text{and} \quad w(y) = \sqrt{\frac{9}{\gamma^2} + \frac{6y}{\gamma} + 1} - \frac{3}{\gamma}. \tag{3.75}$$

From Section 2.5 we know that $w(q(u)) = u$ and $q(w(y)) = y$. Furthermore, $q(\cdot)$ and $w(\cdot)$ are monotonically increasing, and $q(u) \geq y \Leftrightarrow w(y) \leq u$. Let Z be a random variable with expected value 0, standard deviation 1 and skewness $\gamma > 0$. We will derive the stop-loss premiums of random variables X with $\mathrm{E}[X] = \mu$, $\mathrm{Var}[X] = \sigma^2$ and skewness γ from those of Z with the help of (3.68).

The NP approximation states that

$$\Pr[Z > q(u)] = \Pr[w(Z) > u] \approx 1 - \Phi(u) \quad \text{for } u \geq 1. \tag{3.76}$$

Assume that $U \sim N(0,1)$ and define $V = q(U)$ if $U \geq 1$, $V = 1$ otherwise, i.e. $V = q(\max\{U, 1\})$. Then,

$$\Pr[V > q(u)] = \Pr[U > u] = 1 - \Phi(u), \quad u \geq 1. \tag{3.77}$$

Hence,

$$\Pr[Z > y] \approx \Pr[V > y] = 1 - \Phi(w(y)), \quad y \geq 1. \tag{3.78}$$

The stop-loss premium of Z in $d > 1$ can be approximated through the stop-loss premium of V, since

$$\begin{aligned}
\int_d^\infty \Pr[Z > y]dy &\approx \int_d^\infty \Pr[V > y]dy = \mathrm{E}[(V-d)_+] \\
&= \int_{-\infty}^\infty (q(\max\{u,1\}) - d)_+ \phi(u)du \\
&= \int_{w(d)}^\infty (q(u) - d)\phi(u)du.
\end{aligned} \tag{3.79}$$

To calculate this integral, we use the fact that $\frac{d}{du}[u\phi(u)] = (1-u^2)\phi(u)$, and hence

$$\int_t^\infty [u^2 - 1]\phi(u)du = t\phi(t). \tag{3.80}$$

Substituting the relations (3.69) and (3.80) and the function $q(\cdot)$ into (3.79) yields

$$\begin{aligned}
\mathrm{E}[(Z-d)_+] &\approx \int_{w(d)}^\infty \left(u + \frac{\gamma}{6}(u^2-1) - d\right)\phi(u)du \\
&= \phi(w(d)) + \frac{\gamma}{6}w(d)\phi(w(d)) - d[1 - \Phi(w(d))]
\end{aligned} \tag{3.81}$$

as an approximation for the net stop-loss premium for any risk Z with mean 0, variance 1 and skewness γ. ∇

Example 3.9.5 (Comparing CLT and NP stop-loss approximations)
What are approximately the stop-loss premiums for X with $\mathrm{E}[X] = \mu = 0$, $\mathrm{Var}[X] = \sigma^2 = 1$ and skewness $\gamma = 0, \frac{1}{4}, \frac{1}{2}, 1, 2, 4$, for retentions $d = 0, \frac{1}{2}, \ldots, 4$?

If the skewness equals 0, we apply formula (3.71), otherwise (3.81). Although formula (3.81) was only derived for $d \geq 1$, we use it for $d = 0$ and $d = \frac{1}{2}$ anyway. This results in:

d	$\gamma=0$	$\gamma=1/4$	$\gamma=1/2$	$\gamma=1$	$\gamma=2$	$\gamma=4$
0.0	.3989	.3993	.4003	.4044	.4195	.4694
0.5	.1978	.2053	.2131	.2294	.2642	.3385
1.0	.0833	.0934	.1035	.1236	.1640	.2446
1.5	.0293	.0376	.0461	.0637	.1005	.1769
2.0	.0085	.0134	.0189	.0316	.0609	.1280
2.5	.0020	.0042	.0072	.0151	.0365	.0926
3.0	.0004	.0012	.0026	.0070	.0217	.0670
3.5	.0001	.0003	.0009	.0032	.0128	.0484
4.0	.0000	.0001	.0003	.0014	.0075	.0350

So a positive skewness leads to a much larger stop-loss premium. For arbitrary μ and σ, one has to use (3.68). In that case, first determine $d = (t - \mu)/\sigma$, then multiply the corresponding stop-loss premium in the above table by σ, and if necessary, use interpolation. ∇

Example 3.9.6 (Stop-loss premiums of translated gamma distribution)
What are the results if the stop-loss premiums in the previous example are calculated with the translated gamma approximation instead?

The parameters of a translated gamma distributed random variable with expected value 0, variance 1 and skewness γ are $\alpha = 4/\gamma^2$, $\beta = 2/\gamma$ and $x_0 = -2/\gamma$. For $\gamma \downarrow 0$, (3.72) yields the stop-loss premiums for a $\mathrm{N}(0,1)$ distribution. All of the gamma stop-loss premiums are somewhat smaller than those of the NP approximation. Indeed, in (2.60) we see that the tail probabilities of the gamma approximation for $d < \mu + \sigma$ are smaller than those of the NP approximation.

Only in case of a substantial skewness $\gamma = 4$ there is a larger difference.

d	$\gamma = 0$	$\gamma = 1/4$	$\gamma = 1/2$	$\gamma = 1$	$\gamma = 2$	$\gamma = 4$
0.0	.3989	.3984	.3969	.3907	.3679	.3038
0.5	.1978	.2046	.2103	.2184	.2231	.2046
1.0	.0833	.0930	.1017	.1165	.1353	.1424
1.5	.0293	.0374	.0453	.0598	.0821	.1011
2.0	.0085	.0133	.0186	.0297	.0498	.0726
2.5	.0020	.0042	.0072	.0144	.0302	.0527
3.0	.0004	.0012	.0026	.0068	.0183	.0385
3.5	.0001	.0003	.0009	.0032	.0111	.0283
4.0	.0000	.0001	.0003	.0015	.0067	.0209

From this table it would seem that the results for small d cannot be correct. Even the approximation (3.81), although only derived for $d \geq 1$, yields more plausible results for $d = 0$ and $d = 0.5$, since these increase with increasing skewness. But from (3.83) below, it immediately follows that if all stop-loss premiums for one distribution are larger than those of another distribution with the same expected value, then the former has a larger variance. Since in this case the variances are equal, besides larger stop-loss premiums of the translated gamma, there have to be smaller ones as well.

Note that the translated gamma approximation gives the stop-loss premium for a risk with the right expected value and variance. On the other hand, the NP approximation gives approximating stop-loss premiums for a random variable with the appropriate tail probabilities beyond $\mu + \sigma$. Obviously, random variables exist having the NP tail probabilities and the correct first three moments at the same time. ∇

3.10 STOP-LOSS PREMIUMS IN CASE OF UNEQUAL VARIANCES

In this section we compare the stop-loss premiums of two risks with equal expected value, but with unequal variance. It is impossible to formulate an exact general rule, but we can state some useful approximating results.

Just as one gets the expected value by integrating the distribution function over $(0, \infty)$, one can in turn integrate the stop-loss premiums. In Exercise 3.10.1, the reader is invited to prove that, if $U \geq 0$ with probability 1,

$$\frac{1}{2}\mathrm{Var}[U] = \int_0^\infty \{\mathrm{E}[(U-t)_+] - (\mu - t)_+\}dt. \tag{3.82}$$

The integrand in this equation is always non-negative. From (3.82), it follows that if U and W are risks with equal expectation μ, then

$$\int_0^\infty \{\mathrm{E}[(U-t)_+] - \mathrm{E}[(W-t)_+]\}dt = \frac{1}{2}\{\mathrm{Var}[U] - \mathrm{Var}[W]\}. \tag{3.83}$$

By approximating the integral in (3.83) with the trapezoid rule with interval width 1, we can say the following about the total of all differences in the stop-loss premiums of U and W (notice that we don't use absolute values):

$$\sum_{i=1}^{\infty}\{\mathrm{E}[(U-i)_+] - \mathrm{E}[(W-i)_+]\} \approx \frac{1}{2}\{\mathrm{Var}[U] - \mathrm{Var}[W]\}. \tag{3.84}$$

So, if we replace the actual stop-loss premiums of U by those of W, then (3.84) provides an approximation for the total error in all integer-valued arguments. In Chapter 10 we examine conditions for $\mathrm{E}[(U-d)_+] \geq \mathrm{E}[(W-d)_+]$ to hold for all d. If that is the case, then all terms in (3.84) are positive and consequently, the maximum error in all of these terms will be less than the right-hand side.

It is not very unreasonable to assume that the ratio of two integrands is approximately equal to the ratio of the corresponding integrals. Then, (3.82) yields the following approximation

$$\frac{\mathrm{E}[(U-t)_+] - (\mu - t)_+}{\mathrm{E}[(W-t)_+] - (\mu - t)_+} \approx \frac{\mathrm{Var}[U]}{\mathrm{Var}[W]}. \tag{3.85}$$

This approximation is exact if $\mu = \mathrm{E}[U]$ and $W = (1-I)\mu + IU$ with $I \sim$ Bernoulli(α) independent of U and $\alpha = \mathrm{Var}[W]/\mathrm{Var}[U]$, see Exercise 3.10.2.

If $t \geq \mu$, then $(\mu - t)_+ = 0$, so the approximation (3.85) simplifies to the following rule of thumb:

Rule of thumb 3.10.1 (Ratio of stop-loss premiums)
For retentions t larger than the expectation $\mu = \mathrm{E}[U] = \mathrm{E}[W]$, we have for the stop-loss premiums of risks U and W:

$$\frac{\mathrm{E}[(U-t)_+]}{\mathrm{E}[(W-t)_+]} \approx \frac{\mathrm{Var}[U]}{\mathrm{Var}[W]}. \tag{3.86}$$

This rule works best for intermediate values of t, see below. ∇

Example 3.10.2 ('Undefined wife')
Exercise 3.7.4 deals with the situation where it is unknown for which of the insureds a widows' benefit might have to be paid. If the frequency of being married is 80%, we can either multiply all risk amounts by 0.8 and leave the probability of dying within one year as it is, or we can multiply the mortality probability by 0.8 and leave the payment as it is. We derived that the resulting variance of the total claim amount in the former case is approximately 80% of the variance in the latter case. So, if we use the former method to calculate the stop-loss premiums instead of the correct method, then the resulting stop-loss premiums for retentions which are larger than the expected claim cost are approximately 20% too small. ∇

We will check Rule of thumb 3.10.1 by considering the case $\mathrm{N}(\mu, \sigma^2)$ with fixed μ and σ^2. Write $\pi(d; \mu, \sigma^2)$ for the stop-loss premium of a $\mathrm{N}(\mu, \sigma^2)$ distributed random variable, $\pi(\cdot)$ for $\pi(\cdot; 0, 1)$, $\Phi(\cdot)$ for the $\mathrm{N}(0,1)$ cdf and $\phi(\cdot) = \Phi'(\cdot)$ for the corresponding pdf. With $d^* = (d-\mu)/\sigma$, we can rewrite (3.71) as follows:

$$\pi(d; \mu, \sigma^2) = \sigma\pi(d^*; 0, 1) = \sigma[\phi(d^*) - d^*(1 - \Phi(d^*))]. \tag{3.87}$$

To see how $\pi(d; \mu, \sigma^2)$ varies by changing σ^2 and keeping μ constant, we calculate the partial derivative with respect to σ^2:

$$\begin{aligned}\frac{\partial}{\partial\sigma^2}\pi(d; \mu, \sigma^2) &= \frac{1}{2\sigma}\frac{\partial}{\partial\sigma}\sigma\pi\left(\frac{d-\mu}{\sigma}\right)\\ &= \frac{1}{2\sigma^2}\left[\sigma\pi\left(\frac{d-\mu}{\sigma}\right) + (d-\mu)\left\{1 - \Phi\left(\frac{d-\mu}{\sigma}\right)\right\}\right].\end{aligned} \tag{3.88}$$

Hence if we replace σ^2 by $\sigma^2 + \delta^2$ for small δ, this roughly affects the stop-loss premium as follows:

$$\begin{aligned}&\pi(d; \mu, \sigma^2 + \delta^2)\\ &\approx \pi(d; \mu, \sigma^2) + \frac{\delta^2}{2\sigma^2}\left[\sigma\pi\left(\frac{d-\mu}{\sigma}\right) + (d-\mu)\left\{1 - \Phi\left(\frac{d-\mu}{\sigma}\right)\right\}\right]\\ &= \frac{\sigma^2 + \delta^2}{\sigma^2}\pi(d; \mu, \sigma^2)\\ &\quad + \frac{\delta^2}{2\sigma^2}\left[(d-\mu)\left\{1 - \Phi\left(\frac{d-\mu}{\sigma}\right)\right\} - \sigma\pi\left(\frac{d-\mu}{\sigma}\right)\right].\end{aligned} \tag{3.89}$$

The first term in (3.89) is precisely the Rule of thumb. One can show that integrating the second term over $d \in [\mu, \infty)$ yields 0. This term is negative if d is close to μ,

d	$\pi(d;0,1)$	Correction factor	
		$1+0.01\times$	$1+0.25\times$
0.0	0.39894	0.50	0.47
0.5	0.19780	0.89	0.85
1.0	0.08332	1.45	1.45
1.5	0.02931	2.22	2.35
2.0	0.00849	3.20	3.73
2.5	0.00200	4.43	5.84
3.0	0.00038	5.92	9.10

Table 3.1 Factors by which the $\mathrm{N}(0, 1.01)$ and $\mathrm{N}(0, 1.25)$ stop-loss premiums deviate from those of $\mathrm{N}(0, 1)$, expressed in terms of the Rule of thumb correction factor

zero if $d \approx 0.745$ and positive for large d. From this, we may conclude that the Rule of thumb will work best for retentions approximately equal to $\mu + \frac{3}{4}\sigma$.

Example 3.10.3 (Numerical evaluation of the Rule of thumb)
We calculated the stop-loss premiums for a $\mathrm{N}(0, 1.01)$ and a $\mathrm{N}(0, 1.25)$ distribution at retentions $d = 0, \frac{1}{2}, 1, \ldots, 3$, to compare them with those of a $\mathrm{N}(0, 1)$ distribution. According to Rule of thumb 3.10.1, these should be 1.01 and 1.25 times as big respectively. Table 3.1 gives the factor by which that factor should be multiplied to get the real error. For instance, for $d = 0$ the quotient $\pi(d; 0, 1.01)/\pi(d; 0, 1)$ equals 1.005 instead of 1.01, so the error is only 50% of the one predicted by the Rule of thumb. As can be seen, the Rule of thumb correction factor is too large for retentions close to the expected value, too small for large retentions and approximately correct for retentions equal to the expected value plus 0.75 standard deviation. The Rule of thumb correction factor has a large error for retentions in the far tail where the stop-loss premiums of the distribution with the smaller variance are negligible but those of the distribution with the larger variance are not.

If one wants to squeeze a little more precision out of the Rule of thumb, one can find an appropriate correction factor in Table 3.1. For instance, if the retention equals $\mu + \sigma$ and if the quotient of the variances equals $1 + \delta$, then one should multiply the stop-loss premium by a factor $1 + 1.45\delta$ to approximate the stop-loss premium, assuming the risks resemble a normal distribution. ∇

3.11 EXERCISES

Section 3.2

1. Calculate (3.3), (3.4) and (3.5) in case N has the following distribution: a) Poisson(λ), b) binomial(n,p) and c) negative binomial(r,p).
2. Give the counterpart of (3.5) for the cumulant generating function.
3. Assume that the number of eggs in a bird's nest is a Poisson(λ) distributed random variable, and that the probability that a female hatches out equals p. Determine the distribution of the number of females in a bird's nest.
4. Let S be compound Poisson distributed with $\lambda = 2$ and $p(x) = x/10$, $x = 1, 2, 3, 4$. Apply (3.10) to calculate the probabilities of $S = s$ for $s \leq 4$.
5. Complete the table in Example 3.2.2 for $x = 0, \ldots, 6$. Determine the expected value and the variance of N, X and S.
6. Determine the expected value and the variance of S, where S is defined as in Example 3.2.2, except that N is Poisson distributed with $\lambda = 2$.
7. Prove relation (3.11) by partial integration. Do the same by differentiating both sides of the equation and examining one value, either $x = 0$ or $x \to \infty$.

Section 3.3

1. Show that the Poisson distribution also arises as the limit of the negative binomial(r,p) distribution if $r \to \infty$ and $p \to 1$ such that $r(1-p) = \lambda$ remains constant.
2. Under which circumstances does the usual Poisson distribution arise instead of the negative binomial in Examples 3.3.1 and 3.3.2?
3. [♠] Prove (3.19).

Section 3.4

1. The same as Exercise 3.2.4, but now with the sparse vector algorithm.
2. What happens with (3.23) if some x_i are equal in (3.22)?
3. Assume that S_1 is compound Poisson with $\lambda_1 = 4$ and claims $p_1(j) = \frac{1}{4}, j = 0, 1, 2, 3$, and S_2 is also compound Poisson with $\lambda_2 = 2$ and $p_2(j) = \frac{1}{2}, j = 2, 4$. If S_1 and S_2 are independent, then what is the distribution of $S_1 + S_2$?
4. In Exercise 3.2.3, prove that the number of males is independent of the number of females.
5. Let N_j, $j = 1, 2$, denote the number of claims of size j in Example 3.2.2. Are N_1 and N_2 independent?
6. Assume that S is compound Poisson distributed with parameter λ and with discrete claims distribution $p(x)$, $x > 0$. Consider S_0, a compound Poisson distribution with parameter $\lambda_0 = \lambda/\alpha$ for some α with $0 < \alpha < 1$, and with claims distribution $p_0(x)$ where $p_0(0) = 1 - \alpha$ and $p_0(x) = \alpha p(x)$ for $x > 0$. Prove that S and S_0 have the same distribution by comparing their

mgf's. Also show that $S \sim S_0$ holds because the frequencies of the claim amounts $x \neq 0$ in (3.22) have the same distribution.

Section 3.5

1. The same as Exercise 3.2.4, but now with Panjer's recursion relation.
2. The same as Exercise 3.4.6, first part, but now by proving with induction that Panjer's recursion yields the same probabilities $f(s)$.
3. Verify Example 3.5.2.
4. In case of a compound Poisson distribution for which the claims have mass points $1, 2, \ldots, m$, determine how many multiplications have to be done to calculate the probability $F(t)$ using Panjer's recursion. Distinguish the cases $m < t$ and $m \geq t$.
5. Prove that $\mathrm{E}[N] = (a+b)/(1-a)$ if $q_n = \Pr[N = n]$ satisfies (3.26).
6. In Example 3.5.4, determine the retention d for which $\pi(d) = 0.3$.
7. Let N_1, N_2 and N_3 be independent and Poisson(1) distributed. For the retention $d = 2.5$, determine $\mathrm{E}[(N_1 + 2N_2 + 3N_3 - d)_+]$.
8. Assume that S_1 is compound Poisson distributed with parameter $\lambda = 2$ and claim sizes $p(1) = p(3) = \frac{1}{2}$. Let $S_2 = S_1 + N$, where N is Poisson(1) distributed and independent of S_1. Determine the mgf of S_2. What is the corresponding distribution? Determine $\Pr[S_2 \leq 2.4]$. Leave the powers of e unevaluated.
9. Determine the parameters of an integer-valued compound Poisson distributed Z if for some $\alpha > 0$, Panjer's recursion relation equals $\Pr[Z = s] = f(s) = \frac{\alpha}{s}[f(s-1) + 2f(s-2)]$, $s = 1, 2, 3, \ldots$. [Don't forget the case $p(0) \neq 0$!]
10. Assume that S is compound Poisson distributed with parameter $\lambda = 3$, $p(1) = \frac{5}{6}$ and $p(2) = \frac{1}{6}$. Calculate $f(x)$, $F(x)$ and $\pi(x)$ for $x = 0, 1, 2, \ldots$. Also calculate $\pi(2.5)$.
11. Derive formulas from (3.34) for the stop-loss premium which only use $f(0), f(1), \ldots, f(d-1)$ and $F(0), F(1), \ldots, F(d-1)$ respectively.
12. Give a formula, analogous to (3.36), to calculate $\mathrm{E}[(S-d)_+^2]$.

Section 3.6

1. Assume that S is compound Poisson distributed with parameter $\lambda = 12$ and uniform$(0, 1)$ distributed claims. Approximate $\Pr[S < 10]$ with the CLT approximation, the translated gamma approximation and the NP approximation.
2. Assume that S is compound Poisson distributed with parameter $\lambda = 10$ and χ_4^2 distributed claims. Approximate the distribution function of S with the translated gamma approximation. With the NP approximation, estimate the quantile s such that $F_S(s) \approx 0.95$, as well as the probability $F_S(\mathrm{E}[S] + 3\sqrt{\mathrm{Var}[S]})$.

Section 3.7

1. Show that $\lambda_j = -\log(1 - q_j)$ yields both a larger expectation and a larger variance of S in (3.49) than $\lambda_j = q_j$ does. For both cases, compare $\Pr[I_i = j]$ and $\Pr[N_i = j]$, $j = 0, 1, 2, \ldots$ in (3.48) and (3.49), as well as the cdf's of I_i and N_i.

2. Consider a portfolio of 100 one-year life insurance policies which are evenly divided between the insured amounts 1 and 2 and probabilities of dying within this year 0.01 and 0.02. Determine the expectation and the variance of the total claims $\widetilde{S}$. Choose an appropriate compound Poisson distribution S to approximate $\widetilde{S}$ and compare the expectations and the variances. Determine for both S and $\widetilde{S}$ the parameters of a suitable approximating translated gamma distribution.

3. Show, by comparing the respective mgf's, that the following representations of *the* collective model are equivalent:

    1. The compound Poisson distribution with parameter $\lambda = n$ and claims distribution $Q(x) = \frac{1}{n}\sum_j \Pr[X_j \leq x]$. [Hence $Q(\cdot)$ is the arithmetic mean of the cdf's of the claims. It can be interpreted as the cdf of a claim from a *randomly* chosen policy, where each policy has probability $\frac{1}{n}$.]
    2. The compound Poisson distribution specified in (3.50) with $\lambda_i = q_i$.
    3. The random variable $\sum_i N_i b_i$ from (3.49) with $\lambda_i = q_i$.
    4. The random variable $Z_1 + \cdots + Z_n$ where the Z_i are compound Poisson distributed with claim number parameter 1 and claims distribution equal to those of $I_i b_i$.

4. In a portfolio of n one-year life insurance policies for men, the probability of dying in this year equals q_i for the ith policyholder. In case of death, an amount b_i has to be paid out, but only if it turns out that the policy holder leaves a widow behind. This information is not known to the insurer in advance ('undefined wife'), but from tables we know that this probability equals 80% for each policy. In this situation, we can approximate the individual model by a collective one in two ways: by replacing the insured amount for policy i by $0.8b_i$, or by replacing the claim probability for policy i by $0.8q_i$. Which method is correct? Determine the variance of the total claims for both methods. Show how we can proceed in both cases, if we have a program at our disposal that calculates stop-loss premiums from a mortality table and an input file containing the sex, the age and the risk amount.

5. [♠] At what value of x in (3.56) may we stop the summation if an absolute precision ε is required?

6. Consider a portfolio with 2 classes of policies. Class i contains 1000 policies with claim size $b_i = i$ and claim probability 0.01, for $i = 1, 2$. Let B_i denote the number of claims in class i. Write the total claims S as $S = B_1 + 2B_2$ and let $N = B_1 + B_2$ denote the number of claims. Consider the compound binomial distributed random variable $T = X_1 + X_2 + \cdots + X_N$ with $\Pr[X_i = 1] = \Pr[X_i = 2] = 1/2$. Compare S and T as regards the maximum value, the expected value, the variance, the claim number distribution and the distribution. Do the same for B_1 and B_2 ~Poisson(10).

7. Consider an excess of loss reinsurance on some portfolio. In case of a claim x, the reinsurer pays out an amount $h(x) = (x - \beta)_+$. The claims process is a compound Poisson process with claim number parameter 10 and uniform(1000,2000) distributed claim sizes. For $\beta \in [1000, 2000]$, determine the distribution of the total amount to be paid out by the reinsurer in a year.

8. Consider two portfolios P1 and P2 with the following characteristics:

	Risk amount	Number of policies	Claim probability
P1	z_1	n_1	q_1
	z_2	n_2	q_2
P2	z_1	$2n_1$	$\frac{1}{2}q_1$
	z_2	$2n_2$	$\frac{1}{2}q_2$

For the *individual* risk models for P1 and P2, determine the difference of the variance of the total claims amount. Check if the *collective* approximation of P1 equals the one of P2, both constructed with the recommended methods.

9. A certain portfolio contains two types of contracts. For type k, $k = 1, 2$, the claim probability equals q_k and the number of policies equals n_k. If there is a claim, then with probability $p_k(x)$ it equals x, as follows:

	n_k	q_k	$p_k(1)$	$p_k(2)$	$p_k(3)$
Type 1	1000	0.01	0.5	0	0.5
Type 2	2000	0.02	0.5	0.5	0

Assume that all policies are independent. Construct a collective model T to approximate the total claims. Make sure that both the expected number of positive claims and the expected total claims agree. Give the simplest form of Panjer's recursion relation in this case; also give a starting value. With the help of T, approximate the capital that is required to cover all claims in this portfolio with probability 95%. Use an approximation based on three moments, and compare the results with those of Exercise 2.5.13.

10. Consider a portfolio containing n contracts that all produce a claim 1 with probability q. What is the distribution of the total claims according to the individual model, *the* collective model and the *open* collective model? If $n \to \infty$, with q fixed, does the individual model S converge to the collective model T, in the sense that the difference of the probabilities $\Pr[(S - \mathrm{E}[S])/\sqrt{\mathrm{Var}[S]} \leq x] - \Pr[(T - \mathrm{E}[S])/\sqrt{\mathrm{Var}[S]} \leq x]$ converges to 0?

Section 3.8

1. Determine the mean and the variance of the lognormal and the Pareto distribution, see also Table A. Proceed as follows: if $Y \sim \text{lognormal}(\mu, \sigma^2)$, then $\log Y \sim N(\mu, \sigma^2)$; if $Y \sim \text{Pareto}(\alpha, x_0)$, then $Y/x_0 \sim \text{Pareto}(\alpha, 1)$ and $\log(Y/x_0) \sim \text{exponential}(\alpha)$.

2. Determine which parameters of the distributions in this section are scale parameters, in the sense that λX, or more general $f(\lambda)X$ for some function f, has a distribution that does not depend on λ. Show that neither the skewness γ_X nor the coefficient of variation σ_X/μ_X depend on such parameters. Determine these two quantities for the given distributions.

3. [♠] Prove that the expression in (3.57) is indeed a cdf, which is 0 in $x = 0$, tends to 1 for $x \to \infty$ and has a positive derivative (3.58). Also verify that (3.59) is the mgf, and confirm the other statements about the inverse Gaussian distributions.

4. Show that the given conditions on q in (3.60) are sufficient for $p(\cdot)$ to be a pdf.
5. Determine the cdf $\Pr[Z \leq d]$ and the stop-loss premium $\mathrm{E}[(Z-d)_+]$ for a mixture or combination Z of exponential distributions as in (3.60). Also determine the conditional distribution of $Z - z$, given $Z > z$.
6. Determine the mode of mixtures and combinations of exponential distributions. Also determine the mode and the median of the lognormal distribution.
7. [♠] Determine the mode of the inverse Gaussian(α, α) distribution. For the parameter values of Figure 3.1, use your computer to determine the median of this distribution.

Section 3.9

1. Assume that X is normally distributed with expectation 10000 and standard deviation 1000. Determine the stop-loss premium for a retention 13000. Do the same for a random variable Y that has the same first two moments as X, but skewness 1.
2. Show that $\mathrm{E}[(S-d)_+] = \mathrm{E}[S] - d + \int_0^d (d-x)dF(x) = \mathrm{E}[S] - \int_0^d [1 - F(x)]dx$.
3. If $X \sim N(\mu, \sigma^2)$, show that $\int_\mu^\infty \mathrm{E}[(X-t)_+]dt = \frac{1}{4}\sigma^2$ and determine $\mathrm{E}[(X-\mu)_+]$.
4. Verify (3.72). Also verify (3.73) and (3.74), and show how these can be used to approximate the variance of the retained loss.
5. Give an expression for the net premium if the number of claims is Poisson(λ) distributed and the claim size is Pareto distributed. Assume that there is a deductible d.
6. [♠] Let $X \sim$ lognormal(μ, σ^2). Determine the stop-loss premium $\mathrm{E}[(X-d)_+]$ for $d > 0$. Compare your result to the Black-Scholes option pricing formula, and explain.
7. In the table from Example 3.9.5, does using linear interpolation to calculate the stop-loss premium in e.g. $d = 0.4$ for one of the given values for γ yield a result that is too high or too low?
8. Assume that N is an integer-valued risk with $\mathrm{E}[(N-d)_+] = \mathrm{E}[(U-d)_+]$ for $d = 0, 1, 2, \ldots$, where $U \sim N(0,1)$. Determine $\Pr[N = 1]$.
9. Let $\pi(t) = \mathrm{E}[(U-t)_+]$ denote the stop-loss premium for $U \sim N(0,1)$ and retention t, $-\infty < t < \infty$. Show that $\pi(-t), t \geq 0$ satisfies $\pi(-t) = t + \pi(+t)$. Sketch $\pi(t)$.
10. In Sections 3.9 and 3.10, the retention is written as $\mu + k\sigma$, so it is expressed in terms of a number of standard deviations above the expected loss. However, in the insurance practice, the retention is always expressed as a percentage of the expected loss. Consider two companies for which the risk of absence due to illness is to be covered by stop-loss insurance. This risk is compound Poisson distributed with parameter λ_i and exponentially distributed individual losses X with $\mathrm{E}[X] = 1000$. Company 1 is small: $\lambda_1 = 3$; company 2 is large: $\lambda_2 = 300$. What are the net stop-loss premiums for both companies in case the retention d equals 80%, 100% and 120% of the expected loss respectively? Express these amounts as a percentage of the expected loss and use the normal approximation.

Section 3.10

1. Prove (3.82) and (3.83) and verify that the integrand in (3.82) is non-negative.

2. Show that (3.85) is exact if $W = (1 - I)\mu + IU$ with $\mu = \mathrm{E}[U]$ and $I \sim$ Bernoulli(α), for $\alpha = \mathrm{Var}[W]/\mathrm{Var}[U]$.
3. Verify (3.88) and (3.89). Also verify that integrating the last term in (3.89) yields 0.
4. Assume that $X_1, X_2, \ldots$ are independent and identically distributed risks that represent the loss on a portfolio in consecutive years. We could insure these risks with separate stop-loss contracts for one year with a retention d, but we could also consider only one contract for the whole period of n years with a retention nd. Show that $\mathrm{E}[(X_1 - d)_+] + \cdots + \mathrm{E}[(X_n - d)_+] \geq \mathrm{E}[(X_1 + \cdots + X_n - nd)_+]$. If $d \geq \mathrm{E}[X_i]$, examine how the total net stop-loss premium for the one-year contracts $\mathrm{E}[(X_1 - d)_+]$ relates to the stop-loss premium for the n-year period $\mathrm{E}[(X_1 + \cdots + X_n - nd)_+]$.
5. Let $B_1 \sim$ binomial(4,0.05), $B_2 \sim$ binomial(2,0.1), $S = B_1 + B_2$ and $T \sim$ Poisson(0.4). For the retentions $d = \frac{1}{2}, 1, \frac{3}{2}$, use the Rule of thumb 3.10.1 and discuss the results.
6. Derive (3.84) from the trapezoid rule $\int_0^\infty f(x)dx \approx \frac{1}{2\delta}\sum_1^\infty [f(i\delta) + f((i-1)\delta)]$ with interval width $\delta = 1$.

4

Ruin theory

4.1 INTRODUCTION

In this chapter we focus again on collective risk models, but now in the long term. We consider the development in time of the capital $U(t)$ of an insurer. This is a stochastic process which increases continuously because of the earned premiums, and decreases stepwise because of the payment of claims. When the capital becomes negative, we say that ruin occurs. Let $\psi(u)$ denote the probability that this ever happens, provided that the annual premium and the claims process remain unchanged. This probability is a useful tool for the management since it serves as an indication of the soundness of the insurer's combined premiums and claims process, given the available initial capital $u = U(0)$. A high probability of ruin indicates instability: measures such as reinsurance or raising some premiums should be considered, or the insurer should attract extra working capital.

The probability of ruin enables one to compare portfolios with each other, but we cannot attach any absolute meaning to the probability of ruin, as it doesn't actually represent the probability that the insurer will go bankrupt in the near future. First of all, it might take centuries for ruin to actually happen. Moreover, potential interventions in the process, for instance paying out dividends or raising the premium for risks with an unfavorable claims performance, are ruled out in the determination of the probability of ruin. Furthermore, the effects of inflation on the one hand and the return on the capital on the other hand are supposed to cancel each other out exactly. The ruin probability only accounts for the insurance risk, not the managerial blunders that might occur. Finally, the state of ruin is nothing but a mathematical abstraction: with a capital of -1 Euro, the insurer isn't broke in practice, and with a capital of $+1$ Euro, the insurer can hardly be called solvent.

The calculation of the probability of ruin is one of the classical problems in actuarial science. Although it is possible to determine the moment generating function with the probability $1 - \psi(u)$ of not getting ruined (the non-ruin probability), only two types of claim distributions are known for which the probability of ruin can easily be calculated. These are the exponential distributions and sums, mixtures and combinations of these distributions, as well as the distributions with only a finite number of values. For other distributions, however, an elegant and usually sufficiently tight upper bound $\psi(u) \leq e^{-Ru}$ can be found. The real number R in this expression is called the *adjustment coefficient*. This so-called *Lundberg upper bound* can often be used instead of the actual ruin probability: the higher R, the lower the upper bound for the ruin probability and, hence, the safer the situation. The adjustment coefficient R can be calculated by solving an equation which contains the mgf of the claims, their expectation and the ratio of premium and expected claims.

Multiplying both the premium rate and the expected claim frequency by the same factor does not change the probability of eventual ruin: it doesn't matter if we make the clock run faster. There have been attempts to replace the ruin probability by a more 'realistic' quantity, for instance the *finite* ruin probability, which is the probability of ruin before time t_0. But this quantity behaves somewhat less orderly and introduces an extra problem, namely the choice of the length of the time interval. Another alternative arises if we consider the capital in discrete time points $0, 1, 2, \ldots$ only, for instance at the time of the closing of the books. For this *discrete time model*, we will derive some results.

First, we will discuss the Poisson process as a model to describe the development in time of the number of claims. A characteristic feature of the Poisson process is that it is *memoryless*: the occurrence of a claim in the next second is independent of the history of the process. The advantage of a process being memoryless is the mathematical simplicity; the disadvantage is that it is often not realistic. The total of the claims paid in a Poisson process constitutes a compound Poisson process.

In the second part of this chapter, we will derive the mgf of the non-ruin probability by studying the maximal aggregate loss, which represents the maximum

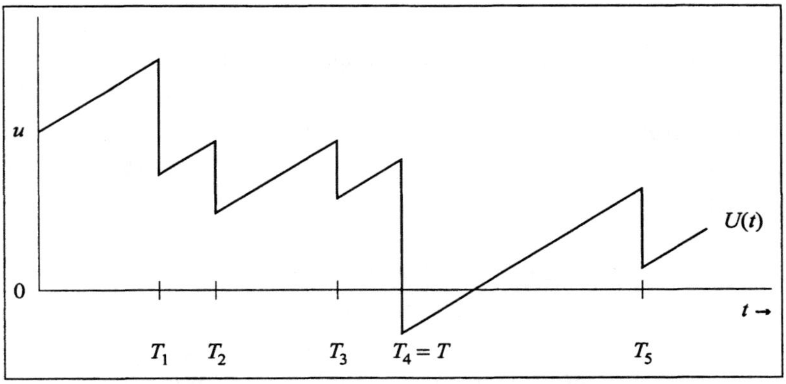

Fig. 4.1 A realization of the risk process $U(t)$.

difference between the earned premiums and the total payments up to any moment. Using this mgf, we will determine the value of the ruin probability in case the claims are distributed according to variants of the exponential distribution. Next, we will consider some approximations for the ruin probability.

4.2 THE RISK PROCESS

A stochastic process consists of related random variables, indexed by the time t. We define the *surplus process* or *risk process* as follows:

$$U(t) = u + ct - S(t), \quad t \geq 0, \tag{4.1}$$

where

$$\begin{aligned} U(t) &= \text{the insurer's capital at time } t; \\ u = U(0) &= \text{the initial capital;} \\ c &= \text{the (constant) premium income per unit of time;} \\ S(t) &= X_1 + X_2 + \cdots + X_{N(t)}, \end{aligned}$$

with

$$\begin{aligned} N(t) &= \text{the number of claims up to time } t, \text{ and} \\ X_i &= \text{the size of the } i\text{th claim, assumed to be non-negative.} \end{aligned}$$

A typical realization of the risk process is depicted in Figure 4.1. The random variables $T_1, T_2, \ldots$ denote the time points at which a claim occurs. The slope of the process is c if there are no claims; if, however, $t = T_j$ for some j, then the capital drops by X_j, which is the size of the jth claim. Since in Figure 4.1, at time T_4 the total of the incurred claims $X_1 + X_2 + X_3 + X_4$ is larger than the initial capital u plus the earned premium cT_4, the remaining surplus $U(T_4)$ is less than 0. This state of the process is called *ruin* and the point in time at which this occurs for the first time is denoted by T. So,

$$\begin{aligned} T &= \min\{t | t \geq 0 \;\&\; U(t) < 0\}; \\ &= \infty \quad \text{if } U(t) \geq 0 \text{ for all } t. \end{aligned} \tag{4.2}$$

The random variable T is *defective*, as the probability of $T = \infty$ is positive. The probability that ruin ever occurs, i.e., the probability that T is finite, is called the ruin probability. It is written as follows:

$$\psi(u) = \Pr[T < \infty]. \tag{4.3}$$

Before we turn to the claim process $S(t)$, i.e., the total claims up to time t, we first look at the process $N(t)$ of the number of claims up to t. We will assume that $N(t)$ is a so-called Poisson process:

Definition 4.2.1 (Poisson process)
The process $N(t)$ is a *Poisson process* if for some intensity $\lambda > 0$, the increments of the process have the following property:

$$N(t + h) - N(t) \sim \text{Poisson}(\lambda h) \tag{4.4}$$

for all $t > 0$, $h > 0$ and each history $N(s)$, $s \leq t$. ∇

As a result, a Poisson process has the following properties:

- the increments are *independent*: if the intervals $(t_i, t_i + h_i)$, $i = 1, 2, \ldots$, are disjoint, then the increments $N(t_i + h_i) - N(t_i)$ are independent;
- the increments are *stationary*: $N(t + h) - N(t)$ is Poisson(λh) distributed for every value of t.

Next to this global definition of the claim number process, we can also consider *infinitesimal* increments $N(t + dt) - N(t)$, where the infinitesimal 'number' dt

again is positive, but smaller than any real number larger than 0. For the Poisson process we have:

$$\begin{aligned}
&\Pr[N(t+dt)-N(t)=1|N(s),0\le s\le t]=e^{-\lambda dt}\lambda dt=\lambda dt,\\
&\Pr[N(t+dt)-N(t)=0|N(s),0\le s\le t]=e^{-\lambda dt}=1-\lambda dt,\\
&\Pr[N(t+dt)-N(t)\ge 2|N(s),0\le s\le t]=0.
\end{aligned} \tag{4.5}$$

Actually, these equalities are not really quite equalities: they are only valid if we ignore terms of order $(dt)^2$.

A third way to define such a process is by considering the *waiting times*

$$W_1=T_1,\quad W_j=T_j-T_{j-1},\ j=2,3,\ldots \tag{4.6}$$

Because Poisson processes are memoryless, these waiting times are independent exponential(λ) random variables, and they are also independent of the history of the process. This can be shown as follows: if the history H represents an arbitrary realization of the process up to time t with the property that $T_{i-1}=t$, then

$$\Pr[W_i>h|H]=\Pr[N(t+h)-N(t)=0|H]=e^{-\lambda h}. \tag{4.7}$$

If $N(t)$ is a Poisson process, then $S(t)$ is a compound Poisson process; for a fixed $t=t_0$, the aggregate claims $S(t_0)$ have a compound Poisson distribution with parameter λt_0.

Some more notation: the cdf and the moments of the individual claims X_i are

$$P(x)=\Pr[X_i\le x];\quad \mu_j=\mathrm{E}[X_i^j],\ i,j=1,2,\ldots \tag{4.8}$$

The *loading factor* or *safety loading* θ is defined by $c=(1+\theta)\lambda\mu_1$, hence

$$\theta=\frac{c}{\lambda\mu_1}-1. \tag{4.9}$$

4.3 EXPONENTIAL UPPER BOUND

In this section we give a short and elegant proof of F. Lundberg's exponential upper bound. Later on, we will derive more accurate results. First we introduce the adjustment coefficient.

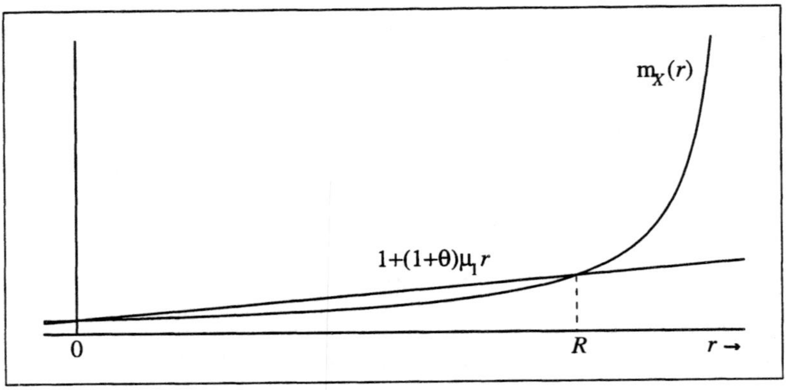

Fig. 4.2 Determining the adjustment coefficient R.

Definition 4.3.1 (Adjustment coefficient)
The *adjustment coefficient* R for claims $X \geq 0$ with $\mathrm{E}[X] = \mu_1 > 0$ is the positive solution of the following equation in r:

$$1 + (1+\theta)\mu_1 r = m_X(r). \tag{4.10}$$

See also Figure 4.2. ∇

In general, the adjustment coefficient equation (4.10) has one positive solution: $m_X(t)$ is strictly convex since $m_X''(t) = \mathrm{E}[X^2 e^{tX}] > 0$, $m_X'(0) < (1+\theta)\mu_1$, and, almost without exception, $m_X(t) \to \infty$ continuously. Note that for $\theta \downarrow 0$, the limit of R is 0, while for $\theta \uparrow \infty$, we see that R tends to the asymptote of $m_X(r)$, or to ∞.

Remark 4.3.2 (Equivalent equations for the adjustment coefficient)
The adjustment coefficient can also be found as the positive solution of any of the following equivalent equations, see Exercise 4.3.1:

$$\begin{aligned}
&\lambda + cR = \lambda m_X(R), \\
&\int_0^\infty [e^{Rx} - (1+\theta)][1-P(x)]dx = 0, \qquad (4.11)\\
&e^{Rc} = \mathrm{E}[e^{RS}] \quad \text{or} \quad m_{c-S}(-R) = 1 \quad \text{or} \quad c = \frac{1}{R}\log m_S(R),
\end{aligned}$$

where S denotes the total claims in an interval of length 1 and consequently $c - S$ is the profit in that interval. Note that S is compound Poisson distributed with parameter λ, and hence $m_S(r) = \exp\{\lambda(m_X(r) - 1)\}$. From the last equation we see that the adjustment coefficient R corresponds to the risk aversion α in case of an exponential utility function which leads to an annual premium c, see (1.20). In the second equation of (4.11), which can be proven by partial integration, $R = 0$ is no longer a root. The other equations still admit the solution $R = 0$. ∇

Example 4.3.3 (Adjustment coefficient for an exponential distribution)
Assume that X is exponentially distributed with parameter $\beta = 1/\mu_1$. The corresponding adjustment coefficient is the positive solution of

$$1 + (1+\theta)\mu_1 r = m_X(r) = \frac{\beta}{\beta - r}. \tag{4.12}$$

The solutions of this equation are the trivial solution $r = 0$ and

$$r = R = \frac{\theta\beta}{1+\theta}. \tag{4.13}$$

This situation admits an explicit expression for the adjustment coefficient. ∇

For most distributions, there is no explicit expression for the adjustment coefficient. To facilitate solving (4.10) by a spreadsheet or a computer program, one can use the fact that $R \in [0, 2\theta\mu_1/\mu_2]$, see Exercise 4.3.2.

In the next theorem, we prove F. Lundberg's famous exponential inequality for the ruin probability. Surprisingly, the proof involves mathematical induction.

Theorem 4.3.4 (Lundberg's exponential bound for the ruin probability)
For a compound Poisson risk process with an initial capital u, a premium per unit of time c, claims with cdf $P(\cdot)$ and mgf $m_X(t)$, and an adjustment coefficient R that satisfies (4.10), we have the following inequality for the ruin probability:

$$\psi(u) \leq e^{-Ru}. \tag{4.14}$$

Proof. Define $\psi_k(u)$, $-\infty < u < \infty$ and $k = 0, 1, 2, \ldots$, as the probability that ruin occurs at or before the kth claim. Since the limit of $\psi_k(u)$ for $k \to \infty$ equals $\psi(u)$ for all u, it suffices to prove that $\psi_k(u) \leq e^{-Ru}$ for each k. For $k = 0$ the inequality holds, since $\psi_0(u) = 1$ if $u < 0$, and $\psi_0(u) = 0$ if $u \geq 0$. Assume that the first claim occurs at time t. This event has a 'probability' $\lambda e^{-\lambda t} dt$. Also assume it has a size x, which has a probability $dP(x)$. Then the capital at that moment equals $u+ct-x$. Integrating over x and t yields

$$\psi_k(u) = \int_0^\infty \int_0^\infty \psi_{k-1}(u+ct-x)dP(x)\lambda e^{-\lambda t}dt. \tag{4.15}$$

Now assume that the induction hypothesis holds for $k-1$, i.e., $\psi_{k-1}(u) \leq e^{-Ru}$ for all real u. Then, (4.15) leads to

$$\begin{aligned}\psi_k(u) &\leq \int_0^\infty \int_0^\infty \exp\{-R(u+ct-x)\}dP(x)\lambda e^{-\lambda t}dt \\ &= e^{-Ru}\int_0^\infty \lambda \exp\{-t(\lambda+Rc)\}dt \int_0^\infty e^{Rx}dP(x) \\ &= e^{-Ru}\frac{\lambda}{\lambda+cR}m_X(R) = e^{-Ru},\end{aligned} \tag{4.16}$$

where the last equality follows from (4.11). ∇

Remark 4.3.5 (Interpretation of the adjustment coefficient; martingale)
The adjustment coefficient R has the property that $\mathrm{E}[e^{-RU(t)}]$ is constant in t. In other words, $e^{-RU(t)}$ is a *martingale*: it can be interpreted as the fortune of a gambler who is involved in a sequence of fair games. This can be shown as follows: since $U(t) = u + ct - S(t)$ and $S(t) \sim$ compound Poisson with parameter λt, we have, using again (4.11):

$$\begin{aligned}\mathrm{E}[e^{-RU(t)}] &= \mathrm{E}[e^{-R\{u+ct-S(t)\}}] \\ &= e^{-Ru}[e^{-Rc}\exp\{\lambda(m_X(R)-1)\}]^t \\ &= e^{-Ru}.\end{aligned} \tag{4.17}$$

Note that if R is replaced by any other real number, the expression in square brackets in (4.17) is unequal to 1, so in fact the adjustment coefficient is the unique positive number R with the property that $e^{-RU(t)}$ is a martingale. ∇

4.4 RUIN PROBABILITY AND EXPONENTIAL CLAIMS

In this section we give an expression for the ruin probability which involves the mgf of $U(T)$, i.e., the capital at the moment of ruin, conditionally given the event that ruin occurs in a finite time period. This expression enables us to give an exact expression for the ruin probability in case of an exponential distribution.

Theorem 4.4.1 (Ruin probability)
The ruin probability for $u \geq 0$ satisfies

$$\psi(u) = \frac{e^{-Ru}}{\mathrm{E}[e^{-RU(T)}|T < \infty]}. \tag{4.18}$$

Proof. Let $R > 0$ and $t > 0$. Then,

$$\begin{aligned}\mathrm{E}[e^{-RU(t)}] = \mathrm{E}[e^{-RU(t)}|T \leq t]\,\Pr[T \leq t]\\ + \mathrm{E}[e^{-RU(t)}|T > t]\,\Pr[T > t].\end{aligned} \tag{4.19}$$

From Remark 4.3.5, we know that the left-hand side equals e^{-Ru}. For the first conditional expectation in (4.19) we take $v \in [0, t]$ and write, using $U(t) = U(v) + c(t - v) - [S(t) - S(v)]$, see also (4.17):

$$\begin{aligned}&\mathrm{E}[e^{-RU(t)}|T = v] = \mathrm{E}[e^{-R\{U(v)+c(t-v)-[S(t)-S(v)]\}}|T = v]\\ &= \mathrm{E}[e^{-RU(v)}|T = v]e^{-Rc(t-v)}\mathrm{E}[e^{R\{S(t)-S(v)\}}|T = v]\\ &= \mathrm{E}[e^{-RU(v)}|T = v]\left\{e^{-Rc}\exp[\lambda(m_X(R) - 1)]\right\}^{t-v}\\ &= \mathrm{E}[e^{-RU(T)}|T = v].\end{aligned} \tag{4.20}$$

The total claims $S(t) - S(v)$ between v and t has again a compound Poisson distribution. What happens after v is independent of what happened before v, so $U(v)$ and $S(t) - S(v)$ are independent. The term in curly brackets equals 1. Equality (4.20) holds for all $v \leq t$, so $\mathrm{E}[e^{-RU(t)}|T \leq t] = \mathrm{E}[e^{-RU(T)}|T \leq t]$ also holds.

Since $\Pr[T \leq t] \uparrow \Pr[T < \infty]$ for $t \to \infty$, it suffices to show that the last term in (4.19) vanishes for $t \to \infty$. For that purpose, we split the event $T > t$ according to the size of $U(t)$. More precisely, we consider the cases $U(t) \leq u_0(t)$ and $U(t) > u_0(t)$ for some function $u_0(t)$. Notice that $T > t$ implies that we are not in ruin at time t, i.e., $U(t) \geq 0$, so $e^{-RU(t)} \leq 1$. We have

$$\begin{aligned}&\mathrm{E}[e^{-RU(t)}|T > t]\,\Pr[T > t]\\ &= \mathrm{E}[e^{-RU(t)}|T > t \;\&\; 0 \leq U(t) \leq u_0(t)]\,\Pr[T > t \;\&\; 0 \leq U(t) \leq u_0(t)]\\ &\quad + \mathrm{E}[e^{-RU(t)}|T > t \;\&\; U(t) > u_0(t)]\,\Pr[T > t \;\&\; 0 \leq U(t) > u_0(t)]\\ &\leq \Pr[U(t) \leq u_0(t)] + \mathrm{E}[\exp(-Ru_0(t))].\end{aligned} \tag{4.21}$$

The second term vanishes if $u_0(t) \to \infty$. For the first term, note that $U(t)$ has an expected value $\mu(t) = u + ct - \lambda t\mu_1$ and a variance $\sigma^2(t) = \lambda t\mu_2$. Because of Chebyshev's inequality, it suffices to choose the function $u_0(t)$ such that $(\mu(t) - u_0(t))/\sigma(t) \to \infty$. We can for instance take $u_0(t) = t^{2/3}$. ∇

Corollary 4.4.2 (Some consequences of Theorem 4.4.1)

1. If $\theta \downarrow 0$, then the chord in Figure 4.2 tends to a tangent line and, because of Theorem 4.4.1, $\psi(u) \to 1$; if $\theta \leq 0$ then the ruin probability equals 1, see Exercise 4.4.1.

2. If $T < \infty$, then $U(T) < 0$. Hence, the denominator in (4.18) is larger than or equal to 1, so $\psi(u) \leq e^{-Ru}$; this is yet another proof of Theorem 4.3.4.

3. If the claims cannot be larger than b, then $U(T) \geq -b$, hence we get an exponential lower bound for the ruin probability: $\psi(u) \geq e^{-R(u+b)}$.

4. It is quite plausible that the denominator of (4.18) has a finite limit for $u \to \infty$, say c. Then, of course, $c > 1$. This yields the following asymptotic approximation for $\psi(\cdot)$: for large u, we have $\psi(u) \approx \frac{1}{c}e^{-Ru}$.

5. If $R > 0$, then $1-\psi(u) > 0$ for all $u \geq 0$. As a consequence, if $1-\psi(u_0) = 0$ for some $u_0 \geq 0$, then $R = 0$ and $1 - \psi(u) = 0$ for all $u \geq 0$. ∇

Example 4.4.3 (Expression for the ruin probability, exponential claims)
From (4.18), we can derive an exact expression for the ruin probability if the claims have an exponential(β) distribution. For this purpose, assume that ruin occurs at a finite time $T = t$ and that the capital $U(T-0)$ just before ruin equals v. Then, for each value of v, t and y, if H represents an arbitrary history of the process with $U(T-0) = v$ and $T = t$, we have:

$$\Pr[-U(T) > y|H] = \Pr[X > v + y|X > v] = \frac{e^{-\beta(v+y)}}{e^{-\beta v}} = e^{-\beta y}. \tag{4.22}$$

Apparently, the deficit $-U(T)$ at ruin also has an exponential(β) distribution, so the denominator of (4.18) equals $\beta/(\beta - R)$. With $\beta = 1/\mu_1$ and $R = \theta\beta/(1+\theta)$, see (4.13), and thus $\beta/(\beta - R) = 1 + \theta$, we have the following exact expression for the ruin probability in case of exponential(β) claims:

$$\begin{aligned}\psi(u) &= \frac{1}{1+\theta}\exp\left(-\frac{\theta\beta u}{1+\theta}\right) = \frac{1}{1+\theta}\exp\left(-\frac{\theta}{1+\theta}\frac{u}{\mu_1}\right) \\ &= \psi(0)e^{-Ru}.\end{aligned} \tag{4.23}$$

Notice that Lundberg's exponential upper bound boils down to an equality here except for the constant $1/(1+\theta)$. In this case, the denominator of (4.18) does not depend on u. In general, however, it will depend on u. ∇

4.5 DISCRETE TIME MODEL

In the discrete time model, we consider more general risk processes $U(t)$ than the compound Poisson process from the previous sections, but now only on the time points $0, 1, 2, \ldots$ Instead of $U(n)$, we write U_n, $n = 0, 1, \ldots$ Let G_n denote the profit between the time points $n-1$ and n, therefore

$$U_n = u + G_1 + G_2 + \cdots + G_n, \quad n = 0, 1, \ldots \tag{4.24}$$

Later on, we will discuss what happens if we assume that $U(t)$ is a compound Poisson process, but for the moment we only assume that the profits $G_1, G_2, \ldots$ are independent and identically distributed, with $\Pr[G_n < 0] > 0$, but $\mathrm{E}[G_n] = \mu > 0$. We define a discrete time version of the ruin time $\widetilde{T}$, the ruin probability $\widetilde{\psi}(u)$ and the adjustment coefficient $\widetilde{R} > 0$, as follows:

$$\widetilde{T} = \min\{n : U_n < 0\}; \quad \widetilde{\psi}(u) = \Pr[\widetilde{T} < \infty]; \quad m_G(-\widetilde{R}) = 1. \tag{4.25}$$

The last equation has a unique solution. This can be seen as follows: since $\mathrm{E}[G] > 0$ and $\Pr[G < 0] > 0$, we have $m_G'(0) > 0$ and $m_G(-r) \to \infty$ for $r \to \infty$, while $m_G''(-r) = \mathrm{E}[G^2 e^{-Gr}] > 0$, so $m_G(\cdot)$ is a convex function.

Example 4.5.1 (Compound Poisson distributed annual claims)
In the special case that $U(t)$ is a compound Poisson process, we have $G_n = c - Z_n$ where Z_n denotes the compound Poisson distributed total claims in year n. From (4.11), we know that R satisfies the equation $m_{c-Z}(-R) = 1$. Hence, $R = \widetilde{R}$. ∇

Example 4.5.2 (Normally distributed annual claims)
If $G_n \sim N(\mu, \sigma^2)$, with $\mu > 0$, then $\widetilde{R} = 2\mu/\sigma^2$ follows from:

$$\log(m_G(-r)) = 0 = -\mu r + \frac{1}{2}\sigma^2 r^2. \tag{4.26}$$

Combining this result with the previous example, we observe the following. If we consider a compound Poisson process with a large Poisson parameter, i.e., with many claims between the time points $0, 1, 2, \ldots$, then S_n will approximately follow a normal distribution. Consequently, the adjustment coefficients will be close to each other, so $R \approx 2\mu/\sigma^2$. On the other hand, if we take $\mu = c - \lambda\mu_1 = \theta\lambda\mu_1$ and $\sigma^2 = \lambda\mu_2$ in Exercise 4.3.2, then it turns out that $2\mu/\sigma^2$ is an upper bound for R. ∇

Analogously to Theorem 4.4.1, one can prove the following equality:

$$\widetilde{\psi}(u) = \frac{e^{-\widetilde{R}u}}{\mathrm{E}[e^{-\widetilde{R}U(\widetilde{T})}|\widetilde{T} < \infty]}. \tag{4.27}$$

So in the discrete time model one can give an exponential upper bound for the ruin probability, too, which is

$$\widetilde{\psi}(u) \leq e^{-\widetilde{R}u}. \tag{4.28}$$

4.6 REINSURANCE AND RUIN PROBABILITIES

In the economic environment we postulated, reinsurance contracts should be compared by their expected utility. In practice, however, this method is not applicable. As an alternative, one could compare the ruin probabilities after a reinsurance policy. This too is quite difficult. Therefore we will concentrate on the adjustment coefficient and try to obtain a more favorable one by reinsurance. It is exactly from this possibility that the adjustment coefficient takes its name.

In reinsurance we transfer some of our expected profit to the reinsurer, in exchange for more stability in our position. These two conflicting criteria cannot be optimized at the same time. A similar problem arises in statistics where one finds a trade-off between the power and the size of a test. In our situation, we can follow the same procedure as it is used in statistics, i.e., maximizing one criterion while restricting the other. We could, for instance, maximize the expected profit subject to the condition that the adjustment coefficient R is larger than some R_0.

We will consider two situations. First, we use the discrete time ruin model, take out a reinsurance policy on the total claims in one year and then examine the discrete adjustment coefficient $\widetilde{R}$. In the continuous time model, we compare R for two types of reinsurance, namely proportional reinsurance and excess of loss reinsurance, with a retention for each claim.

Example 4.6.1 (Discretisized compound Poisson claim process)
Again consider the compound Poisson distribution with $\lambda = 1$ and $p(1) = p(2) =$

$\frac{1}{2}$ from Example 3.5.4. What is the discrete adjustment coefficient $\widetilde{R}$ for the total claims S in one year, if the loading factor θ equals 0.2, i.e., the annual premium c equals 1.8?

The adjustment coefficient $\widetilde{R}$ is calculated as follows:

$$\lambda + cr = \lambda m_X(r) \Leftrightarrow 1 + 1.8r = \frac{1}{2}e^r + \frac{1}{2}e^{2r} \Rightarrow \widetilde{R} \approx 0.211. \tag{4.29}$$

Now assume that we take out a stop-loss reinsurance with $d = 3$. For a reinsurance with payment Y, the reinsurer asks a premium $(1+\xi)\mathrm{E}[Y]$ with $\xi = 0.8$. If $d = 3$, the reinsurance premium amounts to $(1+\xi)\mathrm{E}[(S-d)_+] = 1.8\pi(3) = 0.362$. To determine the adjustment coefficient, we calculate the distribution of the profit in one year G_i, which consists of the premium income minus the reinsurance premium minus the retained loss. Hence,

$$G_i = \begin{cases} 1.8 - 0.362 - S_i & \text{if } S_i = 0, 1, 2, 3; \\ 1.8 - 0.362 - 3 & \text{if } S_i > 3. \end{cases} \tag{4.30}$$

The corresponding discrete adjustment coefficient $\widetilde{R}$, which is the solution of (4.25), is approximately 0.199.

Because of the reinsurance, our expected annual profit is reduced. It is equal to our original expected profit minus the one of the reinsurer. For instance, for $d = 3$ it equals $1.8 - 1.5 - \xi\pi(3) = 0.139$. In the following table, we show the results for different values of the retention d:

Retention d	$\widetilde{R}$	Expected profit
3	0.199	0.139
4	0.236	0.234
5	0.230	0.273
∞	0.211	0.300

We see that the decision $d = 3$ is not rational: it is dominated by $d = 4$, $d = 5$ as well as $d = \infty$, i.e., no reinsurance, since they all yield both a higher expected profit and more stability in the sense of a larger adjustment coefficient. ∇

Example 4.6.2 (Reinsurance, individual claims)
Reinsurance may also affect each individual claim, instead of only the total claims in a period. Assume that the reinsurer pays an amount $h(x)$ if the claim amount

is x. In other words, the retained loss equals $x - h(x)$. We consider two special cases:

$$\begin{array}{lll} h(x) = \alpha x & 0 \le \alpha \le 1 & \text{proportional reinsurance} \\ h(x) = (x - \beta)_+ & 0 \le \beta & \text{excess of loss reinsurance} \end{array} \tag{4.31}$$

Obviously, proportional reinsurance can be considered as a reinsurance on the total claims just as well. We will examine the usual adjustment coefficient R_h, which is the root of

$$\lambda + (c - c_h)r = \lambda \int_0^\infty e^{r[x-h(x)]} dP(x), \tag{4.32}$$

where c_h denotes the reinsurance premium. The reinsurer uses a loading factor ξ on the net premium. Assume that $\lambda = 1$, and $p(x) = \frac{1}{2}$ for $x = 1$ and $x = 2$. Furthermore, let $c = 2$, so $\theta = \frac{1}{3}$, and consider two values $\xi = \frac{1}{3}$ and $\xi = \frac{2}{5}$.

In case of proportional reinsurance $h(x) = \alpha x$, the premium equals

$$c_h = (1 + \xi)\lambda \mathrm{E}[h(X)] = (1 + \xi)\frac{3}{2}\alpha, \tag{4.33}$$

so, because of $x - h(x) = (1 - \alpha)x$, (4.32) leads to the equation

$$1 + [2 - (1 + \xi)\frac{3}{2}\alpha]r = \frac{1}{2}e^{r(1-\alpha)} + \frac{1}{2}e^{2r(1-\alpha)}. \tag{4.34}$$

For $\xi = \frac{1}{3}$, we have $c_h = 2\alpha$ and $R_h = \frac{0.325}{1-\alpha}$; for $\xi = \frac{2}{5}$, we have $c_h = 2.1\,\alpha$.

Next, we consider the excess of loss reinsurance $h(x) = (x - \beta)_+$, with $0 \le \beta \le 2$. The reinsurance premium equals

$$\begin{aligned} c_h &= (1 + \xi)\lambda[\frac{1}{2}h(1) + \frac{1}{2}h(2)] \\ &= \frac{1}{2}(1 + \xi)[(1 - \beta)_+ + (2 - \beta)_+], \end{aligned} \tag{4.35}$$

while $x - h(x) = \min\{x, \beta\}$, and therefore R_h is the root of

$$\begin{aligned} 1 + (2 - \frac{1}{2}(1 + \xi)[(1 - \beta)_+ + (2 - \beta)_+])r \\ = \frac{1}{2}[e^{\min\{\beta,1\}r} + e^{\min\{\beta,2\}r}]. \end{aligned} \tag{4.36}$$

In the table below, we give the results R_h for different values of β, compared with the same results in case of proportional reinsurance with the same expected payment by the reinsurer: $\frac{3}{2}\alpha = \frac{1}{2}(1 - \beta)_+ + \frac{1}{2}(2 - \beta)_+$.

For $\xi = \frac{1}{3}$, the loading factors of the reinsurer and the insurer are equal, and the more reinsurance we take, the larger the adjustment coefficient is. If the reinsurer's loading factor equals $\frac{2}{5}$, then for $\alpha \geq \frac{5}{6}$ the expected retained loss $\lambda\mathrm{E}[X-h(X)] = \frac{3}{2}(1-\alpha)$ is not less than the retained premium $c-c_h = 2-2.1\alpha$. Consequently, the resulting retained loading factor is not positive, and eventual ruin is a certainty. The same phenomenon occurs in case of excess of loss reinsurance with $\beta \leq \frac{1}{4}$. In the table below, this situation is denoted by the symbol $*$.

	β	2.0	1.4	0.9	0.6	0.3	0.15	0.0
	α	0.0	0.2	0.4	0.6	0.8	0.9	1.0
$\xi = \frac{1}{3}$	XL	.326	.443	.612	.918	1.84	3.67	∞
	Prop.	.326	.407	.542	.813	1.63	3.25	∞
$\xi = \frac{2}{5}$	XL	.326	.426	.541	.667	.425	$*$	$*$
	Prop.	.326	.390	.482	.602	.382	$*$	$*$

From the table we see that all adjustment coefficients for excess of loss coverage (XL) are at least as large as those for proportional reinsurance (Prop.) with the same expected payment. This is not a coincidence: by using the theory on ordering of risks, it can be shown that XL coverage always yields the best R-value as well as the smallest ruin probability among all reinsurance contracts with the same expected value of the payment, see Example 10.4.4. ∇

4.7 BEEKMAN'S CONVOLUTION FORMULA

In this section we show that the non-ruin probability can be written as a compound geometric distribution function. For this purpose, we consider the *maximal aggregate loss*, i.e., the maximal difference between the payments and the earned premium up to time t:

$$L = \max\{S(t) - ct | t \geq 0\}. \tag{4.37}$$

Since $S(0) = 0$, we have $L \geq 0$. The event $L > u$ occurs if, and only if, a finite point in time t exists for which $U(t) < 0$. In other words, the inequalities $L > u$ and $T < \infty$ are equivalent and consequently

$$\psi(u) = 1 - F_L(u). \tag{4.38}$$

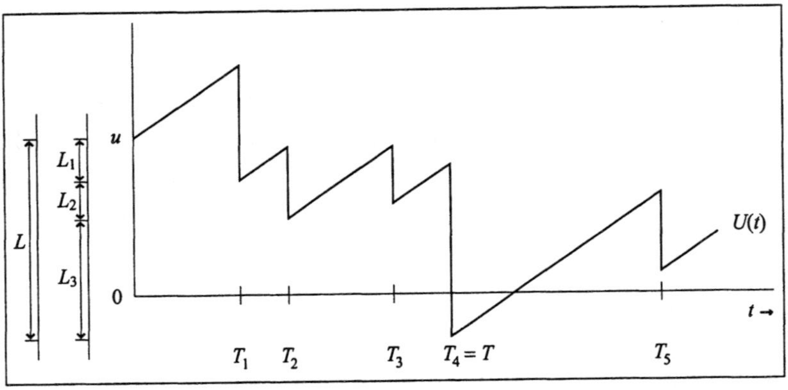

Fig. 4.3 The quantities L, L_1, L_2, . . .

Next, we consider the points where the surplus process reaches a new record low. This happens necessarily at points in time when a claim is paid. Let the random variables $L_j, j = 1, 2, \ldots$ denote the amounts by which the jth record low is less than the $j - 1$st one, see Figure 4.3 where there are three new record lows, assuming that the process drifts away to ∞ in the time period not shown. Let M be the random number of new records. We have

$$L = L_1 + L_2 + \cdots + L_M. \tag{4.39}$$

From the fact that a Poisson process is memoryless, it follows that the probability that a particular record low is the last one is the same every time. Hence, M follows a geometric distribution. For the same reason, the amounts of the improvements $L_1, L_2, \ldots$ are independent and identically distributed. The parameter of M, i.e., the probability that the previous record is the last one, equals the probability to avoid ruin starting with initial capital 0, hence it equals $1 - \psi(0)$.

So L has a compound geometric distribution. Both the value of the geometric parameter $1 - \psi(0)$ and the distribution of L_1, conditionally given $M \geq 1$, follow from the following theorem:

Theorem 4.7.1 (Distribution of the capital at time of ruin)
If the initial capital u equals 0, then for all $y > 0$ we have:

$$\Pr[U(T) \in (-y - dy, -y) \;\&\; T < \infty] = \frac{\lambda}{c}[1 - P(y)]dy. \tag{4.40}$$

Proof. In a compound Poisson process, the probability of having a claim in the interval $(t, t+dt)$ equals λdt, which is independent of t and of the history of the process up to that time. So, between 0 and dt there is either no claim (with probability $1-\lambda dt$), and the capital increases from u to $u+cdt$, or one claim with size X. In the latter case, there are two possibilities. If the claim size is less than u, then the process continues with capital $u+cdt-X$. Otherwise ruin occurs, but the capital at ruin is only larger than y if $X > u+y$. Defining

$$G(u,y) = \Pr[U(T) \in (-\infty, -y) \;\&\; T < \infty | U(0) = u], \tag{4.41}$$

we can write

$$\begin{aligned} G(u,y) &= (1-\lambda dt) G(u+cdt, y) \\ &\quad + \lambda dt \left\{ \int_0^u G(u-x,y)dP(x) + \int_{u+y}^{\infty} dP(x) \right\}. \end{aligned} \tag{4.42}$$

If G' denotes the partial derivative of G with respect to u, then

$$G(u+cdt, y) = G(u,y) + cdt\, G'(u,y). \tag{4.43}$$

Substitute (4.43) into (4.42), subtract $G(u,y)$ from both sides and divide by cdt. Then we get

$$G'(u,y) = \frac{\lambda}{c} \left\{ G(u,y) - \int_0^u G(u-x,y)dP(x) - \int_{u+y}^{\infty} dP(x) \right\}. \tag{4.44}$$

Integrating this over $u \in [0,z]$ yields

$$\begin{aligned} G(z,y) - G(0,y) = \frac{\lambda}{c} \Big\{ &\int_0^z G(u,y)du - \int_0^z \int_0^u G(u-x,y)dP(x)du \\ &- \int_0^z \int_{u+y}^{\infty} dP(x)du \Big\}. \end{aligned} \tag{4.45}$$

The double integrals in (4.45) can be reduced to single integrals as follows. For the first double integral, exchange the order of integration, substitute $v = u - x$ and again exchange the integration order. This leads to

$$\begin{aligned} \int_0^z \int_0^u G(u-x,y)dP(x)du &= \int_0^z \int_0^{z-v} G(v,y)dP(x)dv \\ &= \int_0^z G(v,y)P(z-v)dv. \end{aligned} \tag{4.46}$$

In the second double integral in (4.45), we substitute $v = u + y$. Then,

$$\int_0^z \int_{u+y}^{\infty} dP(x)du = \int_y^{z+y} [1 - P(v)]dv. \tag{4.47}$$

Hence,

$$G(z,y) - G(0,y) = \frac{\lambda}{c}\left\{\int_0^z G(u,y)[1 - P(z-u)]du - \int_y^{z+y} [1 - P(u)]du\right\}. \tag{4.48}$$

For $z \to \infty$, the first term on both sides of (4.48) vanishes, leaving

$$G(0,y) = \frac{\lambda}{c}\int_y^{\infty} [1 - P(u)]du, \tag{4.49}$$

which completes the proof. ∇

This theorem has many important consequences.

Corollary 4.7.2 (Consequences of Theorem 4.7.1)

1. The ruin probability at 0 depends on the safety loading only. Integrating (4.40) for $y \in (0, \infty)$ yields $\Pr[T < \infty]$, so regardless of $P(\cdot)$ we have

$$\psi(0) = \frac{\lambda}{c}\int_0^{\infty} [1 - P(y)]dy = \frac{\lambda}{c}\mu_1 = \frac{1}{1+\theta}. \tag{4.50}$$

2. Assuming that there is at least one new record low, L_1 has the same distribution as the amount with which ruin occurs starting from $u = 0$ (if ruin occurs). So we have the following expression for the density function of the record improvements:

$$f_{L_1}(y) = \frac{1 - P(y)}{(1+\theta)\mu_1} \frac{1}{\psi(0)} = \frac{1 - P(y)}{\mu_1}, \quad y > 0. \tag{4.51}$$

3. Let $H(x)$ denote the cdf of L_1 and p the parameter of M. Then, since L has a compound geometric distribution, the non-ruin probability of a risk process is given by Beekman's convolution formula:

$$1 - \psi(u) = \sum_{m=0}^{\infty} p(1-p)^m H^{m*}(u), \tag{4.52}$$

where

$$p = \frac{\theta}{1+\theta} \quad \text{and} \quad H(x) = 1 - \frac{1}{\mu_1}\int_x^\infty [1 - P(y)]dy. \tag{4.53}$$

4. The mgf of the maximal aggregate loss L which because of (4.38) is also the mgf of the non-ruin probability $1 - \psi(u)$, is given by

$$m_L(r) = \frac{\theta}{1+\theta} + \frac{1}{1+\theta}\frac{\theta(m_X(r) - 1)}{1 + (1+\theta)\mu_1 r - m_X(r)}. \tag{4.54}$$

Proof. Only the last assertion requires a proof. Since $L = L_1 + \cdots + L_M$ with $M \sim$ geometric(p) for $p = \frac{\theta}{1+\theta}$, we have

$$m_L(r) = m_M(\log m_{L_1}(r)) = \frac{p}{1 - (1-p)m_{L_1}(r)}. \tag{4.55}$$

The mgf of L_1 follows from its density (4.51):

$$\begin{aligned} m_{L_1}(r) &= \frac{1}{\mu_1}\int_0^\infty e^{ry}(1 - P(y))dy \\ &= \frac{1}{\mu_1}\left\{\frac{1}{r}[e^{ry} - 1][1 - P(y)]\Big|_0^\infty + \int_0^\infty \frac{1}{r}[e^{ry} - 1]dP(y)\right\} \\ &= \frac{1}{\mu_1 r}[m_X(r) - 1], \end{aligned} \tag{4.56}$$

since the integrated term disappears at ∞ because for $t \to \infty$:

$$\begin{aligned} \int_0^\infty e^{ry}dP(y) < \infty &\Rightarrow \int_t^\infty e^{ry}dP(y) \downarrow 0 \\ &\Rightarrow e^{rt}\int_t^\infty dP(y) = e^{rt}(1 - P(t)) \downarrow 0. \end{aligned} \tag{4.57}$$

Substituting (4.56) into (4.55) then yields (4.54). ∇

Remark 4.7.3 (Recursive formula for ruin probabilities)
The ruin probability in u can be expressed in the ruin probabilities at smaller initial capitals, as follows:

$$\psi(u) = \frac{\lambda}{c}\int_0^u [1 - P(y)]\psi(u - y)dy + \frac{\lambda}{c}\int_u^\infty [1 - P(y)]dy. \tag{4.58}$$

To prove this, note that $T < \infty$ implies that the surplus eventually will drop below the initial level, so

$$\begin{aligned}
\psi(u) &= \Pr[T < \infty] = \Pr[T < \infty \;\&\; M > 0] \\
&= \Pr[T < \infty | M > 0] \Pr[M > 0] \\
&= \frac{1}{1+\theta} \int_0^\infty \Pr[T < \infty | L_1 = y] f_{L_1}(y) dy \\
&= \frac{\lambda}{c} \left(\int_0^u \psi(u-y)(1-P(y))dy + \int_u^\infty (1-P(y))dy \right),
\end{aligned} \tag{4.59}$$

where we have substituted $c = (1+\theta)\lambda\mu_1$. ∇

4.8 EXPLICIT EXPRESSIONS FOR RUIN PROBABILITIES

Two situations exist for which we can give expressions for the ruin probabilities. In case of exponential distributions, and mixtures or combinations of these, an analytical expression arises. For discrete distributions, we can derive an algorithm.

In the previous section, we derived the mgf with the non-ruin probability $1 - \psi(u)$. In some cases, it is possible to identify this mgf, and thus give an expression for the ruin probability. We will describe how this works for mixtures and combinations of two exponential distributions, see Section 3.7. Since $1 - \psi(0) = \theta/(1+\theta)$ and

$$m_L(r) = \int_0^\infty e^{ru} d[1-\psi(u)] = 1 - \psi(0) + \int_0^\infty e^{ru}(-\psi'(u))du, \tag{4.60}$$

it follows from (4.54) that the 'mgf' of the function $-\psi'(u)$ equals

$$\int_0^\infty e^{ru}(-\psi'(u))du = \frac{1}{1+\theta} \frac{\theta(m_X(r)-1)}{1+(1+\theta)\mu_1 r - m_X(r)}. \tag{4.61}$$

Note that, except for a constant, $-\psi'(u)$ is a density function, see Exercise 4.8.1. Now, if X is a combination or a mixture of two exponential distributions as in (3.27), i.e., for some $\alpha < \beta$ and $0 \le q \le \frac{\beta}{\beta-\alpha}$ it has density function

$$p(x) = q\alpha e^{-\alpha x} + (1-q)\beta e^{-\beta x}, \quad x > 0, \tag{4.62}$$

then the right-hand side of (4.61), after multiplying both the numerator and the denominator by $(r-\alpha)(r-\beta)$, can be written as the ratio of two polynomials in r. By using partial fractions, this can be written as a sum of terms of the form $\delta\gamma/(\gamma - r)$, corresponding to δ times an exponential(γ) distribution. We give two examples to clarify this method.

Example 4.8.1 (Ruin probability for exponential distributions)
In (4.62), let $q = 0$ and $\beta = 1$, hence the claims distribution is exponential(1). Then, for $\delta = 1/(1+\theta)$ and $\gamma = \theta/(1+\theta)$, the right-hand side of (4.61) leads to

$$\frac{1}{1+\theta} \frac{\theta\left(\frac{1}{1-r} - 1\right)}{1 + (1+\theta)r - \frac{1}{1-r}} = \frac{\theta}{(1+\theta)[\theta - (1+\theta)r]} = \frac{\delta\gamma}{\gamma - r}. \tag{4.63}$$

Except for the constant δ, this is the mgf of an exponential(γ) distribution. We conclude from (4.61) that $-\psi'(u)/\delta$ is equal to the density function of this distribution. By using the boundary condition $\psi(\infty) = 0$, we see that for the exponential(1) distribution

$$\psi(u) = \frac{1}{1+\theta} \exp\left(\frac{-\theta u}{1+\theta}\right), \tag{4.64}$$

which corresponds to (4.23) in Section 4.4 for $\beta = \mu_1 = 1$. ∇

Example 4.8.2 (Ruin probability, mixtures of exponential distributions)
Choose $\theta = 0.4$ and $p(x) = \frac{1}{2} \times 3e^{-3x} + \frac{1}{2} \times 7e^{-7x}$, $x > 0$. Then

$$m_X(r) = \frac{1}{2}\frac{3}{3-r} + \frac{1}{2}\frac{7}{7-r}; \quad \mu_1 = \frac{1}{2}\frac{1}{3} + \frac{1}{2}\frac{1}{7} = \frac{5}{21}. \tag{4.65}$$

So, after some calculations, the right-hand side of (4.61) leads to

$$\frac{6(5-r)}{7(6-7r+r^2)} = \frac{\delta}{1-r} + \frac{6\varepsilon}{6-r} \quad \text{for } \delta = \frac{24}{35} \text{ and } \varepsilon = \frac{1}{35}. \tag{4.66}$$

The ruin probability for this situation is given by

$$\psi(u) = \frac{24}{35}e^{-u} + \frac{1}{35}e^{-6u}. \tag{4.67}$$

Notice that $\psi(0) = \frac{1}{1+\theta}$ indeed holds. ∇

This method works fine for combinations of exponential distributions, too, and also for the limiting case gamma(2,β), see Exercises 4.8.5–7. It is possible to generalize the method to mixtures/combinations of more than two exponential

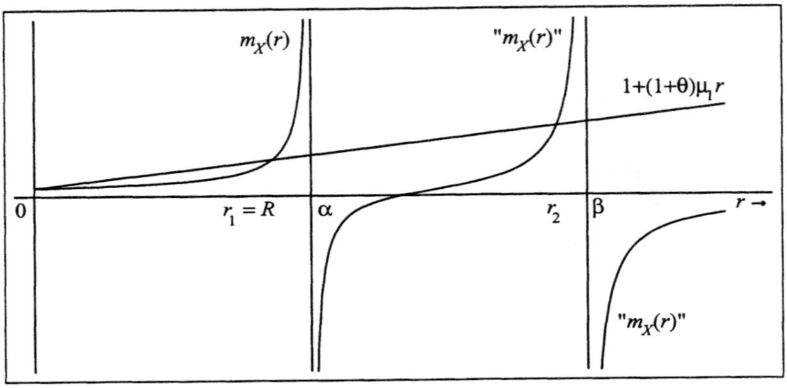

Fig. 4.4 Solutions of (4.68). Only the left branch of the graph is actually the mgf of X.

distributions, but then roots of polynomials of order three and higher have to be determined.

To find the coefficients in the exponents of expressions like (4.67) for the ruin probability, i.e., the asymptotes of (4.66), we need the roots of the denominator of the right-hand side of (4.61). Assume that, in the density (4.62), $\alpha < \beta$ and $q \in (0, 1)$. We have to solve the following equation:

$$1 + (1 + \theta)\mu_1 r = q\frac{\alpha}{\alpha - r} + (1 - q)\frac{\beta}{\beta - r}. \tag{4.68}$$

Notice that the right-hand side of this equation corresponds to the mgf of the claims only if r is to the left of the asymptotes, i.e., if $r < \alpha$. If r is larger, then this mgf is $+\infty$; hence we write "$m_X(r)$" instead of $m_X(r)$ for these branches in Figure 4.4. From this figure, one sees immediately that the positive roots r_1 and r_2 are real numbers that satisfy

$$r_1 = R < \alpha < r_2 < \beta. \tag{4.69}$$

Remark 4.8.3 (Ruin probability for discrete distributions)
If the claims X can have only a finite number of positive values $x_1, x_2, \ldots, x_m$, with probabilities $p_1, p_2, \ldots, p_m$, the ruin probability equals

$$\psi(u) = 1 - \frac{\theta}{1+\theta} \sum_{k_1,\ldots,k_m} (-z)^{k_1+\cdots+k_m} e^z \prod_{j=1}^{m} \frac{p_j^{k_j}}{k_j!} \tag{4.70}$$

where $z = \frac{\lambda}{c}(u - k_1 x_1 - \cdots - k_m x_m)_+$. The summation extends over all values of $k_1, \ldots, k_m = 0, 1, 2, \ldots$ leading to $z > 0$, and hence is finite. For a proof of (4.70), see Gerber (1989). ∇

4.9 APPROXIMATION OF RUIN PROBABILITIES

For other distributions than the ones above, it is difficult to calculate the exact value of the ruin probability $\psi(u)$. Furthermore, one may argue that this exact value is not very important, since in case of doubt, other factors will be decisive. So there is a need for good and simple approximations for the ruin probability.

First of all, we give some global properties of the ruin probability that should preferably be satisfied by the approximations. Equation (4.50) yields

$$\psi(0) = \frac{1}{1+\theta}. \tag{4.71}$$

Next, we know that $\psi(u) = 1 - F_L(u)$, and thus, with partial integration,

$$\begin{aligned} \int_0^\infty u \, d[1 - \psi(u)] &= \int_0^\infty \psi(u) du = \mathrm{E}[L], \\ \int_0^\infty u^2 \, d[1 - \psi(u)] &= \int_0^\infty 2u\psi(u) du = \mathrm{E}[L^2]. \end{aligned} \tag{4.72}$$

These moments of the maximal aggregate loss L follow easily since $L = L_1 + \cdots + L_M$ has a compound geometric distribution, with the distribution of M and L_j given in Section 4.7. The required moments of L_j are

$$\mathrm{E}[L_j^k] = \frac{\mu_{k+1}}{\mu_1(k+1)}, \quad k = 1, 2, \ldots \tag{4.73}$$

Since $\mathrm{E}[M] = \frac{1}{\theta}$, we have

$$\int_0^\infty \psi(u) du = \frac{\mu_2}{2\theta\mu_1}. \tag{4.74}$$

It can also be shown that

$$\mathrm{Var}[L] = \frac{\mu_3}{3\theta\mu_1} + \frac{\mu_2^2}{4\theta^2\mu_1^2}, \tag{4.75}$$

hence

$$\int_0^\infty u\psi(u)du = \frac{1}{2}\mathrm{E}[L^2] = \frac{\mu_3}{6\theta\mu_1} + \frac{\mu_2^2}{4\theta^2\mu_1^2}. \tag{4.76}$$

After this groundwork, we are ready to introduce a number of possible approximations.

1. Replacing the claims distribution by an exponential distribution with the same expected value, we get, see (4.23):

$$\psi(u) \approx \frac{1}{1+\theta}\exp\left(-\frac{\theta}{1+\theta}\frac{u}{\mu_1}\right). \tag{4.77}$$

   For $u = 0$, the approximation is correct, but in general, the integrals over the left-hand side and the right-hand side are different.

2. Approximating $\psi(u)$ by $\psi(0)e^{-ku}$ with k chosen such that (4.74) holds yields as an approximation

$$\psi(u) \approx \frac{1}{1+\theta}\exp\left(\frac{-2\theta\mu_1 u}{(1+\theta)\mu_2}\right). \tag{4.78}$$

   Note that if the claims are exponential($1/\mu_1$) distributed, then $\mu_2 = 2\mu_1^2$, so not only (4.77) but also (4.78) gives the correct ruin probability.

3. We can approximate the ruin probability by a gamma distribution:

$$\psi(u) \approx \frac{1}{1+\theta}(1 - G(u,\alpha,\beta)), \quad u \geq 0. \tag{4.79}$$

   To fit the first two moments, the parameters α and β of the gamma cdf $G(\cdot;\alpha,\beta)$ must meet the following conditions:

$$\mathrm{E}[L] = \frac{1}{1+\theta}\frac{\alpha}{\beta}; \quad \mathrm{E}[L^2] = \frac{1}{1+\theta}\left(\frac{\alpha^2}{\beta^2} + \frac{\alpha}{\beta^2}\right). \tag{4.80}$$

4. Just as in the first approximation, one can replace the claims distribution by another with a few moments in common, for which the corresponding ruin probability can be easily calculated. A suitable candidate for such a replacement is a mixture or combination of exponential distributions.

5. Another possible replacement is a discrete distribution. The ruin probabilities can easily be computed from (4.70). For each claims distribution, one can find a two-point distribution with the same first three moments. This is not always possible in case of a mixture/combination of two exponential distributions. Both methods yield good approximations.

6. From the theory of ordering of risks, it follows that one gets a lower bound for the ruin probability if one replaces the claims distribution with expectation μ by a one-point distribution on μ. A simple upper bound can be obtained if one knows the maximum value b of the claims. If one takes a claims distribution with probability μ/b for b, and probability $1-\mu/b$ for 0, then a Poisson process arises which is equivalent to a Poisson process with claims always equal to b and claim number parameter $\lambda\mu/b$ instead of λ. So, both the lower bound and the upper bound can be calculated by using (4.70) with $m = 1$.

7. The geometric distribution allows the use of Panjer's recursion, provided the individual terms are integer-valued. This is not the case for the terms L_j of L, see (4.51). But we can easily derive lower and upper bounds this way, by simply rounding the L_j down to an integer multiple of δ to get a random variable L' which is suitable for Panjer's recursion, and gives an upper bound for $F_L(u)$ since $\Pr[L \le u] \le \Pr[L' \le u]$. Rounding up leads to a lower bound for $F_L(u)$. By taking δ small, we get quite good upper and lower bounds with little computational effort.

4.10 EXERCISES

Section 4.2

1. Assume that the waiting times $W_1, W_2, \ldots$ are independent and identically distributed random variables with cdf $F(x)$ and density function $f(x)$, $x \ge 0$. Given $N(t) = i$ and $T_i = s$ for some $s \le t$, what is the *conditional* probability of a claim occurring between points in time t and $t + dt$? (This generalization of a Poisson process is called a *renewal process*.)

2. Let $\{N(t), t \ge 0\}$ be a Poisson process with parameter λ, and let $p_n(t) = \Pr[N(t) = n]$ and $p_{-1}(t) \equiv 0$. Show that $p_n'(t) = -\lambda p_n(t) + \lambda p_{n-1}(t)$, $n = 0, 1, 2, \ldots$, and interpret these formulas by comparing $p_n(t)$ with $p_n(t + dt)$.

Section 4.3

1. Prove that the expressions in (4.11) are indeed equivalent to (4.10).
2. Use $e^{rx} > 1 + rx + \frac{1}{2}(rx)^2$ for $r > 0$ and $x > 0$ to prove that $R < 2\theta\mu_1/\mu_2$.
3. For $\theta = 0.4$ and $p(x) = \frac{1}{2}(3e^{-3x} + 7e^{-7x})$, determine the values of t for which $m_X(t)$ is finite, and also determine R.
4. If the claims distribution is discrete with $p(1) = p(2) = \frac{1}{2}$, then determine θ if it is given that $R = \log 3$.
5. Which premium yields $e^{-Ru} = \varepsilon$?
6. [♠] If $\Pr[X = 0, 1, 2, 4] = \frac{1}{4}$, then determine R by using a spreadsheet, for $\lambda = 1$ and $c = 3$.
7. Assume that the claims X in a ruin process with $\theta = \frac{2}{5}$ arise as follows: first, a value Y is drawn from two possible values 3 and 7, each with probability $\frac{1}{2}$. Next, conditionally on $Y = y$, the claim X is drawn from an exponential(y) distribution. Determine the adjustment coefficient R. If $R = 2$ for the same distribution, is θ larger or smaller than $\frac{2}{5}$?
8. In some ruin process, the individual claims have a gamma(2, 1) distribution. Determine the loading factor θ as a function of the adjustment coefficient R. Also, determine $R(\theta)$. If the adjustment coefficient equals $\frac{4}{3}$, does $\theta = 2$ hold? Using a sketch of the graph of the mgf of the claims, discuss the behavior of R as a function of θ.
9. [♠] Discuss the determination of the adjustment coefficient R if in a ruin process the claims are lognormally distributed. Also, if the claims are inverse Gaussian.
10. Argue that $dc/dR \geq 0$. Use the relation $c = \frac{1}{R}\log(m_S(R))$, where S denotes the total claim in some period of length 1, to derive that an exponential premium increases with the parameter (risk aversion) α.

Section 4.4

1. From Theorem 4.4.1, we know that $\psi(u) \to 1$ if $\theta \downarrow 0$. Why does this imply that $\psi(u) = 1$ if $\theta < 0$?
2. Which compound Poisson processes have a ruin probability $\psi(u) = \frac{1}{2}e^{-u}$?
3. For a compound Poisson process, it is known that the continuous ruin probability depends on the initial capital u in the following way: $\psi(u) = \alpha e^{-u} + \beta e^{-2u}$. Determine the adjustment coefficient for this process. Can anything be said about the Poisson parameter in this risk process? What is $\mathrm{E}[\exp(-RU(T))|T < \infty]$?
4. Assume that $\psi(\varepsilon) < 1$. By looking at the event "non-ruin & no claim before ε/c", with c denoting the premium income per unit of time, show that $\psi(0) < 1$ must hold.
5. For a certain risk process, it is given that $\theta = 0.4$ and $p(x) = \frac{1}{2}(3e^{-3x} + 7e^{-7x})$. Which of the numbers 0, 1 and 6 are roots of the adjustment coefficient equation $1 + (1+\theta)\mu_1 R = m_X(R)$? Which one is the real adjustment coefficient?
One of the four expressions below is the ruin probability for this process; determine which expression is the correct one, and argue why the other expressions can't be the ruin probability.

1. $\psi(u) = \frac{24}{35}e^{-u} + \frac{1}{35}e^{-6u}$;

2. $\psi(u) = \frac{24}{35}e^{-u} + \frac{11}{35}e^{-6u}$;

3. $\psi(u) = \frac{24}{35}e^{-0.5u} + \frac{1}{35}e^{-6.5u}$;

4. $\psi(u) = \frac{24}{35}e^{-0.5u} + \frac{11}{35}e^{-6.5u}$.

6. The ruin probability for some ruin process equals $\psi(u) = \frac{1}{5}e^{-u} + \frac{2}{5}e^{-0.5u}$, $u \geq 0$. By using the fact that for ruin processes, in general, $\lim_{u\to\infty} \psi(u)/e^{-Ru} = c$ for some $c \in (0,1)$, determine the adjustment coefficient R and the appropriate constant c in this case.

Section 4.5

1. Assume that the distribution of G_i satisfies $\Pr[G_i = +1] = p$ and $\Pr[G_i = -1] = q = 1 - p$. Further, $p > \frac{1}{2}$ and u is an integer. Determine $U(\widetilde{T})$ if $\widetilde{T} < \infty$. Express $\widetilde{\psi}(u)$ in terms of $\widetilde{R}$, and both $\widetilde{R}$ and $\widetilde{\psi}(u)$ in terms of p and q.
2. [♠] Assume that an insurer uses an exponential utility function $w(\cdot)$ with risk aversion α. Prove that $\mathrm{E}[w(U_{n+1})|U_n = x] \geq w(x)$ if and only if $\alpha \leq \widetilde{R}$, and interpret this result.
3. Show that $\widetilde{T} \geq T$ with probability 1, as well as $\widetilde{\psi}(u) \leq \psi(u)$ for all u, if both are determined for a compound Poisson risk process.
4. Assume that the continuous infinite ruin probability for a compound Poisson process equals αe^{-u} in case of an initial capital u, for some constant α. Furthermore, the claims follow an exponential distribution with parameter 2 and the expected number of claims a year is 50. Determine the safety loading for this process. Also determine an upper bound for the discrete infinite ruin probability.

Section 4.6

1. The claim process on some insurance portfolio is compound Poisson with $\lambda = 1$ and $p(x) = e^{-x}$, $x > 0$. The loading factor is θ. Calculate the adjustment coefficient in case one takes out a proportional reinsurance $h(x) = \alpha x$ with a loading factor $\xi > 0$. Calculate the relative loading factor after this reinsurance. Which restrictions apply to α?
2. For the same situation as in the previous exercise, but now with excess of loss coverage $h(x) = (x - \beta)_+$, write down the adjustment coefficient equation, and determine the loading factor after reinsurance.
3. Assume that the claims per year W_i, $i = 1, 2, \ldots$, are $N(5, 1)$ distributed and that $\theta = 0.25$. A reinsurer covers a fraction α of each risk, applying a premium loading factor $\xi = 0.4$. Give the adjustment coefficient $\widetilde{R}$ for the reinsured portfolio, as a function of α. Which value optimizes the security of the insurer?
4. A total claims process is compound Poisson with $\lambda = 1$ and $p(x) = e^{-x}$, $x \geq 0$. The relative loading factor is $\theta = \frac{1}{2}$. One takes out a proportional reinsurance $h(x) = \alpha x$. The relative loading factor of the reinsurer equals 1. Determine the adjustment coefficient R_h. For which values of α is ruin not a certainty?

Section 4.7

1. What is the mgf of L_1 if the claims (a) are equal to b with probability 1, and (b) have an exponential distribution?
2. Prove that $\Pr[L = 0] = 1 - \psi(0)$.
3. In Exercises 4.4.3 and 4.4.6, what is θ?

Section 4.8

1. For which constant γ is $\gamma(-\psi'(u))$, $u > 0$ a density?
2. Make sketches like in Figure 4.4 to determine the asymptotes of (4.61), for a proper combination of exponential distributions and for a gamma(2, β) distribution.
3. Calculate θ and R if $\psi(u) = 0.3e^{-2u} + 0.2e^{-4u} + \alpha e^{-6u}$, $u \geq 0$. Which values of α are possible taking into account that $\psi(u)$ decreases in u and that the safety loading θ is positive?
4. If $\lambda = 3$, $c = 1$ and $p(x) = \frac{1}{3}e^{-3u} + \frac{16}{3}e^{-6u}$, then determine μ_1, θ, m_X, (4.61), and an explicit expression for $\psi(u)$.
5. Determine $\mathrm{E}[e^{-RU(t)}]$ in the previous exercise, with the help of (4.17). Determine independent random variables X, Y and I such that $IX + (1-I)Y$ has density $p(\cdot)$.
6. Just as Exercise 4.8.4, but now $p(x)$ is a gamma(2, $\frac{3}{5}$) density, $\lambda = 1$ and $c = 10$.
7. Determine $\psi(u)$ if $\theta = \frac{5}{7}$ and the claims X_i are equal to $X_i = Y_i/4 + Z_i/3$, with Y_i and $Z_i \sim$ exponential(1) and independent.
8. Sketch the density of L_j in case of a discrete claims distribution.
9. [♠] Prove (4.70) in case of $m = 1$ and $m = 2$.
10. Assume that the individual claims in a ruin process are equal to the maximum of two independent exponential(1) random variables, i.e., $X_i = \max\{Y_{i1}, Y_{i2}\}$ with $Y_{ik} \sim$ exponential(1). Determine the cdf of X_i, and use this to prove that the corresponding density $p(x)$ is a combination of exponential distributions. Determine the loading factor θ in the cases that for the adjustment coefficient, we have $R = 0.5$ and $R = 2.5$.
11. Two companies have independent compound Poisson ruin processes with intensities $\lambda_1 = 1$ and $\lambda_2 = 8$, claims distributions exponential(3) and exponential(6), initial capitals u_1 and u_2 and loading factors $\theta_1 = 1$ and $\theta_2 = \frac{1}{2}$. These companies decide to merge, without changing their premiums. Determine the intensity, claims distribution, initial capital and loading factor of the ruin process for the merged company. Assuming $u_1 = u_2 = 0$, compare the probabilities of the following events (*continuous infinite ruin probabilities*): "both companies never go bankrupt" with "the merged company never goes bankrupt". Argue that for any choice of u_1 and u_2, the former event has a smaller probability than the latter.

Section 4.9

1. Verify (4.72), (4.73), (4.75)/(4.76), and (4.80). Solve α and β from (4.80).
2. Work out the details of the final approximation.

5

Premium principles

5.1 INTRODUCTION

The activities of an insurer can be described as an input-output system, in which the surplus increases because of (earned) premiums and interest, and decreases because of claims and costs, see also the previous chapter. In this chapter we discuss some mathematical methods to determine the premium from the distribution of the claims. The actuarial aspect of a premium calculation is to calculate a minimum premium, sufficient to cover the claims and, moreover, to increase the expected surplus sufficiently for the portfolio to be considered stable.

Bühlmann (1985) described a top-down approach for the premium calculation. One primarily looks at the premium required by the total portfolio. Secondly, one considers the problem of spreading the total premium over the policies in a 'fair' way. To determine the minimum annual premium, we use the discrete ruin probability as introduced in the previous chapter (with some simplifying assumptions). The result is an exponential premium (see Chapter 1), where the parameter follows from the maximal ruin probability allowed and the initial capital. Assuming that the suppliers of the initial capital are to be rewarded with a certain annual dividend, and that the resulting premium should be as low as possible, therefore as competitive as possible, we can derive the optimal initial capital.

Furthermore we show how the total premium can be spread over the policies in a fair way, while the total premium keeps meeting our objectives.

For the policy premium, a lot of premium principles can be justified. Some of them can be derived from models like the zero utility model, where the expected utility before and after insurance are equal. Other premium principles can be derived as an approximation of the exponential premium principle. We will verify to which extent these premium principles satisfy a number of reasonable requirements. We will also consider some characterizations of premium principles. For instance, it turns out that the only utility preserving premium principles for which the total premium for independent policies equals the sum of the individual premiums are the net premium and the exponential premium.

As an application, we analyze how insurance companies should handle if they want to form a 'pool'. It turns out that the most competitive total premium is obtained when the companies each take a fixed part of the pooled risk (coinsurance), where the proportion is inversely proportional to their risk aversion. See also Gerber (1979).

5.2 PREMIUM CALCULATION FROM TOP-DOWN

As argued in Chapter 4, insuring a certain portfolio of risks leads to a surplus which increases because of collected premiums and decreases in the event of claims. The following equalities hold in the discrete time ruin model:

$$U_t = U_{t-1} + c - S_t, \quad t = 1, 2, \ldots \tag{5.1}$$

Ruin occurs if $U_t < 0$ for some t. We assume that the annual total claims S_t, $t = 1, 2, \ldots$, are independent and identically compound Poisson distributed, say $S_t \sim S$. The following question then arises: how large should the initial capital $U_0 = u$ and the premium $c = \pi[S]$ be for ruin not to occur with high probability? The probability of ruin is bounded from above by e^{-Ru} where R denotes the adjustment coefficient, i.e. the root of the equation $e^{Rc} = \mathrm{E}[e^{RS}]$, see Section 4.5. Note that, for the selected conditions, the discrete adjustment coefficient $\widetilde{R}$ and the usual adjustment coefficient R coincide. If we set the upper bound equal to ε, then $R = |\log \varepsilon|/u$. Hence, we get a ruin probability bounded by ε by choosing the premium c as

$$c = \frac{1}{R}\log(\mathrm{E}[e^{RS}]), \quad \text{where } R = \frac{1}{u}|\log \varepsilon|. \tag{5.2}$$

This premium is the exponential premium (1.20) with parameter R. From Example 1.3.1, we know that the adjustment coefficient can be interpreted as a measure for the risk aversion: for the utility function $-\alpha e^{-\alpha x}$ with risk aversion α, the utility preserving premium is $c = \frac{1}{\alpha}\log(\mathrm{E}[e^{\alpha X}])$.

A characteristic of the exponential premium is that choosing this premium for each policy also yields the right total premium for S. So, if the X_j, denoting the payment on policy j, $j = 1, \ldots, n$, are independent, then, as the reader may verify,

$$S = X_1 + \cdots + X_n \quad \Rightarrow \quad \frac{1}{R}\log(\mathrm{E}[e^{RS}]) = \sum_{j=1}^{n} \frac{1}{R}\log(\mathrm{E}[e^{RX_j}]). \tag{5.3}$$

Another premium principle which is additive in this sense is the variance principle, where for a certain parameter $\alpha \geq 0$ the premium is determined by

$$\pi[S] = \mathrm{E}[S] + \alpha \mathrm{Var}[S]. \tag{5.4}$$

This premium can also be obtained as an approximation of the exponential premium by considering only two terms of the Taylor expansion of the cgf, assuming that the risk aversion R is small, since

$$\pi[S] = \frac{1}{R}\kappa_S(R) = \frac{1}{R}\left(\mathrm{E}[S]R + \mathrm{Var}[S]\frac{R^2}{2} + \cdots\right). \tag{5.5}$$

For the approximation of (5.2) by (5.4), α should thus be taken equal to $\frac{1}{2}R$. From (5.2) and $\widetilde{\psi}(u) \leq e^{-Ru}$, we can roughly state that:

- doubling the loading factor α in (5.4) decreases the upper bound for the ruin probability from ε to ε^2;
- halving the initial capital requires the loading factor to be doubled if one wants to keep the same maximal ruin probability.

We will introduce a new aspect in the discrete time ruin model (5.1): how large should u be, if the premium c is to contain a yearly dividend for the shareholders who have supplied the initial capital? A premium at the portfolio level which takes this into account is

$$\pi[S] = \mathrm{E}[S] + \frac{|\log\varepsilon|}{2u}\mathrm{Var}[S] + i\,u, \tag{5.6}$$

i.e. the premium according to (5.2), (5.4) and (5.5), plus the dividend $i\,u$. We choose u such that the premium is as competitive as possible, therefore as low as possible. By setting the derivative equal to zero, we see that a minimum is reached for $u = \sigma[S]\sqrt{|\log\varepsilon|/2i}$. Substituting this value into (5.6), it turns out that the optimal premium is a *standard deviation premium*:

$$\pi[S] = \mathrm{E}[S] + \sigma[S]\sqrt{2i|\log\varepsilon|}. \tag{5.7}$$

In the optimum, the loading $\pi[S] - \mathrm{E}[S] - i\,u$ equals the dividend $i\,u$; notice that, if i increases, then u decreases, but $i\,u$ increases.

Finally, we have to determine which premium should be asked at the down level. We can't just use a loading proportional to the standard deviation. The sum of these premiums for independent risks doesn't equal the premium for the sum, and consequently the top level wouldn't be in balance: if we add a contract, the total premium no longer satisfies the specifications. On the other hand, as stated before, the variance principle is additive, just like the exponential and the net premium. Hence, (5.6) and (5.7) lead to the following recommendation for the premium calculation:

1. Compute the optimal initial capital $u = \sigma[S]\sqrt{|\log\varepsilon|/2i}$ for S, i and ε;

2. Spread the total premium over the individual risks X_j by charging the following premium:

$$\pi[X_j] = \mathrm{E}[X_j] + R\mathrm{Var}[X_j], \quad \text{where } R = |\log\varepsilon|/u. \tag{5.8}$$

Note that in this case the loading factor $R = \alpha$ of the variance premium is twice as large as it would be without dividend, see (5.4) and (5.5). The total dividend and the necessary contribution to the expected growth of the surplus which is required to avoid ruin are spread over the policies in a similar way.

Bühlmann gives an example of a portfolio consisting of two kinds (A and B) of exponential risks:

Type	Number of risks	Expected value	Variance	Exponential premium	Variance premium	Stand. dev. premium
A	5	5	25	$-\frac{1}{R}\log(1-5R)$	$5+\frac{R}{2}25$	
B	20	1	1	$-\frac{1}{R}\log(1-R)$	$1+\frac{R}{2}1$	
Total	25	45	145			$45+(2i\lvert\log\varepsilon\rvert 145)^{\frac{1}{2}}$

Choose $\varepsilon = 1\%$, hence $|\log \varepsilon| = 4.6052$. Then, for the model with dividend, we have the following table of variance premiums for different values of i.

	Portfolio premium	Optimal u	Optimal R	Premium for A	Premium for B
$i = 2\%$	50.17	129.20	0.0356	5.89	1.0356
$i = 5\%$	53.17	81.72	0.0564	6.41	1.0564
$i = 10\%$	56.56	57.78	0.0797	6.99	1.0797

The portfolio premium and the optimal u follow from (5.7), R from (5.2), and the premiums for A and B are calculated according to (5.8). We observe that:

- the higher the required return i on the supplied initial capital u, the lower the optimal value for u;
- the loading is far from proportional to the risk premium: the loading as a percentage for risks of type A is 5 times the one for risks of type B;
- the resulting exponential premiums are almost the same: if $i = 2\%$, then the premium with parameter $2R$ is 6.18 for risks of type A and 1.037 for risks of type B.

5.3 VARIOUS PREMIUM PRINCIPLES

In this section, we give a list of premium principles which can be applied at the policy level as well as at the portfolio level. In the next section, we give a number of mathematical properties that one might argue a premium principle should have. Premium principles depend exclusively on the marginal distribution function of the random variable. Consequently, we will use both notations $\pi[F_X]$ and $\pi[X]$ for the premium of X, if F_X is the cdf of X. We will assume that X is a *bounded* random variable. Most premium principles can also be applied to unbounded and possibly negative claims. This may result in an infinite premium, which implies that the risk at hand is uninsurable.

We have encountered the following five premium principles in Section 5.2:

(a) **Net premium:** $\pi[X] = \mathrm{E}[X]$
Also known as the equivalence principle; this premium is sufficient for a risk neutral insurer only.

(b) **Expected value principle:** $\pi[X] = (1+\alpha)\mathrm{E}[X]$
Here, the loading equals $\alpha\mathrm{E}[X]$, where $\alpha > 0$ is a parameter.

(c) **Variance principle:** $\pi[X] = \mathrm{E}[X] + \alpha\mathrm{Var}[X]$
Here, the loading is proportional to $\mathrm{Var}[X]$, and again $\alpha > 0$.

(d) **Standard deviation principle:** $\pi[X] = \mathrm{E}[X] + \alpha\sigma[X]$
Here also $\alpha > 0$.

(e) **Exponential principle:** $\pi[X] = \frac{1}{\alpha}\log(m_X(\alpha))$
The parameter $\alpha > 0$ is called the risk aversion. We already showed in the first chapter that the exponential premium increases if α increases. For $\alpha \downarrow 0$, the net premium arises; for $\alpha \to \infty$, the resulting premium equals the maximal value of X, see Exercise 5.3.11.

In the following two premium principles, the 'parameter' is a function; therefore, one could call them premium models.

(f) **Zero utility premium:** $\pi[X] \leftarrow u(0) = \mathrm{E}[u(\pi[X] - X)]$
This concept was already considered in Chapter 1. The function $u(x)$ represents the utility a decision maker attaches to his present capital plus x. So, $u(0)$ is the utility of the present capital and $u(\pi[X] - X)$ is the utility after insurance of a risk X against premium $\pi[X]$. The premium which solves the utility equilibrium equation is called the zero utility premium. Each linear transform of $u(\cdot)$ yields the same premium. The function $u(\cdot)$ is usually assumed to be non-decreasing and concave. Accordingly it has positive but decreasing marginal utility $u'(x)$. The special choice $u(x) = \frac{1}{\alpha}(1 - e^{-\alpha x})$ leads to exponential utility; the net premium results for linear $u(\cdot)$. See Chapter 1.

(g) **Mean value principle:** $\pi[X] = v^{-1}(\mathrm{E}[v(X)])$
The function $v(\cdot)$ is a convex and increasing valuation function. Again, the net premium and the exponential premium are special cases with $v(x) = x$ and $v(x) = e^{\alpha x}$, $\alpha > 0$.

The following premium principles are chiefly of theoretical importance:

(h) **Percentile principle:** $\pi[X] = \min\{p | F_X(p) \geq 1 - \varepsilon\}$
The probability of a loss on contract X is at most ε, $0 \leq \varepsilon \leq 1$.

(i) **Maximal loss principle**: $\pi[X] = \min\{p|F_X(p) = 1\}$
This premium arises as a limiting case of other premiums: (e) for $\alpha \to \infty$ and (h) for $\varepsilon \downarrow 0$. A 'practical' example: a pregnant woman pays some premium for an insurance contract, which guarantees that the baby will be a girl; if it's a boy, the entire premium is refunded.

(j) **Esscher principle**: $\pi[X] = \text{E}[Xe^{hX}]/\text{E}[e^{hX}]$
Here, h is a parameter with $h > 0$. This premium is actually the net premium for a risk $Y = Xe^{hX}/m_X(h)$. As one sees, Y results from X by enlarging the large values of X, while reducing the small values. It is also the expectation for the so-called Esscher transformation of $dF_X(x)$, which has as a 'density':

$$dG(x) = \frac{e^{hx}dF_X(x)}{\int e^{hy}dF_X(y)}. \tag{5.9}$$

This is the differential of a cdf with the same range as X, but for which the probabilities of small values are reduced in favor of the probabilities of large values. By doing so, a 'safe' premium arises.

5.4 PROPERTIES OF PREMIUM PRINCIPLES

Below, we give five desirable properties for premium principles $\pi[X]$. Other useful properties such as order preserving, which means that premiums for 'smaller' risks should indeed be smaller, will not be covered. For this property, see Chapter 10.

(1) **Non-negative loading**: $\pi[X] \geq \text{E}[X]$
A premium without a loading will lead to ruin with certainty.

(2) **No rip-off**: $\pi[X] \leq \min\{p|F_X(p) = 1\}$
The maximal loss principle (i) is a boundary case. If X is unbounded, this premium is infinite.

(3) **Consistency**: $\pi[X + c] = \pi[X] + c$ for each c
If we raise the claim by some fixed amount c, then the premium should also be higher by the same amount. A probably clearer synonym for consistency is *translation invariance*. Note that in this chapter, a 'risk' is not necessarily a non-negative random variable, though to avoid some technical problems it is assumed to be bounded from below.

(4) **Additivity**: $\pi[X+Y] = \pi[X] + \pi[Y]$ for independent X, Y
Joining independent risks together doesn't influence the total premium.

(5) **Iterativity**: $\pi[X] = \pi[\pi[X|Y]]$ for all X, Y
The premium for X can be calculated in two steps. First, apply $\pi[\cdot]$ to the conditional distribution of X, given $Y = y$. This yields a function of y, so again a random variable, denoted by $\pi[X|Y]$. Then, apply the same premium principle to this random variable. For an iterative premium principle, the same premium results as when one applies the premium principle to X.

For the net premium, iterativity follows from the iterativity property for expected values (2.7). At first sight, this criterion seems to be artificial. It can be explained as follows: assume that a certain driver causes a Poisson number N of accidents in one year, where the parameter λ is drawn from the distribution of the structure variable Λ. The number of accidents varies because of the Poisson deviation from the expectation λ, and because of the variation of the structure distribution. In case of iterativity, if we set premiums for both sources of variation one after another, we get the same premium as if we determined the premium for N directly.

Example 5.4.1 (Iterativity of the exponential principle)
The exponential premium principle is iterative. This can be shown as follows:

$$\begin{aligned}\pi[\pi[X|Y]] &= \frac{1}{\alpha}\log \mathrm{E}[e^{\alpha\pi[X|Y]}] = \frac{1}{\alpha}\log \mathrm{E}\left[\exp(\alpha\frac{1}{\alpha}\log \mathrm{E}[e^{\alpha X}|Y])\right] \\ &= \frac{1}{\alpha}\log \mathrm{E}\left[\mathrm{E}[e^{\alpha X}|Y])\right] = \frac{1}{\alpha}\log \mathrm{E}[e^{\alpha X}] = \pi[X].\end{aligned} \tag{5.10}$$

After taking the expectation in an exponential premium, the transformations that were done before are successively undone. ∇

Example 5.4.2 (Compound distribution)
Assume that $\pi[\cdot]$ is additive as well as iterative, and that S is a compound distribution with N terms distributed as X. The premium for S then equals

$$\pi[S] = \pi[\pi[S|N]] = \pi[N\pi[X]]. \tag{5.11}$$

Furthermore, if $\pi[\cdot]$ is also *proportional*, (or *homogeneous*), which means that $\pi[\alpha X] = \alpha\pi[X]$ for all $\alpha \geq 0$, then $\pi[S] = \pi[X]\pi[N]$. In general, proportionality doesn't hold, see for instance Section 1.2. However, this property is used as a

Principle	(a) μ	(b) $1+\lambda$	(c) σ^2	(d) σ	(e) exp	(f) $u(\cdot)$	(g) $v(\cdot)$	(h) %	(i) max	(j) E
Property										
1) $\pi \geq \mathrm{E}[X]$	+	+	+	+	+	+	+	−	+	+
2) $\pi \leq \max[X]$	+	−	−	−	+	+	+	+	+	+
3) $\pi[X+c]$	+	−	+	+	+	+	e	+	+	+
4) $\pi[X+Y]$	+	+	+	−	+	e	e	−	+	+
5) $\pi[\pi[X\|Y]]$	+	−	−	−	+	e	+	−	+	−

Table 5.1 Various premium principles and their properties

local working hypothesis for the calculation of the premium for similar contracts; without proportionality, the use of a tariff is meaningless. ∇

In Table 5.1, we summarize the properties of our various premium principles. A "+" means that the property holds in general, a "−" that it doesn't, while especially an "e" means that the property only holds in case of an exponential premium (including the net premium). We assume that S is bounded from below. The proofs of these properties are asked in the exercises, but for the proof of most of the characterizations that zero utility and mean value principles with a certain additional property must be exponential, we refer to the literature. See also the following section.

Summarizing, one may state that only the exponential premium, the maximal loss principle and the net premium principle satisfy all these properties. Since the maximal loss premium principle and the net premium principle are of minor practical importance, only the exponential premium principle survives this selection. See also Section 5.2. A drawback of the exponential premium has already been mentioned: it has the property that a decision maker's decisions do not depend on the capital he has currently acquired. On the other hand, this is also a strong point of this premium principle, since it is very convenient not to have to know one's current capital, which is generally either random or simply not precisely known at each point in time.

5.5 CHARACTERIZATIONS OF PREMIUM PRINCIPLES

In this section we investigate the properties marked with "e" in Table 5.1, and also some more characterizations of premium principles. Note that linear transforms of the functions $u(\cdot)$ and $v(\cdot)$ in (f) and (g) yield the same premiums. The technique to prove that only exponential utility functions $u(\cdot)$ have a certain property consists of applying this property to risks with a simple structure, and derive a differential equation for $u(\cdot)$ which holds only for exponential and linear functions. Since the linear utility function is a limit of the exponential utility functions, we won't mention them explicitly in this section. For full proofs of the theorems in this section, we refer to Gerber (1979, 1985) as well as Goovaerts et al. (1984).

The entries "e" in Table 5.1 are studied in the following theorem.

Theorem 5.5.1 (Characterizing exponential principles)
The following assertions hold:

1. A consistent mean value principle is exponential.
2. An additive mean value principle is exponential.
3. An additive zero utility principle is exponential.
4. An iterative zero utility principle is exponential.

Proof. Since for a mean value principle we have $\pi[X] = c$ if $\Pr[X = c] = 1$, consistency is just additivity with the second risk degenerate, so the second assertion follows from the first. The proof of the first, which will be given below, involves applying consistency to risks that are equal to x plus some Bernoulli(q) random variable, and computing the second derivative at $q = 0$ to show that a valuation function $v(\cdot)$ with the required property necessarily satisfies the differential equation $\frac{v''(x)}{v'(x)}$ = some constant, which is satisfied only by the linear and exponential valuation functions. The final assertion is proven in much the same way. The proof that an additive zero utility principle is exponential proceeds by deriving a similar equation, for which it turns out to be considerably more difficult to prove that the exponential utility function is the unique solution.

To prove that a consistent mean value principle is exponential, assume that $v(\cdot)$, which is a convex increasing function, yields a consistent mean value principle. Let $P(q)$ denote the premium, considered as a function of q, for a Bernoulli(q) risk S_q. Then, by definition,

$$v(P(q)) = qv(1) + (1 - q)v(0). \tag{5.12}$$

The right-hand derivative of this equation in $q = 0$ yields

$$P'(0)v'(0) = v(1) - v(0), \tag{5.13}$$

so $P'(0) > 0$. The second derivative in $q = 0$ gives

$$P''(0)v'(0) + P'(0)^2 v''(0) = 0. \tag{5.14}$$

Because of the consistency, the premium for $S_q + x$ equals $P(q) + x$ for each constant x, and therefore

$$v(P(q) + x) = qv(1 + x) + (1 - q)v(x). \tag{5.15}$$

The second derivative at $q = 0$ of this equation yields

$$P''(0)v'(x) + P'(0)^2 v''(x) = 0, \tag{5.16}$$

and, since $P'(0) > 0$, we have for all x that

$$\frac{v''(x)}{v'(x)} = \frac{v''(0)}{v'(0)}. \tag{5.17}$$

Consequently, $v(\cdot)$ is linear if $v''(0) = 0$, and exponential if $v''(0) > 0$. ∇

Remark 5.5.2 (Continuous and mixable premiums)
Another interesting characterization is the following one. A premium principle $\pi[\cdot]$ is continuous if $F_n \to F$ in distribution implies $\pi[F_n] \to \pi[F]$. If furthermore $\pi[\cdot]$ admits mixing, which means that $\pi[tF + (1-t)G] = t\pi[F] + (1-t)\pi[G]$ for cdf's F and G, then it can be shown that $\pi[\cdot]$ must be the expected value principle $\pi[X] = (1 + \lambda)\mathrm{E}[X]$. ∇

Finally, the Esscher premium principle can be justified as follows.

Theorem 5.5.3
Assume an insurer has an exponential utility function with risk aversion α. If he charges a premium of the form $\mathrm{E}[\varphi(X)X]$ where $\varphi(\cdot)$ is a continuous increasing function with $\mathrm{E}[\varphi(X)] = 1$, his utility is maximized if $\varphi(x) \propto e^{\alpha x}$, hence if he uses the Esscher premium principle with parameter α.

Proof. The proof of this statement is based on the technique of variational calculus and adapted from Goovaerts et al. (1984). Let $u(\cdot)$ be a convex increasing utility function, and introduce $Y = \varphi(X)$. Then, because $\varphi(\cdot)$ increases continuously, we have $X = \varphi^{-1}(Y)$. Write $f(y) = \varphi^{-1}(y)$. To derive a condition for $\mathrm{E}[u(-f(Y)+\mathrm{E}[f(Y)Y])]$ to be maximal for all choices of continuous increasing functions when $\mathrm{E}[Y] = 1$, consider a function $f(y)+\varepsilon g(y)$ for some arbitrary continuous function $g(\cdot)$. A little reflection will lead to the conclusion that the fact that $f(y)$ is optimal, and this new function is not, must mean that

$$\frac{d}{d\varepsilon}\mathrm{E}\big[u\big(- f(Y) + \mathrm{E}[f(Y)Y] + \varepsilon\{-g(Y) + \mathrm{E}[g(Y)Y]\}\big)\big]\bigg|_{\varepsilon=0} = 0. \quad (5.18)$$

But this derivative is equal to

$$\begin{aligned}&\mathrm{E}\big[u'\big(- f(Y) + E[f(Y)Y] + \varepsilon\{-g(Y) + \mathrm{E}[g(Y)Y]\}\big)\\ &\quad\{-g(Y) + \mathrm{E}[g(Y)Y]\}\big].\end{aligned} \quad (5.19)$$

For $\varepsilon = 0$, this derivative equals zero if

$$\begin{aligned}&\mathrm{E}\left[u'(-f(Y) + \mathrm{E}[f(Y)Y])g(Y)\right] =\\ &\mathrm{E}\left[u'(-f(Y) + \mathrm{E}[f(Y)Y])\right]\mathrm{E}[g(Y)Y].\end{aligned} \quad (5.20)$$

Writing $c = \mathrm{E}\left[u'(-f(Y) + \mathrm{E}[f(Y)Y])\right]$, this can be rewritten as

$$\mathrm{E}\left[\{u'(-f(Y) + \mathrm{E}[f(Y)Y]) - cY\}\{g(Y)\}\right] = 0. \quad (5.21)$$

Since the function $g(\cdot)$ is arbitrary, by a well-known theorem from variational calculus we find that necessarily

$$u'(-f(y) + \mathrm{E}[f(Y)Y]) - cy = 0. \quad (5.22)$$

Using $x = f(y)$ and $y = \varphi(x)$, we see that

$$\varphi(x) \propto u'(-x + \mathrm{E}[X\varphi(X)]). \quad (5.23)$$

Now, if $u(x)$ is exponential(α), so $u(x) = -\alpha e^{-\alpha x}$, then

$$\varphi(x) \propto e^{-\alpha(-x+\mathrm{E}[X\varphi(X)])} \propto e^{\alpha x}. \quad (5.24)$$

Since $\mathrm{E}[\varphi(X)] = 1$, we obtain $\varphi(x) = e^{\alpha x}/\mathrm{E}[e^{\alpha X}]$ for the optimal standardized weight function. The resulting premium is an Esscher premium with parameter $h = \alpha$. ∇

Notice that the insurer uses a different weighting function for risks having different values of $\mathrm{E}[\varphi(X)]$, though these functions differ only by a constant factor.

5.6 PREMIUM REDUCTION BY COINSURANCE

Consider n cooperating insurers which individually have exponential utility functions with parameter α_i, $i = 1, 2, \dots, n$. Together, they want to insure a risk S by defining random variables $S_1, \dots, S_n$ with

$$S \equiv S_1 + \cdots + S_n, \tag{5.25}$$

with S_i denoting the risk insurer i faces. S might for instance be a new risk they want to take on together, or it may be their combined insurance portfolios that they want to redistribute. The total premium they need is

$$P = \sum_{i=1}^{n} \frac{1}{\alpha_i} \log \mathrm{E}\left[e^{\alpha_i S_i}\right]. \tag{5.26}$$

This total premium depends on the choice of the S_i. How should the insurers split up the risk S in order to make the pool as competitive as possible, hence to minimize the total premium P?

It turns out that the optimal choice $\widetilde{S}_i$ for the insurers is when each of them insures a fixed part of S, to be precise

$$\widetilde{S}_i = \frac{\alpha}{\alpha_i} S \quad \text{with } \frac{1}{\alpha} = \sum_{i=1}^{n} \frac{1}{\alpha_i}. \tag{5.27}$$

So, each insurer covers a fraction of the pooled risk which is proportional to the reciprocal of his risk aversion. By (5.27), the corresponding total minimum premium is

$$\widetilde{P} = \sum_{i=1}^{n} \frac{1}{\alpha_i} \log \mathrm{E}\left[e^{\alpha_i \widetilde{S}_i}\right] = \frac{1}{\alpha} \log \mathrm{E}\left[e^{\alpha S}\right]. \tag{5.28}$$

This shows that the pool of cooperating insurers acts as one insurer with an exponential premium principle with risk aversion α.

The proof that $\widetilde{P} \le P$ for all other appropriate choices of $S_1 + \cdots + S_n \equiv S$ goes as follows. We have to prove that (5.28) is smaller than (5.26), so

$$\frac{1}{\alpha} \log \mathrm{E}\left[\exp\left(\alpha \sum_{i=1}^{n} S_i\right)\right] \le \sum_{i=1}^{n} \frac{1}{\alpha_i} \log \mathrm{E}\left[e^{\alpha_i S_i}\right], \tag{5.29}$$

which can be rewritten as

$$\mathrm{E}\left[\prod_{i=1}^{n} e^{\alpha S_i}\right] \leq \prod_{i=1}^{n} \left(\mathrm{E}\left[e^{\alpha_i S_i}\right]\right)^{\alpha/\alpha_i}. \tag{5.30}$$

This in turn is equivalent to

$$\mathrm{E}\left[\prod_{i=1}^{n} \frac{e^{\alpha S_i}}{\mathrm{E}\left[e^{\alpha_i S_i}\right]^{\alpha/\alpha_i}}\right] \leq 1, \tag{5.31}$$

or

$$\mathrm{E}\left[\exp \sum_i \frac{\alpha}{\alpha_i} T_i\right] \leq 1, \quad \text{with } T_i = \log \frac{e^{\alpha_i S_i}}{\mathrm{E}\left[e^{\alpha_i S_i}\right]}. \tag{5.32}$$

We can prove inequality (5.32) as follows. Note that $\mathrm{E}[\exp(T_i)] = 1$ and that by definition $\sum_i \alpha/\alpha_i = 1$. Since e^x is a convex function, we have for all real $t_1, \ldots, t_n$

$$\exp\left(\sum_i \frac{\alpha}{\alpha_i} t_i\right) \leq \sum_i \frac{\alpha}{\alpha_i} \exp(t_i), \tag{5.33}$$

and this implies that

$$\mathrm{E}\left[\exp\left(\sum_i \frac{\alpha}{\alpha_i} T_i\right)\right] \leq \sum_i \frac{\alpha}{\alpha_i} \mathrm{E}\left[e^{T_i}\right] = \sum_i \frac{\alpha}{\alpha_i} = 1. \tag{5.34}$$

Hölder's inequality, which is well-known, arises by choosing $X_i = \exp(\alpha S_i)$ and $r_i = \alpha/\alpha_i$ in (5.30). See the exercises for the case $n = 2$, $r_1 = p$, $r_2 = q$.

5.7 EXERCISES

Section 5.2

1. Show that (5.7) is valid.
2. What are the results in the table in case of a dividend $i = 2\%$ and $\varepsilon = 5\%$? Calculate the variance premium as well as the exponential premium.

Section 5.3

1. Let $X \sim$ exponential(1). Determine the premiums (a)–(e) and (h)–(j).

2. [♠] Prove that $\pi[X;\alpha] = \log(\mathrm{E}[e^{\alpha X}])/\alpha$ is an increasing function of α, by showing that the derivative with respect to α is positive (see also Example 1.3.1).
3. Assume that the total claims for a car portfolio has a compound Poisson distribution with gamma distributed claims per accident. Determine the expected value premium if the loading factor equals 10%.
4. Determine the exponential premium for a compound Poisson risk with gamma distributed individual claims.
5. Calculate the variance premium for the claims distribution as in Exercise 5.3.3.
6. Show that the Esscher premium equals $\kappa_X'(h)$, where κ_X is the cgf of X.
7. What is the Esscher transformed density with parameter h for the following densities: exponential(α), binomial(n,p) and Poisson(λ)?
8. Show that the Esscher premium for X increases with the parameter h.
9. Calculate the Esscher premium for a compound Poisson distribution.
10. Show that the Esscher premium for small values of α boils down to a variance premium principle.
11. Assume that X is a finite risk with maximal value b, hence $\Pr[X \leq b] = 1$ but $\Pr[X \geq b-\varepsilon] > 0$ for all $\varepsilon > 0$. Let π_α denote the exponential premium for X. Show that $\lim_{\alpha\to\infty} \pi_\alpha = b$.

Section 5.4

1. In Table 5.1, prove the properties which are marked "+".
2. Construct counterexamples for the first 4 rows and the second column for the properties which are marked "−".
3. Investigate the additivity of a mixture of Esscher principles of the following type: $\pi[X] = p\pi[X;h_1] + (1-p)\pi[X;h_2]$ for some $p \in [0,1]$, where $\pi[X;h]$ is the Esscher premium for risk X with parameter h.
4. Formulate a condition for dependent risks X and Y that implies that $\pi[X+Y] \leq \pi[X]+\pi[Y]$ for the variance premium (*subadditivity*). Also show that this property holds for the standard deviation principle, no matter what the joint distribution of X and Y is.

Section 5.5

1. For a proof of Hölder's inequality in case of $n = 2$, let $p > 1$ and $q > 1$ satisfy $\frac{1}{p} + \frac{1}{q} = 1$. Successively prove that
   - if $u > 0$ and $v > 0$, then $uv \leq \frac{u^p}{p} + \frac{v^q}{q}$; (write $u = e^{s/p}$ and $v = e^{t/q}$);
   - if $\mathrm{E}[U^p] = \mathrm{E}[V^q] = 1$ and $\Pr[U > 0] = \Pr[V > 0] = 1$, then $\mathrm{E}[UV] \leq 1$;
   - $|\mathrm{E}[XY]| \leq \mathrm{E}[|X|^p]^{1/p}\mathrm{E}[|Y|^q]^{1/q}$.
2. Whose inequality arises for $p = q = 2$ in the previous exercise?

6

Bonus-malus systems

6.1 INTRODUCTION

This chapter deals with the theory behind bonus-malus methods for automobile insurance. This is an important branch of non-life insurance, in many countries even the largest in total premium income. A special feature of automobile insurance is that quite often and to everyone's satisfaction, a premium is charged which depends for a great deal on the claims filed on the policy in the past. In experience rating systems such as these, bonuses can be earned by not filing claims, and a malus is incurred when many claims have been filed. Experience rating systems are common practice in reinsurance, but in this case, it affects the consumer directly. Actually, by charging a randomly fluctuating premium, the ultimate goal of insurance, namely being in a completely secure financial position, is not reached. But it can be shown that in this type of insurance, the uncertainty is greatly reduced. This same phenomenon can also be observed in other types of insurance; think for instance of the part of the claims that is not reimbursed by the insurer because there is a deductible.

That 'lucky' policyholders pay for the damages caused by less lucky insureds is the essence of insurance (*probabilistic solidarity*). But in private insurance, solidarity should not lead to inherently good risks paying for bad ones. An insurer trying to impose such *subsidizing solidarity* on his customers will see his good risks take their business elsewhere, leaving him with the bad risks. This may occur in the automobile insurance market when there are regionally operating insurers. Charging the same premiums nationwide will cause the regional risks, which for automobile insurance tend to be good risks because traffic is not so heavy there, to go to the regional insurer, who with mainly good risks in his portfolio can afford to charge lower premiums.

There is a psychological reason why experience rating is broadly accepted with car insurance, and not, for instance, with health insurance. Bonuses are seen as rewards for careful driving, premium increases as an additional and well-deserved fine for the accident-prone. Many think that traffic offenses cannot be punished harshly and often enough. But someone who is ill is generally not to blame, and does not deserve to suffer in his pocket as well.

Traditionally, car insurance covers third party liability, as well as the damage to one's own vehicle. The latter is more relevant for rather new cars, since for reasons of moral hazard, insurers do not reimburse more than the current value of the car.

In Section 6.2, we describe the Dutch bonus-malus system, which we consider to be typical for such systems. Also, we briefly describe the reasons which have led to this system. Bonus-malus systems lend themselves for analysis by Markov chains, see Section 6.3. In this way, we will be able to determine the Loimaranta efficiency of such systems, which is the elasticity of the mean asymptotic premium with respect to the claim frequency. In Chapter 7, we present a bonus-malus system that is a special case of a so-called credibility method. In Chapter 8, we study among other things some venerable non-life actuarial methods for automobile premium rating in the light of generalized linear models.

6.2 AN EXAMPLE OF A BONUS-MALUS SYSTEM

Every country has his own bonus-malus system, the wheel having been reinvented quite a few times. The Dutch system is the result of a large-scale investigation of the Dutch market by five of the largest companies in 1982, prompted by the fact that the market was chaotic and in danger of collapsing. Many Dutch insurers still utilize variants of the proposed system.

First, a basic premium is determined using rating factors like weight, catalogue price or capacity of the car, type of use of the car (privately or for business), and of course the type of coverage (comprehensive, third party only, or a mixture).

Step	Percentage	New bonus-malus step after				
		0	1	2	3+	claims:
14	30	14	9	5	1	
13	32.5	14	8	4	1	
12	35	13	8	4	1	
11	37.5	12	7	3	1	
10	40	11	7	3	1	
9	45	10	6	2	1	
8	50	9	5	1	1	
7	55	8	4	1	1	
6	60	7	3	1	1	
5	70	6	2	1	1	
4	80	5	1	1	1	
3	90	4	1	1	1	
2	100	3	1	1	1	
1	120	2	1	1	1	

Table 6.1 Transition rules and premium percentages for the Dutch bonus-malus system

This is the premium that drivers without a known claims history have to pay. The bonus and malus for good and bad claims experience are implemented through the use of a so-called bonus-malus scale. One ascends one step, getting a greater bonus, after a claim-free year, and descends several steps after having filed one or more claims. The bonus-malus scale, including the percentages of the basic premium to be paid and the transitions made after 0, 1, 2, and 3 or more claims, is depicted in Table 6.1. In principle, new insureds enter at the step with premium level 100%. Other countries might use different rating factors and a different bonus-malus scale. The group of actuaries that proposed the new rating system in the Netherlands investigated about 700000 policies of which 50 particulars were known, and which produced 80000 claims. Both claim frequency and average claim size were studied.

The factors that were thought relevant about each policy were not all usable as rating factors. Driving capacity, swiftness of reflexes, aggressiveness behind the wheel and knowledge of the highway code are hard to measure, while mileage is prone to deliberate misspecification. For some of these relevant factors, proxy measures can be found. One can get a good idea about mileage by looking at factors like weight and age of the car, as well as the type of fuel used, or type of usage (private or professional). Diesel engines, for instance, tend to be used only by drivers with a high mileage. Traffic density can be deduced from region of residence, driving speed from horse power and weight of the car. But it will remain impossible to assess the average future claim behavior completely using data known in advance, hence the need arises to use the actual claims history as a rating factor. Claims history is an ex post factor, which becomes fully known only just before the next policy year. Hence one speaks of ex post premium rating, where generally premiums are fixed ex ante.

In the investigation, the following was found. Next to the car weight, cylinder capacity and horse power of the car provided little extra predicting power. It proved that car weight correlated quite well with the total claim size, which is the product of claim frequency and average claim size. Heavier cars tend to be used more often, and also tend to produce more damage when involved in accidents. Car weight is a convenient rating factor, since it can be found on official car papers. In many countries, original catalogue price is used as the main rating factor for third party damage. This method has its drawbacks, however, because it is not reasonable to assume that someone would cause a higher third-party claim total if he has a metallic finish on his car or a more expensive audio system. It proved that when used next to car weight, catalogue price also did not improve predictions about third party claims. Of course for damage to the own vehicle, it remains the dominant rating factor. Note that the premiums proposed were not just any function of car weight and catalogue price, but they were directly proportional to these numbers.

The factor 'past claims experience', implemented as 'number of claim-free years', proved to be a good predictor for future claims, even when used in connection with other rating factors. After six claim-free years, the risk still diminishes, although slower. This is reflected in the percentages in the bonus-malus scale given in Table 6.1. Furthermore, it proved that drivers with a bad claims history are worse than beginning drivers, justifying the existence of a malus class with a premium percentage of more than 100%.

An analysis of the influence of the region on the claims experience proved that in less densely populated regions, fewer claims occurred, although somewhat larger. It appeared that the effect of region did not vanish with an increasing number of claim-free years. Hence the region effect was incorporated by a fixed discount, in fact enabling the large companies to compete with the regionally operating insurers on an equal footing.

The age of the policyholder is very important for his claim behavior. The claim frequency at age 18 is about four times the one drivers of age 30–70 have. Part of this bad claim behavior can be traced back to lack of experience, because after some years, the effect slowly vanishes. That is why it was decided not to let the basic premium vary by age, but merely to let young drivers enter at a more unfavorable step in the bonus-malus scale.

For commercial reasons, the profession of the policy holder as well as the make of the car were not incorporated in the rating system, even though these factors did have a noticeable influence.

Note that for the transitions in the bonus-malus system, only the number of claims filed counts, not their size. Although it is clear that a bonus-malus system based on claim sizes is possible, such systems are hardly ever used with car insurance.

6.3 MARKOV ANALYSIS

Bonus-malus systems are special cases of Markov processes. In such processes, one goes from one state to another in time. The Markov property says that the process is in a sense memoryless: the probability of such transitions does not depend on how one arrived in a particular state. Using Markov analysis, one may determine which proportion of the drivers will eventually be on which step of the bonus-malus scale. Also, it gives a means to determine how effective the bonus-malus system is in determining adjusted premiums representing the driver's actual risk.

To fix ideas, let us look at a simple example. In a particular bonus-malus system, a driver pays a high premium c if he files claims in either of the two preceding years, otherwise he pays a, with $a < c$. To describe this system by a bonus-malus scale, notice first that there are two groups of drivers paying the high premium, the ones who claimed last year, and the ones that filed a claim only in the year before. So we have three states (steps):

1. Claim in the previous policy year; paid c at the previous policy renewal;

2. No claim in the previous policy year, claim in the year before; paid c;

3. Claim-free in the two latest policy years; paid a.

First we determine the transition probabilities for a driver with probability p of having one or more claims in a policy year. In the event of a claim, he falls to state 1, otherwise he goes one step up, if possible. We get the following matrix P of transition probabilities p_{ij} to go from state i to state j:

$$P = \begin{pmatrix} p & q & 0 \\ p & 0 & q \\ p & 0 & q \end{pmatrix}. \tag{6.1}$$

The matrix P is a stochastic matrix: every row represents a probability distribution over states to be entered, so all elements of it are non-negative. Also, all row sums $\sum_j p_{ij}$ are equal to 1, since from any state i, one has to go to some state j. Apparently we have

$$P \begin{pmatrix} 1 \\ 1 \\ 1 \end{pmatrix} = \begin{pmatrix} 1 \\ 1 \\ 1 \end{pmatrix} \tag{6.2}$$

Hence the matrix P has $(1, 1, 1)^T$ as a right-hand eigenvector for eigenvalue 1. Assume that initially at time $t = 0$, the probability f_j for each driver to be in state $j = 1, 2, 3$ is given by the row-vector $l(0) = (f_1, f_2, f_3)$ with $f_j \geq 0$ and $f_1 + f_2 + f_3 = 1$. Often, the initial state is known to be i, and then f_i will be equal to one. The probability to start in state i and to enter state j after one year is equal to $f_i p_{ij}$, so the total probability of being in state j after one year, starting from an initial class i with probability f_i, equals $\sum_i f_i p_{ij}$. In matrix notation, the following vector $l(1)$ gives the probability distribution of drivers over the states after one year:

$$l(1) = l(0)P = (f_1, f_2, f_3) \begin{pmatrix} p & q & 0 \\ p & 0 & q \\ p & 0 & q \end{pmatrix} = (p, qf_1, q(f_2 + f_3)). \tag{6.3}$$

Drivers that produce a claim go to state 1. The probability of entering that state equals $p = p(f_1 + f_2 + f_3)$. Non-claimers go to a higher state, if possible. The distribution $l(2)$ over the states after two years is independent of $l(0)$, since

$$l(2) = l(1)P = (p, qf_1, q(f_2 + f_3)) \begin{pmatrix} p & q & 0 \\ p & 0 & q \\ p & 0 & q \end{pmatrix} = (p, pq, q^2). \tag{6.4}$$

The state two years from now does not depend on the current state, but only on the claims filed in the coming two years. Proceeding like this, one sees that $l(3) = l(4) = l(5) = \cdots = l(2)$. So we also have $l(\infty) := \lim_{t\to\infty} l(t) = l(2)$. The vector $l(\infty)$ is called the steady state distribution. Convergence will not always happen this quickly and thoroughly. Taking the square of a matrix, however, can be done very quickly, and doing it ten times starting from P already gives P^{1024}. Each element r_{ij} of this matrix can be interpreted as the probability of going from initial state i to state j in 1024 years. For regular bonus-malus systems, this probability will not depend heavily on the initial state i, nor will it differ much from the probability of reaching j from i in an infinite number of years. Hence all rows of P^{1024} will be virtually equal to the steady state distribution. But there is also a more formal way to determine it. This goes as follows. First, notice that

$$\lim_{t\to\infty} l(t+1) = \lim_{t\to\infty} l(t)P, \quad \text{hence} \quad l(\infty) = l(\infty)P. \tag{6.5}$$

But this means that the steady state distribution $l(\infty)$ is a left-hand eigenvector of P with eigenvalue 1. To determine $l(\infty)$ we only have to find a non-trivial solution for the linear system of equations (6.5), which is equivalent to the homogeneous system $(P^T - I)l^T(\infty) = (0, 0, \ldots, 0)^T$, and to divide it by the sum of its components to make $l(\infty)$ a probability distribution. Note that all components of $l(\infty)$ are necessarily non-negative, because of the fact that $l_j(\infty) = \lim_{t\to\infty} l_j(t)$.

Remark 6.3.1 (Initial distribution over the states)
It is not necessary to take $l(0)$ to be a probability distribution. It also makes sense to take for instance $l(0) = (1000, 0, 0)$. In this way, one considers a thousand drivers with initial state 1. Contrary to $l(0)$, the vectors $l(1), l(2), \ldots$ as well as $l(\infty)$ do not represent the exact number of drivers in a particular state, but just the expected values of these numbers. The actual numbers are binomial random variables with as probability of success in a trial, the probability of being in that particular state at the given time. ∇

Efficiency
The ultimate goal of a bonus-malus system is to make everyone pay a premium which is as near as possible the expected value of his yearly claims. If we want to investigate how efficient a bonus-malus system performs this task, we have to look at how the premium depends on the claim frequency λ. To this end, assume that the random variation about this theoretical claim frequency can be described as a Poisson process, see Chapter 4. Hence, the number of claims in each year is

a Poisson(λ) variate, and the probability of a year with one or more claims equals $p = 1 - e^{-\lambda}$. The expected value of the asymptotic premium to be paid is called the steady state premium. It of course depends on λ, and in our example where $l(\infty) = (p, pq, q^2)$ and the premiums are (c, c, a), it equals

$$b(\lambda) = c(p + pq) + aq^2 = c(1 - e^{-2\lambda}) + ae^{-2\lambda}. \tag{6.6}$$

This is the premium one pays on the average after the effects of in which state one initially started have vanished. In principle, this premium should be proportional to λ, since the average of the total annual claims for a driver with claim frequency intensity parameter λ is equal to λ times the average size of a single claim, which in all our considerations we have taken to be independent of the claim frequency. Define the following function for a bonus-malus system:

$$e(\lambda) := \frac{\lambda}{b(\lambda)} \frac{db(\lambda)}{d\lambda} = \frac{d \log b(\lambda)}{d \log \lambda}. \tag{6.7}$$

This is the so-called *Loimaranta efficiency*; the final equality is justified by the chain rule. It represents the 'elasticity' of the steady state premium $b(\lambda)$ with respect to λ. For 'small' h, it can be shown that if λ increases by a factor $1 + h$, $b(\lambda)$ increases by a factor which is approximately $1 + e(\lambda)h$, so we have

$$b(\lambda(1 + h)) \approx b(\lambda)(1 + e(\lambda)h). \tag{6.8}$$

Ideally, the efficiency should satisfy $e(\lambda) \approx 1$. In view of the explicit expression (6.6) for $b(\lambda)$, for our particular three-state example the efficiency amounts to

$$e(\lambda) = \frac{2\lambda e^{-2\lambda}(c - a)}{c(1 - e^{-2\lambda}) + ae^{-2\lambda}}. \tag{6.9}$$

As the steady state premium doesn't depend on the initial state, the same holds for the efficiency, though both of course depend on the claim frequency λ.

Remark 6.3.2 (Efficiency less than one means subsidizing bad drivers)
The premium percentages in all classes are positive and finite, hence $b(0) > 0$ and $b(\infty) < \infty$ hold. In many practical bonus-malus systems, we have $0 < e(\lambda) < 1$ over the whole range of λ. This is for instance the case for formula (6.9) and all $a < c$, see Exercise 6.3.4. Then we get

$$\frac{d}{d\lambda} \log \frac{b(\lambda)}{\lambda} = \frac{b'(\lambda)}{b(\lambda)} - \frac{1}{\lambda} = \frac{1}{\lambda}(e(\lambda) - 1) < 0. \tag{6.10}$$

As $\log \frac{b(\lambda)}{\lambda}$ decreases with λ, so does $\frac{b(\lambda)}{\lambda}$, from ∞ as $\lambda \downarrow 0$ to 0 as $\lambda \to \infty$. So there is a claim frequency λ_0 such that the steady state premium for $\lambda = \lambda_0$ exactly equals the net premium. Drivers with $\lambda > \lambda_0$ pay less than they should, drivers with $\lambda < \lambda_0$ pay more. This means that there is a capital transfer from the good risks to the bad risks. The rules of the bonus-malus system punish the claimers insufficiently. See again Exercise 6.3.4. ∇

Remark 6.3.3 (Hunger for bonus)
Suppose a driver with claim probability p, who is in state 3 in the above system, causes a damage of size t in an accident. If he is not obliged to file this claim with his insurance company, when exactly is it profitable for him to do so?

Assume that, as some policies allow, he only has to decide on December 31st whether to file this claim, so it is certain that he has no claims after this one concerning the same policy year. Since after two years the effect of this particular claim on his position on the bonus-malus scale will have vanished, we use a planning horizon of two years. His costs in the coming two years (premiums plus claim), depending on whether or not he files the claim and whether he is claim-free next year, are as follows:

	No claim next year	Claims next year
Claim not filed	$a+a+t$	$a+c+t$
Claim filed	$c+c$	$c+c$

Of course he should only file the claim if it makes his expected loss lower, which is the case if

$$(1-p)(2a+t)+p(a+c+t) \geq 2c \quad \Leftrightarrow \quad t \geq (2-p)(c-a). \tag{6.11}$$

From (6.11) we see that it is unwise to file very small claims, because of the loss of bonus in the near future. This phenomenon, which is not unimportant in practice, is called *hunger for bonus*. On the one hand, the insurer misses premiums that are his due, because the insured in fact conceals that he is a bad driver. But this is compensated by the fact that small claims also involve handling costs.

Many articles have appeared in the literature, both on actuarial science and on stochastic operational research, about this phenomenon. The model used can be much refined, involving for instance a longer or infinite time-horizon, with discounting. Also the time in the year that a claim occurs is important. ∇

Remark 6.3.4 (Steady state premiums and Loimaranta efficiency)
To determine the steady state premium as well as the Loimaranta efficiency for a certain bonus-malus system, one may proceed as follows. Let n denote the number of states. For notational convenience, introduce the functions $t_{ij}(k)$ with $i, j = 1, 2, \ldots, n$ to describe the transition rules, as follows:

$$\begin{aligned} t_{ij}(k) &= 1 \quad \text{if by } k \text{ claims in a year, one goes from state } i \text{ to } j; \\ t_{ij}(k) &= 0 \quad \text{otherwise.} \end{aligned} \tag{6.12}$$

The probability of a transition from state i to state j, when the parameter equals λ, is

$$P_{ij}(\lambda) = \sum_{k=0}^{\infty} p_k(\lambda) t_{ij}(k). \tag{6.13}$$

Next consider the initial distribution $l(0) = (l_1(0), \ldots, l_n(0))$, where $l_j(0)$ is the probability of finding a contract initially, at time $t = 0$, in state j, for $j = 1, 2, \ldots, n$. Then the vector of probabilities to find a driver in class j at time $t + 1$ can be expressed in the state vector $l(t)$ as follows:

$$l_j(t+1) = \sum_{i=1}^{n} l_i(t) P_{ij}(\lambda), t = 0, 1, 2, \ldots \tag{6.14}$$

The sum of the $l_j(t)$ is unity for each t. In the steady state we find, taking limits for $t \to \infty$:

$$l_j(\infty) = \sum_{i=1}^{n} l_i(\infty) P_{ij}(\lambda) \quad \text{with} \quad \sum_{j=1}^{n} l_j(\infty) = 1. \tag{6.15}$$

As noted before, the steady state vector $l(\infty) = (l_1(\infty), \ldots, l_n(\infty))$ is a left-hand eigenvector of the matrix P corresponding to the eigenvalue 1. In the steady state, we get for the asymptotic average premium (steady state premium) with claim frequency λ:

$$b(\lambda) = \sum_{j=1}^{n} l_j(\infty) b_j, \tag{6.16}$$

with b_j the premium for state j. Note that $l_j(\infty)$ depends on λ, but not on the initial distribution over the states.

Having an algorithm to compute $b(\lambda)$ as in (6.16), we can easily approximate the Loimaranta efficiency $e(\lambda)$. All it takes is to apply (6.8). But it is also possible to compute the efficiency $e(\lambda)$ exactly. Write $l_j(\lambda) = l_j(\infty)$, then

$$\frac{db(\lambda)}{d\lambda} = \sum_{j=1}^{n} b_j \frac{dl_j(\lambda)}{d\lambda} = \sum_{j=1}^{n} b_j g_j(\lambda), \tag{6.17}$$

where $g_j(\lambda) = \frac{dl_j(\lambda)}{d\lambda}$. These derivatives can be determined by taking derivatives in the system (6.15). One finds the following equations:

$$g_j(\lambda) = \sum_{i=1}^{n} g_i(\lambda) P_{ij}(\lambda) + \sum_{i=1}^{n} l_i(\lambda) P'_{ij}(\lambda), \tag{6.18}$$

where the derivatives of $P_{ij}(\lambda)$ can be found as

$$P'_{ij}(\lambda) = \frac{d}{d\lambda} \sum_{k=0}^{\infty} e^{-\lambda} \frac{\lambda^k}{k!} t_{ij}(k) = \sum_{k=0}^{\infty} e^{-\lambda} \frac{\lambda^k}{k!} [t_{ij}(k+1) - t_{ij}(k)]. \tag{6.19}$$

Using the fact that $\sum_j g_j(\lambda) = 0$, the efficiency $e(\lambda)$ can be computed for every λ by solving the resulting system of linear equations. In this way, one can compare various bonus-malus systems as regards efficiency, for instance by comparing the graphs of $e(\lambda)$ for the plausible values of λ ranging from 0.05 to 0.2, or by looking at some weighted average of $e(\lambda)$ values. ∇

6.4 EXERCISES

Section 6.2

1. Determine the percentage of the basic premium to be paid by a Dutch driver, who originally entered the bonus-malus scale at level 100%, drove without claim for 7 years, then filed one claim during the eighth policy year, and has been driving claim-free for the three years since then. Would the total of the premiums he paid have been different if his one claim occurred in the second policy year?

Section 6.3

1. Prove (6.8).
2. Determine P^2 with P as in (6.1). What is the meaning of its elements? Can you see directly from this that $l(2) = l(\infty)$ must hold?

3. Determine $e(\lambda)$ in the example with three steps in this section if in state 2, instead of c the premium is a. Argue that the system can now be described by only two states, and determine P and $l(\infty)$.
4. Show that $e(\lambda) < 1$ in (6.9) for every a and c with $a < c$. When is $e(\lambda)$ close to 1?
5. Recalculate (6.11) for a claim at the end of the policy year when the interest is i.
6. [♠] Calculate the Loimaranta efficiency (6.9) by method (6.17)–(6.19).
7. Determine the value of α such that the transition probability matrix P has vector $(\frac{5}{12}, \frac{7}{12})$ as its steady state vector, if P is given by

$$P = \begin{pmatrix} \alpha & 1-\alpha \\ \frac{1}{2} & \frac{1}{2} \end{pmatrix} \tag{6.20}$$

8. If for the steady state premium we have $b(\lambda) = 100$ if $\lambda = 0.050$ and $b(\lambda) = 101$ for $\lambda = 0.051$, estimate the Loimaranta efficiency $e(\lambda) = \frac{d \log b(\lambda)}{d \log \lambda}$ at $\lambda = 0.05$.
9. For the following transition probability matrix:

$$P = \begin{pmatrix} t & 1-t \\ s & 1-s \end{pmatrix}, \tag{6.21}$$

determine the relation between s and t that holds if the steady state vector equals $(p, 1-p)$.

7

Credibility theory

7.1 INTRODUCTION

In insurance practice it often occurs that one has to set a premium for a group of insurance contracts for which there is some claim experience regarding the group itself, but a lot more on a larger group of contracts that are more or less related. The problem is then to set up an experience rating system to determine next year's premium, taking into account not only the individual experience with the group, but also the collective experience. There are two extreme positions possible. One is to charge the same premium to everyone, estimated by the overall mean $\overline{X}$ of the data. This makes sense if the portfolio is homogeneous, which means that all risk cells have identical mean claims. But if this is not the case, the 'good' risks will take their business elsewhere, leaving the insurer with only 'bad' risks. The other extreme is to charge to group j its own average claims $\overline{X}_j$ as a premium. Such premiums are justified if the portfolio is heterogeneous, but they can only be applied if the claims experience with each group is large enough. As a compromise, already since the beginning of the 20th century one often asks a premium which is a weighted average of these two extremes:

$$z_j\overline{X}_j + (1 - z_j)\overline{X}. \tag{7.1}$$

The factor z_j that expresses how 'credible' the individual experience of cell j is, is called the *credibility factor*; a premium such as (7.1) is called a *credibility premium*. Charging a premium based on collective as well as individual experience is justified because the portfolio is in general neither completely homogeneous, nor completely heterogeneous. The risks in group j have characteristics in common with the risks in other groups, but they also possess unique group properties.

One would choose z_j close to one under the following circumstances: the risk experience with cell j is vast, it exhibits only little variation, or the variation between groups is substantial. There are two methods to try and determine a value for z_j. In *limited fluctuation credibility theory*, a cell is given full credibility $z_j = 1$ if the experience with it is large enough. This means that the probability of having at least a certain relative error in the individual mean does not exceed a given threshold. If not, the credibility factor equals the ratio of the experience actually present and the experience needed for full credibility. More interesting is the *greatest accuracy credibility theory*, where the credibility factors are derived as optimal coefficients in a Bayesian model with variance components. This model was developed in the 1960's by Bühlmann.

Note that apart from claim amounts, the data can also concern *loss ratios*, i.e., claims divided by premiums, or claims as a percentage of the sum insured, and so on. Quite often, the claims experience in a cell relates to just one contract, observed in a number of periods, but it is also possible that a cell contains various 'identical' contracts.

In practice, one should use credibility premiums only if one only has very few data. If one has additional information in the form of collateral variables, for instance, probably using a generalized linear model (GLM) such as described in the following chapter is indicated. The main problem is to determine how much virtual experience, see Remark 7.2.7 and Exercise 7.4.7, one should incorporate.

In Section 7.2 we present a basic model to illustrate the ideas behind credibility theory. In this model the claims total X_{jt} for contract j in period t is decomposed into three separate components. The first component is the overall mean m, the second a deviation from this mean which is specific for this contract, the third is a deviation for the specific time period. By taking these deviations to be independent random variables, we see that there is a covariance structure between the claim amounts, and under this structure we can derive estimators of the components which minimize a certain sum of squares. In Section 7.3 we show that these exact covariance structures, and hence the same optimal estimators, also arise in more general models. Furthermore, we give a short review of possible generalizations of the basic model. In Section 7.4, we investigate the Bühlmann-Straub model, in which the observations are measured in different precisions. In Section 7.5 we give an application from motor insurance, where the numbers of claims are Poisson random variables with as a parameter the outcome of a structure parameter which is assumed to follow a gamma distribution.

7.2 THE BALANCED BÜHLMANN MODEL

To clarify the ideas behind credibility theory, we study in this section a stylized credibility model. Consider the random variable X_{jt}, representing the claim statistic of cell j, $j = 1, 2, \dots, J$, in year t. For simplicity, we assume that the cell contains a single contract only, and that every cell has been observed during T observation periods. So for each j, the index t has the values $t = 1, 2, \dots, T$. Assume that this claim statistic is the sum of a cell mean m_j plus 'white noise', i.e., that all X_{ij} are independent and $N(m_j, s^2)$ distributed, with possibly unequal mean m_j for each cell, but with the same variance $s^2 > 0$. We can test for equality of all group means using the familiar statistical technique of *analysis of variance* (ANOVA). If the null-hypothesis that all m_j are equal fails to hold, this means that there will be more variation between the cell averages $\overline{X}_j$ around the overall average $\overline{X}$ than can be expected in view of the observed variation within the cells. For this reason we look at the following random variable, called the *sum-of-squares-between* or SSB:

$$SSB = \sum_{j=1}^{J} T(\overline{X}_j - \overline{X})^2. \tag{7.2}$$

One may show that, under the null-hypothesis that all group means m_j are equal, the random variable SSB has mean $(J-1)s^2$. Since s^2 is unknown, we must estimate this parameter separately. This estimate is derived from the *sum-of-squares-within* or SSW, which is defined as

$$SSW = \sum_{j=1}^{J}\sum_{t=1}^{T}(X_{jt} - \overline{X}_j)^2. \tag{7.3}$$

It is easy to show that the random variable SSW has mean $J(T-1)s^2$. Dividing SSB by $J-1$ and SSW by $J(T-1)$ we get two random variables, each with mean s^2, called the *mean-square-between* (MSB) and the *mean-square-within* (MSW) respectively. We can perform an F-test now, where large values of the MSB compared to the MSW indicate that the null-hypothesis that all group means are equal should be rejected. The test statistic to be used is the so-called *variance ratio* or F-ratio:

$$F = \frac{MSB}{MSW} = \frac{\frac{1}{J-1}\sum_j T(\overline{X}_j - \overline{X})^2}{\frac{1}{J(T-1)}\sum_j \sum_t (X_{jt} - \overline{X}_j)^2}. \tag{7.4}$$

Under the null-hypothesis, SSB divided by s^2 has a $\chi^2(J-1)$ distribution, while SSW divided by s^2 has a $\chi^2(J(T-1))$ distribution. Furthermore, it is possible to show that these random variables are independent. Therefore, the ratio F has an $F(J-1, J(T-1))$ distribution. Proofs of these statements can be found in many texts on mathematical statistics, under the heading 'one-way analysis of variance'. The critical values of F can be found in an F-table (Fisher distribution).

Example 7.2.1 (A heterogeneous portfolio)
Suppose that we have the following observations for 3 groups and 5 years:

	$t=1$	$t=2$	$t=3$	$t=4$	$t=5$	$\overline{X}_j$
$j=1$	99.3	93.7	103.9	92.5	110.6	100.0
$j=2$	112.5	108.3	118.0	99.4	111.8	110.0
$j=3$	129.2	140.9	108.3	105.0	116.6	120.0

As the reader may verify, the MSB equals 500 with 2 degrees of freedom, while the MSW is 109 with 12 degrees of freedom. This gives a value $F = 4.6$, which is significant at the 95% level, the critical value being 3.89. The conclusion is that the data show that the mean claims per group are not all equal. ∇

If the null-hypothesis fails to be rejected, there is apparently no convincing statistical evidence that the portfolio is heterogeneous. Accordingly, we should ask the same premium for each contract. In case of rejection, apparently there is variation between the cell means m_j. In this case one may treat these numbers as fixed unknown numbers, and try to find a system behind these numbers, for instance by doing a regression on collateral data. Another approach is to assume that the numbers m_j have been produced by a chance mechanism, hence by 'white noise' similar to the one responsible for the deviations from the mean within each cell. This means that we can decompose the claim statistics as follows:

$$X_{jt} = m + \Xi_j + \Xi_{jt}, \quad j = 1, \ldots, J, \; t = 1, \ldots, T, \tag{7.5}$$

with Ξ_j and Ξ_{jt} independent random variables for which

$$\mathrm{E}[\Xi_j] = \mathrm{E}[\Xi_{jt}] = 0, \quad \mathrm{Var}[\Xi_j] = a, \quad \mathrm{Var}[\Xi_{jt}] = s^2. \tag{7.6}$$

Because the variance of X_{jt} in (7.5) equals the sum of the variances of its components, models such as (7.5) are called *variance components models*. Model (7.5) is a simplified form of the so-called classical Bühlmann model, because we assumed independence of the components where Bühlmann only assumes the correlation to be zero. We call our model which has equal variance for all observations, as well as equal numbers of policies in all cells, the *balanced Bühlmann model.*

The interpretation of the separate components in (7.5) is the following.

1. m is the overall mean; it is the expected value of the claim amount for an arbitrary policyholder in the portfolio.

2. Ξ_j denotes a random deviation from this mean, specific for contract j. The conditional mean, given $\Xi_j = \xi$, of the random variables X_{jt} equals $m + \xi$. It represents the long-term average of the claims each year if the length of the observation period T goes to infinity. The component Ξ_j describes the risk quality of this particular contract; the mean $\mathrm{E}[\Xi_j]$ equals zero, its variation describes differences between contracts. The distribution of Ξ_j depicts the risk structure of the portfolio, hence it is known as the *structure distribution.* The parameters m, a and s^2 characterizing the risk structure are called the *structural parameters.*

3. The components Ξ_{jt} denote the deviation for year t from the long-term average. They describe the within-variation of a contract. It is the variation of the claim experience in time through good and bad luck of the policyholder.

Note that in the model described above, the random variables X_{jt} are *dependent* for fixed j, since they share a common risk quality component Ξ_j. One might say that independent random variables with the same probability distribution involving unknown parameters in a sense are dependent anyway, since their values all depend on these same unknown parameters.

In the next theorem, we are looking for a predictor of the as yet unobserved random variable $X_{j,T+1}$. We require this predictor to be a linear combination of the observable data $X_{11}, \dots, X_{JT}$ with the same mean as $X_{j,T+1}$. Furthermore, its mean squared error must be minimal. We prove that under model (7.5), this predictor has the credibility form (7.1), so it is a weighted average of the individual claims experience and the overall mean claim. The theorem also provides us with the optimal value of the credibility factor z_j. We want to know the optimal predictor of the amount to be paid out in the next period $T+1$, since that is the premium we should ask for this contract. The distributional assumptions are assumed to hold for all periods $t = 1, \dots, T+1$. Note that in the theorem below, normality is not required.

Theorem 7.2.2 (Balanced Bühlmann model; homogeneous estimator)
Assume that the claim figures X_{jt} for contract j in period t can be written as the sum of stochastically independent components, as follows:

$$X_{jt} = m + \Xi_j + \Xi_{jt}, \quad j = 1, \dots, J, \ t = 1, \dots, T+1, \tag{7.7}$$

where the random variables Ξ_j are iid with mean $\mathrm{E}[\Xi_j] = 0$ and $\mathrm{Var}[\Xi_j] = a$, and also the random variables Ξ_{jt} are iid with mean $\mathrm{E}[\Xi_{jt}] = 0$ and $\mathrm{Var}[\Xi_{jt}] = s^2$ for all j and t. Furthermore, assume the random variables Ξ_j to be independent of the Ξ_{jt}.

Then, the homogeneous linear combination $g_{11}X_{11} + \cdots + g_{JT}X_{JT}$ which is the best unbiased predictor of $X_{j,T+1}$ in the sense of minimal mean squared error (MSE)

$$\mathrm{E}[\{X_{j,T+1} - g_{11}X_{11} - \cdots - g_{JT}X_{JT}\}^2] \tag{7.8}$$

equals the credibility premium

$$z\overline{X}_j + (1-z)\overline{X}, \tag{7.9}$$

where

$$z = \frac{aT}{aT + s^2} \tag{7.10}$$

is the resulting best credibility factor (which in this case is equal for all j),

$$\overline{X} = \frac{1}{JT}\sum_{j=1}^{J}\sum_{t=1}^{T} X_{jt} \tag{7.11}$$

is the collective estimator of m, and

$$\overline{X}_j = \frac{1}{T}\sum_{t=1}^{T} X_{jt} \tag{7.12}$$

is the individual estimator of m.

Proof. Because of the independence assumptions and the equal distributions, the random variables X_{it} with $i \neq j$ are interchangeable. By convexity, (7.8) has a unique minimum. For symmetry reasons, in the optimum all values of $g_{it}, i \neq j$ must be identical. The same goes for all values $g_{jt}, t = 1, \ldots, T$. Combining this with the unbiasedness restriction, we see that the homogeneous linear estimator with minimal MSE must be of the form (7.9) for some z. We only have to find its optimal value.

Since X_{jt}, $\overline{X}_j$ and $\overline{X}$ all have mean m, we can rewrite the MSE (7.8) as:

$$\begin{aligned}
&\mathrm{E}[\{X_{j,T+1} - (1-z)\overline{X} - z\overline{X}_j\}^2] = \mathrm{E}[\{X_{j,T+1} - \overline{X} - z(\overline{X}_j - \overline{X})\}^2] \\
&= \mathrm{E}[\{X_{j,T+1} - \overline{X}\}^2] - 2z\mathrm{E}[\{X_{j,T+1} - \overline{X}\}\{\overline{X}_j - \overline{X}\}] + z^2\mathrm{E}[\{\overline{X}_j - \overline{X}\}^2] \\
&= \mathrm{Var}[X_{j,T+1} - \overline{X}] - 2z\mathrm{Cov}[X_{j,T+1} - \overline{X}, \overline{X}_j - \overline{X}] + z^2\mathrm{Var}[\overline{X}_j - \overline{X}].
\end{aligned} \tag{7.13}$$

This quadratic form in z is minimal for the following choice of z:

$$z = \frac{\mathrm{Cov}[X_{j,T+1} - \overline{X}, \overline{X}_j - \overline{X}]}{\mathrm{Var}[\overline{X}_j - \overline{X}]} = \frac{aT}{aT + s^2}, \tag{7.14}$$

where it is left to the reader (Exercise 7.2.1) to verify the final equality by proving and filling in the necessary covariances:

$$\begin{aligned}
&\mathrm{Cov}[X_{jt}, X_{ju}] = a \text{ for } t \neq u; \\
&\mathrm{Var}[X_{jt}] = a + s^2; \\
&\mathrm{Cov}[X_{jt}, \overline{X}_j] = \mathrm{Var}[\overline{X}_j] = a + \frac{s^2}{T}; \\
&\mathrm{Cov}[\overline{X}_j, \overline{X}] = \mathrm{Var}[\overline{X}] = \frac{1}{J}(a + \frac{s^2}{T}).
\end{aligned} \tag{7.15}$$

So indeed predictor (7.9) leads to the minimal MSE (7.8) for the value of z given in (7.10). ∇

Remark 7.2.3 (Asymptotic properties of the optimal credibility factor)
The credibility factor z in (7.10) has a number of plausible asymptotic properties:

1. If $T \to \infty$, then $z \to 1$. The more claims experience there is, the more faith we can have in the individual risk premium. This asymptotic case is not very relevant in practice, because it assumes that the risk does not change over time.

2. If $a \downarrow 0$, then $z \downarrow 0$. If the expected individual claim amounts are identically distributed, there is no heterogeneity in the portfolio. But then the collective mean m, see (7.16) below, or its best homogeneous estimator $\overline{X}$ in (7.9), are optimal linear estimators of the risk premium.

3. If $a \to \infty$, then $z \to 1$. This is also intuitively clear. In this case, the result on the other contracts does not provide information about risk j.

4. If $s^2 \to \infty$, then $z \to 0$. If for a fixed risk parameter, the claims experience is extremely variable, the individual experience is not useful for estimating the real risk premium. ∇

Note that (7.9) is only a *statistic* if the ratio s^2/a is known; otherwise its distribution will contain unknown parameters. In Example 7.2.5 below we show how this ratio can be estimated as a by-product of the ANOVA. The fact that the credibility factor (7.14) does not depend on j is due to the simplifying assumption we have made that the number of observation periods is the same for each j, as well as that all observations have the same variance.

If we allow that our linear estimator contains a constant term, hence look at the best *inhomogeneous* linear predictor $g_0 + g_{11}X_{11} + \cdots + g_{JT}X_{JT}$, we get the next theorem. Two things should be noted. One is that it will prove that the unbiasedness restriction is now superfluous. The other is that (7.16) below looks just like (7.9), except that the quantity $\overline{X}$ is replaced by m. But this means that the inhomogeneous credibility premium for group j does not depend on the data from other groups $i \neq j$. The homogeneous credibility premium assumes the ratio s^2/a to be known; the inhomogeneous credibility premium additionally assumes that m is known.

Theorem 7.2.4 (Balanced Bühlmann model; inhomogeneous estimator)
Under the same distributional assumptions about X_{jt} as in the previous theorem, the inhomogeneous linear combination $g_0 + g_{11}X_{11} + \cdots + g_{JT}X_{JT}$ to predict

next year's claim total $X_{j,T+1}$ which is optimal in the sense of mean squared error is the credibility premium

$$z\overline{X}_j + (1-z)m, \tag{7.16}$$

where z and $\overline{X}_j$ are as in (7.10) and (7.12).

Proof. The same symmetry considerations as in the previous proof tell us that the values of $g_{it}, i \neq j$ are identical in the optimal solution, just as those of $g_{jt}, t = 1, \ldots, T$. So for certain g_0, g_1 and g_2, the inhomogeneous linear predictor of $X_{j,T+1}$ with minimal MSE is of the following form:

$$g_0 + g_1\overline{X} + g_2\overline{X}_j. \tag{7.17}$$

The MSE can be written as variance plus squared bias, as follows:

$$\begin{aligned} &\mathrm{E}[\{X_{j,T+1} - g_0 - g_1\overline{X} - g_2\overline{X}_j\}^2] \\ &= \mathrm{Var}[X_{j,T+1} - g_1\overline{X} - g_2\overline{X}_j] + \{\mathrm{E}[X_{j,T+1} - g_0 - g_1\overline{X} - g_2\overline{X}_j]\}^2. \end{aligned} \tag{7.18}$$

The second term on the right hand side is zero, and hence minimal, if we choose $g_0 = m(1-g_1-g_2)$. This entails that the estimator we are looking for is necessarily unbiased. The first term on the right hand side of (7.18) can be rewritten as

$$\begin{aligned} &\mathrm{Var}[X_{j,T+1} - (g_2 + g_1/J)\overline{X}_j - g_1(\overline{X} - \overline{X}_j/J)] \\ &= \mathrm{Var}[X_{j,T+1} - (g_2 + g_1/J)\overline{X}_j] + \mathrm{Var}[g_1(\overline{X} - \overline{X}_j/J)] + 0, \end{aligned} \tag{7.19}$$

because the covariance term vanishes since $g_1(\overline{X} - \overline{X}_j/J)$ depends only of X_{it} with $i \neq j$. Hence any solution (g_1, g_2) with $g_1 \neq 0$ can be improved, since a lower value of (7.19) is obtained by taking $(0, g_2 + g_1/J)$. Therefore choosing $g_1 = 0$ is optimal. So all that remains to be done is to minimize the following expression for g_2:

$$\begin{aligned} &\mathrm{Var}[X_{j,T+1} - g_2\overline{X}_j] \\ &= \mathrm{Var}[X_{j,T+1}] - 2g_2\mathrm{Cov}[X_{j,T+1}, \overline{X}_j] + g_2^2\mathrm{Var}[\overline{X}_j], \end{aligned} \tag{7.20}$$

which has as an optimum

$$g_2 = \frac{\mathrm{Cov}[X_{j,T+1}, \overline{X}_j]}{\mathrm{Var}[\overline{X}_j]} = \frac{aT}{aT + s^2}, \tag{7.21}$$

so the optimal g_2 is just z as in (7.10). The final equality can be verified by filling in the relevant covariances (7.15). This means that the predictor (7.16) for $X_{j,T+1}$ has minimal MSE. ∇

Example 7.2.5 (Credibility estimation in Example 7.2.1)
Consider again the portfolio of Example 7.2.1. It can be shown (see Exercise 7.2.8), that in model (7.5) the numerator of F in (7.4) (the MSB) has mean $aT + s^2$, while the denominator MSW has mean s^2. Hence $\frac{1}{F}$ will be close to $s^2/\{aT + s^2\}$, which means that we can use $1 - \frac{1}{F}$ to estimate z. Note that this is not an unbiased estimator, since $\mathrm{E}[1/MSB] \neq 1/\mathrm{E}[MSB]$. The resulting credibility factor is $z = 0.782$ for each group. So the optimal forecasts for the claims next year in the three groups are $0.782\overline{X}_j + (1 - 0.782)\overline{X}, j = 1, 2, 3$, resulting in 102.18, 110 and 117.82. Notice the 'shrinkage effect': the credibility estimated premiums are closer together than the original group means 100, 110 and 120. ∇

Remark 7.2.6 (Estimating the risk premium)
One may argue that instead of aiming to predict next year's claim figure $X_{j,T+1}$, including the fluctuation $\Xi_{j,T+1}$, we actually should estimate the *risk premium* $m + \Xi_j$ of group j. But we will show that, whether we allow a constant term in our estimator or not, in each case we get the same optimum that we found before. Indeed we have for every random variable Y:

$$\begin{aligned} &\mathrm{E}[\{m + \Xi_j + \Xi_{j,T+1} - Y\}^2] \\ &= \mathrm{E}[\{m + \Xi_j - Y\}^2] + \mathrm{Var}[\Xi_{j,T+1}] + 2\mathrm{Cov}[m + \Xi_j - Y, \Xi_{j,T+1}]. \end{aligned} \tag{7.22}$$

If Y depends only on the X_{jt} that are already observed, hence with $t \leq T$, the covariance term must be equal to zero. Since it follows from (7.22) that the MSE's for Y as an estimator of $m + \Xi_j$ and of $X_{j,T+1} = m + \Xi_j + \Xi_{j,T+1}$ differ only by a constant $\mathrm{Var}[\Xi_{j,T+1}] = s^2$, we conclude that both MSE's are minimized by the same estimator Y. ∇

The credibility premium (7.16) is a weighted average of the estimated individual mean claim, with as a weight the credibility factor z, and the estimated mean claim for the whole portfolio. Because we assumed that the number of observation years T for each contract is the same, by asking premium (7.16) on the lowest level we receive the same premium income as when we would ask $\overline{X}$ as a premium from everyone. For $z = 0$ the individual premium equals the collective premium. This is acceptable in a homogeneous portfolio, but in general not in a heterogeneous one. For $z = 1$, a premium is charged which is fully based on individual experience. In general, this individual information is scarce, making this estimator unusable in practice. Sometimes it even fails completely, like when a prediction is wanted for a contract that up to now has not produced any claim.

The quantity $a > 0$ represents the heterogeneity of the portfolio as depicted in the risk quality component Ξ_j, and s^2 is a global measure for the variability within the homogeneous groups.

Remark 7.2.7 (Virtual experience)
Write $X_{j\Sigma} = X_{j1} + \cdots + X_{jT}$, then an equivalent expression for the credibility premium (7.16) is the following:

$$\frac{s^2 m + aT\overline{X}_j}{s^2 + aT} = \frac{ms^2/a + X_{j\Sigma}}{s^2/a + T}. \tag{7.23}$$

So if we add a virtual claims total ms^2/a to the actually observed claim total $X_{j\Sigma}$, and also extend the number of observation periods by an extra s^2/a periods, the credibility premium is nothing but the average claim total, adjusted for virtual experience. ∇

7.3 MORE GENERAL CREDIBILITY MODELS

In model (7.5) of the previous section, we assumed the components Ξ_j and Ξ_{jt} to be independent random variables. But from (7.14) and (7.15) one sees that actually only the covariances of the random variables X_{jt} are essential. We get the same results if we impose a model with weaker requirements, as long as the covariance structure remains the same. An example is to only require independence and identical distributions of the Ξ_{jt}, conditionally given Ξ_j, with $\mathrm{E}[\Xi_{jt}|\Xi_j = \xi] = 0$ for all ξ. If the joint distribution of Ξ_j and Ξ_{jt} is like that, the Ξ_{jt} are not necessarily independent, but they are uncorrelated, as can be seen from the following lemma:

Lemma 7.3.1 (Conditionally iid random variables are uncorrelated)
Suppose that given Ξ_j, the random variables $\Xi_{j1}, \Xi_{j2}, \ldots$ are iid with mean zero. Then we have

$$\mathrm{Cov}[\Xi_{jt}, \Xi_{ju}] = 0,\ t \neq u; \quad \mathrm{Cov}[\Xi_j, \Xi_{jt}] = 0. \tag{7.24}$$

Proof. Because of the decomposition rule for conditional covariances, see Exercise 7.3.1, we can write for $t \neq u$:

$$\text{Cov}[\Xi_{ju}, \Xi_{jt}] = \text{E}[\text{Cov}[\Xi_{ju}, \Xi_{jt}|\Xi_j]] + \text{Cov}[\text{E}[\Xi_{ju}|\Xi_j], \text{E}[\Xi_{jt}|\Xi_j]]. \quad (7.25)$$

This equals zero since, by our assumptions, $\text{Cov}[\Xi_{ju}, \Xi_{jt}|\Xi_j] \equiv 0$ and $\text{E}[\Xi_{ju}|\Xi_j] \equiv 0$. Clearly, $\text{Cov}[\Xi_j, \Xi_{jt}|\Xi_j] \equiv 0$ as well. Because

$$\text{Cov}[\Xi_j, \Xi_{jt}] = \text{E}[\text{Cov}[\Xi_j, \Xi_{jt}|\Xi_j]] + \text{Cov}[\text{E}[\Xi_j|\Xi_j], \text{E}[\Xi_{jt}|\Xi_j]], \quad (7.26)$$

the random variables Ξ_j and Ξ_{jt} are uncorrelated as well. ∇

Note that in the model of this lemma, the random variables X_{jt} are not marginally uncorrelated, let alone independent.

Example 7.3.2 (Mixed Poisson distribution)
Assume that the X_{jt} random variables represent the numbers of claims in a year on a particular motor insurance policy. The driver in question has a number of claims in that year which has a Poisson(Λ_j) distribution, where the parameter Λ_j is a drawing from a certain non-degenerate structure distribution. Then the first component of (7.5) represents the expected number of claims $m = \text{E}[X_{jt}] = \text{E}[\Lambda_j]$ of an arbitrary driver. The second is $\Xi_j = \Lambda_j - m$; it represents the difference in average numbers of claims between this particular driver and an arbitrary driver. The third term $\Xi_{jt} = X_{jt} - \Lambda_j$ equals the annual fluctuation around the mean number of claims of this particular driver. In this case, the second and third component, though uncorrelated, are not independent, for instance because $\text{Var}[X_{jt} - \Lambda_j|\Lambda_j - m] = \text{Var}[X_{jt}|\Lambda_j] = \Lambda_j$. See also Section 7.5. ∇

Remark 7.3.3 (Parametrization through risk parameters)
The variance components model (7.5), even with relaxed independence assumptions, sometimes is too restricted for practical applications. Suppose that X_{jt} as in (7.5) now represents the annual claims total of the driver from Example 7.3.2, and also suppose that this has a compound Poisson distribution. Then apart from the Poisson parameter, there are also the parameters of the claim size distribution. The conditional variance of the noise term, given the second term (mean annual total claim costs), is now no longer a function of the second term. To remedy this, Bühlmann studied slightly more general models, having a latent random variable Θ_j, that might be vector-valued, as a structure parameter. The risk premium is the conditional mean $\mu(\Theta_j) := \text{E}[X_{jt}|\Theta_j]$ instead of simply $m + \Xi_j$. If $\text{E}[X_{jt}|\Theta_j]$

is not a one-to-one function of Θ_j, it might occur that contracts having the same Ξ_j in the basic model above, have a different pattern of variation $\mathrm{Var}[\Xi_{jt}|\Theta_j]$ in Bühlmann's model, therefore the basic model is insufficient here. But it can be shown that in this case the same covariances, and hence the same optimal estimators, are found.

Unfortunately, Bühlmann's way of describing the risk structure is copied in many texts and articles about credibility theory. The gain in generality and flexibility is slight, and the resulting models are much more cumbersome technically as well as conceptually. ∇

It is possible to extend credibility theory to models that are more complicated than (7.5). Results resembling the ones from Theorems 7.2.2 and 7.2.4 can be derived for such models. In essence, to find an optimal predictor in the sense of least squares one minimizes the quadratic MSE over its coefficients, if needed with an additional unbiasedness restriction. Because of the symmetry assumptions in the balanced Bühlmann model, only a one-dimensional optimization was needed there. But in general we must solve a system of linear equations that arises by differentiating either the MSE or a Lagrange function. The latter situation occurs when there is an unbiasedness restriction. One should not expect to obtain analytical solutions such as above.

Possible generalizations of the basic model are the following.

Example 7.3.4 (Bühlmann-Straub model; varying precision)
Credibility models such as (7.5) can be generalized by looking at X_{jt} that are averages over a number of policies. It is also conceivable that there are other reasons to assume that not all X_{jt} have been measured equally precisely, i.e., have the same variance. For this reason, it may be expedient to introduce weights in the model. By doing this, we get the Bühlmann-Straub model. In principle, these weights should represent the total number of observation periods of which the figure X_{jt} is the mean *(natural weights)*. Sometimes this number is unknown. In that case, one has to make do with approximate weights, like for instance the total premium paid. If the actuary deems it appropriate, he can adjust these numbers to express the degree of confidence he has in the individual claims experience of particular contracts. In Section 7.4 we prove a result, analogous to Theorem 7.2.2, for the homogeneous premium in the Bühlmann-Straub model. ∇

Example 7.3.5 (Jewell's hierarchical model)
A further generalization is to subdivide the portfolio into sectors, and to assume that

each sector p has its own deviation from the overall mean. The claims experience for contract j in sector p in year t can then be decomposed as follows:

$$X_{pjt} = m + \Xi_p + \Xi_{pj} + \Xi_{pjt}. \tag{7.27}$$

This model is called Jewell's hierarchical model. Splitting up each sector p into subsectors q, each with its own deviation $\Xi_p + \Xi_{pq}$, and so on, leads to a hierarchical chain of models with a tree structure. ∇

Example 7.3.6 (Cross classification models)
It is conceivable that X_{pjt} is the risk in sector p, and that index j corresponds to some other general factor to split up the policies, for instance if p is the region and j the gender of the driver. For such two-way cross classifications it doesn't make sense to use a hierarchical structure for the risk determinants. Instead, one could add to (7.27) a term Ξ'_j, to describe the risk characteristics of group j. In this way, one gets

$$X_{pjt} = m + \Xi_p + \Xi'_j + \Xi_{pj} + \Xi_{pjt}. \tag{7.28}$$

This is a cross classification model. In Chapter 8, we study similar models, where the row and column effects are fixed but unknown, instead of being modelled as random variables such as here. ∇

Example 7.3.7 (De Vijlder's credibility model for IBNR)
Credibility models are also useful to tackle the problem of estimating IBNR reserves to be held, see also Chapter 9. These are provisions for claims that are not, or not fully, known to the insurer. In a certain calendar year T, realizations are known for random variables X_{jt} representing the claim figure for policies written in year j, in their tth year of development, $t = 0, 1, \ldots, T - j$. A credibility model for this situation is

$$X_{jt} = (m + \Xi_j)d_t + \Xi_{jt}, \tag{7.29}$$

where the numbers d_t are development factors, for instance with a sum equal to 1, that represent the fraction of the claims paid on average in the tth development period, and where $m + \Xi_j$ represents the claims, aggregated over all development periods, on policies written in year j. ∇

Example 7.3.8 (Regression models; Hachemeister)
We can also generalize (7.5) by introducing collateral data. If for instance y_{jt} represents a certain risk characteristic of contract j, like for instance the age of the

policy holder in year t, Ξ_j might be written as a linear, stochastic, function of y_{jt}. Then the claims in year t are equal to

$$\{m^{(1)} + \Xi_j^{(1)}\} + \{m^{(2)} + \Xi_j^{(2)}\}y_{jt} + \Xi_{jt}, \tag{7.30}$$

which is a credibility-regression model. Classical one-dimensional regression arises when $\Xi_j^{(k)} \equiv 0, k = 1, 2$. This means that there are no latent risk characteristics. Credibility models such as (7.30) were first studied by Hachemeister. ∇

7.4 THE BÜHLMANN-STRAUB MODEL

Just as in (7.7), in the Bühlmann-Straub model the observations can be decomposed as follows:

$$X_{jt} = m + \Xi_j + \Xi_{jt}, \quad j = 1, \ldots, J, \; t = 1, \ldots, T+1, \tag{7.31}$$

where the unobservable risk components $\Xi_j, j = 1, 2, \ldots, J$ are iid with mean zero and variance a; the Ξ_{jt} are also independent with mean zero. The components Ξ_j and Ξ_{jt} are assumed to be independent, too. The difference between the Bühlmann and the Bühlmann-Straub models is that in the latter the variance of the Ξ_{jt} components is s^2/w_{jt}, where w_{jt} is the *weight* attached to observation X_{jt}. This weight represents the relative precision of the various observations. Observations with variances like this arise when X_{jt} is an average of w_{jt} replications, hence $X_{jt} = \sum_k X_{jtk}/w_{jt}$ where $X_{jtk} = m + \Xi_j + \Xi_{jtk}$ with Ξ_{jtk} iid with zero mean and variance s^2. The random variables Ξ_{jtk} then denote deviations from the risk premium $m + \Xi_j$ for the kth individual contract in time period t and group j. In this case, the weights are called *natural weights*. Sometimes the natural weights are not available, or there is another mechanism that leads to different variances. In that case we can approximate the volume by the total premium for a cell.

To find the best homogeneous linear predictor of the *risk premium* $m + \Xi_j$ (cf. Remark 7.2.6), we must minimize the following MSE:

$$\begin{aligned} &\min_{h_{it}} \mathrm{E}[\{m + \Xi_j - \sum_{i,t} h_{it} X_{it}\}^2] \\ &\text{subject to } \mathrm{E}[m + \Xi_j] = \sum_{i,t} h_{it} \mathrm{E}[X_{it}]. \end{aligned} \tag{7.32}$$

The following notation will be used, cf. (7.10)–(7.12):

$$w_{j\Sigma} = \sum_{t=1}^{T} w_{jt}; \qquad w_{\Sigma\Sigma} = \sum_{j=1}^{J} w_{j\Sigma};$$

$$z_j = \frac{a w_{j\Sigma}}{s^2 + a w_{j\Sigma}}; \qquad z_{\Sigma} = \sum_{j=1}^{J} z_j;$$

$$X_{jw} = \sum_{t=1}^{T} \frac{w_{jt}}{w_{j\Sigma}} X_{jt}; \qquad X_{ww} = \sum_{j=1}^{J} \frac{w_{j\Sigma}}{w_{\Sigma\Sigma}} X_{jw}; \qquad X_{zw} = \sum_{j=1}^{J} \frac{z_j}{z_{\Sigma}} X_{jw}. \tag{7.33}$$

Notice the difference between, e.g., X_{jw} and X_{ju}. If a w appears as an index, this indicates that there has been a weighted summation over this index, using the (natural or other) weights of the observations. An index z denotes a weighted summation with credibility weights, while a Σ is used for an unweighted summation. We do not allow for different numbers of observation periods T in our notation. The easiest way to remedy this is to add observations with weight zero when necessary.

In Theorem 7.4.1 below, we derive the optimal values in (7.32) for the coefficients h_{it}. They produce the following MSE-best estimator of the risk premium $m + \Xi_j$, cf. (7.9):

$$z_j X_{jw} + (1 - z_j) X_{zw}. \tag{7.34}$$

Here X_{jw} is the individual estimator of the risk premium, X_{zw} is the credibility weighted collective estimator, and z_j is the credibility factor for contract j.

The proof that of all the linear combinations of the observations to estimate $m + \Xi_j$ that have the same mean, (7.34) has the smallest MSE, can be given by Lagrange optimization. One has to solve the first order conditions to find an extremum. In the proof below, we prove the result by capitalizing on the fact that linear combinations of uncorrelated random variables with a given mean have minimal variance if the coefficients are inversely proportional to the variances; see Exercise 7.4.1. First we derive the optimal 'mix' $h_{it}/h_{i\Sigma}$ of the contracts in group i. The best choice proves to be $h_{it}/h_{i\Sigma} = w_{it}/w_{i\Sigma}$; from this we see that the observations X_{it} have to appear in (7.32) in the form X_{iw}. Then we derive that the totals $h_{i\Sigma}$ of the coefficients with group $i, i \neq j$ are best taken proportional to z_j. Finally, the optimal value of $h_{j\Sigma}$ is derived.

Theorem 7.4.1 (Bühlmann-Straub model; homogeneous estimator)
The MSE-best homogeneous unbiased predictor $\sum_{i,t} h_{it} X_{it}$ of the risk premium $m + \Xi_j$ in model (7.31) is the credibility estimator (7.34).

Proof. From (7.32) we see that the following problem must be solved to find the best predictor of $m + \Xi_j$:

$$\min_{h_{it}:h_{\Sigma\Sigma}=1} \mathrm{E}\left[\{m + \Xi_j - \sum_{i,t} h_{it} X_{it}\}^2\right]. \tag{7.35}$$

The restriction $h_{\Sigma\Sigma} = 1$ is the unbiasedness constraint in (7.32). By this constraint, the expectation in (7.35) is also the variance. Substituting decomposition (7.31) for X_{it}, we get from (7.35):

$$\min_{h_{it}:h_{\Sigma\Sigma}=1} \mathrm{Var}\left[(1 - h_{j\Sigma})\Xi_j - \sum_{i\neq j} h_{i\Sigma}\Xi_i - \sum_{i,t} h_{it}\Xi_{it}\right], \tag{7.36}$$

or, what is the same because of the variances of the components Ξ_j and Ξ_{jt} and the independence of these components:

$$\min_{h_{it}:h_{\Sigma\Sigma}=1} (1 - h_{j\Sigma})^2 a + \sum_{i\neq j} h_{i\Sigma}^2 a + \sum_i h_{i\Sigma}^2 \sum_t \frac{h_{it}^2}{h_{i\Sigma}^2} \frac{s^2}{w_{it}}. \tag{7.37}$$

First we optimize the inner sum. Because of Exercise 7.4.1 the optimal values of $h_{it}/h_{i\Sigma}$ prove to be $w_{it}/w_{i\Sigma}$. So we can replace the observations $X_{it}, t = 1, 2, \ldots, T$ by their weighted averages X_{iw}, and we see that the credibility estimator has the form $\sum_i h_{i\Sigma} X_{iw}$, where the values of $h_{i\Sigma}$ are still to be determined.

The minimal value for the inner sum equals $s^2/w_{i\Sigma}$. From (7.33) we see that $a + s^2/w_{i\Sigma} = a/z_i$. So we can rewrite (7.37) in the form

$$\min_{h_{i\Sigma}:h_{\Sigma\Sigma}=1} (1 - h_{j\Sigma})^2 a + h_{j\Sigma}^2 \frac{s^2}{w_{j\Sigma}} + (1 - h_{j\Sigma})^2 \sum_{i\neq j} \frac{h_{i\Sigma}^2}{(1 - h_{j\Sigma})^2} \frac{a}{z_i}. \tag{7.38}$$

As $h_{\Sigma\Sigma} = 1$, we have $\sum_{i\neq j} h_{i\Sigma}/(1 - h_{j\Sigma}) = 1$. So again because of Exercise 7.4.1, the optimal choice in (7.38) for the factors $h_{i\Sigma}, i \neq j$ is

$$\frac{h_{i\Sigma}}{1 - h_{j\Sigma}} = \frac{z_i}{z_\Sigma - z_j}. \tag{7.39}$$

The minimal value for the sum in (7.38) is $a/(z_\Sigma - z_j)$, so (7.38) leads to

$$\min_{h_{j\Sigma}} (1 - h_{j\Sigma})^2 (a + \frac{a}{z_\Sigma - z_j}) + h_{j\Sigma}^2 \frac{s^2}{w_{j\Sigma}}. \tag{7.40}$$

The optimal value for $h_{j\Sigma}$, finally, can be found by once again applying Exercise 7.4.1. This optimal value is, as the reader may verify,

$$\begin{aligned} h_{j\Sigma} &= \frac{w_{j\Sigma}}{\frac{s^2}{a+a/(z_\Sigma - z_j)} + w_{j\Sigma}} = \frac{1}{\frac{1/z_j - 1}{1+1/(z_\Sigma - z_j)} + 1} \\ &= \frac{z_j(z_\Sigma - z_j + 1)}{(1 - z_j)(z_\Sigma - z_j) + z_j(z_\Sigma - z_j + 1)} = z_j + (1 - z_j)\frac{z_j}{z_\Sigma}. \end{aligned} \tag{7.41}$$

Because of (7.39) we see that $h_{i\Sigma} = (1 - z_j)z_i/z_\Sigma$, which implies that (7.34) is indeed the MSE-optimal homogeneous unbiased linear predictor of the risk premium $m + \Xi_j$. ∇

Notice that if we replace Ξ_j in (7.31) by the constant ξ_j, i.e., we take $a = 0$, we get the classical weighted mean X_{ww}. This is because in that case the relative weight $w_{j\Sigma}$ for X_{jw} is equal to the credibility weight z_j.

The *inhomogeneous* estimator of $m + \Xi_j$ contains a constant h, next to the homogeneous linear combination of the X_{jt} in (7.32). One may show, just as in Theorem 7.2.4, that the unbiasedness restriction is superfluous in this situation. The inhomogeneous estimator is equal to the homogeneous one, except that X_{zw} in (7.34) is replaced by m. The observations outside group j do not occur in the estimator. For the inhomogeneous estimator, both the ratio s^2/a and the value of m must be known. By replacing m by its best estimator X_{zw} under model (7.31), we get the homogeneous estimator again. Just as in Remark 7.2.6, the optimal predictor of $m + \Xi_j$ is also the optimal predictor of $X_{j,T+1}$. The asymptotic properties of (7.34) are analogous to those given in Remark 7.2.3. Also, the credibility premium can be found by combining the actual experience with virtual experience, just as in Remark 7.2.7. See the exercises.

Parameter estimation in the Bühlmann-Straub model

The credibility estimators of this chapter depend on the generally unknown structure parameters m, a and s^2. To be able to apply them in practice, one has to estimate these portfolio characteristics. Some unbiased estimators (not depending on the structure parameters that are generally unknown) are derived in the theorem below. We can replace the unknown structure parameters in the credibility estimators by these estimates, hoping that the quality of the resulting estimates is still good. The estimators of s^2 and a are based on the weighted sum-of-squares-within:

$$SSW = \sum_{j,t} w_{jt}(X_{jt} - X_{jw})^2, \tag{7.42}$$

and the weighted sum-of-squares-between

$$SSB = \sum_{j} w_{j\Sigma}(X_{jw} - X_{ww})^2. \tag{7.43}$$

Note that if all weights w_{jt} are taken equal to one, these expressions reduce to (7.2) and (7.3), defined in the balanced Bühlmann model.

Theorem 7.4.2 (Unbiased parameter estimates)
In the Bühlmann-Straub model, the statistics

$$\begin{aligned}
\widetilde{m} &= X_{ww}, \\
\widetilde{s^2} &= \frac{1}{J(T-1)} \sum_{j,t} w_{jt}(X_{jt} - X_{jw})^2, \\
\widetilde{a} &= \frac{\sum_j w_{j\Sigma}(X_{jw} - X_{ww})^2 - (J-1)\widetilde{s^2}}{w_{\Sigma\Sigma} - \sum_j w_{j\Sigma}^2 / w_{\Sigma\Sigma}},
\end{aligned} \tag{7.44}$$

are unbiased estimators of the corresponding structure parameters.

Proof. The proof of $\mathrm{E}[X_{ww}] = m$ is easy. Using the covariance relations (7.15), we get for $\widetilde{s^2}$:

$$\begin{aligned}
J(T-1)\mathrm{E}[\widetilde{s^2}] &= \sum_{j,t} w_{jt} \left\{ \mathrm{Var}[X_{jt}] + \mathrm{Var}[X_{jw}] - 2\mathrm{Cov}[X_{jt}, X_{jw}] \right\} \\
&= \sum_{j,t} w_{jt} \left\{ a + \frac{s^2}{w_{jt}} + a + \frac{s^2}{w_{j\Sigma}} - 2(a + \frac{s^2}{w_{j\Sigma}}) \right\} \\
&= J(T-1)s^2.
\end{aligned} \tag{7.45}$$

For $\widetilde{a}$ we have

$$
\begin{aligned}
& \mathrm{E}\left[\sum_j w_{j\Sigma}(X_{jw} - X_{ww})^2\right] \\
& = \sum_j w_{j\Sigma}\left\{\mathrm{Var}[X_{jw}] + \mathrm{Var}[X_{ww}] - 2\mathrm{Cov}[X_{jw}, X_{ww}]\right\} \\
& = \sum_j w_{j\Sigma}\left\{a + \frac{s^2}{w_{j\Sigma}} + a\sum_k \frac{w_{k\Sigma}^2}{w_{\Sigma\Sigma}^2} + \frac{s^2}{w_{\Sigma\Sigma}} - 2\left(\frac{s^2}{w_{\Sigma\Sigma}} + \frac{a w_{j\Sigma}}{w_{\Sigma\Sigma}}\right)\right\} \qquad (7.46) \\
& = a\sum_j w_{j\Sigma}\left(1 + \sum_k \frac{w_{k\Sigma}^2}{w_{\Sigma\Sigma}^2} - 2\frac{w_{j\Sigma}}{w_{\Sigma\Sigma}}\right) + s^2\sum_j w_{j\Sigma}\left(\frac{1}{w_{j\Sigma}} - \frac{1}{w_{\Sigma\Sigma}}\right) \\
& = a\left(w_{\Sigma\Sigma} - \sum_j \frac{w_{j\Sigma}^2}{w_{\Sigma\Sigma}}\right) + (J-1)s^2.
\end{aligned}
$$

Taking $\mathrm{E}[\widetilde{a}]$ in (7.44), using (7.45) and (7.46) we see that $\widetilde{a}$ is unbiased as well. ∇

Remark 7.4.3 (Negativity of estimators)
The estimator $\widetilde{s^2}$ is of course non-negative, but $\widetilde{a}$ might well be negative. Although this may be an indication that $a = 0$ holds, it can also happen if $a > 0$. Let us elaborate on Example 7.2.1, returning to the balanced Bühlmann model where all weights w_{jt} are equal to one. In that case, defining MSW and MSB as in (7.4), the estimators of s^2 and a in Theorem 7.4.2 reduce to

$$\widetilde{s^2} = MSW; \qquad \widetilde{a} = \frac{MSB - MSW}{T}. \tag{7.47}$$

To estimate z, we substitute these estimators into $z = \frac{aT}{aT+s^2}$, and we get the following statistic:

$$\widetilde{z} = 1 - \frac{MSW}{MSB}. \tag{7.48}$$

Using $X_{jt} = m + \Xi_j + \Xi_{jt}$ and defining $\overline{\Xi}_j = \frac{1}{T}\sum_t \Xi_{jt}$, we see that the SSW can be written as

$$SSW = \sum_{j=1}^{J}\sum_{t=1}^{T}(X_{jt} - \overline{X}_j)^2 = \sum_{j=1}^{J}\sum_{t=1}^{T}(\Xi_{jt} - \overline{\Xi}_j)^2. \tag{7.49}$$

Under the assumption that the Ξ_{jt} are iid $N(0, s^2)$, the right hand side, divided by s^2, has a $\chi^2(J(T-1))$ distribution. It is independent of the averages $\overline{\Xi}_j$, and hence also of the averages $\overline{X}_j = m + \Xi_j + \overline{\Xi}_j$. So MSW is independent of the $\overline{X}_j$, hence also of MSB.

Assuming that the components Ξ_j are iid $N(0, a)$, we find in similar fashion that

$$\frac{SSB}{a + s^2/T} = \frac{J-1}{aT + s^2} MSB \tag{7.50}$$

is $\chi^2(J-1)$ distributed. So under the normality assumptions made, if it is multiplied by the constant $s^2/(aT + s^2) = 1 - z$, the variance ratio MSB/MSW of Section 7.2 is still $F(J-1, J(T-1))$ distributed. Thus,

$$(1-z)\frac{MSB}{MSW} = \frac{1-z}{1-\widetilde{z}} \sim F(J-1, J(T-1)). \tag{7.51}$$

In this way, $\Pr[\widetilde{a} < 0]$ can be computed for different values of J, T and s^2/a, see for instance Exercise 7.4.9.

Note that by (7.47), the event $\widetilde{a} < 0$ is the same as $MSB/MSW < 1$. In Section 7.2 we established that the data indicates rejection of equal means, which boils down to $a = 0$ here, only if MSB/MSW exceeds the right-hand $F(J-1, J(T-1))$ critical value, which is surely larger than one. Thus we conclude that, although $\Pr[\widetilde{a} < 0] > 0$ for every $a > 0$, obtaining such a value means that a Fisher test for $a = 0$ based on this data would not have led to rejection. This in turn means that there is in fact no statistical reason not to charge every contract the same premium.

In order to estimate $a = \mathrm{Var}[\Xi_j]$ in practice, one would be inclined to use $\max\{0, \widetilde{a}\}$ as an estimator, but, though still consistent, this is of course no longer an unbiased estimator. ∇

Remark 7.4.4 (Credibility weighted mean and ordinary weighted mean)
The best unbiased estimator of m in model (7.31) is not X_{ww}, but X_{zw}. This is in line with Exercise 7.4.1, since both X_{ww} and X_{zw} are linear combinations of the random variables X_{jw}, and the variances thereof are not proportional to the original weights $w_{j\Sigma}$, but rather to the credibility adjusted weights z_j. So a lower variance is obtained if we estimate m by the credibility-weighted mean X_{zw} instead of by the ordinary weighted mean X_{ww}. The problem of course is that we do not know the credibility factors z_j to be used, because they depend on the unknown parameters that we are actually estimating. One way to achieve better

estimators is to use iterative *pseudo-estimators*, that determine estimates of the structure parameters by determining a fixed point of certain equations. For these methods, we refer to more advanced literature on credibility theory. ∇

7.5 NEGATIVE BINOMIAL MODEL FOR THE NUMBER OF CAR INSURANCE CLAIMS

In this section, we expand on Example 7.3.2, considering a driver with an accident proneness which is a drawing from a non-degenerate distribution, and, given that his accident proneness equals λ, a Poisson(λ) distributed number of claims in a year. Charging a credibility premium in this situation leads to an experience rating system which resembles the bonus-malus systems we described in Chapter 6.

If for a motor insurance policy, all relevant variables for the claim behavior of the policyholder can be observed as well as used, the number of claims still is generated by a stochastic process. Assuming that this process is a Poisson process, the rating factors cannot do more than provide us with the exact Poisson intensity, i.e., the Poisson parameter of the number of claims each year. Of the claim size, we know the probability distribution. The cell with policies sharing common values for all the risk factors would be homogeneous, in the sense that all policy holders have the same Poisson parameter and the same claims distribution. In reality, however, some uncertainty about the parameters remains, because it is impossible to obtain all relevant information on these parameters. So the cells are heterogeneous. This heterogeneity is the actual justification of using a bonus-malus system. In case of homogeneity, each policy represents the same risk, and there is no reason to ask different premiums within a cell.

The heterogeneity of the claim frequency can be modelled by assuming that the Poisson parameter λ has arisen from a structure variable Λ, with structure distribution $U(\lambda) = \Pr[\Lambda \leq \lambda]$. In this section, we look at the number of claims X_{jt} of driver j in period t. There are J drivers, who have been observed for T_j periods. For convenience, we drop the index j from our notation, unless in case we refer back to earlier sections. Just as in (7.5), we can decompose the number of claims $X_t = X_{jt}$ for driver j in time period t as follows:

$$X_{jt} = \mathrm{E}[\Lambda] + \{\Lambda_j - \mathrm{E}[\Lambda]\} + \{X_{jt} - \Lambda_j\}. \tag{7.52}$$

Here $\Lambda_j \sim \Lambda$ iid. The last two components are not independent, although uncorrelated. See Exercise 7.5.6. Component $\Lambda_j - \mathrm{E}[\Lambda]$ has variance $a = \mathrm{Var}[\Lambda]$, for component $X_{jt} - \Lambda_j$, just as in Example 3.3.1, $\mathrm{Var}[X_{jt}] - \mathrm{Var}[\Lambda_j] = \mathrm{E}[\Lambda]$ remains. As one sees, the structural parameters m and s^2 coincide because of the Poisson distributions involved.

Up to now, except for its first few moments, we basically ignored the structure distribution. Several models for it come to mind. Because of its mathematical properties and good fit (see later on for a convincing example), we will prefer the gamma distribution. Another possibility is the structure distribution that produces a 'good' driver, having claim frequency λ_1, with probability p, or a 'bad' driver with claim frequency $\lambda_2 > \lambda_1$. The number of claims of an arbitrary driver then has a mixed Poisson distribution with a two-point mixing distribution. Though one would expect more than two types of drivers to be present, this 'good driver/bad driver' model quite often fits rather closely to the data that is found in practice.

It is known, see again Example 3.3.1, that if the structure distribution is gamma(α, τ), the marginal distribution of the number of claims X_t of driver j in time period t has a negative binomial distribution with α as the number of successes required, and $\tau/(\tau+1)$ as the probability of a success. In Lemaire (1985), we find data from a Belgian portfolio with $J = 106\,974$ policies. The number n_k denotes the number of policies with k accidents, $k = 0, 1, \ldots$ If $X_t \sim \text{Poisson}(\lambda)$, the maximum likelihood estimate $\hat{\lambda}$ for λ equals the average number of claims. It can be shown (see the exercises), that fitting α and τ by maximum likelihood in the gamma-Poisson model gives the following parameter estimates $\hat{\alpha}$ and $\hat{\tau}$:

$$\hat{\tau} = \frac{\hat{\alpha}}{\overline{x}}, \quad \text{where} \quad \overline{x} = \sum_{k=0}^{\infty} k\, n_k \Big/ \sum_{k=0}^{\infty} n_k, \tag{7.53}$$

and $\hat{\alpha}$ is the solution to the equation

$$\sum_{k=0}^{\infty} n_k \left(\frac{1}{\alpha} + \frac{1}{\alpha+1} + \cdots + \frac{1}{\alpha+k-1} \right) = \sum_{k=0}^{\infty} n_k \log(1 + \frac{\overline{x}}{\alpha}). \tag{7.54}$$

As one sees from (7.53), the first moment of the estimated structure distribution, hence also of the marginal distribution of the number of claims, coincides with the first sample moment. The parameters p, λ_1 and λ_2 of the good driver/bad driver model have been estimated by the method of moments. Note that this method does not with certainty produce admissible estimates $\hat{\lambda}_i \geq 0$ and $0 \leq \hat{p} \leq 1$. The resulting estimates for the three models considered were

$$\begin{aligned} &\hat{\lambda} = 0.1011; \\ &\hat{\alpha} = 1.6313; \qquad \hat{\tau} = 16.1384; \\ &\hat{p} = 0.9112; \qquad \hat{\lambda}_1 = 0.0762; \quad \hat{\lambda}_2 = 0.3576. \end{aligned} \tag{7.55}$$

Observed and estimated frequencies can be tabulated as follows:

k	n_k	$\hat{n}_k$ (Poisson)	$\hat{n}_k$ (Neg.Bin.)	$\hat{n}_k$ (good/bad)
0	96 978	96 690	96 981	96 975
1	9 240	9 774	9 231	9 252
2	704	494	709	685
3	43	16.6	50.1	56.9
4	9	0.4	3.4	4.6
5+	0	0.0	0.2	0.3
χ^2		191.	0.1	2.1

The χ^2-value in the bottom row represents the usual χ^2-statistic, computed as $\chi^2 = \sum_k (n_k - \hat{n}_k)^2/\hat{n}_k$. When computing χ^2-statistics, one usually combines cells with estimated numbers less than 5 with neighboring cells. By doing this, the last three rows are joined together into one row representing 3 or more claims. The two mixed models provide an excellent fit; in fact, the fit of the negative binomial model is almost too good to be true. Note that we fit 4 numbers using 2 or 3 parameters. But homogeneity for this portfolio is rejected without any doubt whatsoever.

Though the null-hypothesis that the numbers of claims for each policy holder are independent Poisson random variables with the same parameter is rejected, while the mixed Poisson models are not, we cannot just infer that policy holders have a fixed unobservable risk parameter, drawn from a structure distribution. It might well be that the numbers of claims are just independent negative binomial random variables, for instance because the number of claims follows a Poisson process in which the intensity parameter is drawn independently from a gamma structure distribution each year.

With the model of this section, we want to predict as accurately as possible the number of claims that a policy holder produces in the next time period $T+1$. This number is a Poisson(λ) random variable, with λ an observation of Λ, of which the prior distribution is known to be, say, gamma(α, τ). Furthermore, observations $X_1, \ldots, X_T$ from the past are known. We may show that the posterior distribution of Λ, given $X_1 = x_1, \ldots, X_T = x_T$ is also a gamma distribution, with adjusted parameters $\tau' = \tau + T$ and $\alpha' = \alpha + x_\Sigma$ with $x_\Sigma = x_1 + \cdots + x_T$. Assuming a quadratic loss function, in view of Exercise 7.2.9, the best predictor of the number of claims next year is the posterior expectation of Λ:

$$\lambda_{T+1}(x_1, \ldots, x_T) = \frac{\alpha + x_\Sigma}{\tau + T}. \tag{7.56}$$

We can interpret (7.56) as the observed average number of claims per time unit, provided we include for everyone a virtual prior experience of α claims in a time period of length τ. See also Remark 7.2.7.

Prediction (7.56) is a special case of a credibility forecast. The forecast is proportional to a linear combination of a priori premium and policy average, because, cf. (7.10):

$$\frac{\alpha + x_\Sigma}{\tau + T} = z\frac{x_\Sigma}{T} + (1 - z)\frac{\alpha}{\tau} \quad \text{for} \quad z = \frac{T}{\tau + T}. \tag{7.57}$$

Remark 7.5.1 (Non-linear estimators; exact credibility)
In Theorems 7.2.2 and 7.2.4 it was required that the predictors of $X_{j,T+1}$ were linear in the observations. Though such linear observations are in general the easiest to deal with, one may also look at more general functions of the data. Without linearity restriction, the best predictor in the sense of MSE for $X_{j,T+1}$ is the so-called *posterior Bayes estimator*, which is just the conditional mean $\mathrm{E}[X_{j,T+1}|X_{11}, \ldots, X_{JT}]$. See also (7.56). If the Ξ_j and the Ξ_{jt} are independent *normal* random variables, the optimal linear estimator coincides with the Bayes-estimator. In the literature, this is expressed as 'the credible mean is exact Bayesian'. Also combining a gamma prior and a Poisson posterior distribution gives such 'exact credibility', because the posterior Bayes estimator happens to be linear in the observations. See Exercise 7.5.2. The posterior mean of the claim figure is equal to the credibility premium (7.57). ∇

If we split up the premium necessary for the whole portfolio according to the mean value principle, we get a solid experience rating system based on credibility, because of the following reasons, see also Lemaire (1985):

1. The system is fair. Upon renewal of the policy, every insured pays a premium which is proportional to his estimated claim frequency (7.56), taking into account all information from the past.

2. The system is balanced financially. Write $X_\Sigma = X_1 + \cdots + X_T$ for the total number of claims generated, then $\mathrm{E}[X_\Sigma] = \mathrm{E}[\mathrm{E}[X_\Sigma|\Lambda]] = T\mathrm{E}[\Lambda]$, so

$$\mathrm{E}\left[\frac{\alpha + X_\Sigma}{\tau + T}\right] = \frac{\alpha + T\frac{\alpha}{\tau}}{\tau + T} = \frac{\alpha}{\tau}. \tag{7.58}$$

This means that for every policy, the mean of the proportionality factor (7.56) is equal to its overall mean α/τ. So the expected value of the premium to be paid by an arbitrary driver remains constant over the years.

3. The premium only depends on the number of claims filed in the previous T years, and not on how these are distributed over this period. So for the premium next year, it makes no difference if the claim in the last five years was in the first or in the last year of this period. The bonus-malus system in Section 6.2 doesn't have this property. But it is questionable if this property is even desirable. If one assumes, like here, the intensity parameter λ to remain constant, K is a sufficient statistic. In practice, however, the value of λ is not constant. One gets past his youth, or past his prime, or one's son gets old enough to borrow the family car. Following this reasoning, later observations should count more heavily than old ones.

4. Initially, at time $t = 0$, everyone pays the same premium, proportional to α/τ. If T tends to ∞, the expected value $(\alpha + x_\Sigma)/(\tau + T)$ converges to x_Σ/T, which in the limit represents the actual risk on the policy. The variance $(\alpha + x_\Sigma)/(\tau + T)^2$ converges to zero. So in the long run, everyone pays the premium corresponding to his own risk; the influence of the virtual experience vanishes.

Using the values $\alpha = 1.6$ and $\tau = 16$, see (7.55) and Lemaire (1985), we have constructed Table 7.1 giving the optimal estimates of the claim frequencies in case of various lengths of the observation period and numbers of claims observed. The initial premium is set to 100%, the other a posteriori premiums are computed by the formula:

$$100\frac{\lambda_{T+1}(x_1, \ldots, x_T)}{\lambda_1} = \frac{100\frac{\alpha + x_\Sigma}{\tau + T}}{\alpha/\tau} = 100\frac{\tau(\alpha + x_\Sigma)}{\alpha(\tau + T)} \tag{7.59}$$

One sees that in Table 7.1, a driver who caused exactly one claim in the past ten years represents the same risk as a new driver, who is assumed to carry with him

	Number of claims k				
Number of years t	0	1	2	3	4
0	100				
1	94	153	212	271	329
2	89	144	200	256	311
3	84	137	189	242	295
4	80	130	180	230	280
5	76	124	171	219	267
6	73	118	164	209	255
7	70	113	157	200	243
8	67	108	150	192	233
9	64	104	144	184	224
10	62	100	138	177	215

Table 7.1 Optimal estimates of the claim frequency next year as a percentage of the one of a new driver

a virtual experience of 1.6 claim in 16 years. A person who drives claim-free for ten years gets a discount of $1 - \tau/(\tau + 10) = 38\%$. After a claims experience of 16 years, actual and virtual experience count just as heavily in the premium.

Example 7.5.2 (Contrast with the bonus-malus system of Chapter 6)
As an example, we look at the premiums to be paid by a driver in the 6th year of insurance if he has had one claim in the first year of observation. In Table 7.1, his premium next year equals 124%. In the system of Table 6.1, his path on the ladder has been $2 \to 1 \to 2 \to 3 \to 4$, so now he pays the premium of step 5, which equals 70%. The total of the premiums paid according to Table 7.1 is $100+153+144+137+130+124 = 788\%$ of the premium for a new entrant. In the system of Table 6.1, he has paid only $100+120+100+90+80+70 = 560\%$. Note that for the premium next year in Table 7.1, it makes no difference if the claim occurred in the first or the fifth year of observation, though this does affect the total claims paid. ∇

Remark 7.5.3 (Overlapping claim frequencies)
Consider a policyholder for which T years of claims experience is known. The posterior distribution of the expected number of claims Λ is gamma$(\alpha + x_\Sigma, \tau + T)$

if x_Σ claims were filed. As noted in Lemaire (1985), if $T = 3$, in the two situations $x_\Sigma = 0$ and $x_\Sigma = 2$ the premium to be paid next year differs by a factor $189/84 = 2.25$. But the posterior distributions of both claim frequencies overlap to a large extent. Indeed, in the first situation the probability is 60.5% to have a claim frequency lower than the average $\alpha/(\tau + T) = 0.0842$ for drivers with a similar claims experience, since $G(0.0842; \alpha, \tau + T) = 0.605$, but in the second situation there also is a substantial probability to have a better Poisson parameter than the average of drivers as above, since $G(0.0842; \alpha + x_\Sigma, \tau + T) = 0.121$ for $x_\Sigma = 2$ and $T = 3$. Experience rating by any bonus-malus system will turn out to be very unfair for all 'good' drivers that are unlucky enough to produce claims. ∇

7.6 EXERCISES

Section 7.2

1. Finish the proofs of Theorems 7.2.2 and 7.2.4 by filling in and deriving the relevant covariance relations (7.15). Use and verify the linearity properties of covariances: for all random variables X, Y and Z, we have $\text{Cov}[X, Y + Z] = \text{Cov}[X, Y] + \text{Cov}[X, Z]$, while for all real α, $\text{Cov}[X, \alpha Y] = \alpha\text{Cov}[X, Y]$.
2. Let $X_1, \dots, X_T$ be uncorrelated random variables with mean m and variance s^2. Consider the weighted average $X_w = \sum_t w_t X_t$, where the weights $w_t \geq 0, t = 1, \dots, T$ satisfy $\sum_t w_t = 1$. Show that $\text{E}[X_w] = m$, $\text{Cov}[X_t, X_w] = w_t s^2$ and $\text{Var}[X_w] = \sum_t w_t^2 s^2$. [If especially $w_t \equiv \frac{1}{T}$, we get $X_w = \overline{X}$ and $\text{E}[\overline{X}] = m$; $\text{Cov}[X_t, \overline{X}] = \text{Var}[\overline{X}] = \frac{s^2}{T}$.]
3. Show that the sample variance $S^2 = \frac{1}{T-1}\sum_1^T \{X_t - \overline{X}\}^2$ is an unbiased estimator of s^2.
4. Show that the best predictor of $X_{j,T+1}$ is at the same time the best estimator of the risk premium $m + \Xi_j$ in the situation of Theorem 7.2.2. What is the best linear unbiased estimator (BLUE) of Ξ_j?
5. Determine the variance of the credibility premium (7.9). What is the MSE? Also determine the MSE of (7.9) as an estimator of $m + \Xi_j$.
6. Determine the credibility estimator if the unbiasedness restriction is not imposed in Theorem 7.2.2. Also investigate the resulting bias.
7. Show that if each contract pays the homogeneous premium, the sum of the credibility premiums equals the average annual outgo in the observation period.
8. Show that in model (7.5), the MSB has mean $aT + s^2$, while the MSW has mean s^2.
9. Prove that for each random variable Y, the real number p which is the best predictor of it in the sense of MSE is $p = \text{E}[Y]$.
10. Let $\vec{X} = (X_{11}, \dots, X_{1T}, X_{21}, \dots, X_{2T}, \dots, X_{J1}, \dots, X_{JT})^T$ be the vector containing the observable random variables in (7.7). Describe the covariance matrix $\text{Cov}[\vec{X}, \vec{X}]$.

Section 7.3

1. Derive the formula $\text{Cov}[X,Y] = \text{E}[\text{Cov}[X,Y|Z]] + \text{Cov}[\text{E}[X|Z],\text{E}[Y|Z]]$ for the decomposition of covariances into conditional covariances.

Section 7.4

1. Let $X_1,\ldots,X_T$ be independent random variables with variances $\text{Var}[X_t] = s^2/w_t$ for certain positive numbers w_t, $t = 1,\ldots,T$. Show that the variance $\sum_t \alpha_t^2 s^2/w_t$ of the linear combination $\sum_t \alpha_t X_t$ with $\alpha_\Sigma = 1$ is minimal when we take $\alpha_t \propto w_t$, where the symbol $\propto$ means 'proportional to'. Hence the optimal solution has $\alpha_t = w_t/w_\Sigma$. Prove also that the minimal value of the variance in this case is s^2/w_Σ.
2. Prove that in model (7.31), we have $\text{Var}[X_{zw}] \leq \text{Var}[X_{ww}]$. See Remark 7.4.4.
3. Determine the best homogeneous linear estimator of m.
4. Show that in determining the best inhomogeneous linear estimator of $m + \Xi_j$, the unbiasedness restriction is superfluous.
5. Show that, just as in Remark 7.2.6, the optimal predictors of $X_{j,T+1}$ and $m + \Xi_j$ coincide in the Bühlmann-Straub model.
6. Describe the asymptotic properties of z_j in (7.33); cf. Remark 7.2.3.
7. In the same way as in Remark 7.2.7, describe the credibility premium (7.34) as a mix of actual and virtual experience.
8. Show that (7.9) follows from (7.34) in the special case (7.5)–(7.6) of the Bühlmann-Straub model given in (7.31).
9. In the situation of Remark 7.4.3, for $s^2/a = 0.823$, $J = 5$ and $T = 4$, use an F-table to show that the probability of the event $\widetilde{a} < 0$ equals 0.05.
10. Estimate the credibility premiums in the Bühlmann-Straub setting when the claims experience for three years is given for three contracts, each with weight $w_{jt} \equiv 1$. The claims on the contracts are as follows:

	$t=1$	$t=2$	$t=3$
$j=1$	10	12	14
$j=2$	13	17	15
$j=3$	14	10	6

Section 7.5

1. [♠] Consider a sample $X_1,\ldots,X_J$ from a negative binomial distribution with parameters α and $\tau/(\tau+1)$. Define the number of these random variables with value k as $N_k = \#\{j|X_j = k\}, k = 0,1,\ldots$ If $N_k = n_k$, $k = 0,1,\ldots$, show that the maximum likelihood estimators of α and τ indeed are given by (7.53) and (7.54).
2. [♠] Suppose that Λ has a gamma(α,τ) prior distribution, and that given $\Lambda = \lambda$, the annual numbers of claims $X_1,\ldots,X_T$ are independent Poisson(λ) random variables. Prove that the

posterior distribution of Λ, given $X_1 = x_1, \ldots, X_T = x_T$, is gamma($\alpha + x_\Sigma, \tau + T$), where $x_\Sigma = x_1 + \cdots + x_T$.

3. By comparing $\Pr[X_2 = 0]$ with $\Pr[X_2 = 0 | X_1 = 0]$ in the previous exercise, show that the numbers of claims X_t are not marginally independent. Also show that they are not uncorrelated.
4. Show that the mode of a gamma(α, τ) distribution, which represents the argument where the density is maximal, is $(\alpha - 1)_+ / \tau$.
5. [♠] Determine the estimated values for n_k and the χ^2-test statistic if α and τ are estimated by the method of moments.
6. Show that in the model (7.52) of this section, Λ_j and $X_{jt} - \Lambda_j$ are uncorrelated. Taking $\alpha = 1.6$ and $\tau = 16$, determine the ratio $\text{Var}[\Lambda_j]/\text{Var}[X_{jt}]$. [Since no model for X_{jt} can do more than determine the value of Λ_j as precisely as possible, this ratio provides an upper bound for the attainable 'percentage of explained variation' on an individual level.]
7. [♠] What is the Loimaranta efficiency of the system in Table 7.1? What is the steady state distribution?

8

Generalized linear models

8.1 INTRODUCTION

In econometrics, the most widely used statistical technique is multiple linear regression. Actuarial statistics models situations that do not always fit in this framework. Regression assumes normally distributed disturbances with a constant variance around a mean that is linear in the collateral data. In actuarial applications, a symmetric normally distributed random variable with a fixed variance does not adequately describe the situation. For counts, a Poisson distribution is generally a good model, if the assumptions of the Poisson processes such as described in Chapter 4 are valid. For these random variables, the mean and variance are the same, but the data sets encountered in practice generally exhibit a variance greater than the mean. A distribution to describe the claim size should have a thick right-hand tail. Rather than a variance not depending of the mean, one would expect the coefficient of variation to be constant. Furthermore, the phenomena to be modelled are rarely additive in the collateral data. A multiplicative model is much more plausible. Moving from downtown to the country, or replacing the car by a car 200 kilograms lighter, without changing other policy characteristics, would result in a reduction in the average total claims by some fixed percentage of it, not by a fixed amount independent of the original risk.

Both these problems can be solved by not working with ordinary linear models, but with Generalized Linear Models (GLM). The generalization is twofold. First, it is allowed that the random deviations from the mean obey another distribution than the normal. In fact, one can take any distribution from the exponential dispersion family, including apart from the normal distribution also the Poisson, the (negative) binomial, the gamma and the inverse Gaussian distributions. Second, it is no longer necessary that the mean of the random variable is a linear function of the explanatory variables, but it only has to be linear on a certain scale. If this scale for instance is logarithmic, we have in fact a multiplicative model instead of an additive model.

Often, one does not look at the observations themselves, but at transformed values that are better suited for the ordinary multiple regression model, with normality, hence symmetry, with a constant variance and with additive systematic effects. This, however, is not always possible. A transformation to make a Poisson random variable Y symmetric (skewness $\approx$ zero) is $Y^{2/3}$, while taking $Y^{1/2}$ stabilizes the variance and taking $\log Y$ reduces multiplicative systematic effects to additive ones. It should be noted that some of the optimality properties in the transformed model, notably unbiasedness and in some cases even consistency, may be lost when transforming back to the original scale.

In this chapter, we will not deal with Generalized Linear Models in their full generality. For simplicity, we restrict to cross-classified observations, which can be put into a two-dimensional table in a natural way. The relevant collateral data with random variable X_{ij} are the row number i and the column number j. In the next chapter, we will also include the 'diagonal number' $i+j-1$ as an explanatory variable. For more general models, e.g., tables with more than two dimensions, we refer to other texts. In general, the observations are arranged in a vector of n independent but not identically distributed random variables, and there is a design matrix containing the explanatory variables in a directly usable form.

Many actuarial problems can be tackled using specific Generalized Linear Models, such as ANOVA, Poisson regression and logit and probit models, to name a few. They can also be applied to IBNR problems, as demonstrated in the next chapter, to survival data, and to compound Poisson distributions. Furthermore, it proves that many venerable heuristic actuarial techniques are really instances of GLM's. In the investigation that led to the bonus-malus system of Chapter 6, estimation techniques were chosen on the basis of their simple heuristic foundation, but they also turn out to produce maximum likelihood estimates in specific GLM's. The same holds for some widely used techniques for IBNR estimation, as explained in the next chapter. As opposed to credibility theory, there is a lot of commercial software that is able to handle GLM's. Apart from the specialized program GLIM (Generalized Linear Interactive Modelling), developed by the Numerical Algorithms Group (NAG), we mention the module GenMod included in the widely used program SAS, as well as the program S-Plus. The study of Generalized Linear Models was initiated by Nelder and Wedderburn. They gave a unified description, in the form of a GLM, of a multitude of statistical methods, including ANOVA, probit-analysis and many others. Also, they gave an algorithm to estimate all these models optimally and efficiently. In later versions of GLIM, other algorithms were implemented to improve stability in some situations.

In Section 8.2, we briefly present the ordinary and the generalized linear models. In Section 8.3, we show how some rating techniques used in actuarial practice can be written as instances of GLM's. In Section 8.4, we study the deviance (and the scaled deviance) as a measure for the goodness of fit. For normal distributions, these quantities are sums of squared residuals, hence χ^2 related statistics, but in general they are related to the loglikelihood. In Section 8.5 we present an example. In Section 8.6, we provide some additional theory about GLM's, in line with other texts on GLM's. We give the general definition of a GLM, briefly describe the all-purpose algorithm of Nelder and Wedderburn, and explain what the canonical link is. For the application of GLM's to IBNR problems, see the next chapter.

8.2 GENERALIZED LINEAR MODELS

Generalized Linear Models have three characteristics:

1. There is a *stochastic component*, which states that the observations are *independent* random variables $Y_i, i = 1, \ldots, n$ with a density in the exponential dispersion family. The most important examples for our goal are:

   - $\mathrm{N}(\mu_i, \psi_i)$ random variables;
   - $\mathrm{Poisson}(\mu_i)$ random variables;
   - means of samples with size $n_i = 1/\psi_i$ of $\mathrm{Poisson}(\mu_i)$ distributed random variables;
   - $\psi_i \times \mathrm{binomial}(\frac{1}{\psi_i}, \mu_i)$ random variables (hence, the proportion of successes in $1/\psi_i$ trials);
   - $\mathrm{gamma}(\frac{1}{\psi_i}, \frac{1}{\psi_i \mu_i})$ random variables;

- inverse Gaussian($\frac{1}{\psi_i \mu_i}, \frac{1}{\psi_i \mu_i^2}$) random variables.

It can be seen that in all these examples, the parametrization chosen leads to the mean being equal to μ_i, while ψ_i is a parameter that does not affect the mean, but only the variance of the random variable. See Exercise 8.2.1. We take ψ_i to be equal to ϕ/w_i, where ϕ is the so-called *dispersion parameter*, and w_i the *weight* of observation i. Just as for the weight in the Bühlmann-Straub setting of the previous chapter, in principle it represents the number of iid observations of which our observation Y_i is the arithmetic average (natural weight). Note that, e.g., doubling ψ_i has the same effect on the variance as doubling the weight (sample size) has.

2. The *systematic component* of the model attributes to every observation a *linear predictor* $\eta_i = \sum_j x_{ij}\beta_j$, linear in the parameters $\beta_1, \ldots, \beta_p$.

3. The expected value μ_i of Y_i is linked to the linear predictor η_i by the *link function*: $\eta_i = g(\mu_i)$.

Remark 8.2.1 (Canonical link)
Each of the distributions has a natural link function associated with it, called the *canonical link function*. Using these link functions has some technical advantages, see Section 8.6. For the normal distribution, the canonical link is the identity, leading to additive models, for the Poisson it is the logarithmic function, leading to loglinear, multiplicative models. For the gamma, it is the reciprocal. ∇

Remark 8.2.2 (Variance function)
Note that the parametrizations used in the stochastic component above are not always the usual, nor the most convenient ones. The μ_i parameter is the mean, and it can be shown that in each case, the variance equals $V(\mu_i)\psi_i$ for some function $V(\cdot)$ which is called the *variance function*. Assume for the moment that $w_i = 1$, hence $\psi_i = \phi$, for every observation i. The list of distributions above contains distributions with a variety of variance functions, making it possible to adequately model many actuarial statistical problems. In increasing order of the exponent of μ in the variance function, we have:

1. the normal distribution with a constant variance $\sigma^2 = \mu^0 \phi$ (homoscedasticity).

2. the Poisson distribution with a variance equal to the mean, hence $\sigma^2 = \mu^1$, and the class of Poisson sample means which have a variance proportional to the mean, hence $\sigma^2 = \mu^1 \phi$.

3. the gamma(α, β) distributions, having, in the parametrization as listed, a fixed shape parameter, and hence a constant coefficient of variation σ/μ, therefore $\sigma^2 = \mu^2 \phi$.

4. the inverse Gaussian(α, β) distributions, having in the μ, ϕ parametrization as listed, a variance equal to $\frac{\alpha}{\beta^2} = \sigma^2 = \mu^3 \phi$.

The variance of Y_i describes the precision of the ith observation. Apart from weight, this precision is constant for the normally distributed random variables. Poisson random variables are less precise for large parameter values than for small ones so the residuals for smaller observations should be smaller than for larger ones. This is even more strongly the case for gamma distributions, as well as for the inverse Gaussian distributions. ∇

Remark 8.2.3 ('Null' and 'full' models)
The least refined linear model that we study uses as a systematic component only the constant term, hence ascribes all variation to chance and denies any influence of the collateral data. In the GLM-literature, this model is called the *null model.* Every observation is assumed to have the same distribution, and the average $\overline{Y}$ is the best estimator for every μ_i. At the other extreme, one finds the so-called *full model*, where every unit of observation i has its own parameter. Maximizing the total likelihood then produces the observation Y_i as an estimator. The model merely repeats the data, without condensing it at all, and without imposing any structure. In this model, all variation between the observations is due to the systematic effects. The null model will in general be too crude, the full model has too many parameters for practical use. Somewhere between these two extremes, one has to find an 'optimal' model. This model has to fit well, in the sense that the predicted outcomes should be close to the actually observed values. On the other hand, the fewer parameters it has, the easier the model is to 'sell', not just to potential policy holders, but especially to the manager. The latter will insist on thin tariff books and a workable and understandable model. There is a trade-off between the *predictive power* of a model and its *manageability.* ∇

In GLM analyses, the criterion to determine the quality of a model is the loglikelihood of the model. It is known that under the null-hypothesis that a certain refinement of the model is not an actual improvement, the gain in loglikelihood ($\times 2$, and divided by the dispersion parameter ϕ), approximately has a χ^2-distribution with degrees of freedom the number of parameters that have to be estimated additionally. Based on this, one can look at a chain of ever refined models and judge which of the refinements lead to a significantly improved fit, expressed in the maximal likelihood. A bound for the loglikelihood is the one of the full model, which can serve as a yardstick. Not only should the models to be compared be nested, with subsets of parameter sets, possibly after reparametrization by linear combinations, but also should the link function and the error distribution be the same.

Remark 8.2.4 (Residuals)
To judge if a model is good enough and where it can be improved, we look at the *residuals*, the differences between actual observations and the values predicted for them by the model, standardized by taking into account the variance function as well as parameter estimates. We might look at the ordinary Pearson residuals, but in this context it is preferable to look at residuals based on the contribution of this observation to the maximized loglikelihood. For the normal distribution with as a link the identity function, the sum of the squares of the standardized (Pearson) residuals has a χ^2 distribution and is proportional to the difference in maximized likelihoods; for other distributions, this quantity provides an alternative for the difference in maximized likelihoods to compare the goodness of fit. ∇

8.3 SOME TRADITIONAL ESTIMATION PROCEDURES AND GLM'S

In this section, we illustrate the ideas behind GLM's using $I \times J$ contingency tables. We have a table of observations Y_{ij}, $i = 1, \dots, I$, $j = 1, \dots, J$, classified by two rating factors into I and J risk classes. Hence, we have IJ independent observations indexed by i and j instead of n observations indexed by i as before. Generalization to more than two dimensions is straightforward. The collateral data with each observation consists of the row number i and the column number j in the table. With these factors, we try to construct a model for the expected values of the observations. There are many situations in which this example applies. For instance, the row number may indicate a certain region/gender combination such as in the example of Section 8.5, the column number may be a weight class for a car or a step in the bonus-malus scale. The observations might then be the observed total number of accidents for all drivers with the characteristics i and j. Other examples, see also the next chapter, arise if i is the year that a certain policy was written, and j the development year, and the observations denote the total amount paid in year $i + j - 1$ regarding claims pertaining to policies of the year i. The calendar year $i + j - 1$ is then used as a third collateral variable. We will assume that the probability distribution of the observations Y_{ij} obeys a GLM, more specifically, a loglinear model with i and j as explanatory variables. This means that for the expected values of the Y_{ij} we have

$$\mathrm{E}[Y_{ij}] = \mu\, \alpha_i\, \beta_j, \quad i = 1, \ldots, I,\ j = 1, \ldots, J. \tag{8.1}$$

The parameters of the model are μ, α_i and β_j. There are at least two parameters too many; without loss of generality we will first assume that $\mu = \beta_1 = 1$ holds. Later on, we will find it more convenient to fix $\alpha_1 = 1$ instead of $\mu = 1$, so μ can be interpreted as the expected value of the reference cell $(i, j) = (1, 1)$. One gets an additive model in (8.1) by adding the parameters instead of multiplying them. As stated earlier, such models are not often relevant for actuarial practice.

Remark 8.3.1 (Connection with loglinear models)
One may wonder how our model (8.1) can be reconciled with the second and third characteristic of a GLM as listed above. A loglinear model in i and j arises, obviously, when $\mathrm{E}[Y_{ij}] = \exp(i \log\alpha + j \log\beta + \log\mu)$ for some α, β and μ. In that case we call the regressors i and j *variates*. They must be measured on an interval scale; the contribution of i to the linear predictor has the form $i \log\alpha$ and the parameter α_i has the special form $\alpha_i = \alpha^i$ (the first i is an index, the second an exponent). If, as in (8.1), variable i classifies the data, and the numerical values of i act only as labels, we call i a *factor*. The parameters with a factor are arbitrary numbers α_i, $i = 1, \ldots, I$. To achieve this within the GLM model as stated, i.e., to express $\mathrm{E}[Y_{ij}]$ as a loglinear form of the collateral data, for each observation we recode the row number by a series of I *dummy variables* $d_1, \ldots, d_I$, of which $d_i = 1$ if the row number for this observation is i, the others are zero. The contribution to (8.1) of a cell in row i can then be written in the loglinear form $\exp(\sum_{t=1}^{I} d_t \log\alpha_t)$. ∇

Remark 8.3.2 (Aliasing)
To avoid the identification problems arising from redundant parameters in the model such as occur when a constant term is present in the model or when more than one factor is replaced by a set of dummies, we leave out the redundant dummies. In GLIM parlance, these parameters are *aliased*. This phenomenon is also known as 'multicollinearity' and as the 'dummy trap'. ∇

Remark 8.3.3 (Interaction between variables)
Sometimes two factors, or a factor and a variate, 'interact', for instance when gender and age (class) are regressors, but the age effect for males and females is different. Then these two variables can be combined into one that describes the combined effect of these variables and is called their *interaction*. If two factors have I and J levels, their interaction has IJ levels. See further Section 8.5. ∇

Remark 8.3.4 (Weights of observations)
For every cell (i, j), next to an observed claim figure Y_{ij} there is also a weight w_{ij}. In actuarial applications, several interpretations are possible for these quantities:

1. Y_{ij} is the average claim frequency if $S_{ij} = Y_{ij}\, w_{ij}$ is the number of claims and w_{ij} is the *exposure* of cell (i, j), which is the total number of years that policies in it have been insured;

2. Y_{ij} is the average claim size if S_{ij} is the total claim amount for the cell and w_{ij} is the number of claims;

3. Y_{ij} is the observed pure premium if S_{ij} is the total claim amount for the cell and w_{ij} is the exposure.

Any of these interpretations may apply in the examples below. The weights w_{ij} are assumed to be constants, measured with full precision, while the S_{ij} and hence the Y_{ij} are random variables with outcomes denoted as s_{ij} and y_{ij}. ∇

In the sequel, we give some methods to produce estimates $\hat{\alpha}_i$ and $\hat{\beta}_j$ of the parameters α_i and β_j in such a way that $\hat{\alpha}_i\, \hat{\beta}_j \approx y_{ij}$; we fix $\mu = 1$. These methods have been used in actuarial practice without some users being aware that they were actually statistically quite well founded methods. For each method we give a short description, and indicate also for which GLM this method computes the maximum likelihood estimates, or which other estimates are computed.

Property 8.3.5 (Bailey-Simon = Minimal chi-square with Poisson)
In the Bailey-Simon method, the parameter estimates $\hat{\alpha}_i$ and $\hat{\beta}_j$ in the multiplicative model are determined as the solution of

$$\min_{\alpha_i, \beta_j} BS \quad \text{with} \quad BS = \sum_{i,j} \frac{w_{ij}(y_{ij} - \alpha_i \beta_j)^2}{\alpha_i \beta_j}. \tag{8.2}$$

A justification of this method is that if the S_{ij} denote Poisson distributed numbers of claims, BS in (8.2) is just the χ^2-statistic, since (8.2) can be rewritten as

$$BS = \sum_{i,j} \frac{(s_{ij} - w_{ij}\alpha_i\beta_j)^2}{w_{ij}\alpha_i\beta_j} = \sum_{i,j} \frac{(s_{ij} - \mathrm{E}[S_{ij}])^2}{\mathrm{Var}[S_{ij}]}. \tag{8.3}$$

So minimizing BS is nothing but determining the minimal-χ^2 estimator. The model hypotheses can be easily tested.

Solving the normal equations arising from differentiating BS in (8.2) with respect to each parameter, we get a system of equations that can be written as follows:

$$\begin{aligned} \alpha_i &= \left(\sum_j \frac{w_{ij}\, y_{ij}^2}{\beta_j} \Big/ \sum_j w_{ij}\,\beta_j\right)^{\frac{1}{2}}, \quad i = 1, \ldots, I; \\ \beta_j &= \left(\sum_i \frac{w_{ij}\, y_{ij}^2}{\alpha_i} \Big/ \sum_i w_{ij}\,\alpha_i\right)^{\frac{1}{2}}, \quad j = 1, \ldots, J. \end{aligned} \tag{8.4}$$

One method to solve this system of equations iteratively is as follows. First we choose initial values for β_j, for instance $\beta_j = 1$ for all $j = 1, \ldots, J$. From these, we get first estimates for α_i by using the first set of equations. Substitute these values in the second set to get updated values of β_j. Repeat this procedure until the parameter values do not change any longer; an equilibrium has been reached. This method is known as *successive substitution*. Generally, it converges rather quickly. If it doesn't, one should try some other initial solution, or look for another method to determine the required minimum altogether. From the many possible equivalent solutions, we choose the one with $\beta_1 = 1$. See also the numerical Example 8.3.12 at the end of this section. Essentially, successive substitution provides us with a fixed point of the equation $a = g(a)$ with a the parameter vector and $g(\cdot)$ denoting the right hand side of (8.4). ∇

Remark 8.3.6 (Compound Poisson distributions)
In the case of compound Poisson distributed total claims we can apply χ^2-tests under some circumstances. Let S_{ij} denote the total claim amount and w_{ij} the total exposure of cell (i, j). Assume that the number of claims caused by each insured is Poisson(λ_{ij}) distributed. The individual claim amounts are iid random variables, distributed as X. Hence the mean claim frequency varies, but the claim size distribution is the same for each cell. Then we have

$$\mathrm{E}[S_{ij}] = w_{ij}\,\lambda_{ij}\,\mathrm{E}[X] \quad \text{and} \quad \mathrm{Var}[S_{ij}] = w_{ij}\,\lambda_{ij}\,\mathrm{E}[X^2], \tag{8.5}$$

hence with $\mathrm{E}[Y_{ij}] = \alpha_i\beta_j$ we get

$$\mathrm{Var}[Y_{ij}] = \frac{\alpha_i\beta_j}{w_{ij}} \frac{\mathrm{E}[X^2]}{\mathrm{E}[X]}. \tag{8.6}$$

So the random variable BS is the sum of the squares of random variables with mean zero and a constant variance. This is also the case when only the ratio $\mathrm{E}[X^2]/\mathrm{E}[X]$ is the same for all cells. If we correct BS for this factor and if moreover our estimation procedure produces best asymptotic normal estimators (BAN), such as maximum likelihood estimation does, asymptotically we get a χ^2-distribution with $(I-1)(J-1)$ degrees of freedom. This is not necessarily true if Y_{ij} represents the observed pure premium, even if the claim sizes are iid and we standardize BS by dividing by $\mathrm{E}[X^2]/\mathrm{E}[X]$. ∇

Property 8.3.7 (Bailey-Simon leads to a 'safe' premium)
The Bailey-Simon method in the multiplicative model has a property that will certainly appeal to actuaries. It proves that with this method, the resulting total premium is larger than the observed loss. We can even prove that this holds when premiums and losses are accumulated over rows or over columns. In other words, we can prove that, assuming that $\hat{\alpha}_i$ and $\hat{\beta}_j$ solve (8.4), we have

$$\sum_{i(j)} w_{ij}\,\hat{\alpha}_i\,\hat{\beta}_j \geq \sum_{i(j)} w_{ij}\,y_{ij} \quad \text{for all } j(i). \tag{8.7}$$

A summation over $i(j)$ for all $j(i)$ means that the sum has to be taken not only over i for all j, but also over j for all i. To prove (8.7) we rewrite the first set of equations in (8.4) as

$$\hat{\alpha}_i^2 = \sum_j \frac{w_{ij}\,\hat{\beta}_j}{\sum_h w_{ih}\,\hat{\beta}_h} \frac{y_{ij}^2}{\hat{\beta}_j^2}, \quad i = 1, 2, \ldots, I. \tag{8.8}$$

But this is just $\mathrm{E}[U^2]$ if U is a random variable with $\Pr[U = d_j] = p_j$, where

$$p_j = \frac{w_{ij}\hat{\beta}_j}{\sum_h w_{ih}\hat{\beta}_h} \quad \text{and} \quad d_j = \frac{y_{ij}}{\hat{\beta}_j}. \tag{8.9}$$

Since $\mathrm{E}[U^2] \geq (\mathrm{E}[U])^2$ for any random variable U, we have immediately

$$\hat{\alpha}_i \geq \sum_j \frac{w_{ij}}{\sum_h w_{ih}\,\hat{\beta}_h} y_{ij}, \quad \text{hence} \quad \sum_j w_{ij}\,\hat{\alpha}_i\,\hat{\beta}_j \geq \sum_j w_{ij}\,y_{ij}. \tag{8.10}$$

In the same way one proves that the estimated column totals are at least the observed totals. ∇

Property 8.3.8 (Marginal Totals = ML with Poisson)
The basic idea behind the method of marginal totals is the same as the one behind the actuarial equivalence principle: in a 'good' tariff system, for large groups of insureds, the total premium equals the observed loss. We determine the values $\hat{\alpha}_i$ and $\hat{\beta}_j$ in such a way that this condition is met for all groups of risks for which one of the risk factors, either the row number i or the column number j, is constant. The equivalence does not hold for each cell, but it does on the next-higher aggregation level of rows and columns.

In the multiplicative model, to estimate the parameters we have to solve the following system of equations consisting of $I+J$ equations in as many unknowns:

$$\sum_{i(j)} w_{ij}\,\alpha_i\,\beta_j = \sum_{i(j)} w_{ij}\,y_{ij} \quad \text{for all } j(i). \tag{8.11}$$

If all estimated and observed row totals are the same, the same holds for the sum of all these row totals. So the total of all observations equals the sum of all estimates. Hence, one of the equations in the system (8.11) is superfluous, since each equation in it can be written as a linear combination of all the others. This is in line with the fact that the α_i and the β_j in (8.11) are only identified up to a multiplicative constant.

One way to solve (8.11) is by successive substitution, starting from any positive initial value for the β_j. For this, rewrite the system in the form:

$$\begin{aligned} \alpha_i &= \sum_j w_{ij}\,y_{ij} \Big/ \sum_j w_{ij}\,\beta_j, \qquad i = 1,\ldots,I; \\ \beta_j &= \sum_i w_{ij}\,y_{ij} \Big/ \sum_i w_{ij}\,\alpha_i, \qquad j = 1,\ldots,J. \end{aligned} \tag{8.12}$$

A few iterations generally suffice to produce the optimal estimates. ∇

The heuristic justification of the method of marginal totals applies for every interpretation of the Y_{ij}. But if the Y_{ij} denote claim numbers, there is another explanation, as follows.

Property 8.3.9 (Loglinear Poisson GLM = Marginal totals method)
Suppose the number of claims caused by each of the w_{ij} insureds in cell (i,j) has a Poisson(λ_{ij}) distribution with $\lambda_{ij} = \alpha_i\beta_j$. Then estimating α_i and β_j by maximum likelihood or by the marginal totals method gives the same results.

Proof. The total number of claims in cell (i,j) has a Poisson($w_{ij}\lambda_{ij}$) distribution. The likelihood of the parameters λ_{ij} with the observed numbers of claims s_{ij} then equals

$$L = \prod_{i,j} e^{-w_{ij}\lambda_{ij}} \frac{(w_{ij}\lambda_{ij})^{s_{ij}}}{s_{ij}!}. \tag{8.13}$$

By substituting into (8.13) the relation

$$\mathrm{E}[Y_{ij}] = \mathrm{E}[S_{ij}]/w_{ij} = \lambda_{ij} = \alpha_i\beta_j \tag{8.14}$$

and maximizing (8.13) for α_i and β_j we get exactly the equations (8.11). ∇

Property 8.3.10 (Least squares = ML with normality)
In the method of least squares, estimators are determined that minimize the total of the squared differences of observed loss and estimated premium, weighted by the exposure in a cell. This weighting is necessary to ensure that the numbers added have the same order of magnitude. If the variance of Y_{ij} is proportional to $1/w_{ij}$, which is for instance the case when S_{ij} is the sum of w_{ij} iid random variables with the same variance, all terms in (8.15) below have the same mean, hence it makes sense to add them up. The parameters α_i and β_j are estimated by solving:

$$\min_{\alpha_i,\beta_j} SS \quad \text{with} \quad SS = \sum_{i,j} w_{ij}(y_{ij} - \alpha_i\beta_j)^2. \tag{8.15}$$

The normal equations produce the following system, written in a form that is suitable to be tackled by successive substitution:

$$\begin{aligned} \alpha_i &= \sum_j w_{ij}\, y_{ij}\, \beta_j \Big/ \sum_j w_{ij}\, \beta_j^2, \quad i = 1,\ldots,I; \\ \beta_j &= \sum_i w_{ij}\, y_{ij}\, \alpha_i \Big/ \sum_i w_{ij}\, \alpha_i^2, \quad j = 1,\ldots,J. \end{aligned} \tag{8.16}$$

Because of the form of the likelihood of the normal distribution, one may show that minimizing SS is tantamount to maximizing the normal loglikelihood. See also Exercise 8.3.7. ∇

Property 8.3.11 (Direct method = ML with gamma distribution)
The direct method determines estimates for the parameters α_i and β_j by solving, for instance by successive substitution, the following system:

$$\begin{aligned} \alpha_i &= \sum_j w_{ij} \frac{y_{ij}}{\beta_j} \Big/ \sum_j w_{ij}, \quad i = 1, \ldots, I; \\ \beta_j &= \sum_i w_{ij} \frac{y_{ij}}{\alpha_i} \Big/ \sum_i w_{ij}, \quad j = 1, \ldots, J. \end{aligned} \tag{8.17}$$

The justification for this method is as follows. Assume that we know the correct multiplicities β_j, $j = 1, \ldots, J$. Then all random variables Y_{ij}/β_j have mean α_i. Estimating α_i by a weighted average, we get the equations (8.17) of the direct method. The same reasoning applied to Y_{ij}/α_i gives estimates for β_j. See also Exercise 8.3.4.

The direct method also amounts to determining the maximum likelihood in a certain GLM. We will prove that it produces ML-estimators when $S_{ij} \sim \text{gamma}(\gamma w_{ij}, \frac{\gamma}{\alpha_i \beta_j})$. This means that S_{ij} is the sum of w_{ij} gamma$(\gamma, \frac{\gamma}{\alpha_i \beta_j})$ random variables, with a *fixed* coefficient of variation $\gamma^{-1/2}$, and a mean $\alpha_i \beta_j$. The likelihood of the observation in cell (i, j) can be written as

$$f_{S_{ij}}(s_{ij}; \alpha_i, \beta_j) = \frac{1}{\Gamma(\gamma w_{ij})} \left(\frac{\gamma}{\alpha_i \beta_j} \right)^{\gamma w_{ij}} s_{ij}^{\gamma w_{ij} - 1} e^{\frac{-\gamma s_{ij}}{\alpha_i \beta_j}}. \tag{8.18}$$

With $L = \prod_{i,j} f_{S_{ij}}(s_{ij}; \alpha_i, \beta_j)$, we find by differentiating with respect to α_k:

$$\begin{aligned} \frac{\partial \log L}{\partial \alpha_k} &= \frac{\partial}{\partial \alpha_k} \sum_{i,j} \{ \gamma w_{ij} \log \frac{\gamma}{\alpha_i \beta_j} - \frac{\gamma s_{ij}}{\alpha_i \beta_j} \} + 0 \\ &= \sum_j \{ \frac{-\gamma w_{kj}}{\alpha_k} + \frac{\gamma s_{kj}}{\alpha_k^2 \beta_j} \}. \end{aligned} \tag{8.19}$$

The derivatives with respect to β_h produce analogous equations. Setting the normal equations (8.19) arising from ML-estimation equal to zero produces, after a little algebra, exactly the system (8.17) of the direct method. ∇

Example 8.3.12 (Numerical illustration of the above methods)
We applied the four methods given above to the data given in the following table, which gives $w_{ij} \times y_{ij}$ for $i, j = 1, 2$:

	$j=1$	$j=2$
$i=1$	300×10	500×15
$i=2$	700×20	100×35

The following fitted values $\hat{\alpha}_i \hat{\beta}_j$ arose from the different methods:

Bailey-Simon		marginal totals		least squares		direct method	
9.40	15.38	9.39	15.37	9.04	15.34	9.69	15.29
20.27	33.18	20.26	33.17	20.18	34.24	20.27	31.97
$\Delta = 28.85$		$\Delta = 28.86$		$\Delta = 37.06$		$\Delta = 36.84$	

Here $\Delta = \sum_{i,j} w_{ij}(y_{ij} - \hat{\alpha}_i \hat{\beta}_j)^2/(\hat{\alpha}_i \hat{\beta}_j)$ describes the goodness of the fit; it is of course minimal for the Bailey-Simon method. The systems of equations from which the $\hat{\alpha}_i$ and the $\hat{\beta}_j$ have to be determined are alike, but not identical. See also Exercise 8.3.2. The results of the methods are very similar. The reader is invited to either try and duplicate the optimizations needed above, or merely to verify if the solutions obtained are correct by checking if they satisfy the equations for the optimum given. ∇

In the preceding we emphasized the method of successive substitution, which has the advantage of being simple to implement, once the system of equations has been written in a suitable form. Of course many other algorithms may be used to handle the likelihood maximization.

8.4 DEVIANCE AND SCALED DEVIANCE

As a measure for the difference between vectors of fitted values and of observations one generally looks at the Euclidean distance, i.e., the sum of the squared differences. If the observations are from a normal distribution, minimizing this distance is the same as maximizing the likelihood of the parameter values with the given observations. In GLM-analyses, one looks at the difference of the 'optimal' likelihood of a certain model, compared with the maximally attainable likelihood if one doesn't impose a model on the parameters, hence for the *full model* with a parameter for every observation.

The *scaled deviance* of a model is -2 times the logarithm of the likelihood ratio, which equals the quotient of the likelihood maximized under our particular model, divided by the likelihood of the full model. The *deviance* equals the scaled deviance multiplied by the dispersion parameter ϕ. From the theory of mathematical statistics it is known that the scaled deviance is approximately χ^2 distributed, with as degrees of freedom the number of observations minus the number of estimated parameters. Also, if one model is a submodel of another, it is known that the difference between the scaled deviances has a χ^2-distribution.

For three suitable choices of the distribution of the random variation around the mean in a GLM, we will give expressions for their deviances. We will always assume that the expected values μ_i of our observations Y_i, $i = 1, \ldots, n$ follow a certain model, for instance a multiplicative model with rows and columns such as above. We denote by $\hat{\mu}_i$ the optimally estimated means under this model, and by $\tilde{\mu}_i$ the mean, optimally estimated under the full model, where every observation has its own parameter and the maximization of the total likelihood can be done term by term. We will always take the ith observation to be the mean of w_i single iid observations. All these have a common dispersion parameter ϕ. We already remarked that this dispersion parameter is proportional to the variances, which, as a function of the mean μ, are equal to $\phi V(\mu)/w$, where the function $V(\cdot)$ is the variance function.

Example 8.4.1 (Normal distribution)

Let $Y_1, \ldots, Y_n$ be independent normal random variables, where Y_i is the average of w_i random variables with an $\mathrm{N}(\mu_i, \phi)$ distribution, hence $Y_i \sim \mathrm{N}(\mu_i, \phi/w_i)$. Let L denote the likelihood of the parameters with the given observations. Further let $\hat{L}$ and $\tilde{L}$ denote the values of L when $\hat{\mu}_i$ and $\tilde{\mu}_i$ are substituted for μ_i. We have

$$L = \prod_{i=1}^{n} \frac{1}{\sqrt{2\pi\phi/w_i}} \exp \frac{-(y_i - \mu_i)^2}{2\phi/w_i}. \tag{8.20}$$

It is clear that in the full model, maximizing (8.20) term by term, we can simply take $\mu_i = \tilde{\mu}_i = y_i$ for each i. If D denotes the deviance, we have

$$\frac{D}{\phi} = -2 \log \frac{\hat{L}}{\tilde{L}} = \frac{1}{\phi} \sum_i w_i (\hat{\mu}_i - y_i)^2. \tag{8.21}$$

This means that for the normal distribution, minimizing the deviance, or what is the same, maximizing the likelihood, is the same as determining the parameter estimates by least squares. ∇

Example 8.4.2 (Poisson sample means)
Now let $Y_i = \phi M_i/w_i$ with $M_i \sim$ Poisson$(w_i\mu_i/\phi)$. When this is the case, we write $Y_i \sim$ Poisson(μ_i, ϕ). In the special case that $w_i \equiv 1$ as well as $\phi = 1$, we have ordinary Poisson random variables. If w_i/ϕ is an integer, Y_i can be regarded as the average of w_i/ϕ Poisson(μ_i) random variables, but without this restriction we also have a valid model. For the likelihood we have

$$\begin{aligned} &L(\mu_1, \ldots, \mu_n;\ \phi, w_1, \ldots, w_n, y_1, \ldots, y_n) \\ &= \prod_{i=1}^{n} \Pr[w_i Y_i/\phi = w_i y_i/\phi] = \prod_{i=1}^{n} \frac{e^{-\mu_i w_i/\phi}(\mu_i w_i/\phi)^{w_i y_i/\phi}}{(w_i y_i/\phi)!}. \end{aligned} \tag{8.22}$$

The ith term in this expression is maximal for the value of μ_i that maximizes $e^{-\mu_i}\mu_i^{y_i}$, which is for $\mu_i = y_i$, so we see that just as with the normal distribution, we get $\tilde{\mu}_i$ by simply taking the ith residual equal to zero. It turns out that this holds for every member of the exponential dispersion family; see also Examples 8.4.1 and 8.4.3, as well as Exercise 8.6.5.

It is easy to see that the scaled deviance is equal to the following expression:

$$\frac{D}{\phi} = -2\log\frac{\hat{L}}{\tilde{L}} = \frac{2}{\phi}\sum_i w_i \left(y_i \log\frac{y_i}{\hat{\mu}_i} - (y_i - \hat{\mu}_i) \right). \tag{8.23}$$

Notice that $\text{E}[Y_i] = \mu_i$ and $\text{Var}[Y_i] = \frac{\phi}{w_i}\mu_i$, hence $V(\mu) = \mu$.

Weights w_i are needed for instance to model the average claim frequency of a driver in a cell with w_i policies in it. By not taking the weights into account, one disregards the fact that the observations in cells with many policies in them have been measured with much more precision than the ones in practically empty cells.

By changing ϕ, we get distributions of which the variance is not equal to the mean, but remains proportional to it. One speaks of *overdispersed* Poisson distributions in this case. The random variable Y_i in this example has as a support the integer multiples of ϕ/w_i, but obviously the deviance (8.23) allows minimization for other non-negative values of y_i as well. This way, one gets *pseudo-likelihood* models. ∇

Example 8.4.3 (Gamma distributions)
Now let $Y_i \sim$ gamma$(w_i/\phi, w_i/\{\phi\,\mu_i\})$, hence Y_i has the distribution of an average of w_i gamma$(1/\phi, 1/\{\phi\,\mu_i\})$ random variables, or equivalently, of w_i/ϕ random variables with an exponential$(1/\mu_i)$ distribution. We have again

$$\text{E}[Y_i] = \mu_i, \quad \text{Var}[Y_i] = \frac{\phi}{w_i}V(\mu_i) = \frac{\phi}{w_i}\mu_i^2. \tag{8.24}$$

For this case, we have $\tilde{\mu}_i = y_i$ for the full model as well, since

$$\begin{aligned}
&\frac{d}{d\mu} \log f_Y\left(y; \frac{w}{\phi}, \frac{w}{\phi\,\mu}\right) \\
&= \frac{d}{d\mu} \log\left(\frac{1}{\Gamma(w/\phi)}\left[\frac{w}{\phi\,\mu}\right]^{w/\phi} y^{w/\phi-1} e^{-wy/(\phi\,\mu)}\right) \\
&= \frac{d}{d\mu}\left(\frac{w}{\phi}\log\frac{w}{\phi\,\mu} + (\frac{w}{\phi} - 1)\log y - \frac{wy}{\phi\,\mu}\right) \\
&= \frac{-w}{\phi\,\mu} + \frac{wy}{\phi\,\mu^2} = 0 \quad \text{if and only if} \quad y = \mu.
\end{aligned} \tag{8.25}$$

One can easily verify that the scaled deviance is equal to the following expression:

$$\frac{D}{\phi} = -2\log\frac{\hat{L}}{\tilde{L}} = \frac{2}{\phi}\sum_i w_i\left(-\log\frac{y_i}{\hat{\mu}_i} + \frac{y_i - \hat{\mu}_i}{\hat{\mu}_i}\right). \tag{8.26}$$

The y_i of course must be positive here. ∇

The value of the deviance D can be computed from the data alone; it is a *statistic* and does not involve unknown parameters. Notice that in each of the three classes of distributions given above, the maximization over μ_i gave results that did not depend on ϕ. Only the relative values of the parameters ϕ/w_i with each observation are relevant. The estimation of ϕ can hence be done independently from the determining of optimal values for the μ_i. To estimate the value of ϕ, one often proceeds as follows. Under the null-hypothesis that $Y_i \sim \mathrm{N}(\mu_i, \phi/w_i)$, the minimized sum of squares (8.21) has a χ^2-distribution with as its parameter *df* the number of observations minus the number of parameter estimates needed in evaluating $\hat{\mu}_i$. Then one can estimate ϕ by the method of moments, setting (8.21) equal to its mean value *df* and solving for ϕ. To ensure that the differences between Y_i and the fitted values are caused by chance and not by systematic deviations because one has used too crude a model, the estimation of ϕ is done in the most refined model that still can be estimated, even though there will generally be too many parameters in this model. Hence, for this model the scaled deviance equals the value of *df*. Another possibility is to estimate ϕ by maximum likelihood.

The interpretation for the dispersion parameter ϕ is different for each class of distributions. For the normal distributions, it is simply the variance of the errors. For a pure Poisson distribution, we have $\phi = 1$; in case of overdispersion it is the ratio of variance and mean, as well as the factor by which all Poisson variables have been multiplied. For the gamma distributions, $\sqrt{\phi}$ denotes the coefficient of variation σ/μ for individual observations.

8.5 EXAMPLE: ANALYSIS OF A CONTINGENCY TABLE

In this section, we analyze an artificial data set created by a computer. We generated numbers that represent the number of days spent in hospital of a group of 14 742 persons for a certain disease. They spent a total of 58 607 days hospitalized because of this disease. See Table 8.1. The group is split up according to characteristic j which represents different region/gender combinations. Odd values of j denote females, while $j = 1, 2$ denote region I, $j = 3, 4$ region II, and $j = 5, 6$ region III. In i, we have coded the age class. Group $i = 1$ has ages 15–25, group 2 has ages 25–35, and so on; the last group $i = 6$ represents the people of 65 and older. We try to predict the number of days spent in hospital by a multiplicative model $\mu\,\alpha_i\,\beta_j$, with μ the expected value in cell (1,1), hence $\alpha_1 = \beta_1 = 1$. We will assume that the observations have a Poisson distribution around this mean. With GLM-fitting programs we can try several models. We can let α_i and β_j be arbitrary, but also let $\alpha_i \equiv 1$ or $\beta_j \equiv 1$. We can require that the α_i follow a geometric pattern with $\alpha_i = \alpha^{i-1}$ for a certain value of α. This requirement is less meaningful for the β_j; it only makes sense if a factor is measured on an 'interval scale', in the sense that the difference between $j = 5$ and $j = 4$ is the same as that between $j = 4$ and $j = 3$ or between $j = 2$ and $j = 1$. But the classification $j = 1, \ldots, 6$ is not even on an ordinal scale. By taking $\alpha_i \equiv 1$, we investigate a model where the age has no influence at all on the hospitalization pattern. Choosing $\alpha_i = \alpha^{i-1}$ we see that with increasing age class, the mean number of days in the hospital grows, or shrinks, by a fixed factor. For an overview of the various models to be used and their performance, see Table 8.2.

Comparing models I–III with IV–VI, one sees that in the latter, a geometric progression with age class is assumed. Judging by the distances between fitted and observed values, the resulting fits are quite comparable. But upon replacing β_j by β^{j-1} or even by 1, the quality of the fit gets so bad that the conclusion is that this variable definitely will have to stay in the model in its most complicated form, as a factor. In Table 8.1, one finds the fitted values for the models I ($\mu\,\alpha_i\,\beta_j$) and IV ($\mu\,\alpha^{i-1}\,\beta_j$). The predictions for model IV have been computed in the following

		$j=1$ F,I	$j=2$ M,I	$j=3$ F,II	$j=4$ M,II	$j=5$ F,III	$j=6$ M,III
1	y_{ij}	4.10	3.50	3.20	2.80	3.70	3.00
15–25	w_{ij}	525.	547.	508.	481.	524.	514.
I	fv_1	3.96	3.81	2.95	2.87	3.41	3.28
IV	fv_2	4.04	3.88	3.01	2.93	3.47	3.35
X	fv_3	4.22	3.57	3.24	2.85	3.71	3.13
2	y_{ij}	4.40	4.00	3.40	3.00	3.80	3.50
25–35	w_{ij}	487.	478.	508.	490.	407.	435.
I	fv_1	4.32	4.16	3.22	3.13	3.71	3.57
IV	fv_2	4.30	4.14	3.21	3.13	3.70	3.57
X	fv_3	4.41	3.94	3.34	3.07	3.84	3.43
3	y_{ij}	5.00	4.50	3.70	3.50	4.00	3.90
35–45	w_{ij}	411.	414.	415.	484.	469.	523.
I	fv_1	4.80	4.62	3.58	3.48	4.12	3.97
IV	fv_2	4.58	4.41	3.42	3.33	3.94	3.80
X	fv_3	4.61	4.36	3.45	3.32	3.97	3.76
4	y_{ij}	4.70	4.70	3.10	3.60	4.20	4.20
45–55	w_{ij}	395.	448.	413.	416.	389.	419.
I	fv_1	4.79	4.61	3.57	3.47	4.11	3.96
IV	fv_2	4.88	4.70	3.64	3.55	4.20	4.05
X	fv_3	4.82	4.81	3.56	3.58	4.12	4.12
5	y_{ij}	4.90	5.30	3.80	3.80	4.20	4.40
55–65	w_{ij}	372.	368.	355.	339.	378.	445.
I	fv_1	5.16	4.97	3.85	3.74	4.43	4.27
IV	fv_2	5.21	5.01	3.88	3.78	4.48	4.32
X	fv_3	5.04	5.32	3.67	3.86	4.26	4.52
6	y_{ij}	5.30	5.90	3.90	4.10	4.40	4.90
65+	w_{ij}	265.	240.	233.	233.	210.	205.
I	fv_1	5.56	5.35	4.15	4.03	4.78	4.61
IV	fv_2	5.55	5.34	4.14	4.03	4.77	4.60
X	fv_3	5.27	5.88	3.78	4.17	4.41	4.95

Table 8.1 Observed average number of days in a hospital y_{ij}, number of observations w_{ij} and fitted values according to models I, IV and X. Observations classified by region/gender combination and age class.

Model	Factors in e^{η}	Degrees of freedom	Scaled deviance
I	$\mu\,\alpha_i\,\beta_j$	25	52.6
II	$\mu\,\alpha_i\,\beta^{j-1}$	29	233.
III	$\mu\,\alpha_i$	30	321.
IV	$\mu\,\alpha^{i-1}\,\beta_j$	29	62.8
V	$\mu\,\alpha^{i-1}\,\beta^{j-1}$	33	242.
VI	$\mu\,\alpha^{i-1}$	34	329.
VII	$\mu\,\beta_j$	30	268.
VIII	$\mu\,\beta^{j-1}$	34	450.
IX	μ	35	536.
X	$\mu\,\alpha_j^{i-1}\,\beta_j$	24	24.0

Table 8.2 Parameters, degrees of freedom and scaled deviance for various models applied to the data of Table 8.1.

way:

$$\text{IV:}\quad \hat{y}_{ij} = \hat{\mu}\,\hat{\alpha}^{i-1}\,\hat{\beta}_j = 4.036 \times 1.066^{i-1} \times \begin{bmatrix} j=1: & 1.000 \\ j=2: & 0.962 \\ j=3: & 0.746 \\ j=4: & 0.727 \\ j=5: & 0.860 \\ j=6: & 0.830 \end{bmatrix} \tag{8.27}$$

Up to now, we only looked at models where the fitted values were determined as the product of two main effects, the row effect and the column effect. In general it is quite conceivable that these effects do not operate independently, but that there is *interaction* between the two. This means that it is possible in this case to have a different row effect for each column. The resulting expected values can be written in a quite general form $\text{E}[Y_{ij}] = \delta_{ij}$. In our examples, where by tabulation we combined all observations for cell (i, j) into one, this model boils down to the *full model*, with a parameter for each observation unit, each with a certain associated precision w_{ij}. We might also look at models in which each region/gender combination has its own geometric progression. Then we get model X, where we have $\text{E}[Y_{ij}] = \mu\,\alpha_j^{i-1}\,\beta_j$. Since even though not all other models are nested in it, this model is the most refined that we want to estimate, we determine an estimate for the scale factor ϕ linking deviance and scaled deviance as the average deviance per degree of freedom of model X. This gives an overdispersion equal to $\hat{\phi} = 3.088$. So, the distances in Table 8.2 have been scaled in such a way that model X has a distance 24 with 24 degrees of freedom. There are 36 observations, and 12 parameters have been estimated, since with every region/gender combination, there is an initial level (for age class 15–25) as well as an increase factor. The estimates for model X have been computed as:

$$\text{X:} \quad \hat{y}_{ij} = (\hat{\mu}\,\hat{\beta}_j)(\hat{\alpha}_j)^{i-1} = \begin{bmatrix} j=1: & 4.218 \times 1.046^{i-1} \\ j=2: & 3.567 \times 1.105^{i-1} \\ j=3: & 3.240 \times 1.031^{i-1} \\ j=4: & 2.848 \times 1.079^{i-1} \\ j=5: & 3.706 \times 1.036^{i-1} \\ j=6: & 3.133 \times 1.096^{i-1} \end{bmatrix} \tag{8.28}$$

In Table 8.2 one sees that model IV, having 4 parameters less than model I which is nested in it, has a scaled deviance between data and fitted values that is 10.2 larger. To test if this is significant, observe that, under the null-hypothesis, this number is a drawing from a distribution which is approximately χ^2 with 4 degrees of freedom. The 95% critical value of a $\chi^2(4)$ distribution is 9.5, so it can be concluded that model I is better than model IV. In the class of models without interaction of rows and columns, IV is good, since all coarser models have a significantly larger distance between observations and fitted values. The more refined model I is significantly better, though, if only by a small margin. But the transition from IV to X, involving dropping the condition that $\alpha_j \equiv \alpha$, does lead to a statistically significant, as well as practically meaningful, improvement of the fit. With only 5 extra parameters, a gain in distance of 38.8 is achieved.

The observations with even values of j concern males. By inspecting the coefficients $\hat{\beta}_j$ in (8.27) for $j = 2k - 1$ as well as $j = 2k$, we see that men spend about 3% less days in the hospital, after correction for age group. The effect of region is slightly stronger, and it would seem that region II is about 75% of region I, regardless of gender, and region III is about 85%. It turns out that a better model than IV arises if one allows three main effects: age class (geometrically), gender and region, without interaction between the two last ones.

Note that the theory above was given for two exogenous variables only. Here we have three, but instead of gender and region separately, we looked at the interaction of these two, by constructing a classifying variable with a separate class for each gender/region combination. But of course it is easy to extend the theory to more than two regressors.

8.6 THE STOCHASTIC COMPONENT OF GLM'S

A possible way to introduce GLM's, which is followed in many texts, is to start by defining the exponential dispersion family of densities, which contains all the examples we introduced above as special cases. Next, starting from this general likelihood, one may derive properties of this family, including the mean and variance. Then, the algorithm to determine ML estimates for this family is derived. The algorithm can be applied with any link function. Since the general formula of the density is essential only for deriving the panacea algorithm and provides no help to the occasional user of a GLM, we postponed its introduction to this separate section, to be skipped at first reading. In this section we also study the so-called canonical link function, which has some very nice properties, and give a very short description of the Nelder and Wedderburn algorithm.

The exponential dispersion family

In Section 8.2, we introduced the distributions to possibly describe the randomness in Generalized Linear Models by listing a number of important examples. Below, we give a more general definition of the family of possible densities to be used for GLM's. It can be shown that all our examples, normal, Poisson, Poisson multiples, gamma, inverse Gaussian and binomial proportions, are special cases of the following family.

Definition 8.6.1 (The exponential dispersion family)

The *exponential dispersion family of densities* consists of the densities of the following type:

$$f_Y(y;\theta,\psi) = \exp\left(\frac{y\theta - b(\theta)}{\psi} + c(y;\psi)\right), \quad y \in D_\psi. \tag{8.29}$$

Here ψ and θ are real parameters, $b(\cdot)$ and $c(\cdot;\cdot)$ are real functions. The support of the density is $D_\psi \subset \mathbb{R}$. ∇

The status of the parameter θ is not the same as that of ψ, because ψ does not affect the mean, in which we are primarily interested. The linear models we described in the earlier sections only aimed to explain this mean. Though except in special cases, the value of ψ is fixed and unknown, too, in GLM-literature the above family is referred to as the one-parameter exponential family. The function $b(\cdot)$ is called the cumulant function, see later. The support D_ψ does not depend on θ. The same goes for the function $c(\cdot;\cdot)$ that acts as a normalizing function, ensuring that the density sums or integrates to 1. For the continuous distributions the support is $\mathbb{R}$ for the normal distribution, and $(0,\infty)$ for the gamma and inverse Gaussian distributions. It may also be a countable set, in case of a discrete density. For the Poisson multiples for instance, D_ψ is the set $\{0,\psi,2\psi,\ldots\}$. In the following, we list some examples of members of the exponential dispersion family. For the specific form of the function $b(\cdot)$ as well as the support D_ψ, we refer to Table E. In the exercises, the reader is asked to verify the entries in this table.

Example 8.6.2 (Some members of the exponential dispersion family)
The following parametric families are the most important members of the exponential dispersion family:

1. The $\mathrm{N}(\mu,\sigma^2)$ distributions, after reparametrizations $\theta(\mu,\sigma^2) = \mu$ and $\psi(\mu,\sigma^2) = \sigma^2$. [Note that since the parameter μ denotes the mean here, θ may not depend on σ^2.]

2. The Poisson(μ) distributions, with parameter $\theta = \log\mu$, while $\psi = 1$.

3. For all natural m, assumed fixed and known, the binomial(m,p) distributions, with $\theta = \log\frac{p}{1-p}$ and $\psi = 1$.

4. For all positive r, assumed fixed and known, the negative binomial(r,p) distributions, for $\theta = \log(1-p)$ and $\psi = 1$.

5. The gamma(α,β) distributions, after the reparametrizations $\theta(\alpha,\beta) = -\beta/\alpha$ and $\psi(\alpha,\beta) = 1/\alpha$. Note that $\theta < 0$ must hold in this case.

6. The inverse Gaussian(α,β) distributions, with $\theta(\alpha,\beta) = -\frac{1}{2}\beta^2/\alpha^2$ and $\psi(\alpha,\beta) = \beta/\alpha^2$. Again, $\theta < 0$ must hold. ∇

Note that there are three different parametrizations involved: the 'standard' parameters used throughout this book, the parametrization by mean μ and dispersion parameter ψ which proved convenient in Section 8.2, and the parametrization with θ and ψ as used in this section. This last parametrization is known as the natural or canonical parametrization, since the factor in the density (8.29) involving both the argument y and the parameter θ which determines the mean has the specific form $y\theta$ instead of $yh(\theta)$ for some function $h(\cdot)$.

Example 8.6.3 (Gamma distribution and exponential dispersion family)
As an example, we will show how the gamma distributions fit in the exponential dispersion family. The customary parametrization, used in the rest of this text, is by a shape parameter α and a scale parameter β. To determine ψ, as well as θ, we compare the logarithm of the gamma(α, β) density with (8.29). This leads to

$$-\log\Gamma(\alpha) + \alpha\log\beta + (\alpha-1)\log y - \beta y = \frac{y\theta - b(\theta)}{\psi} + c(y;\psi). \tag{8.30}$$

The parameters must be chosen in such a way that θ, ψ and y appear together in the log-density only in a term of the form $\theta y/\psi$. This is achieved by taking $\psi = \frac{1}{\alpha}$ and $\theta = -\frac{\beta}{\alpha}$. Note that in this case, we have $\theta < 0$. To make the left and right hand side coincide, we further take $b(\theta) = -\log(-\theta)$, which leaves $c(y;\psi) = \alpha\log\beta + (\alpha-1)\log y - \log\Gamma(\alpha)$ for the terms not involving θ. In the μ, ψ parametrization, μ is simply the mean, so $\mu = \frac{\alpha}{\beta}$. We see that in the θ, ψ parametrization, the mean of these random variables does not depend on ψ, since it equals

$$\mathrm{E}[Y;\theta] =: \mu(\theta) = \frac{\alpha}{\beta} = \mu = -\frac{1}{\theta}. \tag{8.31}$$

The variance is

$$\mathrm{Var}[Y;\theta,\psi] = \frac{\alpha}{\beta^2} = \mu^2\psi = \frac{\psi}{\theta^2}. \tag{8.32}$$

So the variance is $V(\mu)\psi$, where $V(\cdot)$ is the variance function $V(\mu) = \mu^2$. ∇

The density (8.29) in its general form permits one to derive the mgf of Y. From this, we can derive some useful properties of the exponential dispersion family.

Lemma 8.6.4 (Mgf of the exponential dispersion family)
For each real number t such that replacing θ by $\theta + t\psi$ in (8.29) also produces a density, the moment generating function at argument t of the density (8.29) equals

$$m_Y(t) = \exp\frac{b(\theta + t\psi) - b(\theta)}{\psi}. \tag{8.33}$$

Proof. We give a proof for the continuous case only; for the proof of the discrete case, it suffices to replace the integrations over the support D_ψ in this proof by summations over $y \in D_\psi$. We can successively rewrite the mgf as follows:

$$\begin{aligned} m_Y(t) &= \int_{D_\psi} e^{ty} \exp\left[\frac{y\theta - b(\theta)}{\psi} + c(y;\psi)\right] dy = \\ &= \int_{D_\psi} \exp\left[\frac{y\{\theta + t\psi\} - b(\theta + t\psi)}{\psi} + c(y;\psi)\right] dy \\ &\quad \times \exp\frac{b(\theta + t\psi) - b(\theta)}{\psi} \\ &= \exp\frac{b(\theta + t\psi) - b(\theta)}{\psi}. \end{aligned} \tag{8.34}$$

The last equality follows since the second integrand in (8.34) was assumed to be a density. ∇

Corollary 8.6.5 (Cgf, cumulants, mean and variance)
If Y has density (8.29), then its cumulant generating function equals

$$\kappa_Y(t) = \frac{b(\theta + t\psi) - b(\theta)}{\psi}. \tag{8.35}$$

As a consequence, for the cumulants κ_j, $j = 1, 2, \ldots$ we have

$$\kappa_j = \kappa_Y^{(j)}(0) = b^{(j)}(\theta)\psi^{j-1}. \tag{8.36}$$

Because of this, the function $b(\cdot)$ is called the *cumulant function*. From (8.36) with $j = 1, 2$, we see that the mean and variance of Y are given by:

$$\mathrm{E}[Y;\theta] = \kappa_1 = b'(\theta), \quad \mathrm{Var}[Y;\theta,\psi] = \kappa_2 = \psi b''(\theta). \tag{8.37}$$

Note that the mean depends only on θ, while the variance equals the dispersion parameter multiplied by $b''(\theta)$. The *variance function* $V(\mu)$ equals $b''(\theta(\mu))$. ∇

Corollary 8.6.6 (Taking sample means)
Let $Y_1, \ldots, Y_m$ be a sample of m independent copies of the random variable Y, and let $\overline{Y} = (Y_1 + \cdots + Y_m)/m$ be the sample mean. If Y is a member of an exponential dispersion family with fixed functions $b(\cdot)$ and $c(\cdot;\cdot)$ and with parameters θ and ψ, then $\overline{Y}$ is in the same exponential dispersion family with parameters θ and ψ/m, if this pair of parameters is allowed.

Proof. By (8.33), we have

$$m_{\overline{Y}}(t) = \{m_Y(\frac{t}{m})\}^m = \exp \frac{b(\theta + t\psi/m) - b(\theta)}{\psi/m}. \tag{8.38}$$

This is exactly the mgf of a member of the exponential dispersion family with parameters θ and ψ/m. ∇

Note that for the (negative) binomial distributions, only $\psi = 1$ is allowed. For the other error distributions, any positive value of ψ is allowed.

Example 8.6.7 (Poisson multiples and sample means)
By Corollary 8.6.6, the sample means of m Poisson(μ) random variables as introduced earlier have a density in the exponential dispersion family (8.29), with $b(\cdot)$, $c(\cdot;\cdot)$ and θ the same as for the Poisson density, but $\psi = 1/m$ instead of $\psi = 1$, and support $0, \frac{1}{m}, \frac{2}{m} \ldots$ Such a sample mean is a Poisson($m\mu$) random variable, multiplied by $1/m$. Extending this idea, let $\psi > 0$ be arbitrary, not specifically equal to $1/m$ for some integer m, and look at

$$Y = \psi M, \quad \text{where} \quad M \sim \text{Poisson}(\mu/\psi). \tag{8.39}$$

It can be shown that Y has density (8.29) with $\theta = \log \mu$ and $b(\theta) = e^\theta$, just as with ordinary Poisson distributions, but with arbitrary ψ. In this way for each ψ, a subclass of the exponential dispersion family is found with parameter $\theta \in \mathbb{R}$. The possible values for Y are $\{0, \psi, 2\psi, \ldots\}$.

As we saw, for $\psi = 1/m$ we get the average of m Poisson(μ) random variables. When $\psi = n$, the resulting random variable has the property that taking the average of a sample of size n of it, we get a Poisson(μ) distribution. So it is natural to call such random variables Poisson sample means. If $\psi = n/m$, (8.39) is the sample average of m random variables of the type with $\psi = n$. So for these values, too, it is rational to call the random variable Y a Poisson average. But in view of (8.39), we also speak of such random variables as Poisson multiples. Note that for $\psi > 1$, we get a random variable with a variance larger than the mean. Hence we also see the name 'overdispersed Poisson' for such random variables in the literature. ∇

Remark 8.6.8 (Binomial and negative binomial distributions)
The negative binomial(r, p) distributions can be described by (8.29) only if one takes $\phi = 1$ and r fixed. Indeed, suppose that there exists a reparametrization from r, p into θ, ϕ describing all the negative binomial distributions in accordance with

(8.29). Now consider two such distributions with the same θ, hence the same mean, and different variances, hence different ψ. If the negative binomial parameters are r_0, p_0 and r_1, p_1, then in view of (8.36), the ratio of their variances is the ratio of their ψ-parameters, and the ratio of their third cumulants is the square of that ratio, so we must have:

$$
\begin{aligned}
\frac{r_0(1-p_0)}{p_0} &= \frac{r_1(1-p_1)}{p_1};\\
\frac{\psi_0}{\psi_1} &= \frac{r_0(1-p_0)}{p_0^2} \Big/ \frac{r_1(1-p_1)}{p_1^2} = \frac{p_1}{p_0};\\
\left(\frac{\psi_0}{\psi_1}\right)^2 &= \frac{r_0(1-p_0)(2-p_0)}{p_0^3} \Big/ \frac{r_1(1-p_1)(2-p_1)}{p_1^3} = \frac{p_1^2}{p_0^2}\frac{2-p_0}{2-p_1}.
\end{aligned}
\tag{8.40}
$$

The last two inequalities can only hold simultaneously if $p_0 = p_1$ holds, and therefore also $r_0 = r_1$. By a similar reasoning, it follows that the n-parameter of the binomial distributions must be fixed, as well. ∇

Another important consequence of the mgf derived in Lemma 8.6.4 is that we can obtain other members of the exponential dispersion family with the same ψ but with different θ. This is done by using the Esscher transformation that we encountered before, e.g., in Chapter 5.

Corollary 8.6.9 (Exponential dispersion family and Esscher transform)
The Esscher transform with parameter h of a continuous density $f(y)$ is the density

$$
f_h(y) = \frac{e^{hy} f(y)}{\int e^{hz} f(z)dz}, \tag{8.41}
$$

provided the denominator is finite, i.e., the mgf with $f(y)$ exists at h. A similar transformation of the density can be performed for discrete distributions. In both cases, the mgf with the transformed density equals $m_h(t) = \frac{m(t+h)}{m(h)}$. For a density f in the exponential dispersion family, the cgf of f_h has the form

$$
\begin{aligned}
\kappa_h(t) &= \frac{b(\theta + (t+h)\psi) - b(\theta)}{\psi} - \frac{b(\theta + h\psi) - b(\theta)}{\psi}\\
&= \frac{b(\theta + h\psi + t\psi) - b(\theta + h\psi)}{\psi},
\end{aligned}
\tag{8.42}
$$

which is again a cgf of an exponential dispersion family member with parameter $\theta_h = \theta + h\psi$ and the same ψ. ∇

Remark 8.6.10 (Generating the exponential dispersion family)
It can be shown that the Esscher transform with parameter $h \in \mathbb{R}$ transforms

1. $\mathrm{N}(0,1)$ into $\mathrm{N}(h,1)$;
2. Poisson(1) into Poisson(e^h);
3. binomial$(m, \frac{1}{2})$ into binomial$(m, (1+e^h)^{-1})$;
4. negative binomial$(r, \frac{1}{2})$ into negative binomial$(r, 1-\frac{1}{2}e^h)$ when $-\infty < h < \log 2$;
5. gamma(1,1) into gamma$(1, 1-h)$ when $-\infty < h < 1$;
6. inverse Gaussian(1,1) into inverse Gaussian$(1, 1-2h)$ when $-\infty < h < \frac{1}{2}$.

So we see that all the examples of distributions in the exponential dispersion family that we have given can be generated by starting with prototypical elements of each type, and next taking Esscher transforms and multiples of type (8.39), if allowed. ∇

The canonical link
In the definition of the exponential dispersion family we gave, the parametrization used leads to a term of the form $y\theta$ in the loglikelihood. Because of this property, we refer to θ as the *natural* or *canonical* parameter. There is also a natural choice for the link function.

Definition 8.6.11 (Canonical link function)
If the link function $\eta = g(\mu)$ is such that the parameter θ and the linear predictor η coincide, one speaks of the *standard link* or *canonical link.* ∇

Note that $\eta(\theta) = g(\mu(\theta))$, so $\eta \equiv \theta$ holds if the link function $g(\mu)$ is the inverse of $\mu(\theta) = b'(\theta)$. The canonical link has several interesting properties. Recall that $\eta_i = \sum_{j=1}^{p} x_{ij}\,\beta_j$ for the linear predictor.

Property 8.6.12 (Canonical link and marginal totals)
Property 8.3.9 shows that in a Poisson GLM with log-link, the marginal fitted and observed totals coincide. This result can be extended. If $\hat{\mu}_i$ is the fitted value for the observation i, $i = 1, \dots, n$, under a maximum likelihood estimation in any GLM with canonical link, it can be proven that the following equalities hold:

$$\sum_i w_i\, y_i\, x_{ij} = \sum_i w_i\, \hat{\mu}_i\, x_{ij}, \quad j = 1, \dots, p. \tag{8.43}$$

If the x_{ij} are dummies characterizing membership of a certain group like a row or a column of a table, and the y_i are averages of w_i iid observations, on the left hand side we see the observed total, and on the right the fitted total.

To prove that equalities (8.43) hold, we use the fact that the $\hat{\beta}_j$ that maximize the loglikelihood must satisfy the normal equations. The loglikelihood of the parameters when y is observed equals

$$l(\beta_1, \ldots, \beta_p; y) = \log f_Y(y; \beta_1, \ldots, \beta_p). \tag{8.44}$$

An extremum of the total loglikelihood of the entire set of observations $Y_1 = y_1, \ldots, Y_n = y_n$ satisfies the conditions:

$$\sum_i \frac{\partial}{\partial \beta_j} l(\beta_1, \ldots, \beta_p; y_i) = 0, \quad j = 1, \ldots, p. \tag{8.45}$$

For the partial derivative of l with respect to β_j we have by the chain rule and by the fact that $\theta \equiv \eta$ for the canonical link:

$$\frac{\partial l}{\partial \beta_j} = \frac{dl}{d\theta} \frac{\partial \theta}{\partial \beta_j} = \frac{dl}{d\theta} \frac{\partial \eta}{\partial \beta_j}, \quad j = 1, \ldots, p. \tag{8.46}$$

With dispersion parameter ϕ and known a priori weights w_i, using (8.29) and $\mu(\theta) = b'(\theta)$, see (8.37), we get for observation $i = 1, \ldots, n$:

$$\frac{\partial l}{\partial \beta_j} = \frac{w_i(y_i - \mu_i)x_{ij}}{\phi}, \quad j = 1, \ldots, p. \tag{8.47}$$

The loglikelihood with the whole sample $y_1, \ldots, y_n$ is obtained by summing over all observations $i = 1, \ldots, n$. Setting the normal equations equal to zero then directly leads to maximum likelihood equations of the form (8.43). ∇

A related property of the standard link is the following.

Property 8.6.13 (Sufficient statistics and canonical links)
In a GLM, if the canonical link $\theta_i \equiv \eta_i = \sum_j x_{ij}\beta_j$ is used, the quantities $S_j = \sum_i w_i Y_i x_{ij}$, $j = 1, \ldots, p$, are a set of sufficient statistics.

Proof. We will prove this using the factorization criterion, hence by showing that the joint density of $Y_1, \ldots, Y_n$ can be factorized as

$$\begin{aligned} &f_{Y_1,\ldots,Y_n}(y_1, \ldots, y_n; \beta_1, \ldots, \beta_p) \\ &\quad = g(s_1, \ldots, s_p; \beta_1, \ldots, \beta_p) h(y_1, \ldots, y_n), \end{aligned} \tag{8.48}$$

for $s_j = \sum_i w_i\, y_i\, x_{ij}$, $j = 1, \dots, p$ and suitable functions $g(\cdot)$ and $h(\cdot)$. But we have

$$\begin{aligned}
&f_{Y_1,\dots,Y_n}(y_1, \dots, y_n; \beta_1, \dots, \beta_p) \\
&= \prod_{i=1}^{n} \exp\left(\frac{y_i\theta_i - b(\theta_i)}{\phi/w_i} + c(y_i; \phi/w_i)\right) \\
&= \exp \sum_i \frac{y_i \sum_j x_{ij}\, \beta_j - b\left(\sum_j x_{ij}\, \beta_j\right)}{\phi/w_i} \exp \sum_i c(y_i; \phi/w_i) \qquad (8.49)\\
&= \exp \frac{1}{\phi}\left[\sum_j \beta_j \sum_i w_i\, y_i\, x_{ij} - \sum_i w_i\, b\Big(\sum_j x_{ij}\, \beta_j\Big)\right] \\
&\quad \times \exp \sum_i c(y_i; \frac{\phi}{w_i}).
\end{aligned}$$

From this representation, the required functions $g(\cdot)$ and $h(\cdot)$ in (8.48) can be derived immediately. The fact that the support of Y does not depend on θ, nor on the β_j parameters, is essential in this derivation. ∇

Sometimes it happens in actuarial practice that not all the separate entries in a table are given, but only the marginal totals of rows and columns. If one uses a standard link, these marginal totals apparently are sufficient statistics, hence knowing only their outcomes, the maximum likelihood parameter estimates can still be determined. The standard link also has advantages when the optimization algorithm of Nelder and Wedderburn is used. It leads to somewhat less iteration steps being necessary, and also divergence is much more exceptional.

Example 8.6.14 (Canonical links for various error distributions)
As stated above, the canonical link is $\theta(\mu)$, and $\mu(\theta) = b'(\theta)$, so the canonical link is nothing but $g(\mu) = (b')^{-1}(\mu)$. The canonical links are listed in Table E. For the normal distributions with $b(\theta) = \frac{1}{2}\theta^2$, the canonical link is the identity function. For the Poisson and the Poisson multiples, we have $\mu(\theta) = e^\theta$ and hence the log-link is the standard link. For the gamma, the canonical link is the reciprocal, for the binomial it is the logit link $\theta = \log \frac{p}{1-p}$ (log-odds).

If $\theta \equiv \eta$ and moreover $\eta \equiv \mu$, then apparently $b'(\theta) = \theta$ holds, and the sequence of cumulants (8.38) implied by this belongs to the normal distribution. ∇

Example 8.6.15 (Threshold models: logit and probit analysis)
Assume that the observations Y_i denote the fractions of successes in n_i independent trials, $i = 1, \dots, n$, each with probability of success p_i. Further assume that a trial results in a success if the 'dose' administered to a person exceeds his tolerance X_{ik}, $k = 1, \dots, n_i$, which is a random variable having an $\mathrm{N}(\mu_i, \sigma^2)$ distribution. Here μ_i is a linear form in the ancillary variables. Apparently

$$p_i = \Phi(d_i;\, \mu_i, \sigma^2) = \Phi\left(\frac{d_i - \mu_i}{\sigma}\right). \tag{8.50}$$

Therefore, we have a valid GLM with a binomial distribution for the random component and with $\eta = \Phi^{-1}(p)$ as a link function. For the binomial distribution we have the following canonical link function:

$$\theta = \eta = \log\frac{p}{1-p}, \quad \text{so} \quad e^\eta = \frac{p}{1-p}, \quad 0 < p < 1. \tag{8.51}$$

Solving this for p leads to $p = e^\eta/(e^\eta + 1)$. Now if we replace the distribution of the tolerance X_i by a logistic(μ_i, σ) distribution with cdf $F_{X_i}(d) = e^{d^*}/(e^{d^*} + 1)$ for $d^* = (d - \mu_i)/\sigma$, it can easily be seen that we get a binomial GLM with standard link.

In case the threshold X_i is assumed to be normally distributed, we speak of probit analysis, in the other case of logit analysis. The second technique is nothing but a GLM involving a multiplicative model not for the probability of success p itself, but rather for the so-called *odds-ratio* $p/(1-p)$. Probit analysis can be applied in the same situations as logit analysis, and produces similar results.

Logit and probit models can be applied with credit insurance. Based on certain characteristics of the insured, the probability of default is estimated. Another application is the problem to determine probabilities of disability. In econometrics, analyses such as these are used for instance to estimate the probability that some household owns a car, given the number of persons in this household, their total income, and so on. ∇

The algorithm by Nelder and Wedderburn
In (8.45), we gave the set of equations to be fulfilled by the maximum likelihood parameter estimates $\hat{\beta}_j, j = 1, \dots, p$. One way to solve these equations is to use Newton-Raphson iteration, which, in a one-dimensional setting, transforms the current best guess x_t for the root of an equation $f(x) = 0$ into a hopefully better one x_{t+1} as follows:

$$x_{t+1} = x_t - (f'(x_t))^{-1} f(x_t). \tag{8.52}$$

For an n-dimensional optimization, this same formula is valid, except that the points x are now vectors, and the reciprocal is now the inverse of a matrix of partial derivatives. In view of (8.45), this means that we need the matrix of second derivatives of l, i.e., the *Hessian* matrix. The algorithm of Nelder and Wedderburn does not use the Hessian itself, but rather its expected value, the *information matrix*. The technique that arises in this way is called *Fisher's scoring technique*. It can be shown that the iteration step in this case boils down to solving a weighted regression problem.

8.7 EXERCISES

Section 8.2

1. Of the distributions mentioned in the random component of a GLM, give the density (including the range), the mean and the variance.
2. Show that if $X_i \sim \text{gamma}(\alpha, \beta_i)$ with parameters $\alpha = 1/\phi$ and $\beta_i = 1/(\phi\, \mu_i)$, all X_i have the same coefficient of variation, $i = 1, \ldots, n$. What is the skewness?

Section 8.3

1. Verify (8.4), (8.16) and (8.17). Also verify if (8.11) describes the maximum of (8.13) under assumption (8.14).
2. Show that the methods of Bailey-Simon, marginal totals and least squares, as well as the direct method, can all be written as methods of *weighted* marginal totals, where the following system is to be solved:

$$\sum_{i(j)} w_{ij}\, z_{ij}(\alpha_i\beta_j - y_{ij}) = 0 \quad \text{for all } j(i),$$

$$\begin{aligned} \text{where} \quad z_{ij} &= 1 + \frac{y_{ij}}{\alpha_i\, \beta_j} && \text{Bailey-Simon,} \\ &= 1 && \text{marginal totals,} \\ &= \alpha_i\, \beta_j && \text{least squares,} \\ &= \frac{1}{\alpha_i\, \beta_j} && \text{direct method.} \end{aligned}$$

3. Show that the additive model $\mathrm{E}[X_{ij}] = \alpha_i + \beta_j$ of the least squares method coincides with the one of the marginal totals.
4. Which requirement should the means and variances of $Y_{ij}/(\alpha_i\beta_j)$ fulfill in order to make (8.17) produce *optimal* estimates for α_i? (See Exercise 7.4.1.)
5. Starting from $\hat{\alpha}_1 = 1$, determine $\hat{\alpha}_2$, $\hat{\beta}_1$ and $\hat{\beta}_2$ in Example 8.3.12. Verify if the solution found for $\hat{\alpha}_1$ satisfies the corresponding equation in each system of equations. Determine the results for the different models after the first iteration step, with initial values $\hat{\beta}_j \equiv 1$, and after rescaling

such that $\hat{\alpha}_1 = 1$. Explain why the results for the Bailey-Simon method agree so closely with the ones for the marginal totals method.

6. In Example 8.3.12, compare the resulting total premium according to the different models. What happens if we divide all weights w_{ij} by 10?
7. Show that the least squares method leads to maximum likelihood estimators in case the S_{ij} have a normal distribution with variance $w_{ij}\sigma^2$.
8. What can be said about the sum of the residuals $\sum_{i,j}(s_{ij} - w_{ij}\hat{\alpha}_i\hat{\beta}_j)$ if the $\hat{\alpha}_i$ and the $\hat{\beta}_j$ are fitted by the four methods of this section?

Section 8.4

1. Verify if (8.23) is the scaled deviance for a Poisson distribution.
2. Verify if (8.26) is the scaled deviance for a gamma distribution.
3. Show that in the model of Property 8.3.9, the second term of (8.23) is always zero.
4. Also show that the second term of deviance (8.26) is zero in a multiplicative model for the expected values, if the parameters are estimated by the direct method.
5. The *deviance residuals*, see also Remark 8.2.4, for Poisson and gamma GLM's are defined as the ith term of the sum in (8.23) and (8.26) with the sign of $y_i - \hat{\mu}_i$. Using the inequality $t - 1 \geq \log t$ for $t \geq 0$, prove that these ith terms are non-negative.

Section 8.5

1. For $i = j = 3$, check if the models (8.27) and (8.28) lead to the fitted values for models IV and X as given in Table 8.1.
2. From Table 8.1, determine which values $\hat{\mu}$, $\hat{\alpha}_3$ and $\hat{\beta}_3$ were used for computing fv_1. With these, verify the value of $\hat{y}_{33}$.
3. For the models I–X, write down chains, as long as possible, of *nested* models, i.e., with less and less restrictions on the parameters. Sketch a graph with the models as nodes, and with edges between nodes that follow each other directly.
4. Determine how many degrees of freedom the model with main effects age class (geometrically), gender and region described in the closing remarks of this section has. Where can this model be put in the graph of the previous exercise?

Section 8.6

1. Prove the relations $\mathrm{E}\left[\frac{\partial l(Y)}{\partial \theta}\right] = 0$ as well as $\mathrm{E}\left[\frac{\partial^2 l(Y)}{\partial \theta^2}\right] + \mathrm{E}\left[\left(\frac{\partial l(Y)}{\partial \theta}\right)^2\right] = 0$, where $l(y) = \log f_Y(y;\theta,\phi)$ for f_Y as in (8.29). With these relations, derive the mean and the variance with l.
2. Check the validity of the entries in Table E for all distributions listed. Verify the reparametrizations, the canonical link, the cumulant function, the mean as a function of θ and the variance function. Also determine the function $c(y;\phi)$.

3. The marginal totals equations are fulfilled, by (8.43), for the Poisson distribution in case of a log-link. Prove that the same holds for the link functions $g(\mu) = \mu^\alpha$, $\alpha > 0$, by adding up the ML-equations, weighted by β_j. What is the consequence for the deviance of Poisson observations with this link function?
4. The same as the previous exercise, but now for gamma observations.
5. Prove that for all members of the exponential dispersion family, the maximum likelihood estimator for μ_i is $\widetilde{\mu}_i = y_i$ under the full model.
6. Show that in general, the scaled deviance equals

$$\frac{D}{\phi} = \frac{2}{\phi} \sum_i w_i \{y_i(\widetilde{\theta}_i - \hat{\theta}_i) - [b(\widetilde{\theta}_i) - b(\hat{\theta}_i)]\}$$

7. From the expression in the previous exercise, derive expressions for the scaled deviances for the normal, Poisson, binomial, gamma and inverse Gaussian distributions.
8. Prove the statements about Esscher transforms in Remark 8.6.10.
9. What does Property 8.6.12 imply about the sum of the residuals if there is a constant term in the model? And if there is a factor in the model? (See also Exercise 8.6.3.)

9

IBNR techniques

9.1 INTRODUCTION

Up to just a few decades ago, non-life insurance portfolios were financed through a pay-as-you-go system. All claims in a particular year were paid from the premium income of that same year, irrespective of the year in which the claim originated. The financial balance in the portfolio was realized by ensuring that there was an equivalence between the premiums collected and the claims paid in a particular financial year. Technical gains and losses arose because of the difference between the premium income in a year and the claims paid during the year.

The claims originating in a particular year often cannot be finalized in that year. For instance, long legal procedures are the rule with liability insurance claims, but there may also be other causes for delay, such as the fact that the exact size of the claim is hard to assess. Also, the claim may be filed only later, or more payments than one have to be made, as in disability insurance. All these factors will lead to delay of the actual payment of the claims. The claims that have already occurred, but are not sufficiently known, are foreseeable in the sense that one knows that payments will have to be made, but not how much the total payment is going to be. Consider also the case that a premium is paid for the claims in a particular year, and a claim arises of which the insurer is not notified as yet. Here also, we have losses that have to be reimbursed in future years.

As seems proper and logical, such claims are now connected to the years for which the premiums were actually paid. This means that reserves have to be kept regarding claims which are known to exist, but for which the eventual size is unknown at the time the reserves have to be set. For claims like these, several acronyms are in use. One has IBNR claims (Incurred But Not Reported) for claims that have occurred but have not been filed. Hence the name IBNR methods, IBNR claims and IBNR reserves for all quantities of this type. There are also RBNS claims (Reported But Not Settled), for claims which are known but not (completely) paid. Other acronyms are IBNFR, IBNER and RBNFS, where the F is for Fully, the E for Enough. Large claims which are known to the insurer are often handled on a case-by-case basis.

When modelling these situations, one generally starts from a so-called *run-off triangle*, which is for instance compiled in the following way:

1. We start in 2000 with a portfolio consisting of a number of contracts. Let us assume that the total claims to be paid are fully known on January 1, 2008, eight years after the end of this year of origin;

2. The claims occurring in the year 2000 have to be paid from the premiums collected in 2000;

3. These payments have been made in the year 2000 itself, but also in the years 2001–2007;

4. In the same way, for the claims pertaining to the year of origin 2001, one has the claims which are known in the years 2001–2007, and it is unknown what has to be paid in 2008;

5. For the year 2005, the known claims are the ones paid in the period 2005–2007, but there are also unknown ones that will come up in the years 2008 and after;

6. For the claims concerning the premiums paid in 2007, on December 31, 2007 only the payments made in 2007 are known, but we can expect that more payments will have to be made in and after 2008. We may expect that the claims develop in a pattern similar to the one of the claims in 2000–2007.

Year of origin	Development year 1	2	3	4	5	6	7	8
2000	101	153	52	17	14	3	4	1
2001	99	121	76	32	10	3	1	
2002	110	182	80	20	21	2		
2003	160	197	82	38	19			
2004	161	254	85	46				
2005	185	201	86					
2006	178	261						
2007	168							

Table 9.1 A run-off triangle with payments by development year (horizontally) and year of origin (vertically)

The development pattern can schematically be depicted as in the triangle of Table 9.1. The numbers in the triangle are the known total payments, grouped by year of origin i (row-wise) and development year j (column-wise). The row corresponding to year 2002 contains the six numbers which are known on December 31, 2007. The third element in this row, for instance, denotes the claims incurred in 2002, but paid for in the third year of development, hence 2004. In the triangle of Table 9.1, we look at new contracts only, which may occur for instance when a new type of policy was issued for the first time in 2000. The business written in this year on average has had only half a year to produce claims in 2000, which is why the numbers in the first column are somewhat lower than those in the second. The numbers on the diagonal with $i+j-1=c$ denote the payments that were made in calendar year c. There are many ways to group these same data into a triangle, but the one given in Table 9.1 is the customary one. On the basis of the claim figures in Table 9.1, we want to make predictions about claims that will be paid, or filed, in future calendar years. These future years are to be found in the bottom-right part of Table 9.1. The goal of the actuarial IBNR techniques is to predict these figures, so as to complete the triangle into a square. The total of the figures found in the lower right triangle is the total of the claims that will have to be paid in the future from the premiums that were collected in the period 2000–2007. This total is precisely the reserve to be kept. We assume that the development pattern lasts eight years. It is obvious that there are many branches, notably in liability, where claims may still be filed after a time longer than eight years. In that case, we have to make predictions about development years after the seventh, of which our run-off triangle provides no data. We not only have to complete a square, but we have to extend the triangle into a rectangle containing more development years. The usual practice is to assume that the development procedure is stopped after a number of years, and to apply a correction factor for the payments made after the development period considered.

The future payments are estimated following well-established actuarial practice. Sometimes one central estimator is given, but also sometimes a whole range of possibilities is considered, containing both the estimated values and, conceivably, the actual results. Estimates of the mean as well as of the variance of the results are very important. Methods to determine the reserves have been developed that each meet specific requirements, have different model assumptions, and produce different estimates. In practice, the method which is the most likely to produce the 'best' estimator is used to determine the estimate of the expected claims, while the results of other methods are used as a means to judge the variation of the stochastic result, which is of course a rather unscientific approach.

Using the triangle in Table 9.1, we can give various methods that each reflect the influence of a number of exogenous factors. In the direction of the year of origin, variation in the size of the portfolio will have an influence on the claim figures. On the other hand, for the factor development year (horizontally), changes in the claim handling procedure as well as in the speed of finalization of the claims will produce a change. The figures on the diagonals correspond to payments in a particular calendar year. Such figures will change due to monetary inflation, but also by changing jurisprudence or increasing claim proneness. As an example, in liability insurance for the medical profession the risk increases each year, and if the amounts awarded by judges get larger and larger, this is visible along the diagonals. In other words, the separation models which have as factors the year of development and the calendar year would be the best choice to describe the evolution of portfolios like these.

Obviously, one should try to get as accurate a picture as possible about the stochastic mechanism that produced the claims, test this model if possible, and estimate the parameters of this model optimally to construct good predictors for the unknown observations. Very important is how the variance of claim figures is related to the mean value. This variance can be more or less constant, it can be proportional to the mean, proportional to the square of the mean, or have some other relation with it. See the following section, as well as the chapter on Generalized Linear Models.

Just as with many rating techniques, see the previous chapter, in the actuarial literature quite often a heuristic method to complete an IBNR triangle was described first, and a sound statistical fundament was provided only later. There is a very basic GLM for which the ML-estimators can be computed by the well-known *chain ladder method*. On the other hand it is possible to give a model which involves a less rigid statistical structure and in which the calculations of the chain ladder method produce an optimal estimate in the sense of mean squared error. We give a general GLM-model, special cases of which can be shown to boil down to familiar methods of IBNR estimation such as the arithmetic and the geometric separation methods, as well as the chain ladder method. A numerical illustration is provided in Section 9.3.

9.2 A GLM THAT ENCOMPASSES VARIOUS IBNR METHODS

In this section we present a Generalized Linear Model that contains as special cases some often used and traditional actuarial methods to complete an IBNR triangle. For variants of these methods, and for other possible methods, we refer to the literature. In Table 9.2, the random variables X_{ij} for $i, j = 1, 2, \ldots, t$ denote the claim figure for year of origin i and year of development j, meaning that the claims were paid in calendar year $i + j - 1$. For (i, j) combinations with $i + j \leq t + 1$, X_{ij} has already been observed, otherwise it is a future observation. As well as claims actually paid, these figures may also be used to denote quantities such as loss ratios. As a model we take a multiplicative model, with a parameter for each row i, each column j and each diagonal $k = i + j - 1$, as follows:

$$X_{ij} \approx \alpha_i \cdot \beta_j \cdot \gamma_k. \tag{9.1}$$

The deviation of the observation on the left hand side from its model value on the right hand side is attributed to chance. As one sees, if we assume further that the random variables X_{ij} are independent and restrict their distribution to be in the exponential dispersion family, (9.1) is a Generalized Linear Model in the sense of the previous chapter, where the expected value of X_{ij} is the exponent of the linear form $\log \alpha_i + \log \beta_j + \log \gamma_{i+j-1}$, such that there is a logarithmic link. Year of origin, year of development and calendar year act as explanatory variables for the observation X_{ij}. We will determine maximum likelihood estimates of the

Year of origin	Development year 1	$\cdots$	n	$\cdots$	t
1	X_{11}	$\cdots$	X_{1n}	$\cdots$	X_{1t}
$\vdots$	$\vdots$		$\vdots$		$\vdots$
$t-n+1$	$X_{t-n+1,1}$	$\cdots$	$X_{t-n+1,n}$	$\cdots$	$X_{t-n+1,t}$
$\vdots$	$\vdots$		$\vdots$		$\vdots$
t	X_{t1}	$\cdots$	X_{tn}	$\cdots$	X_{tt}

Table 9.2 Random variables in a run-off triangle

parameters α_i, β_j and γ_k, under various assumptions for the probability distribution of the X_{ij}. It will turn out that in this simple way, we can generate many widely used IBNR techniques.

Having found estimates of the parameters, it is easy to extend the triangle to a square, simply by taking

$$\hat{X}_{ij} \approx \hat{\alpha}_i \cdot \hat{\beta}_j \cdot \hat{\gamma}_k. \tag{9.2}$$

A problem is that we have no data on the values of the γ_k for calendar years k with $k > t$. The problem can be solved, for instance, by assuming that the γ_k have a geometric relation, with $\gamma_k \propto \gamma^k$ for some real number γ.

Chain ladder method

The first method that can be derived from model (9.1) is the *chain ladder* method. We assume the following about the distributions:

$$X_{ij} \sim \text{Poisson}(\alpha_i\beta_j) \text{ independent; } \gamma_k \equiv 1; \tag{9.3}$$

the parameters α_i and β_j are estimated by maximum likelihood.

The idea behind the chain ladder method is that in any development year, about the same total percentage of the claims from each year of origin will have been settled. In other words, in the run-off triangle, the columns are proportional. But the same holds for the rows, since all the figures in a row are the same multiple of the payment in year of development 1. One may determine the parameters by least squares or by a heuristic method ('mechanical smoothing'). This last method boils down to maximizing the likelihood, but proves to be less reliable if the assumption

Year of origin	1	⋯	Development year n	⋯	t	Total
1	$\alpha_1\beta_1$		$\alpha_1\beta_n$		$\alpha_1\beta_t$	R_1
⋮						⋮
$t-n+1$	$\alpha_{t-n+1}\beta_1$		$\alpha_{t-n+1}\beta_n$			R_{t-n+1}
⋮						⋮
t	$\alpha_t\beta_1$					R_t
Total	K_1	⋯	K_n	⋯	K_t	

Table 9.3 The marginal totals equations in a run-off triangle

about the proportions settled each year is violated. Since for instance in medical liability, many more lawsuits are started than there used to be, it is clear that the premise of the ratios of the columns remaining constant cannot be upheld. This can be redressed by introducing other assumptions like a linear development of the ratio between successive columns as a function of the year of origin. Such methods are then variants of the chain ladder method.

To show how the likelihood maximization problem (9.3) can be solved, we first remark that one of the parameters is superfluous, since if we replace all α_i and β_j by $\delta\alpha_i$ and β_j/δ we get the same expected values. To resolve this ambiguity, we impose an additional restriction on the parameters. A natural one is to impose $\beta_1 + \cdots + \beta_t = 1$, since this allows the β_j to be interpreted as the fraction of claims settled in development year j, and α_i as the 'volume' of year of origin i: it is the total of the payments made. We know that the observations X_{ij}, $i, j = 1, \ldots, t$; $i + j \leq t$ follow a Poisson distribution with a logarithmic model for the means. By Property 8.3.9 it follows that the marginal totals of the triangle, hence the row sums R_i and the column sums K_j of the observed figures X_{ij}, must be equal to the predictions $\sum_j \hat{\alpha}_i\hat{\beta}_j$ and $\sum_i \hat{\alpha}_i\hat{\beta}_j$ for these quantities. By the special triangular shape of the data, the resulting system of marginal totals equations admits a simple solution method, see also Table 9.3.

1. From the first row sum equality $\hat{\alpha}_1(\hat{\beta}_1 + \cdots + \hat{\beta}_t) = R_1$ it follows that $\hat{\alpha}_1 = R_1$. Then from $\hat{\alpha}_1\hat{\beta}_t = K_t$ we find the value of $\hat{\beta}_t$.

	1	2	3	4	5
1	A	A	A	B	$\bullet$
2	A	A	A	B	
3	C	C	C	$\star$	
4	D	D	$\hat{D}$	$\star\star$	
5	$\bullet$				

Table 9.4 Illustrating the completion of a run-off rectangle with chain ladder predictions

2. Assume that, for a certain $n < t$, we have found estimates $\hat{\beta}_{n+1}, \ldots, \hat{\beta}_t$ and $\hat{\alpha}_1, \ldots, \hat{\alpha}_{t-n}$. Then we look at the following two marginal totals equations:

$$\begin{aligned} \hat{\alpha}_{t-n+1}(\hat{\beta}_1 + \cdots + \hat{\beta}_n) &= R_{t-n+1}; \\ (\hat{\alpha}_1 + \cdots + \hat{\alpha}_{t-n+1})\hat{\beta}_n &= K_n. \end{aligned} \tag{9.4}$$

   By the fact that we take $\hat{\beta}_1 + \cdots + \hat{\beta}_t = 1$, the first of these equations directly produces a value for $\hat{\alpha}_{t-n+1}$, and then we can compute $\hat{\beta}_n$ from the second one.

3. Repeat step 2 for $n = t-1, t-2, \ldots, 1$.

We will illustrate by an example how we can express the predictions for the unobserved part of the rectangle resulting from these parameter estimates in the observations, see Table 9.4. Consider the $(3,4)$ element in this table, which is denoted by $\star$. This is a claim figure for the next calendar year 6, which is just beyond the edge of the observed figures. The prediction of this element is

$$\hat{X}_{34} = \hat{\alpha}_3\hat{\beta}_4 = \frac{\hat{\alpha}_3(\hat{\beta}_1 + \hat{\beta}_2 + \hat{\beta}_3)\hat{\beta}_4(\hat{\alpha}_1 + \hat{\alpha}_2)}{(\hat{\alpha}_1 + \hat{\alpha}_2)(\hat{\beta}_1 + \hat{\beta}_2 + \hat{\beta}_3)} = \frac{C_\Sigma \times B_\Sigma}{A_\Sigma}. \tag{9.5}$$

Here B_Σ, for instance, denotes the total of the B-elements in Table 9.4, which are observed values. The last equality in (9.5) is valid because the estimates $\hat{\alpha}$ and $\hat{\beta}$ satisfy the marginal totals property, and B_Σ and C_Σ are directly row and column sums of the observations, while $A_\Sigma = R_1 + R_2 - (K_5 + K_4)$ is expressible in these quantities as well.

The prediction $\star\star$ for $\hat{X}_{44}$ can be computed from the marginal totals in exactly the same way, by

$$\hat{X}_{44} = \frac{D_\Sigma \times B_\Sigma}{A_\Sigma}, \tag{9.6}$$

where the sum D_Σ includes $\hat{D}$. Note that this is not an actual observation but a prediction for it, constructed as above. In Exercise 9.2.1, the reader is asked to verify that exactly the same prediction is obtained by taking

$$\hat{X}_{44} = \frac{D_\Sigma \times (B_\Sigma + \star)}{A_\Sigma + C_\Sigma}, \tag{9.7}$$

hence by following the same procedure as for an observation in the next calendar year. This procedure is exactly how the rectangle is completed from the run-off triangle in the basic chain ladder method. Note that this procedure produces the same estimates to complete the square if we exchange the roles of development year and year of origin, hence take the mirror image of the triangle around the diagonal.

The basic principle of the chain ladder method admits many variants. One may wonder if there is indeed proportionality between the columns. Undoubtedly, this is determined by effects that operate along the axis describing the year of origin of the claims. By the chain ladder method, only the run-off pattern can be captured, given that all other factors, at least the ones having an influence on the proportion of claims settled, remain unchanged over time.

Arithmetic separation method

In both the arithmetic and the geometric separation method the claim figures X_{ij} are also explained by two aspects of time, namely a calendar year effect γ_k, where $k = i+j-1$, and a development year effect β_j. So inflation and run-off pattern are the determinants for the claim figures in this case. For the *arithmetic separation method* we assume

$$X_{ij} \sim \text{Poisson}(\beta_j \gamma_k) \text{ independent; } \alpha_i \equiv 1. \tag{9.8}$$

Again, β_j and γ_k are estimated by maximum likelihood. Since this is again a Poisson model with log-link, because of Property 8.3.9 the marginal totals property must hold here as well. In model (9.8) these marginal totals are the column sums and the sums over the diagonals, with $i + j - 1 = k$.

In the separation models, one assumes that in each year of development a fixed percentage is settled, and that there are additional effects that operate in the diagonal direction (from top-left to bottom-right) in the run-off triangle. So this model describes best the situation that there is inflation in the claim figures, or when the risk increases by other causes. The medical liability risk, for instance, increases every year. This increase is characterized by an index factor for each calendar year, which is a constant for the observations parallel to the diagonal. One supposes that in Table 9.3, the random variables X_{ij} are average loss figures, where the total loss is divided by the number of claims, for year of origin i and development year j.

By a method very similar to the chain ladder computations, we can also obtain parameter estimates in the arithmetic separation method. This method was originally described in Verbeek (1972), and goes as follows. We have $\mathrm{E}[X_{ij}] = \beta_j \gamma_{i+j-1}$. Again, the parameters β_j, $j = 1, \ldots, t$ describe the proportions settled in development year j. Assuming that the claims are all settled after t development years, we have $\beta_1 + \cdots + \beta_t = 1$. Using the marginal totals equations, cf. Table 9.3, we can determine directly the optimal factor $\hat{\gamma}_t$, reflecting base level times inflation, as the sum of the observations on the long diagonal $\sum_i X_{i,t+1-i}$. Since β_t occurs in the final column only, we have $\hat{\beta}_t = \hat{X}_{1t}/\hat{\gamma}_t$. With this, we can compute $\hat{\gamma}_{t-1}$, and then $\hat{\beta}_{t-1}$, and so on. Just as with the chain ladder method, the estimates thus constructed satisfy the marginal totals equations, and hence are maximum likelihood estimates because of Property 8.3.9.

To fill out the remaining part of the square, we also need values for the parameters $\gamma_{t+1}, \ldots, \gamma_{2t}$, to be multiplied by the corresponding $\hat{\beta}_j$ estimate. We find values for these parameters by extrapolating the sequence $\hat{\gamma}_1, \ldots, \hat{\gamma}_t$ in some way. This can be done with many techniques, for instance loglinear extrapolation.

Geometric separation method

The *geometric separation method* involves maximum likelihood estimation of the parameters in the following statistical model:

$$\log(X_{ij}) \sim N\left(\log(\beta_j \gamma_k), \sigma^2\right) \text{ independent; } \alpha_i \equiv 1. \tag{9.9}$$

Here σ^2 is an unknown variance. We get an ordinary regression model with $\mathrm{E}[\log X_{ij}] = \log \beta_j + \log \gamma_{i+j-1}$. Its parameters can be estimated in the usual way, but they can also be estimated recursively in the way described above, starting from $\prod_j \beta_j = 1$.

Note that the values $\beta_j \gamma_{i+j-1}$ in this model are *not* the expected values of X_{ij}. In fact, they are only the medians; we have

$$\mathrm{E}[X_{ij}] = e^{\sigma^2/2} \beta_j \gamma_{i+j-1} \quad \text{and} \quad \Pr[X_{ij} \leq \beta_j \gamma_{i+j-1}] = \frac{1}{2}. \tag{9.10}$$

De Vijlder's least squares method

In De Vijlder's least squares method, we assume that $\gamma_k \equiv 1$ holds, while α_i and β_j are determined by minimizing the sum of squares $\sum_{i,j}(X_{ij} - \alpha_i \beta_j)^2$. But this is tantamount to determining α_i and β_j by maximum likelihood in the following model:

$$X_{ij} \sim N(\alpha_i \beta_j, \sigma^2) \text{ independent; } \gamma_k \equiv 1. \tag{9.11}$$

Just as with the chain ladder method, in this method we assume that the payments for a particular year of origin/year of development combination result from two elements. First, a parameter characterizing the year of origin, proportional to the size of the portfolio in that year. Second, a parameter determining which proportion of the claims is settled through the period that claims develop. The parameters are estimated by least squares.

9.3 ILLUSTRATION OF SOME IBNR METHODS

Obviously, introducing parameters for the three time aspects year of origin, year of development and calendar year sometimes leads to overparametrization. From all these parameters, many should be dropped, i.e., taken equal to 1. Others might be required to be equal, for instance by grouping classes having different values for some factor together. Admitting classes to be grouped leads to many models being considered simultaneously, and it is sometimes hard to construct proper significance tests in these situations. Also, a classification of which the classes are ordered, such as age class or bonus-malus step, might lead to parameters giving a fixed increase per class, except perhaps at the boundaries or for some other special class. In a loglinear model, replacing arbitrary parameter values, associated with factor levels (classes), by a geometric progression in these parameters is easily achieved by replacing the dummified factor by the actual levels again, or in GLIM parlance, treating this variable as a variate instead of as a factor. Replacing arbitrary values α_i, with $\alpha_1 = 1$, by a geometric progression α^{i-1} for some real α means that we assume the portfolio to grow, or shrink, by a fixed percentage each year. Doing the same to the parameters β_j means that the proportion settled decreases by a fixed fraction with each development year. Quite often, the first development year will be different from the others, for instance because only three quarters are counted as the first year. In that case, one does best to allow a separate parameter for the first year, taking parameters $\beta_1, \beta^2, \beta^3, \ldots$ for some real numbers β_1 and β. Instead of with the original t parameters $\beta_1, \ldots, \beta_t$, one works with only two parameters. By introducing a new dummy explanatory variable to indicate whether the calendar year $k = i+j-1$ with observation X_{ij} is before or after k_0, and letting it contribute a factor 1 or δ to the mean, respectively, one gets a model involving a year in which the inflation was different from the standard fixed inflation of the other years.

From the difference of the maximally attainable likelihood and the one of a particular model, one may determine a certain 'distance' between the data and the predictions. For this distance, we take the (scaled) deviance introduced in the previous chapter. Using this, one may test if it is worthwhile to complicate a model by introducing more parameters. For a nested model, of which the parameter set can be constructed by imposing linear restrictions on the parameters of the original model, it is possible to judge if the distance between data and predictions is 'significantly' larger. It proves that this difference in distance, under the null-hypothesis that the eliminated parameters are superfluous, is approximately χ^2 distributed. In similar fashion, the 'goodness of fit' of non-nested models can be compared.

Some software to solve regression problems leaves it to the user to resolve the problems arising from introducing parameters with variables which are dependent of the others, the so-called 'dummy trap' (multicollinearity). Other programs are more convenient in this respect. For instance if one takes all three effects in (9.1) geometric, with as predictors

$$\hat{X}_{ij} = \hat{\mu}\hat{\alpha}^{i-1}\hat{\beta}^{j-1}\hat{\gamma}^{i+j-2}, \tag{9.12}$$

GLIM simply proceeds as if the last of these three parameters is equal to 1. Notice that by introducing $\hat{\mu}$ in (9.12), all three parameter estimates can have the form $\hat{\alpha}^{i-1}$, $\hat{\beta}^{j-1}$ and $\hat{\gamma}^{i+j-2}$. In the same way, we can take $\alpha_1 = \beta_1 = \gamma_1 = 1$ in (9.1). The parameter $\mu = \mathrm{E}[X_{11}]$ is the level in the first year of origin and development year 1. It can be shown that we get the same predictions using either of the models $\mathrm{E}[X_{ij}] = \mu\alpha_i\beta^{j-1}$ and $\mathrm{E}[X_{ij}] = \mu\alpha_i\gamma^{i+j-2}$. Completing the triangle of Table 9.1 into a square by using Model VIIII produces Table 9.5. The column 'Total' contains the row sums of the estimated future payments, hence exactly the amount to be reserved regarding each year of origin. The figures in the top-left part are estimates

Year of origin	Development year 1	2	3	4	5	6	7	8	Total
2000	102.3	140.1	59.4	25.2	10.7	4.5	1.9	0.8|	0.0
2001	101.6	139.2	59.1	25.0	10.6	4.5	1.9|	0.8	0.8
2002	124.0	169.9	72.1	30.6	13.0	5.5|	2.3	1.0	3.3
2003	150.2	205.8	87.3	37.0	15.7|	6.7	2.8	1.2	10.7
2004	170.7	233.9	99.2	42.1|	17.8	7.6	3.2	1.4	30.0
2005	159.9	219.1	92.9|	39.4	16.7	7.1	3.0	1.3	67.5
2006	185.2	253.8|	107.6	45.7	19.4	8.2	3.5	1.5	185.8
2007	168.0|	230.2	97.6	41.4	17.6	7.4	3.2	1.3	398.7

Table 9.5 The claim figures of Table 9.1 estimated by Model VIII. The last column gives the totals for all the future predicted payments.

of the already observed values, the ones in the bottom-right part are predictions for future payments. To judge which model best fits the data, we estimated a few models for (9.1), all assuming the observations to be Poisson$(\alpha_i\beta_j\gamma_{i+j-1})$. See Table 9.6. Restrictions like $\beta_j = \beta^{j-1}$ or $\gamma_k \equiv 1$ were imposed to reproduce the various models from the previous section. The reader may verify why in model I, one may choose $\gamma_8 = 1$ without loss of generality. This means that model I has only 6 more parameters to be estimated than model II. Notice that for model I with $\mathrm{E}[X_{ij}] = \mu\alpha_i\beta_j\gamma_{i+j-1}$, there are $3(t-1)$ parameters to be estimated from $t(t+1)/2$ observations, hence model I only makes sense if $t \geq 4$.

All other models are nested in Model I, since its set of parameters contains all other ones as a subset. The predictions for model I best fit the data. About the deviances and the corresponding numbers of degrees of freedom, the following can be said. The chain ladder model II is not rejected statistically against the fullest model I on a 95% level, since it contains six parameters less, and the χ^2 critical value is 12.6 while the difference in scaled deviance is only 12.3. The arithmetic separation model III fits the data approximately as well as model II. Model IV with an arbitrary run-off pattern β_j and a constant inflation γ is equivalent to model V, which has a constant rate of growth for the portfolio. In Exercise 9.3.3, the reader is asked to explain why these two models are identical. Model IV, which is nested in III and has six parameters less, predicts significantly worse. In the same way, V is worse than II. Models VI and VII again are identical. Their fit is bad. Model VIII, with a geometric development pattern except for the first year, seems to be the winner: with five parameters less, its fit is not significantly worse than model II in which it is nested. It does fit better than model VII in which the first column

Model	Parameters used	Df	Deviance
I	$\mu, \alpha_i, \beta_j, \gamma_k$	15	25.7
II	μ, α_i, β_j	21	38.0
III	μ, β_j, γ_k	21	36.8
IV	$\mu, \beta_j, \gamma^{k-1}$	27	59.9
V	$\mu, \alpha^{i-1}, \beta_j$	27	59.9
VI	$\mu, \alpha_i, \gamma^{k-1}$	27	504.
VII	$\mu, \alpha_i, \beta^{j-1}$	27	504.
VIII	$\mu, \alpha_i, \beta_1, \beta^{j-1}$	26	46.0
IX	$\mu, \alpha^{i-1}, \beta_1, \beta^{j-1}$	32	67.9
X	$\mu, \alpha^{i-1}, \beta^{j-1}$	33	582.
XI	μ	35	2656

Table 9.6 Parameter set, degrees of freedom (= number of observations minus number of estimated parameters), and deviance for several models applied to the data of Table 9.1.

is not treated separately. Comparing VIII with IX, we see that a constant rate of growth in the portfolio must be rejected in favor of an arbitrary growth pattern. In model X, there is a constant rate of growth as well as a geometric development pattern. The fit is bad, mainly because the first column is so different.

From model XI, having only a constant term, we see that the 'percentage of explained deviance' of model VIII is more than 98%. But even model IX, which contains only a constant term and three other parameters, already explains 97.4% of the deviation.

The estimated model VIII gives the following predictions:

$$\text{VIII:} \quad \hat{X}_{ij} = 102.3 \times \begin{bmatrix} i=1: & 1.00 \\ i=2: & 0.99 \\ i=3: & 1.21 \\ i=4: & 1.47 \\ i=5: & 1.67 \\ i=6: & 1.56 \\ i=7: & 1.81 \\ i=8: & 1.64 \end{bmatrix} \times 3.20^{j\neq 1} \times 0.42^{j-1}, \qquad (9.13)$$

where $j \neq 1$ should be read as a Boolean expression, with value 1 if true, 0 if false (in this case, for the special column with $j = 1$). Model IX leads to the following

Year of origin	Development year 1	2	3	4	5	6	7	8
2000	62	146	117	175	203	212	406	318
2001	133	122	96	379	455	441	429	
2002	148	232	120	481	312	390		
2003	119	185	223	171	162			
2004	93	109	87	190				
2005	33	129	176					
2006	237	179						
2007	191							

Table 9.7 Average payments corresponding to the numbers of payments in Table 9.1.

estimates:

$$\text{IX:}\quad \hat{X}_{ij} = 101.1 \times 1.10^{i-1} \times 3.34^{j\neq 1} \times 0.42^{j-1}. \tag{9.14}$$

The Poisson distribution with year of origin as well as year of development as explanatory variables, thus the chain ladder method, is appropriate to model the number of claims. Apart from the numbers of claims given in Table 9.1, we also know the average claim size; it can be found in Table 9.7. For these claim sizes, the portfolio size, characterized by the factors α_i, is irrelevant. The inflation, hence the calendar year, is an important factor, and so is the development year, since only large claims lead to delay in settlement. So for this situation, the separation models are more suited. We have estimated the average claim sizes under the assumption that they arose from a gamma distribution with a constant coefficient of variation, with a multiplicative model.

The various models resulted in Table 9.8. As one sees, the nesting structure in the models is $7 \subset 6 \subset 4/5 \subset 3 \subset 2 \subset 1$; models 4 and 5 are both between 6 and 3, but they are not nested in one another. We have scaled the deviances in such a way that the fullest model 1 has a scaled deviance equal to the number of degrees of freedom, hence 15. This way, we can test the significance of the model refinements by comparing the gain in scaled deviance to the critical value of the χ^2 distribution with as a parameter the number of extra parameters estimated. A statistically significant step in both chains is the step from model 7 to 6. Taking the development parameters β_j arbitrary as in model 5, instead of geometric β^{j-1}

Model	Parameters used	Df	Deviance
1	$\mu, \alpha_i, \beta_j, \gamma_k$	15	15.0
2	μ, β_j, γ_k	21	30.2
3	$\mu, \beta_j, \gamma^{k-1}$	27	36.8
4	$\mu, \beta^{j-1}, \gamma^{k-1}$	33	39.5
5	μ, β_j	28	38.7
6	μ, β^{j-1}	34	41.2
7	μ	35	47.2

Table 9.8 Parameters, degrees of freedom and deviance for various models applied to the average claim sizes of Table 9.7.

as in model 6, does not significantly improve the fit. Refining model 6 to model 4 by introducing a parameter for inflation γ^{k-1} also does not lead to a significant improvement. Refining model 4 to model 3, nor model 3 to model 2, improves the fit significantly, but model 1 is significantly better than model 2. Still, we prefer the simple model 6, if only because model 6 is not dominated by model 1, because at the cost of 19 extra parameters, the gain in scaled deviance is only 26.2. So the best estimates are obtained from model 6. It gives an initial level of 129 in the first year of development, increasing to $129 \times 1.17^7 = 397$ in the eighth year. Notice that if the fit is not greatly improved by taking the coefficients γ_{i+j-1} arbitrary instead of geometric or constant, it is better either to ignore inflation or to use a fixed level, possibly with a break in the trend somewhere, otherwise one still has the problem of finding extrapolated values of $\gamma_{t+1}, \ldots, \gamma_{2t}$.

By combining estimated average claim sizes by year of origin and year of development with the estimated claim numbers, see Table 9.5, we get the total amounts to be reserved. These are given in Table 9.9, under the heading 'Total est.'. The corresponding model is found by combining both multiplicative models 6 and IX, see (9.14); it leads to the following estimated total payments:

$$6 \times \text{IX:} \quad \hat{X}_{ij} = 13041 \times 1.10^{i-1} \times 3.34^{j\neq 1} \times 0.46^{j-1}. \tag{9.15}$$

This model can also be used if, as is usual in practice, one is not content with a square of observed and predicted values, but also wants estimates concerning these years of origin for development years after the one that has last been observed, hence a rectangle of predicted values. The total estimated payments for year of

Year of origin	1	2	3	Development year 4	5	6	7	8	Total paid	Total est.
'00	6262	22338	6084	2975	2842	636	1624	318|	43079	0
'01	13167	14762	7296	12128	4550	1323	429|	361	53655	361
'02	16280	42224	9600	9620	6552	780|	800	398	85056	1198
'03	19040	36445	18286	6498	3078|	1772	881	438	83347	3092
'04	14973	27686	7395	8740|	3926	1952	971	483	58794	7331
'05	6105	25929	15136|	8696	4324	2150	1069	532	47170	16771
'06	42186	46719|	19262	9578	4762	2368	1178	586	88905	37733
'07	32088|	42665	21215	10549	5245	2608	1297	645	32088	84224

Table 9.9 Observed and predicted total claims corresponding to the Tables 9.1 and 9.5. Under Total paid, one finds the total of the payments made so far, under Total est., the estimated remaining payments that have to be made.

origin i are equal to $\sum_{j=1}^{\infty} \hat{X}_{ij}$. Obviously, these are finite only if the coefficient for each development year in models 6 and IX combined is less than 1 in (9.15).

Remark 9.3.1 (Variance of the estimated IBNR totals)
To estimate the variance of the IBNR totals is vital in practice because it enables one to give a prediction interval for these estimates. If the model chosen is the correct one and the parameter estimates are unbiased, this variance is built up from one part describing parameter uncertainty and another part describing the volatility of the process. If we assume that in Table 9.5 the model is correct and the parameter estimates coincide with the actual values, the estimated row totals are predictions of Poisson random variables. As these random variables have a variance equal to this mean, and the yearly totals are independent, the total estimated process variance is equal to the total estimated mean, hence $0.8 + \cdots + 398.7 = 696.8 = 26.4^2$. If there is overdispersion present in the model, the variance must be multiplied by the estimated overdispersion factor. The actual variance of course also includes the variation of the estimated mean, but this is harder to come by. Again assuming that all parameters have been correctly estimated and that the model is also correct, including the independence of claim sizes and claim numbers, the figures in Table 9.9 are predictions for compound Poisson random variables with mean $\lambda\mu_2$. The parameters λ of the numbers of claims can be obtained from Table 9.5, the second moments μ_2 of the gamma distributed payments can be derived from the estimated means in (9.13) together with the estimated dispersion parameter. Doray (1996) gives UMVUEs of the mean and variance of IBNR claims for a model with lognormal claim figures, explained by row and column factors. ∇

Remark 9.3.2 ('The' stochastic model behind chain ladder)
As we have shown, ML-estimation in a model with independent Poisson$(\alpha_i\beta_j)$ variables X_{ij} can be performed using the algorithm known as the chain ladder method. Mack (1993) has described a less restrictive set of distributional assumptions under which doing these calculations makes sense. Aiming for a distribution-free model, he cannot specify a likelihood to be maximized, so he endeavors to find minimum variance unbiased estimators instead. ∇

9.4 EXERCISES

Section 9.1

1. In how many ways can the data in Table 9.1 be organized in a table, by year of origin, year of development and calendar year, vertically or horizontally, in increasing or decreasing order?

Section 9.2

1. Show that (9.6) and (9.7) indeed produce the same estimate.
2. Prove (9.10). What is the mode of the random variables X_{ij} in model (9.9)?
3. Apply the chain ladder method to the given IBNR triangle with cumulated figures. What could be the reason why run-off triangles to be processed through the chain ladder method are usually given in a cumulated form?

Year of	Development year				
origin	1	2	3	4	5
1	232	338	373	389	391
2	258	373	429	456	
3	221	303	307		
4	359	430			
5	349				

4. Apply the arithmetic separation method to the same data of the previous exercise. Determine the missing γ values by linear or by loglinear interpolation, whichever seems more appropriate.
5. Which distance between data and predicted values is minimized by the chain ladder method? Which by the separation methods?

Section 9.3

1. Verify that the same predictions (9.12) are obtained from the models $\mathrm{E}[X_{ij}] = \mu\alpha_i\beta^{j-1}$ and $\mathrm{E}[X_{ij}] = \mu\alpha_i\gamma^{i+j-2}$.

2. Argue why in model I, where for $i, j = 1, \ldots, t$, we have $\mathrm{E}[X_{ij}] = \mu\alpha_i\beta_j\gamma_{i+j-1}$, the parameter γ_t can be taken equal to 1 without loss of generality, meaning that for $t = 8$, model I has only six more parameters to be estimated than model II. Verify that with model I there are $3(t-1)$ parameters to be estimated from $t(t+1)/2$ observations, so model I makes sense only if $t > 3$.
3. Explain why models IV and V are equivalent.
4. For $i = j = 1, 3, 5, 7$, compute the values predicted by models (9.13) and (9.14), and compare these to the actual observations.
5. Verify (9.15). Use it to determine $\sum_{j=1}^{\infty} \hat{X}_{ij}$.

10

Ordering of risks

10.1 INTRODUCTION

Comparing risks is the very essence of the actuarial profession. This chapter offers some mathematical concepts and tools to do this, and gives some important results of non-life actuarial science that can be derived. A *risk*, by which we mean a non-negative random variable, can be preferable to another for two reasons. One is that the other risk is *larger*, see Section 10.2, the second is that it is *thicker-tailed (riskier)*, see Section 10.3. Thicker-tailed means that the probability of large values is larger, making a risk with equal mean less attractive because it is more spread and therefore less predictable. We show that having thicker tails means having larger stop-loss premiums.

We also show that the latter is equivalent to the common preferences between risks of *all* risk averse decision makers. From the fact that a risk is smaller or less risky than another, one may deduce that it is also preferable in the mean-variance ordering that is used quite generally. In this ordering, one prefers the risk with the smaller mean, and the variance serves as a tie-breaker. This ordering concept, however, is inadequate for actuarial purposes, since it leads to decisions that many sensible decision makers would dispute. We give several invariance properties of the stop-loss order. The most important one for actuarial applications is that it is preserved under compounding, when either the number of claims or the claim size distribution is replaced by a riskier one.

In Section 10.4 we give a number of applications of the theory of ordering risks. One is that the individual model is less risky than the collective model. In Chapter 3, we saw that the canonical collective model has the same mean but a larger variance than the individual model, while the open collective model has a larger mean (and variance). We will prove here some stronger assertions, for instance that any risk averse decision maker would prefer a loss with the distributional properties of the individual model to a loss distributed according to the usual collective model, and also that all stop-loss premiums for it are smaller.

From Chapter 4 we know that the non-ruin probability can be written as the cdf of a compound geometric random variable L, which represents the maximal aggregate loss. We will show that if we replace the individual claims distribution in a ruin model by a distribution which is preferred by all risk averse decision makers, this is reflected in the ruin probability getting lower. Under somewhat more general conditions, the same holds for Lundberg's exponential upper bound for the ruin probability.

Many parametric families are monotonic in their parameters, in the sense that the risk increases (or decreases) with the parameters. We will show that if we look at the subfamily of the gamma(α, β) distributions with a fixed mean $\frac{\alpha}{\beta} = \mu$, the stop-loss premiums at each d grow with the variance $\frac{\alpha}{\beta^2}$, hence with decreasing α. In this way, it is possible to compare all gamma distributions with the gamma(α_0, β_0) distribution. Some will be preferred by all decision makers with increasing utility, some only by those who are also risk averse, while for others, the opinions will differ.

In Chapter 1, we showed that stop-loss reinsurance is optimal in the sense that it gives the lowest variance for the retained risk when the mean is fixed. In this chapter we are able to prove the stronger assertion that stop-loss reinsurance leads to a retained loss which is preferable for any risk averse decision maker.

We also will show that quite often, but not always, the common good opinion of all risk averse decision makers about some risk is reflected in a premium to be asked for it. If every risk averse decision maker prefers X to Y as a loss, X has lower zero utility premiums, including for instance exponential premiums.

Another field of application is given in Section 10.5. Sometimes one has to compute a stop-loss premium for a single risk of which only certain global characteristics are known, such as the mean value μ, an upper bound b and possibly the variance σ^2. We will determine risks with these characteristics that produce upper and lower bounds for such premiums.

It is quite conceivable that the constraints of non-negativity and independence of the terms of a sum imposed above are too restrictive. Many invariance properties depend crucially on non-negativity, but in financial actuarial applications, we must be able to incorporate both gains and losses in our models. The independence assumption is often not even approximately fulfilled, for instance if the terms of a sum are consecutive payments under a random interest force, or in case of earthquake and flooding risks. Also, the mortality patterns of husband and wife are obviously related, both because of the 'broken heart syndrome' and the fact that their environments and personalities will be alike ('birds of a feather flock together'). Nevertheless, most traditional insurance models assume independence. One can force a portfolio of risks to satisfy this requirement as much as possible by diversifying, therefore not including too many related risks like the fire risks of different floors of a building or the risks concerning several layers of the same large reinsured risk.

The assumption of independence plays a very crucial role in insurance. In fact, the basis of insurance is that by undertaking many small independent risks, an insurer's random position gets more and more predictable because of the two fundamental laws of statistics, the Law of Large Numbers and the Central Limit Theorem. One risk is hedged by other risks, since a loss on one policy might be compensated by more favorable results on others. Moreover, assuming independence is very convenient, because mostly, the statistics gathered only give information about the marginal distributions of the risks, not about their joint distribution, i.e., the way these risks are interrelated. Also, independence is mathematically much easier to handle than most other structures for the joint cdf. Note by the way that the Law of Large Numbers does not entail that the variance of an insurer's random capital goes to zero when his business expands, but only that the coefficient of variation, i.e., the standard deviation expressed as a multiple of the mean, does so.

In Section 10.6 we will try to determine how to make safe decisions in case we have a portfolio of insurance policies that produce gains and losses of which the stochastic dependency structure is unknown. It is obvious that the sum of random variables is risky if these random variables exhibit a positive dependence, which means that large values of one term tend to go hand in hand with large values of the other terms. If the dependence is absent such as is the case for stochastic independence, or if it is negative, the losses will be hedged. Their total becomes more predictable and hence more attractive in the eyes of risk averse decision makers. In case of positive dependence, the independence assumption would probably underestimate the risk associated with the portfolio. A negative dependence means that the larger the claim for one risk, the smaller the other ones. The central result here is that sums of random variables are the riskiest if these random variables are maximally dependent (comonotonic).

10.2 LARGER RISKS

In this section and the three that follow, we compare risks, i.e., non-negative random variables. It is easy to establish a condition under which we might call one risk Y larger than (more correctly, larger than or equal to) another risk X: without any doubt a decision maker with increasing utility will consider loss X to be preferable to Y if it is smaller with certainty, hence if $\Pr[X \leq Y] = 1$. This leads to the following definition:

Definition 10.2.1 ('Larger' risk)
For two risks, Y is 'larger' than X if a pair (X', Y) exists with $X' \sim X$ and $\Pr[X' \leq Y] = 1$. ∇

Note that in this definition, we do not just look at the marginal cdf's F_X and F_Y, but at the joint distribution of X' and Y. See the following example.

Example 10.2.2 (Binomial random variables)
Let X denote the number of times heads occur in 7 tosses with a fair coin, and Y the same in 10 tosses with a biased coin having probability $p > \frac{1}{2}$ of heads. If X and Y are independent, event $X > Y$ has a positive probability. Can we set up the experiment in such a way that we can define random variables Y and X' on it, such that X' has the same cdf as X, and such that Y is always at least equal to X'?

To construct an $X' \sim X$ such that $\Pr[X' \leq Y] = 1$, we proceed as follows. Toss a biased coin with probability p of falling heads ten times, and denote the number of heads by Y. Every time heads occurs in the first seven tosses, we toss another coin that falls heads with probability $\frac{1}{2p}$. Let X' be the number of heads shown by the second coin. Then $X' \sim \text{binomial}(7, \frac{1}{2})$, just as X, because the probability of a success with each potential toss of the second coin is $p \times \frac{1}{2p}$. Obviously, X' and Y are not independent, and as required, $\Pr[X' \leq Y] = 1$. ∇

The condition for Y to be 'larger' than X proves to be equivalent to a simple requirement on the marginal cdf's:

Theorem 10.2.3 (A larger random variable has a smaller cdf)
A pair (X', Y) with $X' \sim X$ and $\Pr[X' \leq Y] = 1$ exists if, and only if, $F_X(x) \geq F_Y(x)$ for all $x \geq 0$.

Proof. The 'only if'-part of the theorem is evident. For the 'if'-part, we only give a proof for two important special cases. If both $F_X(\cdot)$ and $F_Y(\cdot)$ are continuous and monotone increasing, we can simply take $X' = F_X^{-1}(F_Y(Y))$. Then $F_Y(Y)$ can be shown to be uniform$(0,1)$, and therefore $F_X^{-1}(F_Y(Y)) \sim X$. Also, $X' \leq Y$ holds.

For X and Y discrete, look at the following functions, which are actually the inverse cdf's with $F_X(\cdot)$ and $F_Y(\cdot)$, and are defined for all u with $0 < u < 1$:

$$\begin{aligned} f(u) &= x \quad \text{if } F_X(x-0) < u \leq F_X(x); \\ g(u) &= y \quad \text{if } F_Y(y-0) < u \leq F_Y(y). \end{aligned} \tag{10.1}$$

Next, take $U \sim$ uniform(0,1). Then $g(U) \sim Y$ and $f(U) \sim X$, while $F_X(x) \geq F_Y(x)$ for all x implies that $f(u) \leq g(u)$ for all u, so $\Pr[f(U) \leq g(U)] = 1$. ∇

Remark 10.2.4 ('Larger' vs. larger risks)
To compare risks X and Y, we look only at their marginal cdf's F_X and F_Y. Since the joint distribution doesn't matter, we can, without loss of generality, look at any copy of X. But this means we can assume that if Y is 'larger' than X in the sense of Definition 10.2.1, actually the stronger assertion $\Pr[X \leq Y] = 1$ holds. So instead of just stochastically larger, we may assume the risk to be larger with probability one. All we do then is replace X by an equivalent risk. ∇

In many situations, we consider a model involving several random variables as input. Quite often, the output of the model increases if we replace any of the input random variables by a larger one. This is for instance the case when comparing $X + Z$ with $Y + Z$, for a risk Z which is independent of X and Y (convolution). A less trivial example is compounding, where both the number of claims and the claim size distributions may be replaced. We have:

Theorem 10.2.5 (Compounding)
If the individual claims X_i are 'smaller' than Y_i for all i, the counting variable M is 'smaller' than N, and all these random variables are independent, then $X_1 + X_2 + \cdots + X_M$ is 'smaller' than $Y_1 + Y_2 + \cdots + Y_N$.

Proof. In view of Remark 10.2.4 we can assume without loss of generality that $X_i \leq Y_i$ as well as $M \leq N$ hold with probability one. Then the second expression has at least as many non-negative terms which are all at least as large. ∇

The order concept 'larger than' used above is called *stochastic order*, and the notation is as follows:

Definition 10.2.6 (Stochastic order)
Risk X precedes risk Y in stochastic order, written $X \leq_{st} Y$, if Y is 'larger' than X. ∇

In the literature, often the term 'stochastic order' is used for any ordering concept between random variables or their distributions. In this book, it is reserved for the specific order of Definition 10.2.6.

Remark 10.2.7 (Stochastically larger risks have a larger mean)
A consequence of stochastic order $X \leq_{st} Y$, i.e., a *necessary condition* for it, is obviously that $\mathrm{E}[X] \leq \mathrm{E}[Y]$, and even $\mathrm{E}[X] < \mathrm{E}[Y]$ unless $X \sim Y$. See for instance formula (1.34) at $d = 0$. The opposite doesn't hold: $\mathrm{E}[X] \leq \mathrm{E}[Y]$ doesn't imply $X \leq_{st} Y$. A counterexample is $X \sim \text{Bernoulli}(p)$ with $p = \frac{1}{2}$ and $\Pr[Y = c] = 1$ for a c with $\frac{1}{2} < c < 1$. ∇

Remark 10.2.8 (Once-crossing densities are stochastically ordered)
An important *sufficient condition* for stochastic order is that the densities exhibit the pattern $f_X(x) \geq f_Y(x)$ for small x and the opposite for large x. A proof of this statement is asked in Exercise 10.2.1. ∇

It can be shown that the order $\leq_{st}$ has a natural interpretation in terms of utility theory. We have

Theorem 10.2.9 (Stochastic order and increasing utility functions)
$X \leq_{st} Y$ holds if and only if $\mathrm{E}[u(-X)] \geq \mathrm{E}[u(-Y)]$ for every non-decreasing utility function $u(\cdot)$.

Proof. If $\mathrm{E}[u(-X)] \geq \mathrm{E}[u(-Y)]$ holds for every non-decreasing $u(\cdot)$, then it holds especially for the functions $h_d(y) = 1 - I_{(-\infty,-d]}(y)$. But $\mathrm{E}[h_d(-X)]$ is just $\Pr[X \leq d]$. For the 'only if' part, if $X \leq_{st} Y$, then $\Pr[X' \leq Y] = 1$ for some $X' \sim X$, and therefore $\mathrm{E}[u(-X)] \geq \mathrm{E}[u(-Y)]$. ∇

So the pairs of risks X and Y with $X \leq_{st} Y$ are exactly those pairs of losses about which *all* decision makers with an increasing utility function agree.

10.3 MORE DANGEROUS RISKS

In economics, when choosing between two potential losses, the usual practice is to prefer the loss with the smaller mean. If two risks have the same mean, some decision makers will simply choose the one with the smaller variance. This mean-variance ordering concept forms the basis for the CAPM-models in economic theory. It is inadequate for the actuary, who also has to keep events in mind with such small probability that they remain invisible in the variance, but have such impact that they might lead to ruin. All risk averse actuaries would, however, agree that one risk is riskier than another if its extreme values have larger probability.

Definition 10.3.1 (Thicker-tailed)
Risk Y is said to have thicker tails than risk X if $\mathrm{E}[X] = \mathrm{E}[Y]$, and moreover some real number x_0 exists such that $\Pr[X \leq x] \leq \Pr[Y \leq x]$ for all $x < x_0$, but $\Pr[X \leq x] \geq \Pr[Y \leq x]$ for all $x > x_0$. ∇

In this definition, the property 'thicker-tailed' is expressed directly in the cdf's of X and Y: there is a number x_0 such that to the left of x_0 the cdf of X is smaller, to the right of x_0, the cdf of Y. The cdf's cross exactly once, in x_0. A sufficient condition for two crossing cdf's to cross exactly once is that the difference of these cdf's increases first, then decreases, and increases again after that. Hence we have:

Theorem 10.3.2 (Densities crossing twice means cdf's crossing once)
Let X and Y be two risks with equal mean but different densities. If intervals I_1, I_2 and I_3 exist with $I_1 \cup I_2 \cup I_3 = [0, \infty)$ and I_2 between I_1 and I_3, such that the densities of X and Y satisfy $f_X(x) \leq f_Y(x)$ both on I_1 and I_3, while $f_X(x) \geq f_Y(x)$ on I_2, then the cdf's of X and Y cross only once.

Proof. Note first that because of $\mathrm{E}[X] = \mathrm{E}[Y]$, the cdf's F_X and F_Y must cross at least once, since we assumed that not $f_X \equiv f_Y$. This is because if they would not, one of the two would be larger in stochastic order by Theorem 10.2.3, and the means would then be different by Remark 10.2.7. Both to the left of 0 and at ∞, the difference of the cdf's equals zero. The densities represent either the derivatives of the cdf's, or the jumps therein, and in both cases it is seen that the difference of the cdf's increases first to a maximum, then decreases to a minimum, and next increases to zero again. So there is just one point, somewhere in I_2, where the difference in the cdf's crosses the x-axis, hence the cdf's cross exactly once. ∇

Note that $I_1 = [0, 0]$ or $I_2 = [b, b]$ may occur if the densities are discrete.

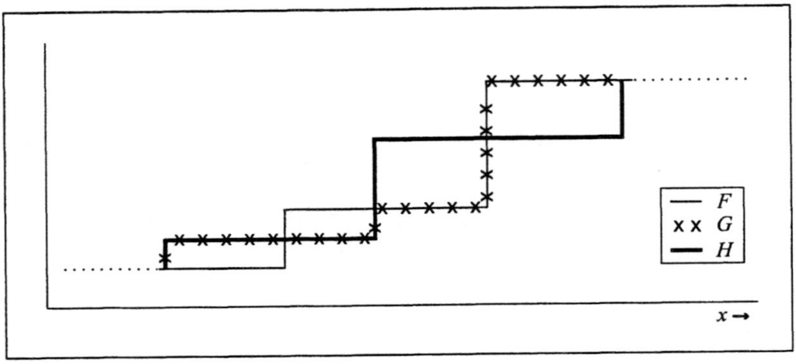

Fig. 10.1 Counterexample of the transitivity of being thicker-tailed: H is thicker-tailed than G, G is thicker-tailed than F, but H is not thicker-tailed than F.

Example 10.3.3 (Binomial has thinner tails than Poisson)
If we compare a binomial(n, p) distribution with a Poisson(np) distribution, we know that they have the same mean, while the latter has a greater variance. Is it also thicker-tailed than the binomial distribution?

We will show that the discrete densities, say $f(x)$ and $g(x)$ respectively, have the crossing properties of the previous theorem. We do this by showing that the ratio of these densities $r(x)$ increases up to a certain value of x, and decreases thereafter. Writing $q = 1 - p$ as usual, we get for this ratio

$$r(x) = \frac{f(x)}{g(x)} = \frac{\binom{n}{x} p^x q^{n-x}}{(np)^x e^{-np}/x!} = \frac{n(n-1)\cdots(n-x+1)}{n^x q^x} q^n e^{np}. \qquad (10.2)$$

Now consider the ratio of successive values of $r(x)$, $x = 1, 2, \ldots$:

$$\frac{r(x)}{r(x-1)} = \frac{n-x+1}{nq} \leq 1 \quad \text{if and only if} \quad x \geq np+1. \qquad (10.3)$$

Because $f(\cdot)$ and $g(\cdot)$ have the same mean, they must cross at least twice. But this means that $r(x)$ must cross the horizontal level 1 twice, so $r(x) < 1$ must hold for small as well as for large values of x, while $r(x) > 1$ must hold for intermediate values x, near $np + 1$. Now apply the previous theorem to see that the Poisson distribution indeed has thicker tails than the binomial distribution. ∇

Remark 10.3.4 (Thicker-tailed is not a transitive ordering)
It is easy to construct examples of random variables X, Y and Z where Y is

thicker-tailed than X, Z is thicker-tailed than Y, but Z is not thicker-tailed than X. In Figure 10.1, the cdf's of X and Y cross once, as do the ones of Y and Z, but those of X and Z cross three times. So being thicker-tailed is not a well-behaved ordering concept: order relations should be *transitive*. Transitivity can be enforced by extending the relation, let's temporarily write $\leq_{tt}$ for it, to pairs X and Z such that a sequence of random variables $Y_1, Y_2, \ldots, Y_n$ exists with $X \leq_{tt} Y_1$, $Y_j \leq_{tt} Y_{j+1}, j = 1, 2, \ldots, n-1$, as well as $Y_n \leq_{tt} Z$. Extending the relation in this way, we get the finite transitive closure of the relation $\leq_{tt}$, which we will call *indirectly thicker-tailed* from now on. ∇

If X precedes Y in stochastic order, their cdf's do not cross. If Y is (indirectly) thicker-tailed than X, it can be shown that their stop-loss transforms $\pi_X(d) = \mathrm{E}[(X-d)_+]$ and $\pi_Y(d)$ do not cross. By proceeding inductively, it suffices to prove this for the case where Y is directly thicker-tailed than X. But in that case, the difference $\pi_Y(d) - \pi_X(d)$ can be seen to be zero at $d = 0$ because the means of X and Y are equal, zero at $d \to \infty$, increasing as long as the derivative of the difference $\pi'_Y(d) - \pi'_X(d) = F_Y(d) - F_X(d)$ is positive, and decreasing thereafter. Hence, Y thicker-tailed than X means that Y has higher stop-loss premiums.

We can prove the reverse of this last statement, too. If Y has larger stop-loss premiums than X and $\mathrm{E}[X] = \mathrm{E}[Y]$, then a possibly infinite sequence of increasingly thicker-tailed cdf's must exist connecting X and Z.

Theorem 10.3.5 (Thicker-tailed vs. higher stop-loss premiums)
If $\mathrm{E}[X] = \mathrm{E}[Z]$ and $\pi_X(d) \leq \pi_Y(d)$ for all $d > 0$, then there exists a sequence $F_1, F_2, \ldots$ of increasingly thicker-tailed cdf's with $X \sim F_1$ and $Z \sim \lim_{n\to\infty} F_n$.

Proof. We sketch the proof for when Z is a random variable with finitely many possible values. Then the cdf of Z is a step-function, so the stop-loss transform is a piecewise linear continuous convex function. Hence, for certain linear functions $A_1, \ldots, A_n$ it can be written in the form

$$\pi_Z(d) = \max\left\{\pi_X(d), A_1(d), A_2(d), \ldots, A_n(d)\right\}, \quad -\infty < d < \infty. \quad (10.4)$$

Now define the following functions $\pi_i(\cdot), i = 1, 2, \ldots, n$:

$$\pi_i(d) = \max\left\{\pi_X(d), A_1(d), A_2(d), \ldots, A_{i-1}(d)\right\}, \quad -\infty < d < \infty. \quad (10.5)$$

These function are stop-loss transforms, say with the cdf's $F_i, i = 1, 2, \ldots, n$. As the reader may check, $X \sim F_1$, $Z \sim F_n$, and F_i has thicker tails than F_{i-1},

$i = 2, 3, \ldots, n$. See also Exercise 10.3.25. If the support of Z is infinite, we must take the limit of the cdf's F_n in the sense of convergence in distribution. ∇

For pairs of random variables with ordered stop-loss premiums we have the following definition.

Definition 10.3.6 (Stop-loss order)
If X has smaller stop-loss premiums than Z, we say that X is smaller than Z in stop-loss order, and write $X \leq_{SL} Z$. ∇

A random variable that is stop-loss larger than another risk with the same mean will be referred to as 'more dangerous' in the sequel. Note that for stop-loss order, equality of the means $\mathrm{E}[X] = \mathrm{E}[Z]$ is not required. In case $\mathrm{E}[X] < \mathrm{E}[Z]$, we may show:

Theorem 10.3.7 (Separation theorem for stop-loss order)
If $X \leq_{SL} Z$ and $\mathrm{E}[X] < \mathrm{E}[Z]$, then there exists a random variable Y for which

1. $X \leq_{st} Y$;
2. $Y \leq_{SL} Z$ and $\mathrm{E}[Y] = \mathrm{E}[Z]$.

Proof. The random variable $Y = \max\{X, b\}$, with $b > 0$ chosen such that $\mathrm{E}[Y] = \mathrm{E}[Z]$, satisfies both these requirements, as the reader is asked to verify in Exercise 10.3.12. ∇

The random variable Y separates X and Y in a sense stronger than merely $\leq_{SL}$. For another separator in a similar sense, with the stochastic inequalities interchanged, see Exercise 10.3.13. A risk Z that is stop-loss larger than X is unattractive for two reasons: it is 'more dangerous' than a risk Y which in turn is 'larger' than X.

Just like stochastic order, stop-loss order can be expressed in a utility context as the common preferences between risks of a group of sensible decision makers:

Theorem 10.3.8 (Stop-loss order, concave increasing utility functions)
$X \leq_{SL} Y$ holds if and only if $\mathrm{E}[u(-X)] \geq \mathrm{E}[u(-Y)]$ for every *concave increasing* utility function $u(\cdot)$.

Proof. In view of Theorem 10.3.7, it suffices to give the proof for the case that $\mathrm{E}[X] = \mathrm{E}[Y]$. Then, it follows as a special case of Theorem 10.6.2 later on. See also Exercise 10.3.17. ∇

So stop-loss order represents the common preferences of all risk averse decision makers. Stop-loss order applies to losses, i.e., non-negative risks. Two general random variables with the same mean and ordered stop-loss premiums for all d are called convex ordered, see Section 10.6. As a consequence of Theorem 10.3.8, expected values of convex functions are ordered. Since all functions x^α with $\alpha \geq 1$ are convex, for the moments of X and Y we have $\mathrm{E}[X^k] \leq \mathrm{E}[Y^k]$, $k = 1, 2, \ldots$ In particular, a more dangerous risk (with the same mean) has a higher variance. But if the means of X and Y are not equal, this is not always the case. A trivial counterexample is $X \sim$ Bernoulli$(\frac{1}{2})$ and $Y \equiv 1$.

Next to stochastic order and stop-loss order, there is another useful ordering concept to be derived from the expected utility model.

Definition 10.3.9 (Exponential order)
If for all $\alpha > 0$, decision makers with an exponential utility function with risk aversion α prefer loss X to Y, we say that X precedes Y in *exponential order*, written $X \leq_e Y$. ∇

Remark 10.3.10 (Exponential order and stop-loss order)
$X \leq_e Y$ is clearly is equivalent to X having a smaller mgf than Y on the interval $(0, \infty)$. A sufficient condition for exponential order between risks is stop-loss order, since the function e^{tx} is a convex function on $[0, \infty)$ for $t > 0$, hence $\mathrm{E}[e^{tX}] \leq \mathrm{E}[e^{tY}]$ holds for all $t > 0$. But this can be seen from utility considerations as well, because the exponential order represents the preferences common to the subset of the risk-averse decision makers for which the risk attitude is independent of their current wealth.

Exponential order represents the common preferences of a smaller group of decision makers than stop-loss order. Indeed there exist pairs of random variables that are exponentially ordered, but not stop-loss ordered. See Exercise 10.4.10. ∇

For stop-loss order, by and large the same invariance properties hold as we derived for stochastic order. So if we replace a particular component of a model by a more dangerous input, we often obtain a stop-loss larger result. For actuarial purposes, it is important whether the order is retained in case of compounding. First we prove that adding independent random variables, as well as taking mixtures, does not disturb the stop-loss order.

Theorem 10.3.11 (Convolution preserves stop-loss order)
If for risks X and Y we have $X \leq_{SL} Y$, and risk Z is independent of X and Y,

then $X + Z \leq_{SL} Y + Z$. If further S_n is the sum of n independent copies of X and T_n is the same for Y, then $S_n \leq_{SL} T_n$.

Proof. The first stochastic inequality can be proven by using the relation:

$$\mathrm{E}[(X + Z - d)_+] = \int_0^\infty \mathrm{E}[(X + z - d)_+] dF_Z(z). \tag{10.6}$$

The second follows by iterating the first inequality. ∇

Theorem 10.3.12 (Mixing preserves stop-loss order)
Let cdf's F_y and G_y satisfy $F_y \leq_{SL} G_y$ for all real y, let $U(y)$ be any cdf, and let $F(x) = \int_{\mathbb{R}} F_y(x) dU(y)$, $G(x) = \int_{\mathbb{R}} G_y(x) dU(y)$. Then $F \leq_{SL} G$.

Proof. The stop-loss premiums with F are equal to

$$\begin{aligned} \int_d^\infty [1 - F(x)] dx &= \int_d^\infty \left[1 - \int_{\mathbb{R}} F_y(x) dU(y)\right] dx \\ &= \int_d^\infty \int_{\mathbb{R}} [1 - F_y(x)] dU(y) dx = \int_{\mathbb{R}} \int_d^\infty [1 - F_y(x)] dx dU(y). \end{aligned} \tag{10.7}$$

Hence, $F \leq_{SL} G$ follows immediately. ∇

Corollary 10.3.13 (Mixing ordered random variables)
The following conclusions are immediate from Theorem 10.3.12:

1. If $F_n(x) = \Pr[X \leq x | N = n]$, $G_n(x) = \Pr[Y \leq x | N = n]$, and $F_n \leq_{SL} G_n$ for all n, then we obtain $X \leq_{SL} Y$ by taking the cdf of N to be $U(\cdot)$. The event $N = n$ might for instance indicate the nature of a particular claim (small or large, liability or comprehensive, bonus-malus class, and so on).

2. Taking especially $F_n(x) = F^{*n}$ and $G_n(x) = G^{*n}$, where F and G are the cdf's of individual claims X_i and Y_i, respectively, produces $X_1 + \cdots + X_N \leq_{SL} Y_1 + \cdots + Y_N$ if $F \leq_{SL} G$. Hence stop-loss order is preserved under compounding, if the individual claim size distribution is replaced by a stop-loss larger one.

3. If Λ is a structure variable with cdf U, and conditionally on the event $\Lambda = \lambda$, $X \sim F_\lambda$ and $Y \sim G_\lambda$, then $F_\lambda \leq_{SL} G_\lambda$ for all λ implies $X \leq_{SL} Y$.

4. Let F_λ denote the cdf of the degenerate random variable on $\mathrm{E}[X|\Lambda = \lambda]$ and G_λ the conditional cdf of X, given the event $\Lambda = \lambda$. Then it is easy to see that $F_\lambda \leq_{SL} G_\lambda$ holds. The function $\int_{\mathbb{R}} F_\lambda(x)dU(\lambda)$ is the cdf of the random variable $\mathrm{E}[X|\Lambda]$, while $\int_{\mathbb{R}} G_\lambda(x)dU(\lambda)$ is the cdf of X. Hence we have $\mathrm{E}[X|\Lambda] \leq_{SL} X$ for all X and Λ; always, *conditional means* are less dangerous than the original random variable. ∇

We saw that if the terms of a compound sum are replaced by stop-loss larger ones, the result is also stop-loss larger. To prove that the same happens when we replace the claim number M by the stop-loss larger random variable N is tougher. The general proof, though short, is not easy, hence we will start by giving an important special case. We take $M \sim \text{Bernoulli}(q)$ and $\mathrm{E}[N] \geq q$. As usual, define $\sum_{i=1}^{n} x_i = 0$ if $n = 0$.

Theorem 10.3.14 (Compounding with a riskier claim number, 1)
If $M \sim \text{Bernoulli}(q)$, N is a counting random variable with $\mathrm{E}[N] \geq q$ and $X_1, X_2, \ldots$ are independent copies of a risk X, then we have

$$MX \leq_{SL} X_1 + X_2 + \cdots + X_N. \tag{10.8}$$

Proof. First we prove that for each $d \geq 0$, the following event has probability one:

$$(X_1 + \cdots + X_n - d)_+ \geq (X_1 - d)_+ + \cdots + (X_n - d)_+. \tag{10.9}$$

There only is something to prove if the right hand side is non-zero. If, say, the first term is positive, then because of $X_i \geq 0$, $i = 1, 2, \ldots$, the first two $(\cdot)_+$-operators in (10.9) can be dropped, leaving

$$X_2 + \cdots + X_n \geq (X_2 - d)_+ + \cdots + (X_n - d)_+, \tag{10.10}$$

which is always fulfilled if $X_i \geq 0$, $i = 2, 3, \ldots$, and $d \geq 0$. Writing $q_n = \Pr[N = n]$, for $d \geq 0$ we have, using (10.9):

$$\begin{aligned}
&\mathrm{E}[(X_1 + X_2 + \cdots + X_N - d)_+] \\
&= \sum_{n=1}^{\infty} q_n \mathrm{E}[(X_1 + X_2 + \cdots + X_n - d)_+] \\
&\geq \sum_{n=1}^{\infty} q_n \mathrm{E}[(X_1 - d)_+ + (X_2 - d)_+ + \cdots + (X_n - d)_+] \\
&= \sum_{n=1}^{\infty} n q_n \mathrm{E}[(X - d)_+] \geq q\mathrm{E}[(X - d)_+] = \mathrm{E}[(MX - d)_+].
\end{aligned} \tag{10.11}$$

The last inequality is valid since $\sum_n nq_n \geq q$ by assumption. ∇

Theorem 10.3.15 (Compounding with a riskier claim number, 2)
If for two counting random variables M and N we have $M \leq_{SL} N$, and $X_1, X_2, \ldots$ are independent copies of a risk X, then $X_1 + X_2 + \cdots + X_M \leq_{SL} X_1 + X_2 + \cdots + X_N$.

Proof. It is sufficient to prove that $f_d(n) = \mathrm{E}[(X_1 + \cdots + X_n - d)_+]$ is a convex and increasing function of n, since by Theorem 10.3.8 this implies $\mathrm{E}[f_d(M)] \leq \mathrm{E}[f_d(N)]$ for all d, which is the same as $X_1 + \cdots + X_M \leq_{SL} X_1 + \cdots + X_N$. Because $X_{n+1} \geq 0$, it is obvious that $f_d(n+1) \geq f_d(n)$. To prove convexity, we need to prove that $f_d(n+2) - f_d(n+1) \geq f_d(n+1) - f_d(n)$ holds for each n. By taking the expectation over the random variables X_{n+1}, X_{n+2} and $S = X_1 + X_2 + \cdots + X_n$, one sees that for this it is sufficient to prove that for all $d \geq 0$ and all $x_i \geq 0, i = 1, 2, \ldots, n+2$, we have

$$\begin{aligned} &(s + x_{n+1} + x_{n+2} - d)_+ - (s + x_{n+1} - d)_+ \\ &\geq (s + x_{n+2} - d)_+ - (s - d)_+, \end{aligned} \tag{10.12}$$

where $s = x_1 + x_2 + \cdots + x_n$. If both middle terms of this inequality are zero, so is the last one and the inequality is valid. If at least one of them is positive, say the one with x_{n+1}, on the left hand side of (10.12), x_{n+2} remains, and the right hand side is equal to this if $s \geq d$, and smaller otherwise, as can be verified easily. ∇

Combining Theorems 10.3.12 and 10.3.15, we see that a compound sum is riskier if the number of claims, the claim size distribution, or both are replaced by stop-loss larger ones.

Remark 10.3.16 (Functional invariance)
Just like stochastic order (see Exercise 10.2.8), stop-loss order has the property of functional invariance. Indeed, if $f(\cdot)$ and $v(\cdot)$ are non-decreasing convex functions, the composition $v \circ f$ is convex and non-decreasing as well, and hence we see immediately that $f(X) \leq_{SL} f(Y)$ holds if $X \leq_{SL} Y$. This holds in particular for the claims paid in case of excess of loss reinsurance, where $f(x) = (x - d)_+$, and proportional reinsurance, where $f(x) = \alpha x$ for $\alpha > 0$. ∇

10.4 APPLICATIONS

In this section, we give some important actuarial applications of the theory of ordering of risks.

Example 10.4.1 (Individual versus collective model)
In Section 3.7 we described how *the* collective model resulted from replacing every policy by a Poisson(1) distributed number of independent copies of it. But from Theorem 10.3.14 with $q = 1$ we see directly that doing this, we in fact replace the claims of every policy by a more dangerous random variable. If subsequently we add up all these policies, which we have assumed to be stochastically independent, then for the portfolio as a whole, a more dangerous total claims distribution ensues. This is because stop-loss order is preserved under convolution, see Theorem 10.3.11.

As an alternative for the canonical collective model, in Remark 3.7.2 we introduced an *open* collective model. If the claims of policy i are $I_i b_i$ for some fixed amount at risk b_i and a Bernoulli(q_i) distributed random variable I_i, the term in *the* collective model corresponding to this policy is $M_i b_i$, with $M_i \sim$ Poisson(q_i). In the open collective model, it is $N_i b_i$, with $N_i \sim$ Poisson(t_i) for $t_i = -\log(1-q_i)$, and hence $I_i \leq_{st} N_i$. So in the open model each policy is replaced by a compound Poisson distribution with a *stochastically* larger claim number distribution than with the individual model. Hence the open model will not only be less attractive than the individual model for all risk averse decision makers, but even for the larger group of all decision makers with increasing utility functions. Also, the canonical collective model is preferable to the open model for this same large group of decision makers. Having a choice between the individual and *the* collective model, some decision makers might prefer the latter. Apparently, these decision makers are not consistently risk averse. ∇

Example 10.4.2 (Ruin probabilities and adjustment coefficients)
In Section 4.7, we derived the result that the non-ruin probability $1 - \psi(u)$ can be written as the cdf of a compound geometric random variable $L = L_1 + L_2 + \cdots + L_M$, where $M \sim$ geometric(p) is the number of record lows in the surplus, L_i is the amount by which a previous record low in the surplus was broken, and L represents the maximal aggregate loss. We have from (4.50) and (4.51):

$$p = 1 - \psi(0) = \frac{\theta}{1+\theta} \quad \text{and} \quad f_{L_1}(y) = \frac{1 - P(y)}{\mu_1}, \; y > 0. \tag{10.13}$$

Here θ is the safety loading, and $P(y)$ is the cdf of the claim sizes in the ruin process. Now suppose that we replace cdf P by Q, where $P \leq_{SL} Q$ and Q has the same mean as P. From (10.13) it is obvious that since the stop-loss premiums with Q are larger than those with P, the probability $\Pr[L_1 > y]$ is increased when P

is replaced by Q. This means that we get a new compound geometric distribution with the same geometric parameter p because μ_1 and hence θ are unchanged, but a *stochastically* larger distribution of the individual terms L_i. This leads to a smaller cdf for L, and hence a larger ruin probability. Note that the equality of the means μ_1 of P and Q is essential here, to ensure that p remains the same and that the L_1 random variables increase stochastically.

Now suppose further that we replace the claim size cdf Q by R, with $Q \leq_{st} R$, while leaving the premium level c unchanged. This means that we replace the ruin process by a process with the same premium per unit time and the same claim number process, but 'larger' claims. By Remark 10.2.4, without loss of generality we can take each claim to be larger with probability one, instead of just stochastically larger. This means that also with probability one, the new surplus $U_R(t)$ will be lower than or equal to $U_Q(t)$, at each instant $t > 0$. This in turn implies that for the ruin probabilities, we have $\psi_R(u) \geq \psi_Q(u)$. It may happen that one gets ruined in the R-process, but not in the Q-process; the other way around is impossible. Because in view of the Separation Theorem 10.3.7, when P is replaced by R we can always find a separating Q with the same expectation as P and with $P \leq_{SL} Q \leq_{st} R$, we see that whenever we replace the claims distribution by any stop-loss larger distribution, the ruin probabilities are increased for every value of the initial capital u.

From Figure 4.2 we see directly that when the mgf with the claims is replaced by one that is larger on $(0, \infty)$, the resulting adjustment coefficient R is smaller. This is already the case when we replace the claims distribution by an exponentially larger one, see Remark 10.3.10. So we get larger ruin probabilities by replacing the claims by stop-loss larger ones, but for the Lundberg exponential upper bound to increase, exponential order suffices.

We saw that stop-loss larger claims lead to uniformly larger ruin probabilities. The weaker exponential order is not powerful enough to enforce this. To give a counterexample, first observe that pairs of exponentially ordered random variables exist that have the same mean and variance. Take for instance $\Pr[X = 0, 1, 2, 3] = \frac{1}{3}, 0, \frac{1}{2}, \frac{1}{6}$ and $Y \sim 3 - X$. See also Exercise 10.4.10. Now if $\psi_X(u) \leq \psi_Y(u)$ for all u would hold, with inequality for some u, the cdf's of the maximal aggregate losses L_X and L_Y would not cross, hence $L_X \leq_{st} L_Y$ would hold, which would imply $\mathrm{E}[L_X] < \mathrm{E}[L_Y]$. But this is not possible since

$$\begin{aligned}\mathrm{E}[L_X] &= \mathrm{E}[M]\mathrm{E}[L_i^{(X)}] = \mathrm{E}[M]\int_0^\infty \mathrm{E}[(X-x)_+]dx/\mathrm{E}[X] \\ &= \mathrm{E}[M]\frac{1}{2}\mathrm{E}[X^2]/\mathrm{E}[X] = \mathrm{E}[M]\frac{1}{2}\mathrm{E}[Y^2]/\mathrm{E}[Y] = \cdots = \mathrm{E}[L_Y].\end{aligned} \tag{10.14}$$

Note that if the two ruin probability functions are equal, the mgf's of L_X and L_Y are equal, and therefore also the mgf's of $L_i^{(X)}$ and $L_i^{(Y)}$, see (4.55), hence in view of (4.51), the claim size distribution must be the same. ∇

Example 10.4.3 (Order in the family of gamma distributions)
The gamma distribution is important as a model for the individual claim size, for instance for damage to the own vehicle, see also Chapter 8. For two gamma distributions, say with parameters α_0, β_0 and α_1, β_1, it is easy to compare means and variances. Is there perhaps more to be said about order between such distributions, for instance about certain tail probabilities or stop-loss premiums?

In general when one thinks of a gamma distribution, one pictures a density which is unimodal with a positive mode, looking a little like a tilted normal density. But if the shape parameter $\alpha = 1$, we get the exponential distribution, which is unimodal with mode 0. In general, the gamma(α, β) density has mode $(\alpha - 1)_+$. The skewness of a gamma distribution is $2/\sqrt{\alpha}$. Thus, the distributions with $\alpha < 1$ are more skewed than the exponential, and have larger tail probabilities.

From the form of the mgf $m(t; \alpha, \beta) = (1 - t/\beta)^{-\alpha}$, one may show that gamma random variables are additive in α. We have $m(t; \alpha_1, \beta)m(t; \alpha_2, \beta) = m(t; \alpha_1 + \alpha_2, \beta)$, so if X and Y are independent gamma random variables with the same β, their sum is a gamma random variable as well. From $\mathrm{E}[e^{t(\beta X)}] = (1-t)^{-\alpha}$ one sees that $\beta X \sim$ gamma$(\alpha, 1)$ if $X \sim$ gamma(α, β), and in this sense, the gamma distributions are multiplicative in the scale parameter β. But from these two properties we have immediately that a gamma(α, β) random variable gets 'larger' if α is replaced by $\alpha + \varepsilon$, and 'smaller' if β is replaced by $\beta(1 + \varepsilon)$ for $\varepsilon > 0$. Hence there is monotonicity in stochastic order in both parameters, see also Exercise 10.2.2.

Now let us compare the gamma(α_1, β_1) with the gamma(α_0, β_0) distribution when it is known that they have the same mean, so $\alpha_1/\beta_1 = \alpha_0/\beta_0$. Suppose that $\alpha_1 < \alpha_0$, therefore also $\beta_1 < \beta_0$. We will show by investigating the densities that the gamma(α_1, β_1) distribution, having the larger variance, is also the more dangerous one. A sufficient condition for this is that the densities cross exactly twice. Consider the ratio of these two densities (where the symbol $\propto$ denotes equality apart from a constant, not depending on x):

$$\frac{\frac{1}{\Gamma(\alpha_1)}\beta_1^{\alpha_1} x^{\alpha_1-1} e^{-\beta_1 x}}{\frac{1}{\Gamma(\alpha_0)}\beta_0^{\alpha_0} x^{\alpha_0-1} e^{-\beta_0 x}} \propto x^{\alpha_1-\alpha_0} e^{-(\beta_1-\beta_0)x} = (x^{\mu} e^{-x})^{\beta_1-\beta_0}. \tag{10.15}$$

The derivative of $x^{\mu}e^{-x}$ is positive if $0 < x < \mu$, negative if $x > \mu$, so the ratio (10.15) crosses each horizontal level at most twice. But because both densities have the same mean, there is no stochastic order, which means that they must intersect more than once. So apparently, they cross exactly twice, which means that one of the two random variables is more dangerous than the other. One can find out which by looking more closely at where each density is larger than the other. But we already know which one is the more dangerous, since it must necessarily be the one having the larger variance, which is the one with parameters α_1, β_1.

We may conclude that going along the diagonal in the (α, β) plane from (α_0, β_0) towards the origin, one finds increasingly more dangerous parameter combinations. Also we see in Figure 10.2 that if a point (α, β) can be reached from (α_0, β_0) by first going along the diagonal in the direction of the origin, and next either to the right or straight down, this points corresponds to a stop-loss larger gamma distribution, because it is stochastically larger than a separating more dangerous distribution. In Figure 10.2, one sees the distributions stochastically larger than (α_0, β_0) in the quarter-plane to the right and below this point. In the opposite quarter-plane are the stochastically smaller ones. The quarter-plane to the left and below (α_0, β_0) has stop-loss larger distributions below the diagonal, while for the distributions above the diagonal one may show that the means are lower, but the stop-loss premiums for $d \to \infty$ are higher than for (α_0, β_0). The latter can be proven by applying the rule of l'Hopital twice. Hence, there is a difference of opinion about such risks between the risk averse decision makers. See also Exercise 10.4.8. ∇

Example 10.4.4 (Optimal reinsurance)

In Theorem 1.4.1, we have proven that among the reinsurance contracts with the same expected value of the reimbursement, stop-loss reinsurance leads to a retained loss that has the lowest possible variance. Suppose the loss equals the random variable X, and compare the cdf of the retained loss $Z = X - (X - d)_+$ under stop-loss reinsurance with another retained loss $Y = X - I(X)$, where $\mathrm{E}[Y] = \mathrm{E}[Z]$. Assume that the function $I(\cdot)$ is non-negative, then it follows that

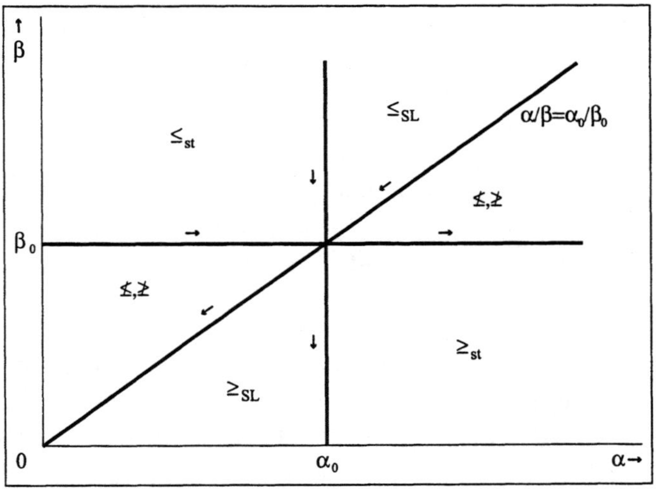

Fig. 10.2 Ordering of gamma(α, β) distributions. The arrows indicate an increase in $\leq_{SL}$.

$Y \leq X$ holds, and hence $F_Y(x) \geq F_X(x)$ for all $x > 0$. Further, $Z = \min\{X, d\}$, so $F_Z(x) = F_X(x)$ for all $x < d$, and $F_Z(x) = 1$ for $x \geq d$. Clearly, the cdf's of Z and Y cross exactly once, at d, and Y is the more dangerous risk. So $Z \leq_{SL} Y$.

Many conclusions can be drawn from this. First, we have $\mathrm{E}[u(-Z)] \geq \mathrm{E}[u(-Y)]$ for every concave increasing utility function $u(\cdot)$. Also, we see confirmed that Theorem 1.4.1 holds, because obviously $\mathrm{Var}[Y] \geq \mathrm{Var}[Z]$. We can also conclude that excess of loss coverage is more effective than any other reinsurance with the same mean that operates on separate claims. Note that these conclusions depend crucially on the fact that the premiums asked for different form of reinsurance depend only on the expected values of the reimbursements. ∇

Example 10.4.5 (Do stop-loss larger claims require larger premiums?)
If a loss X is stop-loss smaller than Y, all risk averse decision makers prefer losing X. Does this show in the premiums that are needed to compensate for this loss?

Surprisingly, the answer to this question is not always affirmative. Consider for instance the standard deviation premium principle, see Chapter 5, leading to a premium $\pi[X] = \mathrm{E}[X] + \alpha\sqrt{\mathrm{Var}[X]}$. If $X \sim$ Bernoulli$(\frac{1}{2})$ and $Y \equiv 1$, while $\alpha > 1$, the premium for X is larger than the one for Y even though $\Pr[X \leq Y] = 1$.

The zero utility premiums, including the exponential premiums, do respect stop-loss order. For these, the premium $\pi[X]$ for a risk X is calculated by solving the utility equilibrium equation (1.11), in this case leading to:

$$\mathrm{E}[u(w + \pi[X] - X)] = u(w). \tag{10.16}$$

The utility function $u(\cdot)$ is assumed to be risk averse, and w is the current wealth. If $X \leq_{SL} Y$ holds, we also have $\mathrm{E}[u(w+\pi[Y]-X)] \geq \mathrm{E}[u(w+\pi[Y]-Y)]$. The right hand side equals $u(w)$. Since $\mathrm{E}[u(w + P - X)]$ increases in P and because $\mathrm{E}[u(w + \pi[X] - X)] = u(w)$ must hold, it follows that $\pi[X] \leq \pi[Y]$. ∇

Example 10.4.6 (Mixtures of Poisson distributions)
In Chapter 7, we have studied, among other things, mixtures of Poisson distributions as a model for the number of claims on an automobile policy, assuming heterogeneity of the risk parameters. In (7.53) for instance we have seen that the estimated structure distribution has the realization $\overline{x}$ as its mean, but we might estimate the parameter $\hat{\alpha}$ in a different way than (7.54). If we replace the structure distribution by a more dangerous one, we increase the uncertainty present in the model. Does it follow from this that the resulting marginal claim number distribution is also stop-loss larger?

A partial answer to this question can be given by combining a few facts that we have seen before. First, by Example 3.3.1, a gamma mixture of Poisson variables has a negative binomial distribution. In Exercise 10.3.9, we saw that a negative binomial distribution is stop-loss larger than a Poisson distribution with the same mean. Hence, a gamma(α, β) mixture of Poisson distributions is stop-loss larger than a pure Poisson distribution with the same mean $\mu = \alpha/\beta$. To give a more general answer, we first introduce some more notation. Suppose that the structure variables are $\Lambda_j, j = 1, 2$, and assume that given $\Lambda_j = \lambda$, the random variables N_j have a Poisson(λ) distribution. Let W_j be the cdf of Λ_j. We want to prove that $W_1 \leq_{SL} W_2$ implies $N_1 \leq_{SL} N_2$. To this end, we introduce the function $f_d(\lambda) = \mathrm{E}[(M_\lambda - d)_+]$, with $M_\lambda \sim$ Poisson(λ). Then $N_1 \leq_{SL} N_2$ holds if and only if $\mathrm{E}[f_d(\Lambda_1)] \leq \mathrm{E}[f_d(\Lambda_2)]$ for all d. So all we have to do is to prove that the function $f_d(\lambda)$ is convex increasing, hence to prove that $f'_d(\lambda)$ is positive and increasing in λ. This proof is rather straightforward:

$$\begin{aligned} f'_d(\lambda) &= \sum_{n>d}(n-d)\frac{d}{d\lambda}\frac{\lambda^n e^{-\lambda}}{n!} = \sum_{n>d}(n-d)\left(\frac{\lambda^{n-1}e^{-\lambda}}{(n-1)!} - \frac{\lambda^n e^{-\lambda}}{n!}\right) \\ &= f_{d-1}(\lambda) - f_d(\lambda) = \int_{d-1}^{d} [1 - F_{M_\lambda}(t)]dt. \end{aligned} \tag{10.17}$$

The last expression is positive, and increasing in λ because $M_\lambda \leq_{st} M_\mu$ for all $\lambda < \mu$. ∇

Example 10.4.7 (Spreading of risks)
Suppose one can invest a total amount 1 in n possible funds. These funds produce iid yields G_i per share. How should one choose the fraction p_i of a share to buy from fund i if the objective is to maximize the expected utility?

Assume that the utility of wealth is measured by the risk averse function $u(\cdot)$. We must solve the following constrained optimization problem:

$$\max_{p_1,\dots,p_n} \mathrm{E}\left[u\left(\sum_i p_i G_i\right)\right] \quad \text{subject to} \sum_i p_i = 1. \tag{10.18}$$

We will prove that taking $p_i = \frac{1}{n}, i = 1, 2, \dots, n$ is optimal. Write $A = \frac{1}{n}\sum_i G_i$ for the average yield. Observe that $\mathrm{E}[G_i|A] \equiv A$, because we have $\sum_i \mathrm{E}[G_i|A] \equiv \mathrm{E}[\sum_i G_i|A] \equiv nA$, and for symmetry reasons the outcome should be the same for every i. This implies

$$\mathrm{E}\left[\sum_i p_i G_i | A\right] \equiv \sum_i p_i \mathrm{E}[G_i|A] \equiv \sum_i p_i A \equiv A. \tag{10.19}$$

By part 4 of Corollary 10.3.13, we have $\mathrm{E}[\sum_i p_i G_i|A] \leq_{SL} \sum_i p_i G_i$, hence because $u(\cdot)$ is concave, the maximum in (10.18) is found when $p_i = \frac{1}{n}, i = 1, 2, \dots, n$. ∇

Remark 10.4.8 (Rao-Blackwell theorem)
The fact that the conditional mean $\mathrm{E}[Y|X]$ is less dangerous than Y itself is also the basis of the Rao-Blackwell theorem, to be found in any text on mathematical statistics, which states that if Y is an unbiased estimator for a certain parameter, then $\mathrm{E}[Y|X]$ is a better unbiased estimator, provided it is a statistic, i.e., it contains no unknown parameters. On every event $X = x$, the conditional distribution of Y is concentrated on its mean $\mathrm{E}[Y|X = x]$, leading to a less dispersed and hence better estimator. ∇

Remark 10.4.9 (Transforming several identical risks)
Consider a sequence of iid risks $X_1, \dots, X_n$ and non-negative functions ρ_i, $i = 1, \dots, n$. Then we can prove that

$$\sum_{i=1}^n \overline{\rho}(X_i) \leq_{SL} \sum_{i=1}^n \rho_i(X_i), \quad \text{where} \quad \overline{\rho}(x) = \frac{1}{n}\sum_{i=1}^n \rho_i(x). \tag{10.20}$$

This inequality expresses the fact that given identical risks, to get the least variable result the same treatment should be applied to all of them. To prove this, we prove that if V is the random variable on the right and W the one on the left in (10.20), we have $W \equiv \mathrm{E}[V|W]$. Next, we use that $\mathrm{E}[V|W] \leq_{SL} V$, see part 4 of Corollary 10.3.13. We have

$$\mathrm{E}\left[\sum_{i=1}^{n} \rho_i(X_i) \middle| \sum_{i=1}^{n} \overline{\rho}(X_i)\right] \equiv \sum_{i=1}^{n} \mathrm{E}\left[\rho_i(X_i) \middle| \sum_{k=1}^{n} \frac{1}{n} \sum_{l=1}^{n} \rho_k(X_l)\right]. \tag{10.21}$$

For symmetry reasons, the result is the same if we replace the X_i by X_j, for each $j = 1, \ldots, n$. But this means that we also have

$$\begin{aligned} &\sum_{i=1}^{n} \mathrm{E}\left[\rho_i(X_i) \middle| \sum_{k=1}^{n} \frac{1}{n} \sum_{l=1}^{n} \rho_k(X_l)\right] \\ &\equiv \sum_{i=1}^{n} \mathrm{E}\left[\frac{1}{n} \sum_{j=1}^{n} \rho_i(X_j) \middle| \sum_{k=1}^{n} \frac{1}{n} \sum_{l=1}^{n} \rho_k(X_l)\right]. \end{aligned} \tag{10.22}$$

This last expression can be rewritten as

$$\begin{aligned} &\mathrm{E}\left[\sum_{i=1}^{n} \frac{1}{n} \sum_{j=1}^{n} \rho_i(X_j) \middle| \sum_{k=1}^{n} \frac{1}{n} \sum_{l=1}^{n} \rho_k(X_l)\right] \\ &\equiv \sum_{k=1}^{n} \frac{1}{n} \sum_{l=1}^{n} \rho_k(X_l) \equiv \sum_{l=1}^{n} \overline{\rho}(X_l). \end{aligned} \tag{10.23}$$

So we have proven that indeed $W \equiv \mathrm{E}[V|W]$, and the required stop-loss inequality in (10.20) follows immediately from Corollary 10.3.13. ∇

Remark 10.4.10 (Law of large numbers and stop-loss order)
The weak law of large numbers expresses that for sequences of iid observations $X_1, X_2, \ldots \sim X$ with finite mean μ and variance σ^2, the average $\overline{X}_n = \frac{1}{n}\sum_{i=1}^{n} X_i$ converges to μ, in the sense that when $\varepsilon > 0$ and $\delta > 0$, we have

$$\Pr[|\overline{X}_n - \mu| < \varepsilon] \geq 1 - \delta \quad \text{for all } n > \sigma^2/\varepsilon^2\delta. \tag{10.24}$$

In terms of stop-loss order, we may prove the following assertion:

$$\overline{X}_1 \geq_{SL} \overline{X}_2 \geq_{SL} \cdots \geq_{SL} \mu. \tag{10.25}$$

Hence the sample averages $\overline{X}_n$, all having the same mean μ, decrease in dangerousness. As $n \to \infty$, the stop-loss premiums $\mathrm{E}[(\overline{X}_n - d)_+]$ at each d converge to $(\mu - d)_+$, which is the stop-loss premium of the degenerate random variable on μ. The proof of (10.25) can be given by taking in the previous remark $\rho_i(x) = \frac{x}{n-1}, i = 1, \ldots, n-1$ and $\rho_n(x) \equiv 0$, resulting in $\overline{\rho}(x) = \frac{x}{n}$. ∇

10.5 INCOMPLETE INFORMATION

In this section we study the situation that we only have limited information about the distribution $F_Y(\cdot)$ of a certain risk Y, and try to determine a safe stop-loss premium at retention d for it. From past experience, from the policy conditions, or from the particular reinsurance that is operative, it is often possible to fix a practical upper bound for the risk. Hence in this section we will assume that we know an upper bound b for the payment Y. We will also assume that we have a good estimate for the mean risk μ as well as sometimes for its variance σ^2. In reinsurance proposals, sometimes these values are prescribed. Also it is conceivable that we have deduced mean and variance from scenario analyses, where for instance the mean payments and the variance about this mean are calculated from models involving return times of catastrophic spring tides or hurricanes. With this data the actuary, much more than the statistician, will tend to base himself on the worst case situation where under the given conditions on μ, σ^2 and the upper bound b, the distribution is chosen that leads to the maximal possible stop-loss premium.

Example 10.5.1 (Dispersion and concentration)
The class of risks Y with a known upper bound b and mean μ contains a most dangerous element Z. It is the random variable with

$$\Pr[Z = b] = 1 - \Pr[Z = 0] = \frac{\mu}{b}. \tag{10.26}$$

This random variable Z has mean μ and upper bound b, so it belongs to the class of feasible risks Y. It is clear that if Y also belongs to this class, their cdf's cross exactly once, hence $Y \leq_{SL} Z$. See Figure 10.3. The distribution of Z arises from the one of Y by *dispersion* of the probability mass to the boundaries 0 and b. The random variable Z is the most dispersed one with this given mean and upper bound. For every retention d, the random variable Z has the maximal possible stop-loss premium $\mathrm{E}[(Z - d)_+]$. The variance $\mathrm{Var}[Z]$ is maximal as well. This is obvious because Z is more dangerous than any feasible risk, but it can also be shown directly, since $\mathrm{E}[Y^2] \leq \mathrm{E}[bY] = b\mu = \mathrm{E}[Z^2]$.

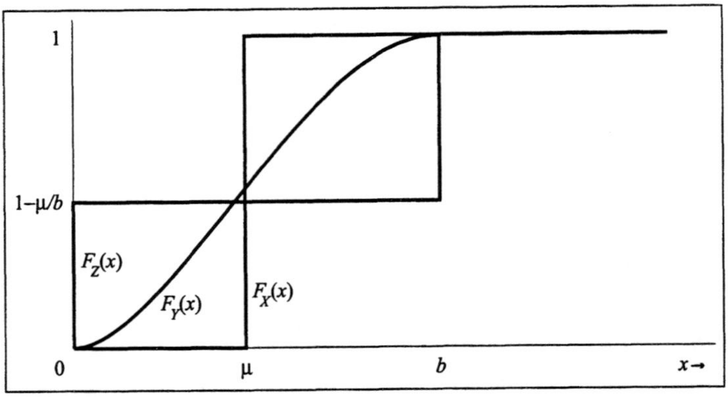

Fig. 10.3 Most and least dangerous cdf's with random variables with mean μ and range $[0, b]$, generated by *dispersion* and *concentration*

This same class of risks on the other hand also contains a least dispersed element. It arises by *concentration* of the probability mass on μ. If $X \equiv \mu$, then $X \leq_{SL} Y$, see again Figure 10.3, and the stop-loss premium of X at each d is minimal, as is its variance. The problem of determining a minimal stop-loss premium is less interesting for practical purposes. Hence in the sequel, we will concentrate on maximal stop-loss premiums.

Note that if the risks X and Y have the same mean and variance, stop-loss order is impossible, because their stop-loss transforms must cross at least once. This is because in view of (3.83), if $\pi_Y(d) \geq \pi_X(d)$ for all d, either $\text{Var}[X] < \text{Var}[Y]$ or $X \sim Y$ must hold.

Dispersal and concentration can also be restricted to only the probability mass in some interval, still resulting in stop-loss larger and stop-loss smaller distributions respectively. See the Exercises 10.5.5 and 10.5.6. ∇

Remark 10.5.2 (Compound distributions and ruin processes)
For each d, we found the same minimal X and maximal Z in Example 10.5.1. Hence $X \leq_{SL} Y \leq_{SL} Z$ holds, implying that we also have results for compound distributions. For instance if $X_i \equiv \mu$, then $X_1 + \cdots + X_N \leq_{SL} Y_1 + \cdots + Y_N$. For ruin processes, if Z as in (10.26) is the claim size distribution in a ruin process, then the ruin probability is maximal for every initial capital u. Notice that this leads to a ruin process with claims zero or b, hence in fact to a process with only one possible claim size. ∇

Now let's further assume that also the variance σ^2 is known. First notice that the following conditions are necessary for feasible distributions to exist at all:

$$0 \leq \mu \leq b, \quad 0 \leq \sigma^2 \leq \mu(b-\mu). \tag{10.27}$$

The need for the first three inequalities is obvious. The last one says that σ^2 is at most the variance of Z in Example 10.5.1, which we proved to be maximal for risks with this range and mean. We will assume the inequalities in (10.27) to be strict, so as to have more than one feasible distribution.

Later on we will prove that the random variable Y with the largest stop-loss premium at d necessarily has a support consisting of two points only. Which support this is depends on the actual value of d. Hence it will not be possible to derive attainable upper bounds for compound stop-loss premiums and ruin probabilities as we did for the case that the variance was unspecified. First we study two-point distributions with mean μ and variance σ^2.

Lemma 10.5.3 (Two-point distributions with given mean and variance)
Suppose a random variable T with $\mathrm{E}[T] = \mu$, $\mathrm{Var}[T] = \sigma^2$, but not necessarily $\Pr[0 \leq T \leq b] = 1$, has a two-point support $\{r, \bar{r}\}$. Then r and $\bar{r}$ are related by

$$\bar{r} = \mu + \frac{\sigma^2}{\mu - r}. \tag{10.28}$$

Proof. We know that $\mathrm{E}[(T-\bar{r})(T-r)] = 0$ must hold. This implies

$$0 = \mathrm{E}[T^2 - (r+\bar{r})T + r\bar{r}] = \mu^2 + \sigma^2 - (r+\bar{r})\mu + r\bar{r}. \tag{10.29}$$

For a given r, we can solve for $\bar{r}$, leading to (10.28). ∇

So for any given r, the number $\bar{r}$ denotes the unique point that can form, together with r, a two-point support with known μ and σ^2. Note the special points $\bar{0}$ and $\bar{b}$. The probability $p_r = \Pr[T = r]$ is uniquely determined by

$$p_r = \frac{\mu - \bar{r}}{r - \bar{r}} = \frac{\sigma^2}{\sigma^2 + (\mu - r)^2}. \tag{10.30}$$

This means that there is exactly one two-point distribution containing $r \neq \mu$. The bar-function assigning $\bar{r}$ to r has the following properties:

$$\begin{aligned} &\overline{(\bar{r})} = r; \\ &\text{for } r \neq \mu, \ \bar{r} \text{ is increasing in } r; \\ &\text{if } r < \mu, \text{ then } \bar{r} > \mu. \end{aligned} \tag{10.31}$$

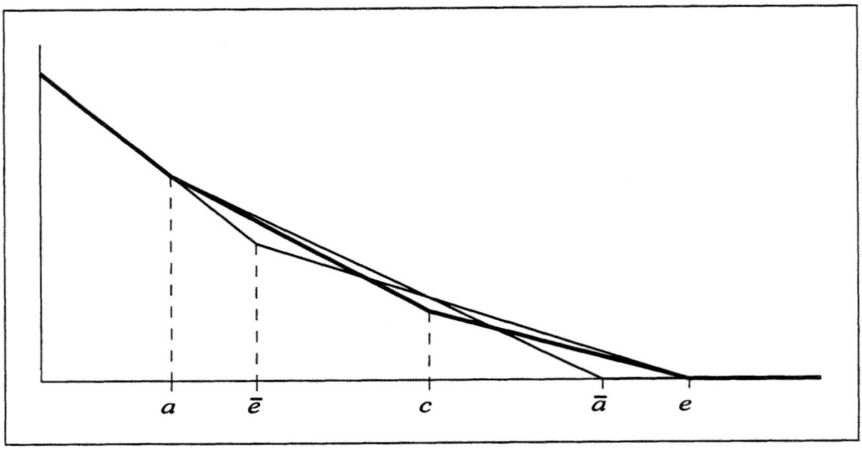

Fig. 10.4 Proof that the stop-loss premium of a 3-point distribution cannot be maximal. For each retention, one of the two-point distributions $\{a, \bar{a}\}$ or $\{\bar{e}, e\}$ has a larger stop-loss premium than the three-point distribution.

So if $\{r, s\}$ and $\{u, v\}$ are two possible two-point supports with $r < s$, $u < v$ and $r < u$, then $r < u < \mu < s < v$ must hold, in line with the fact that because the distributions have equal mean and variance, their stop-loss transforms must cross at least once, their cdf's at least twice, and their densities three or more times.

In our search for the maximal stop-loss premiums, we prove next that the maximal stop-loss premium in any retention d cannot be attained by a distribution with a support contained in $[0, b]$ that consists of more than two points. For this purpose, assume that we have a support $\{a, c, e\}$ of a feasible distribution with $0 \leq a < c < e \leq b$. It can be verified that $c \leq \bar{a} \leq e$, as well as $a \leq \bar{e} \leq c$. From a sketch of the stop-loss transforms, see Figure 10.4, it is easy to see that on $(-\infty, c]$, the two-point distribution on $\{a, \bar{a}\}$ has a stop-loss premium at least equal to the one corresponding to $\{a, c, e\}$, while on $[c, \infty)$, the same holds for $\{e, \bar{e}\}$. In the same fashion, a distribution with n mass points is dominated by one with $n - 1$ mass points. To see why, just let a, c and e be the last three points in the n-point support. The conclusion is that the distribution with a maximal stop-loss premium at retention d is to be found among the distributions with a two-point support.

So to find the random variable X that maximizes $\mathrm{E}[(X - d)_+]$ for a particular value of d and for risks with the properties $\Pr[0 \leq X \leq b] = 1$, $\mathrm{E}[X] = \mu$

and $\mathrm{Var}[X] = \sigma^2$, we only have to look at random variables X with two-point support $\{c, \bar{c}\}$. Note that in case either $d < \bar{c} < c$ or $\bar{c} < c < d$, we have $\mathrm{E}[(X-d)_+] = (\mu - d)_+$, which is in fact the minimal possible stop-loss premium, so we look only at the case $c \geq d \geq \bar{c}$. First we ignore the range constraint $0 \leq \bar{c} < c \leq b$, and solve the following maximization problem:

$$\max_{c>\mu} \mathrm{E}[(X-d)_+] \quad \text{for } \Pr[X=c] = \Pr[X \neq \bar{c}] = \frac{\sigma^2}{\sigma^2 + (c-\mu)^2}. \tag{10.32}$$

This is equivalent to

$$\max_{c>\mu} \frac{\sigma^2(c-d)}{\sigma^2 + (c-\mu)^2}. \tag{10.33}$$

Dividing by σ^2 and taking the derivative with respect to c leads to

$$\frac{d}{dc}\frac{c-d}{\sigma^2 + (c-\mu)^2} = \frac{(c-\mu)^2 + \sigma^2 - 2(c-d)(c-\mu)}{[\sigma^2 + (c-\mu)^2]^2}. \tag{10.34}$$

Setting the numerator equal to zero gives a quadratic equation in c:

$$-c^2 + 2dc + \mu^2 + \sigma^2 - 2d\mu = 0. \tag{10.35}$$

The solution with $c > \mu > \bar{c}$ is given by

$$c^* = d + \sqrt{(d-\mu)^2 + \sigma^2}, \quad \bar{c}^* = d - \sqrt{(d-\mu)^2 + \sigma^2}. \tag{10.36}$$

Notice that we have $d = \frac{1}{2}(c^* + \bar{c}^*)$. The numbers c^* and $\bar{c}^*$ of (10.36) constitute the optimal two-point support if one ignores the requirement that $\Pr[0 \leq X \leq b] = 1$. Imposing this restriction additionally, we get boundary extrema. Since $0 \leq \bar{c}$ implies $\bar{0} \leq c$, we no longer maximize over $c > \mu$, but only over the values $\bar{0} \leq c \leq b$. If $c^* > b$, which is equivalent to $d > \frac{1}{2}(b + \bar{b})$, the optimum is $\{b, \bar{b}\}$. If $\bar{c}^* < 0$, hence $d < \frac{1}{2}\bar{0}$, the optimum is $\{0, \bar{0}\}$. From this discussion we can establish the following theorem about the supports leading to the maximal stop-loss premiums, leaving it to the reader to actually compute the optimal values:

Theorem 10.5.4 (Maximal stop-loss premiums)
For values $\frac{1}{2}\bar{0} \leq d \leq \frac{1}{2}(b + \bar{b})$, the maximal stop-loss premium for a risk with given mean μ, variance σ^2 and upper bound b is the one with the two-point support $\{c^*, \bar{c}^*\}$ with c^* and $\bar{c}^*$ as in (10.36). For $d > \frac{1}{2}(b + \bar{b})$, the distribution with support $\{b, \bar{b}\}$ has the maximal stop-loss premium, and for $d < \frac{1}{2}\bar{0}$, the optimal support is $\{0, \bar{0}\}$. ∇

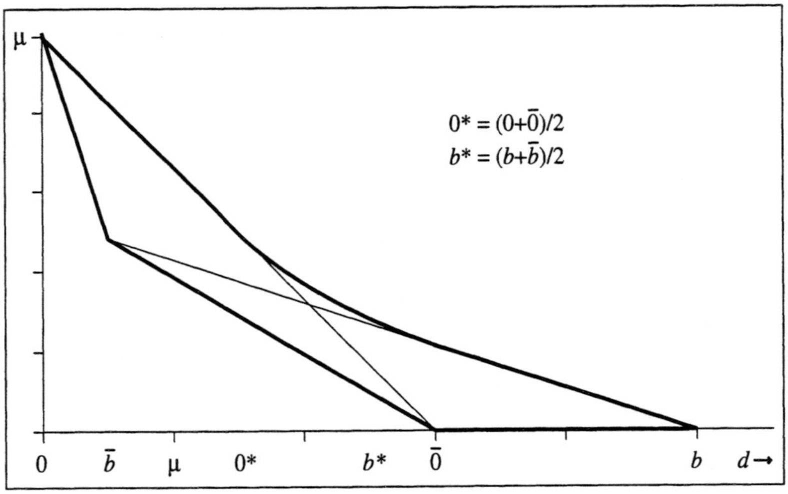

Fig. 10.5 Extremal stop-loss premiums at retention d for $\mu = 1$, $\sigma^2 = 2$ and $b = 5$.

Example 10.5.5 (Minimal and maximal stop-loss premiums)
In Figure 10.5, the minimal and maximal stop-loss premiums are plotted for all $d \in [0, b]$ for the case $\mu = 1$, $\sigma^2 = 2$, and $b = 5$. It can be seen that both the minimal possible stop-loss premiums and the maximal stop-loss premiums constitute a convex decreasing function, hence both are the stop-loss transform with a certain risk. It is evident from the diagram that these have the correct mean μ and upper bound b, but not the right variance σ^2. Further it can be noticed that there are no cdf's that lead to large stop-loss premiums uniformly, since for instance the risk with support $\{0, \bar{0}\}$ has maximal stop-loss premiums for low retentions d, but minimal ones when $d > \bar{0}$.

For reinsurance as occurring in practice, it is the large retentions with $d > \mu+\sigma$, say, that are of interest. One may show that if b is small, for all these d-values the stop-loss premium is maximal for the support $\{b, \bar{b}\}$. This support is optimal as long as $d > \frac{1}{2}(b + \bar{b})$, and $\mu + \sigma > \frac{1}{2}(b + \bar{b})$ holds if $0 < \frac{b-\mu}{\sigma} \leq 1 + \sqrt{2}$, as the reader may check. See Exercise 10.5.8.

The distributions that produce the maximum stop-loss premium have a two-point support, and their stop-loss transforms are tangent lines at d to the graph with the upper bounds. Minima are attained at $(\mu - d)_+$ when $d \leq \bar{b}$ or $d \geq \bar{0}$. In those cases, the support is $\{d, \bar{d}\}$. For intermediate values of d we will argue that the minimal stop-loss premium $l(d)$ is attained by a distribution with support $\{0, d, b\}$.

In a sense, these distributions have a two-point support as well, if one counts the boundary points 0 and b, of which the location is fixed but the associated probability can be chosen freely, for one half. In Figure 10.5 one sees that connecting the points $(0, \mu)$, $(d, l(d))$ and $(b, 0)$ gives a stop-loss transformation $\pi(\cdot)$ with not only the right mean $\pi(0) = \mu$, but also with an upper bound b since $\pi(b) = 0$. Moreover, the variance is equal to σ^2. This is because the area below the stop-loss transform, which equals the second moment of the risk, is equal to the corresponding area for the risks with support $\{0, \bar{0}\}$ as well as with $\{b, \bar{b}\}$. To see this, use the areas of triangles with base line $(b, 0)$ to $(0, \mu)$. Note that $l(d)$ is the minimal value of a stop-loss premium at d, because any stop-loss transform through a point (d, h) with $h < \pi(d)$ leads to a second moment strictly less than $\mu^2 + \sigma^2$. On the interval $\bar{b} < d < \bar{0}$, one may show that the function $l(d)$ runs parallel to the line connecting $(b, 0)$ to $(0, \mu)$. ∇

Remark 10.5.6 (Related problems)
Other problems of this type have been solved as well. There are analytical results available for the extremal stop-loss premiums given up to four moments, and algorithms for when the number of known moments is larger than four. The practical relevance of these methods is somewhat questionable, since the only way to have reliable estimates of the moments of a distribution is to have many observations, and from these one may estimate a stop-loss premium directly. There are also results for the case that Y is unimodal with a known mode M. As well as the extremal stop-loss premiums, also the extremal tail probabilities can be computed. ∇

Example 10.5.7 (Verbeek's inequality; mode zero)
Let Y be a unimodal risk with mean μ, upper bound b and mode 0. As F_Y is concave on $[0, b]$, $2\mu \leq b$ must hold. Further, let X and Z be risks with $\Pr[Z = 0] = 1 - 2\frac{\mu}{b}$, and

$$\begin{aligned} F'_Z(y) &= \frac{2\mu}{b^2}, \quad 0 < y < b; \\ F'_X(y) &= \frac{1}{2\mu}, \quad 0 < y < 2\mu, \end{aligned} \tag{10.37}$$

and zero otherwise. Then X and Z are also unimodal with mode zero, and $\mathrm{E}[X] = \mathrm{E}[Y] = \mathrm{E}[Z]$, as well as $X \leq_{SL} Y \leq_{SL} Z$. See Exercise 10.5.2. So this class of risks also has elements that have uniformly minimal and maximal stop-loss premiums, respectively, allowing results extending to compound distributions and ruin probabilities. ∇

10.6 SUMS OF DEPENDENT RANDOM VARIABLES

In order to be able to handle both gains and losses, we start by extending the concept of stop-loss order somewhat to account for more general random variables with possibly negative values as well as positive ones, instead of the non-negative risks that we studied up to now. Then we state and prove the central result in this theory, which is that the least attractive portfolios are those for which the policies are maximally dependent. Next, we give some examples of how to apply the theory. A lot of research is being done in this field, enough to fill a monograph of its own.

With stop-loss order, we are concerned with large values of a random loss, and call random variable Y less attractive than X if the expected values of all top parts $(Y-d)_+$ are larger than those of X. Negative values for these random variables are actually gains. But with stability in mind, excessive gains are just as unattractive for the decision maker, for instance for tax reasons. Hence X will be more attractive than Y only if both the top parts $(X-d)_+$ and the bottom parts $(d-X)_+$ have a lower mean value than for Y. This leads to the following definition:

Definition 10.6.1 (Convex order)
If both the following conditions hold for every $d \in (-\infty, \infty)$:

$$\begin{aligned} &\mathrm{E}[(X-d)_+] \leq \mathrm{E}[(Y-d)_+], \quad \text{and} \\ &\mathrm{E}[(d-X)_+] \leq \mathrm{E}[(d-Y)_+], \end{aligned} \tag{10.38}$$

then the random variable X is less than Y in convex order, written $X \leq_{cx} Y$. ∇

Note that adding d to the first set of inequalities and letting $d \to -\infty$ leads to $\mathrm{E}[X] \leq \mathrm{E}[Y]$. Subtracting d in the second set of inequalities and letting $d \to +\infty$, on the other hand, produces $\mathrm{E}[X] \geq \mathrm{E}[Y]$. Hence $\mathrm{E}[X] = \mathrm{E}[Y]$ must hold for two random variables to be convex ordered. Also note that the first set of inequalities combined with equal means implies the second set of (10.38), since $\mathrm{E}[(X-d)_+] - \mathrm{E}[(d-X)_+] = \mathrm{E}[X] - d$. So two random variables with equal means and ordered stop-loss premiums are convex ordered, while random variables with unequal means are never convex ordered.

Stop-loss order is the same as having ordered expected values $\mathrm{E}[f(X)]$ for all *non-decreasing* convex functions $f(\cdot)$, see Theorem 10.3.8. Hence it represents the common preferences of all risk averse decision makers. On the other hand, convex order is the same as ordered expectations for *all* convex functions. This is of course where the name convex order derives from. In a utility theory context, it represents the common preferences of all risk averse decision makers between random variables with equal mean. One way to prove that convex order implies ordered expectations of convex functions is to use the fact that any convex function can be obtained as the uniform limit of a sequence of piecewise linear functions, each of them expressible as a linear combination of functions $(x-t)_+$ and $(t-x)_+$. This is the proof that one usually finds in the literature. A simpler proof, involving partial integrations, is given below.

Theorem 10.6.2 (Convex order means ordered convex expectations)
If $X \leq_{cx} Y$ and $f(\cdot)$ is convex, then $\mathrm{E}[f(X)] \leq \mathrm{E}[f(Y)]$.
If $\mathrm{E}[f(X)] \leq \mathrm{E}[f(Y)]$ for every convex function $f(\cdot)$, then $X \leq_{cx} Y$.

Proof. To prove the second assertion, consider the convex functions $f(x) = x$, $f(x) = -x$ and $f(x) = (x-d)_+$ for arbitrary *d*. The first two functions lead to $\mathrm{E}[X] = \mathrm{E}[Y]$, the last one gives $\mathrm{E}[(X-d)_+] \leq \mathrm{E}[(Y-d)_+]$.

To prove the first assertion, consider $g(x) = f(x) - f(a) - (x-a)f'(a)$, where a is some point where the function f is differentiable. Since $\mathrm{E}[X] = \mathrm{E}[Y]$, the inequality $\mathrm{E}[f(X)] \leq \mathrm{E}[f(Y)]$, assuming these expectations exist, is equivalent to $\mathrm{E}[g(X)] \leq \mathrm{E}[g(Y)]$. Write $F(x) = \Pr[X \leq x]$ and $\overline{F}(x) = 1 - F(x)$. Since $g(a) = g'(a) = 0$, the integrated terms below vanish, so by four partial integrations we get

$$\begin{aligned}
\mathrm{E}[g(X)] &= \int_{-\infty}^{a} g(x)\,dF(x) - \int_{a}^{\infty} g(x)\,d\overline{F}(x) \\
&= -\int_{-\infty}^{a} g'(x)F(x)\,dx + \int_{a}^{\infty} g'(x)\,\overline{F}(x)dx \qquad (10.39)\\
&= \int_{-\infty}^{a} \mathrm{E}[(x-X)_+]\,dg'(x) + \int_{a}^{\infty} \mathrm{E}[(X-x)_+]dg'(x),
\end{aligned}$$

from which the result immediately follows because since $f(\cdot)$ is convex, so is $g(\cdot)$, and therefore $dg'(x) \geq 0$ for all x. ∇

The stop-loss transforms $\mathrm{E}[(X-d)_+]$ of two random variables with equal mean μ have common asymptotes. One is the x-axis, the other the line $y = \mu - x$. Generalizing (3.82), it can be shown that $\int_{-\infty}^{\infty}\{\mathrm{E}[(X-t)_+] - (\mu-t)_+\}dt = \frac{1}{2}\mathrm{Var}[X]$. Hence, just as for risks, the integrated difference between the stop-loss transforms of two arbitrary random variables with the same mean is half the difference in their variances. See Figure 10.6.

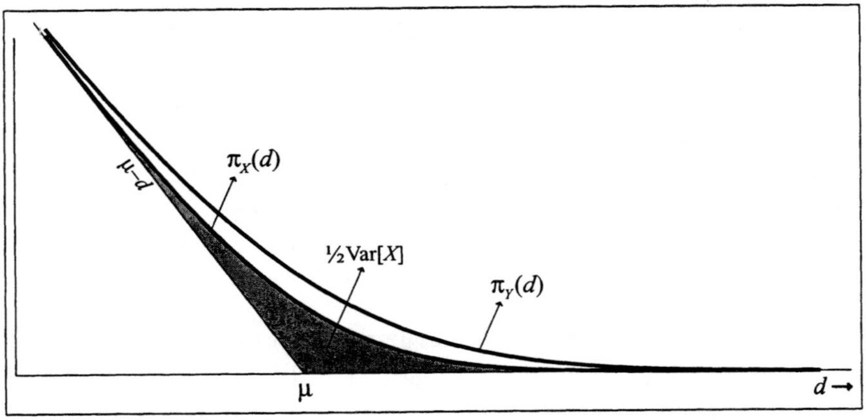

Fig. 10.6 Two stop-loss transforms $\pi_X(d) = \text{E}[(X-d)_+]$ and $\pi_Y(d)$ when $X \leq_{cx} Y$. Note that the asymptotes are equal.

Consider some univariate cumulative distribution function F. It is well-known that if $U \sim$ uniform(0,1), the random variable $F^{-1}(U)$ is distributed according to F (probability integral transform). Note that it is irrelevant how we define $y = F^{-1}(u)$ for arguments u where there is an ambiguity, i.e., where $F(y) = u$ holds for an interval of y-values. Just as the cdf of a random variable can have only countably many jumps, it can be shown that there can only be countably many such horizontal segments. To see this, observe that in the interval $[-2^n, 2^n]$ there are only finitely many intervals with a length over 2^{-n} where $F(y)$ is constant, and let $n \to \infty$. Hence, if $g(\cdot)$ and $h(\cdot)$ are two different choices for the inverse cdf, $g(U)$ and $h(U)$ will be equal with probability one. The customary choice is to take $F^{-1}(u)$ to be the left-hand endpoint of the interval of y-values (generally containing one point only) with $F(y) = u$. Then, $F^{-1}(\cdot)$ is non-decreasing and continuous from the left.

Now consider any random n-vector $(X_1, X_2, \ldots, X_n)$. Define a set in $\mathbb{R}^n$ to be *comonotonic* if each two vectors in it are ordered componentwise, i.e., all components of the larger one are at least the corresponding components of the other. We will also call a distribution comonotonic if its support is comonotonic. Also, any random vector having such a distribution is comonotonic. We have:

Theorem 10.6.3 (Comonotonic joint distribution)
For some $U \sim \text{uniform}(0,1)$, define the following random vector:

$$(Y_1, Y_2, \ldots, Y_n) = (F_{X_1}^{-1}(U), F_{X_2}^{-1}(U), \ldots, F_{X_n}^{-1}(U)). \qquad (10.40)$$

This vector has the same marginals as $(X_1, X_2, \ldots, X_n)$.
Its support is comonotonic.
Its joint cdf equals the so-called *Fréchet/Höffding* upper bound:

$$\Pr[Y_1 \leq y_1, \ldots, Y_n \leq y_n] = \min_{j=1,\ldots,n} \Pr[X_j \leq y_j]. \tag{10.41}$$

Proof. First, we have for all $j = 1, 2, \ldots, n$:

$$\Pr[Y_j \leq y_j] = \Pr[F_{X_j}^{-1}(U) \leq y_j] = \Pr[U \leq F_{X_j}(y_j)] = F_{X_j}(y_j). \tag{10.42}$$

Next, the support of $(Y_1, \ldots, Y_n)$ is a curve $\{(y_1(u), \ldots, y_n(u)) | 0 < u < 1\}$ that increases in all its components. If $(y_1, \ldots, y_n)$ and $(z_1, \ldots, z_n)$ are two elements of it with $F_{X_i}^{-1}(u) = y_i < z_i = F_{X_i}^{-1}(v)$ for some i, then $u < v$ must hold, and hence $y_j \leq z_j$ for all $j = 1, 2, \ldots, n$.

Further, we have

$$\begin{aligned} \Pr[Y_1 \leq y_1, \ldots, Y_n \leq y_n] &= \Pr[F_{X_1}^{-1}(U) \leq y_1, \ldots, F_{X_n}^{-1}(U) \leq y_n] \\ &= \Pr[U \leq F_{X_1}(y_1), \ldots, U \leq F_{X_n}(y_n)] \\ &= \min_{j=1,\ldots,n} \Pr[X_j \leq y_j], \end{aligned} \tag{10.43}$$

which proves the final assertion of the theorem. ∇

The set S that is the support of $(Y_1, \ldots, Y_n)$ consists of a series of connected closed curves, see Figures 10.7 and 10.8, possibly containing just one point. Together they form a comonotonic set. The connected closure $\overline{S}$ of S is a continuous curve which is also comonotonic. It arises by connecting the endpoints of consecutive curves by straight lines. Note that this has to be done only countably many times, at discontinuities of one of the inverse cdf's in the components. The set $\overline{S}$ thus produced is a continuously increasing curve in $\mathbb{R}^n$.

Note that by (10.41), the joint cdf of $Y_1, \ldots, Y_n$, i.e., the probability that all components have small values simultaneously, is as large as it can be without violating the marginal distributions; trivially, the right hand side of this equality is an upper bound for any joint cdf with the prescribed marginals. Also note that comonotonicity entails that no Y_j is in any way a hedge for another component Y_k. In view of the remarks made in the introduction of this chapter, it is not surprising that the following theorem holds.

Theorem 10.6.4 (Comonotonic random vector has convex largest sum)
The random vector $(Y_1, Y_2, \dots, Y_n)$ in Theorem 10.6.3 has the following property:

$$Y_1 + Y_2 + \cdots + Y_n \geq_{cx} X_1 + X_2 + \cdots + X_n. \tag{10.44}$$

Proof. It suffices to prove that the stop-loss premiums are ordered, since it is obvious that the means of these two random variables are equal. The following holds for all $x_1, \dots, x_n$ when $d_1 + \cdots + d_n = d$:

$$\begin{aligned}
&(x_1 + x_2 + \cdots + x_n - d)_+ \\
&= \{(x_1 - d_1) + (x_2 - d_2) + \cdots + (x_n - d_n)\}_+ \\
&\leq \{(x_1 - d_1)_+ + (x_2 - d_2)_+ + \cdots + (x_n - d_n)_+\}_+ \\
&= (x_1 - d_1)_+ + (x_2 - d_2)_+ + \cdots + (x_n - d_n)_+.
\end{aligned} \tag{10.45}$$

Assume that d is such that $0 < \Pr[Y_1 + \cdots + Y_n \leq d] < 1$ holds; if not, the stop-loss premiums of $Y_1 + \cdots + Y_n$ and $X_1 + \cdots + X_n$ can be seen to be equal. The connected curve $\overline{S}$ containing the support S of the comonotonic random vector $(Y_1, \dots, Y_n)$ points upwards in all coordinates, so it is obvious that $\overline{S}$ has exactly one point of intersection with the hyperplane $\{(x_1, \dots, x_n) | x_1 + \cdots + x_n = d\}$. From now on, let $(d_1, \dots, d_n)$ denote this point of intersection. In specific examples, it is easy to determine this point, but for now, we only need the fact that such a point exists. For all points $(y_1, \dots, y_n)$ in the support S of $(Y_1, \dots, Y_n)$, we have the following *equality:*

$$\begin{aligned}
&(y_1 + y_2 + \cdots + y_n - d)_+ \\
&\quad \equiv (y_1 - d_1)_+ + (y_2 - d_2)_+ + \cdots + (y_n - d_n)_+.
\end{aligned} \tag{10.46}$$

This is because for this particular choice of $(d_1, \dots, d_n)$, by the comonotonicity, whenever $y_j > d_j$ for any j, we also have $y_k \geq d_k$ for all k; when all $y_j \leq d_j$, obviously the left hand side is 0 as well. Now replacing constants by the corresponding random variables in the two relations above and taking expectations, we get

$$\begin{aligned}
&\mathrm{E}[(Y_1 + Y_2 + \cdots + Y_n - d)_+] \\
&\quad = \mathrm{E}[(Y_1 - d_1)_+] + \mathrm{E}[(Y_2 - d_2)_+] + \cdots + \mathrm{E}[(Y_n - d_n)_+] \\
&\quad = \mathrm{E}[(X_1 - d_1)_+] + \mathrm{E}[(X_2 - d_2)_+] + \cdots + \mathrm{E}[(X_n - d_n)_+] \\
&\quad \geq \mathrm{E}[(X_1 + X_2 + \cdots + X_n - d)_+],
\end{aligned} \tag{10.47}$$

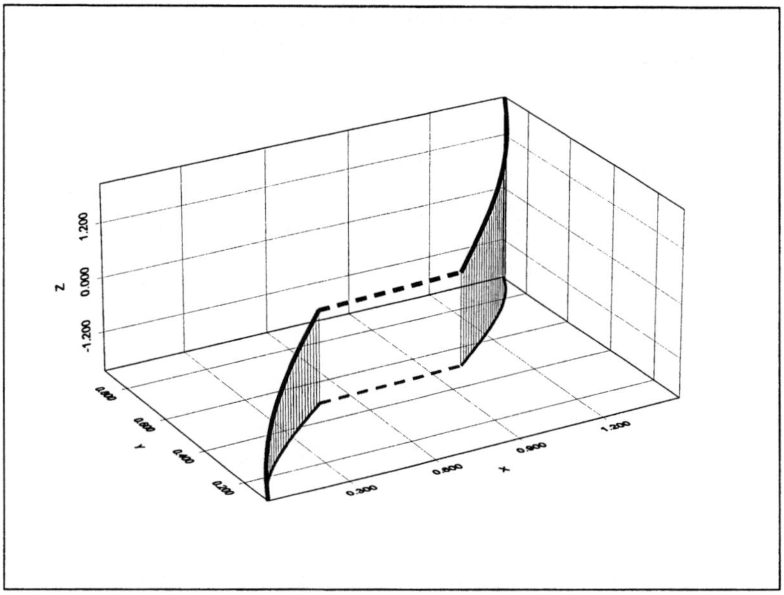

Fig. 10.7 Comonotonic cdf with (X, Y, Z) as in Example 10.6.5, and the marginal comonotonic cdf of (X, Y). The dotted lines serve to make the comonotonic support connected.

since X_j and Y_j have the same marginal distribution for all j. ∇

Example 10.6.5 (A three-dimensional continuous random vector)
Let $X \sim$ uniform on the set $(0, \frac{1}{2}) \cup (1, \frac{3}{2})$, $Y \sim$ Beta(2,2), $Z \sim \mathrm{N}(0, 1)$. The support of the comonotonic distribution is the set

$$\{(F_X^{-1}(u), F_Y^{-1}(u), F_Z^{-1}(u)) | 0 < u < 1\}. \tag{10.48}$$

See Figure 10.7. Actually, not all of the support is depicted. The part left out corresponds to $u \notin (\Phi(-2), \Phi(2))$ and extends along the asymptotes, the vertical lines $(0, 0, z)$ and $(\frac{3}{2}, 1, z)$. The thick continuous line is the support S, while the dotted line is the straight line needed to make S into the connected curve $\overline{S}$. Note that $F_X(x)$ has a horizontal segment between $x = \frac{1}{2}$ and $x = 1$. The projection of $\overline{S}$ along the z-axis can also be seen to constitute an increasing curve, as do projections along the other axes. ∇

Example 10.6.6 (A two-dimensional discrete example)
For a discrete example, take $X \sim$ uniform$\{0, 1, 2, 3\}$ and $Y \sim$ binomial$(3, \frac{1}{2})$. It is easy to verify that

$$\begin{aligned}
(F_X^{-1}(u), F_Y^{-1}(u)) &= (0,0) \text{ for } 0 < u < \frac{1}{8}, \\
&= (0,1) \text{ for } \frac{1}{8} < u < \frac{2}{8}, \\
&= (1,1) \text{ for } \frac{2}{8} < u < \frac{4}{8}, \\
&= (2,2) \text{ for } \frac{4}{8} < u < \frac{6}{8}, \\
&= (3,2) \text{ for } \frac{6}{8} < u < \frac{7}{8}, \\
&= (3,3) \text{ for } \frac{7}{8} < u < 1.
\end{aligned}$$

At the boundaries of the intervals for u, one may take the limit from either the left or the right. The points $(1,1)$ and $(2,2)$ have probability $\frac{1}{4}$, the other points of the support S of the comonotonic distribution have probability $\frac{1}{8}$. The curve $\overline{S}$ arises by simply connecting these points consecutively with straight lines, the dotted lines in Figure 10.8. The straight line connecting $(1,1)$ and $(2,2)$ is not along one of the axes. This happens because at level $u = \frac{1}{2}$, both $F_X(y)$ and $F_Y(y)$ have horizontal segments. Note that any non-decreasing curve connecting $(1,1)$ and $(2,2)$ would have led to a feasible $\overline{S}$. ∇

Example 10.6.7 (Mortality risks of husband and wife)
Let $n = 2$, $X \sim$ Bernoulli(q_x), and Y such that $\frac{1}{2}Y \sim$ Bernoulli(q_y). This describes the situation of life insurances on two lives, one male of age x and with amount at risk 1, and one female of age y with amount at risk 2. Assume the mortality risks to be dependent random variables, and write $z = \Pr[X = 1, Y = 2]$. Then we can represent the joint distribution of (X, Y) as follows:

	$X = 0$	$X = 1$	Total
$Y = 0$	$1 - q_x - q_y + z$	$q_x - z$	$1 - q_y$
$Y = 2$	$q_y - z$	z	q_y
Total	$1 - q_x$	q_x	1

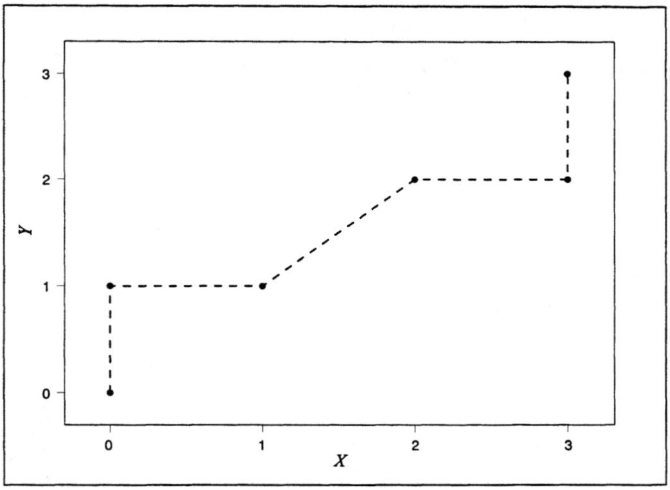

Fig. 10.8 Comonotonic support of (X, Y) as in Example 10.6.6; the dots represent the points with positive probability, the dotted lines connect the support.

For each convex function $f(\cdot)$, the following is increasing in z:

$$\begin{aligned} \mathrm{E}[f(X+Y)] &= f(0)(1-q_x-q_y)+f(1)q_x+f(2)q_y \\ &\quad + [f(0)-f(1)-f(2)+f(3)]z. \end{aligned} \tag{10.49}$$

Hence, one gets the maximal $X+Y$ in convex order by taking the z as large as possible, so $z = \min\{q_x, q_y\}$. Assume that $q_x < q_y$ holds, then we get:

	$X=0$	$X=1$	Total
$Y=0$	$1-q_y$	0	$1-q_y$
$Y=2$	q_y-q_x	q_x	q_y
Total	$1-q_x$	q_x	1

The joint distribution can only be comonotonic if one or both of the events $X = 1, Y = 0$ and $X = 0, Y = 2$ have probability zero. In the comonotonic distribution for $q_x < q_y$, if $X = 1$ occurs, necessarily event $Y = 2$ occurs as well. If $q_x > q_y$, the situation is reversed. So the comonotonic joint mortality pattern is such that if the person with the smaller mortality probability dies, so does the other. For $q_x = q_y$, we have $Y = 2X$ with probability one. ∇

Example 10.6.8 (Cash-flow in a random interest term structure)
Assume that we have to make payments 1 at the end of each year for the coming n years. The interest is not fixed, but it varies randomly. We assume that the discount factor for a payment to be made at time k is equal to

$$X_k = e^{-(Y_1+\cdots+Y_k)}, \tag{10.50}$$

where the annual returns Y_j are assumed to obey some multinormal distribution, for instance a Brownian motion. Hence $X_k \sim$ lognormal, and the total present value of all payments is the sum of dependent lognormal random variables. It is not easy to handle such random variables analytically. In view of Theorem 10.6.4, however, it is easy to find an upper bound in convex order for the total payment $S = \sum_k X_k$ that is easy to handle. It suffices to replace the X_k random variables by their comonotonic versions. For an approximation by a comonotonic sum to be good, the dependence between the terms should be strong to begin with. To see why this might well be the case here, note that for $k < l$ we have $X_l = X_k e^{-(Y_{k+1}+\cdots+Y_l)}$. So for k and l both large, X_k and X_l have a large correlation in many random interest term structures. ∇

Sometimes the dependency structure is known, but it is so cumbersome that we cannot fruitfully use it. In the example below we give stochastic bounds for $X_1 + \cdots + X_n$ for the special case that a random variable Z exists such that the cdf of Z is known and the same holds for all the conditional distributions of X_i, given $Z = z$. A structure variable such as one encounters in credibility contexts is a good example. In view of Corollary 10.3.13, a convex lower bound for $X_1 + \cdots + X_n$ is then $\mathrm{E}[X_1 + \cdots + X_n|Z]$. A better convex upper bound than the comonotonic one arises by replacing, for each z, the conditional distribution of $X_1, \ldots, X_n$, given $Z = z$, by the comonotonic joint distribution, and again taking the weighted average of the resulting distributions. As opposed to the lower bound, the improved upper bound can be shown to have the prescribed marginals, hence it is lower than the comonotonic upper bound which uses only the marginal distributions. See Exercise 10.6.12.

Example 10.6.9 (Stochastic bounds when a structure variable exists)
We illustrate the technique of conditioning on the value of a structure random variable by an example. The multinormal distribution is very useful in this context, because the conditional and marginal distributions are known. Let $n = 2$, and take Y_1, Y_2 to be independent $N(0, 1)$ random variables. Look at the sum $S = X_1 + X_2$

where $X_1 = e^{Y_1} \sim \text{lognormal}(0,1)$, and $X_2 = e^{Y_1+Y_2} \sim \text{lognormal}(0,2)$. For Z, we take a linear combination of Y_1, Y_2, in this case $Z = Y_1 + Y_2$. For the lower bound as described above, denoted by S_l, note that $\mathrm{E}[X_2|Z] = e^Z$, while $Y_1|Y_1 + Y_2 = z \sim N(\frac{1}{2}z, \frac{1}{2})$, and hence

$$\mathrm{E}[e^{Y_1}|Y_1 + Y_2 = z] = m(1; \frac{1}{2}z, \frac{1}{2}), \tag{10.51}$$

where $m(t; \mu, \sigma^2) = e^{\mu t + \frac{1}{2}\sigma^2 t^2}$ is the $N(\mu, \sigma^2)$ moment generating function. This leads to

$$\mathrm{E}[e^{Y_1}|Z] = e^{\frac{1}{2}Z + \frac{1}{4}}. \tag{10.52}$$

So the lower bound is

$$S_l = \mathrm{E}[X_1 + X_2|Z] = e^{\frac{1}{2}Z + \frac{1}{4}} + e^Z. \tag{10.53}$$

The comonotonic upper bound, S_u, say, has $(X_1, X_2) \sim (e^W, e^{\sqrt{2}W})$ for some $W \sim$ N(0,1). The improved upper bound, denoted by S'_u, has as its second term again e^Z. The first term equals $e^{\frac{1}{2}Z + \frac{1}{2}\sqrt{2}W}$, with Z and W mutually independent, $Z \sim$ N(0,2) and $W \sim$ N(0,1). All terms occurring in these bounds are lognormal random variables, so the variances of the bounds are easy to compute. Note that to compare variances is meaningful when comparing stop-loss premiums of convex ordered random variables. This is because half the variance difference between two convex ordered random variables equals the integrated difference of their stop-loss premiums, see, e.g., Figure 10.6. This implies that if $X \leq_{cx} Y$ and in addition Var$[X]$ = Var$[Y]$, then X and Y must necessary be equal in distribution. Moreover, the ratio of the variances for random variables with the same mean is roughly equal to the ratio of the stop-loss premiums, minus their minimal possible value. We have, as the reader may verify,

$$\begin{aligned}
(\mathrm{E}[S])^2 &= e^1 + 2e^{\frac{3}{2}} + e^2, \\
\mathrm{E}[S_l^2] &= e^{\frac{3}{2}} + 2e^{\frac{5}{2}} + e^4, \\
\mathrm{E}[S^2] = \mathrm{E}[S_u'^2] &= e^2 + 2e^{\frac{5}{2}} + e^4, \\
\mathrm{E}[S_u^2] &= e^2 + 2e^{\frac{3}{2}+\sqrt{2}} + e^4.
\end{aligned} \tag{10.54}$$

Hence,

$$\begin{aligned} \text{Var}[\text{E}[S]] &= 0, \\ \text{Var}[S_l] &= 64.374, \\ \text{Var}[S] = \text{Var}[S_u^{'}] &= 67.281, \\ \text{Var}[S_u] &= 79.785. \end{aligned} \qquad (10.55)$$

So a stochastic lower bound S_l for S, much better than just $\text{E}[S]$, is obtained by conditioning on $Y_1 + Y_2$, and the improved upper bound $S_u^{'}$ has in fact the same distribution as S. In general, for pairs of random variables, the distributions of $S_u^{'}$ and S coincide when one conditions on one of the variables. See Exercise 10.6.22.

For the lower bound, recall that $\text{Var}[S] = \text{E}[\text{Var}[S|Z]] + \text{Var}[\text{E}[S|Z]]$. The variance of S_l is just the second term. To maximize the second term is to minimize the first, so we look for a Z which resembles S as closely as possible. Approximating e^{Y_1} and $e^{Y_1+Y_2}$ by $1+Y_1$ and $1+Y_1+Y_2$ respectively, we see that $S \approx 2+2Y_1+Y_2$, hence taking $2Y_1 + Y_2$ instead of $Y_1 + Y_2$ as our conditioning random variable might lead to a better lower bound. It is left as Exercise 10.6.11 to check whether this is indeed the case. ∇

Example 10.6.10 (More related joint db's; PQD)

We have seen that two random variables are maximally related if their joint distribution is comonotonic, hence if their joint cdf is as large as possible. This inspires us to advance a partial order between pairs of random variables having the same marginals. Assume that all random variables X, X', $X^{\perp}$ and X^U below have the same marginal cdf F, and all corresponding random variables Y have marginal cdf G. We call (X, Y) *more related* than (X', Y') if the probability $F_{X,Y}(x, y)$ that X and Y are both small is larger than this probability for X' and Y', for all x and y. If $X^{\perp}$ and $Y^{\perp}$ are independent, and (X^U, Y^U) has a comonotonic joint distribution, then obviously the pair (X^U, Y^U) is more related than $(X^{\perp}, Y^{\perp})$. In fact it is more related than any other pair, hence, 'most related', or maximally dependent. Any pair which is more related than $(X^{\perp}, Y^{\perp})$ will be called PQD, for *positive quadrant dependent*. Hence X and Y are PQD if

$$\Pr[X \le x, Y \le y] \ge \Pr[X \le x]\Pr[Y \le y] \text{ for all } x \text{ and } y. \qquad (10.56)$$

There is also a joint distribution with the right marginals that is 'least related', or 'most antithetic'. It follows from the following lower bound for the joint cdf, also studied by Fréchet/Höffding:

$$\Pr[X \le x, Y \le y] \ge \max\{0, F(x) + G(y) - 1\}. \qquad (10.57)$$

This inequality follows directly from Bonferroni's inequality, see Exercise 10.6.8. A pair with this cdf is $(X, Y) = (F^{-1}(U), G^{-1}(1-U))$; here Y is small when X is large and vice versa. In fact, in this case X and $-Y$ are most related; X and Y are not comonotonic, but countermonotonic.

To compare pairs of random variables as regards degree of relatedness, one might of course simply compare their values of association measures such as the customary correlation coefficient $r(X,Y) = (\mathrm{E}[XY] - \mathrm{E}[X]\mathrm{E}[Y])/\sigma_X\sigma_Y$, also known as the Pearson product-moment correlation, or the Spearman rank correlation defined as $\rho(X,Y) = r(F(X), G(Y))$. This procedure has the advantage of leading to a total order, but it has some drawbacks as well, see e.g. Exercise 10.6.19. An important property of the concept of being 'more related' is that the sum of the more related pair is larger in convex order. This can be inferred from combining the equality $\mathrm{E}[(X+Y-d)_+] = \mathrm{E}[(d-X-Y)_+] + \mathrm{E}[X] + \mathrm{E}[Y] - d$ with the following one, derived by reversing the order of integration (Fubini):

$$\mathrm{E}[(d-X-Y)_+] = \iint\limits_{x+y\le d} \int\limits_{t=y}^{d-x} dt\, dF(x,y) = \int\limits_{t=-\infty}^{\infty} \iint\limits_{y\le t,\, x\le d-t} dF(x,y)dt$$
$$= \int_{t=-\infty}^{\infty} F(t, d-t)dt. \tag{10.58}$$

See the exercises for some more characteristics of the PQD property. In particular, as one would expect, the pair (X, X) is PQD, as well as $(X, X+Z)$ and $(X+Y, X+Z)$ when X, Y and Z are independent. The concept can also be generalized to dimension $n > 2$. ∇

Example 10.6.11 (Copulas)

Consider continuous two-dimensional random vectors (X, Y) with joint distribution $F(x, y)$. The marginals are assumed given, and again written as $F(x, \infty) = F(x)$ and $F(\infty, y) = G(y)$. *Copulas* provide a means to construct random vectors with a wide range of possible joint distributions. A copula is a function $C(u, v)$ that maps the marginals to the joint distribution, hence $F(x, y) = C(F(x), G(y))$. We will illustrate the concept by three special cases, see also the previous example:

$$\begin{aligned} C_1(u,v) &= \min\{u,v\}; \\ C_2(u,v) &= u\,v; \qquad\qquad 0<u<1,\ 0<v<1 \\ C_3(u,v) &= \max\{0, u+v-1\}. \end{aligned} \tag{10.59}$$

As one sees, $C_1(u,v)$ is the Fréchet/Höffding upper bound for any copula function, and it produces the most related (comonotonic) pair in the sense of the previous example. On the other hand, $C_3(u,v)$ is a lower bound; it produces the most antithetic pair. The other copula function $C_2(u,v)$ simply represents the case that X and Y are independent. By considering the special case that $F(x) = x$ and $G(y) = y$ on $(0,1)$, one sees that $C(u,v)$ must itself be a two-dimensional cdf. It has uniform$(0,1)$ marginals, and hence $C(u,1) = u$ and $C(1,v) = v$.

Assume for the moment that (U,V) is a random vector with joint cdf generated by some copula function $C(u,v)$, and that the marginals are both uniform(0,1). Then if $C = C_1$, we have $U \equiv V$, if $C = C_3$, we have $U \equiv 1-V$, and if $C = C_2$, U and V are independent. Mixtures of copulas are again a copula. We will show how by taking a convex combination of the three copulas used above, we can get a random vector with uniform marginals that has any correlation between -1 and $+1$. Indeed if for $p_1, p_2, p_3 \geq 0$ with $p_1 + p_2 + p_3 = 1$, we have

$$C(u,v) = p_1 C_1(u,v) + p_2 C_2(u,v) + p_3 C_3(u,v), \tag{10.60}$$

then the random vector (U,V) has the distribution of

$$\left(U, I_1 U + I_2 U^{\perp} + I_3(1-U)\right), \tag{10.61}$$

where I_i, $i = 1,2,3$ are dependent Bernoulli(p_i) random variables with $I_1 + I_2 + I_3 \equiv 1$, and $U^{\perp} \sim$ uniform(0,1), independent of U. To determine the correlation $r(U,V)$, note that

$$\mathrm{E}[UV] = p_1 \mathrm{E}[U^2] + p_2 \mathrm{E}[U\,U^{\perp}] + p_3 \mathrm{E}[U(1-U)] = \frac{1}{3}p_1 + \frac{1}{4}p_2 + \frac{1}{6}p_3, \tag{10.62}$$

leading to

$$r(U,V) = \frac{\mathrm{E}[UV] - \mathrm{E}[U]\mathrm{E}[V]}{\sqrt{\mathrm{Var}[U]}\sqrt{\mathrm{Var}[V]}} = p_1 - p_3. \tag{10.63}$$

Hence $r(U,V) = 1$ if $p_1 = 1$ (the comonotonic upper bound), $r(U,V) = -1$ if $p_3 = 1$ (the countermonotonic lower bound), and $r(U,V) = 0$ holds if $p_1 = p_3$. Independence holds only if $p_1 = p_3 = 0$.

It is easy to simulate a random drawing from a joint cdf if this cdf is generated by a copula. First generate outcome u of $U \sim$ uniform(0,1), simply taking a computer generated random number. Then, draw an outcome v for V from the conditional cdf of V, given $U = u$. This is a trivial matter in the three cases considered above;

in general, this cdf equals $\frac{\partial C(u,v)}{\partial u}$. Next, to produce an outcome of (X,Y), one simply takes $x = F^{-1}(u)$ and $y = G^{-1}(v)$. Note that the above calculation (10.63) does not produce the ordinary Pearson product-moment correlation $r(X,Y)$, but rather the Spearman rank correlation $\rho(X,Y) = r(F(X), G(Y))$.

Copulas exist that are flexible enough to produce many realistic joint distributions, allowing us to simulate drawings from more and less dangerous sums of random variables. ∇

10.7 EXERCISES

Section 10.2

1. Let $f_X(\cdot)$ and $f_Y(\cdot)$ be two continuous densities (or two discrete densities) that cross exactly once, in the sense that for a certain c, we have $f_X(x) \geq f_Y(x)$ if $x < c$, and $f_X(x) \leq f_Y(x)$ if $x > c$. Show that $X \leq_{st} Y$. Why do the densities $f_X(\cdot)$ and $f_Y(\cdot)$ cross *at least* once?
2. Show that if $X \sim \text{gamma}(\alpha, \beta)$ and $Y \sim \text{gamma}(\alpha, \beta')$ with $\beta > \beta'$, then $X \leq_{st} Y$. The same if $Y \sim \text{gamma}(\alpha', \beta)$ with $\alpha < \alpha'$.
3. Prove that the binomial(n,p) distributions increase in p with respect to stochastic order, by constructing a pair (X,Y) just as in Example 10.2.2 with $X \sim \text{binomial}(n, p_1)$ and $Y \sim \text{binomial}(n, p_2)$ for $p_1 < p_2$, with additionally $\Pr[X \leq Y] = 1$.
4. Prove the assertion in the previous exercise with the help of Exercise 10.2.1.
5. As Exercise 10.2.3, but now for the case that $X \sim \text{binomial}(n_1, p)$ and $Y \sim \text{binomial}(n_2, p)$ for $n_1 < n_2$. Then, give the proof with the help of Exercise 10.2.1.
6. If $N \sim \text{binomial}(2, 0.5)$ and $M \sim \text{binomial}(3, p)$, show that $(1-p)^3 \leq \frac{1}{4}$ is necessary and sufficient for $N \leq_{st} M$.
7. For two risks X and Y having marginal distributions $\Pr[X = j] = \frac{1}{4}, j = 0, 1, 2, 3$ and $\Pr[Y = j] = \frac{1}{4}, j = 0, 4$, $\Pr[Y = 2] = \frac{1}{2}$, construct a simultaneous distribution with the property that $\Pr[X \leq Y] = 1$.
8. Prove that $\leq_{st}$ is functionally invariant, in the sense that for every non-decreasing function f, we have $X \leq_{st} Y$ implies $f(X) \leq_{st} f(Y)$. Apply this property especially to the excess of loss part $f(x) = (x-d)_+$ of a claim x, and to proportional (re-)insurance $f(x) = \alpha x$ for some $\alpha > 0$.

Section 10.3

1. Prove that $M \leq_{SL} N$ if $M \sim \text{binomial}(n,p)$ and $N \sim \text{binomial}(n+1, \frac{np}{n+1})$. Show that in the limit for $n \to \infty$, the Poisson stop-loss premium is found for any retention d.
2. If $N \sim \text{binomial}(2, 0.5)$ and $M \sim \text{binomial}(3, p)$, show that $p \geq \frac{1}{3}$ is necessary and sufficient for $N \leq_{SL} M$.
3. Show that if $X \sim Y$, then $\frac{1}{2}(X+Y) \leq_{SL} X$. Is it necessary that X and Y are independent?

4. Let X and Y be two risks with the same mean and with the same support $\{a, b, c\}$ with $0 \le a < b < c$. Show that either $X \le_{SL} Y$, or $Y \le_{SL} X$ must hold. Also give an example of two random variables, with the same mean and both with support $\{0, 1, 2, 3\}$, that are not stop-loss ordered.
5. Compare the cdf F of a risk with another cdf G with the same mean and with $F(x) = G(x)$ on $(-\infty, a)$ and $[b, \infty)$, but $G(x)$ is constant on $[a, b)$. Note that G results from F by dispersion of the probability mass on (a, b) to the endpoints of this interval. Show that $F \le_{SL} G$ holds. Sketch the stop-loss transforms with F and G.
6. As the previous exercise, but now for the case that the probability mass of F on (a, b) has been concentrated on an appropriate d, i.e., such that $G(x)$ is constant both on $[a, d)$ and $[d, b)$. Also consider that case that all mass on the closed interval $[a, b]$ is concentrated.
7. Consider the following differential of cdf F:

$$dF(x) = \begin{cases} \frac{1}{3}dx & \text{for } 0 < x < 1 \text{ and } 2 < x < 3 \\ \frac{1}{6} & \text{for } x \in \{1, 2\} \\ 0 & \text{otherwise} \end{cases}$$

   Show that this cdf is indirectly more dangerous than the uniform$(0, 3)$ cdf.
8. Let A_1, A_2, B_1 and B_2 be independent Bernoulli random variables with parameters p_1, p_2, q_1 and q_2. If $p_1 + p_2 = q_1 + q_2$, when is $A_1 + A_2 \le_{SL} B_1 + B_2$, when is $A_1 + A_2 \ge_{SL} B_1 + B_2$, and when does neither of these stochastic inequalities hold?
9. Show that a negative binomial random variable N is stop-loss larger than any Poisson random variable M having $\mathrm{E}[M] \le \mathrm{E}[N]$. The same for $M \sim$ binomial.
10. Suppose it is known that for every value of the risk aversion α, the exponential premium for the risk X is less than for Y. Which order relation holds between X and Y?
11. Show that the stop-loss transforms $\pi_i(d)$ in (10.5) correspond to cdf's F_i that increase in dangerousness.
12. Complete the proof of Theorem 10.3.7 by proving that the random variable Y satisfies the requirements, using sketches of the stop-loss transform and the cdf.
13. Let $X \le_{SL} Z$ and $\mathrm{E}[X] < \mathrm{E}[Z]$. Consider the function $\pi(\cdot)$ that has $\pi(t) = \mathrm{E}[(X - t)_+]$ for $t \le 0$, $\pi(t) = \mathrm{E}[(Z - t)_+]$ for $t \ge c$, and $\pi(t) = A(t)$ for $0 \le t \le c$. Here c and $A(\cdot)$ are chosen in such a way that $A(0) = \mu$ and $A(t)$ is the tangent line to $\mathrm{E}[(Z - t)_+]$ at $t = c$. Show that $\pi(\cdot)$ is convex, and hence the stop-loss transform of a certain risk Y. Sketch the cdf's of X, Y and Z. Show that $X \le_{SL} Y \le_{SL} Z$, as well as $\mathrm{E}[X] = \mathrm{E}[Y]$ and $Y \le_{st} Z$. [In this way, Y is another separator between X and Z in a sense analogous to Theorem 10.3.7.]
14. Show that if $X \le_e Y$ and $\mathrm{E}[X^k] = \mathrm{E}[Y^k]$ for $k = 1, 2, \ldots, n-1$, then $\mathrm{E}[X^n] \le \mathrm{E}[Y^n]$. [This means especially that if $X \le_e Y$ and $\mathrm{E}[X] = \mathrm{E}[Y]$, then $\mathrm{Var}[X] \le \mathrm{Var}[Y]$. The moments of X and Y are called *lexicographically ordered*.]
15. For risks X and Y and for a certain $d > 0$ we have $\Pr[Y > d] > 0$ while $\Pr[X > d] = 0$. Can $X \le_{SL} Y$, $X \le_{st} Y$ or $X \le_e Y$ hold?
16. Let $X \sim$ uniform$(0, 1)$, $V = \frac{1}{2}X$, and $W = \min\{X, d\}$ for a certain $d > 0$. Sketch the cdf's of V, W and X. Investigate for which d we have $V \le_{SL} W$ and for which we have $W \le_{SL} V$.

17. Prove Theorem 10.3.8 for the case $\mathrm{E}[X] = \mathrm{E}[Y]$ by using partial integrations. Use the fact that the stop-loss transform is an antiderivative of $F_X(x) - 1$, and consider again $v(x) = -u(-x)$. To make things easier, look at $\mathrm{E}[v(X) - v(0) - Xv'(0)]$ and assume that $v(\cdot)$ is differentiable at 0.

18. The following risks $X_1, \ldots, X_5$ are given.

    1. $X_1 \sim$ binomial$(10, \frac{1}{2})$;
    2. $X_2 \sim$ binomial$(15, \frac{1}{3})$;
    3. $X_3 \sim$ Poisson(5);
    4. $X_4 \sim$ negative binomial$(2, \frac{2}{7})$;
    5. $X_5 \sim 15I$, where $I \sim$ Bernoulli$(\frac{1}{3})$.

    Do any two decision makers with increasing utility function agree about preferring X_1 to X_2? For each pair (i, j) with $i, j = 1, 2, 3, 4$, determine if $X_i \leq_{SL} X_j$ holds. Determine if $X_j \leq_{SL} X_5$ or its reverse holds, $j = 2, 3$. Does $X_3 \leq_e X_5$?

19. Consider the following class of risks $X_p = pY + (1-p)Z$, with Y and Z independent exponential(1) random variables, and p a number in $(0, \frac{1}{2})$. Note that $X_0 \sim$ exponential(1), while $X_{0.5} \sim$ gamma(2,2). Are the risks in this class stochastically ordered? Show that decision makers with an exponential utility function prefer losing X_p to X_q if and only if $p \geq q$. Prove that $X_{1/2} \leq_{SL} X_p \leq_{SL} X_0$.

20. The cdf's $G(\cdot)$ and $V(\cdot)$ are given by

$$G(x) = \frac{1}{4}\left\{F^{*0}(x) + F^{*1}(x) + F^{*2}(x) + F^{*3}(x)\right\}$$
$$V(x) = q_0 F^{*0}(x) + q_1 F^{*1}(x) + q_2 F^{*2}(x)$$

    Here F is the cdf of an arbitrary risk, and F^{*n} denotes the nth convolution power of cdf F. For $n = 0$, F^{*0} is the cdf of the constant 0. Determine $q_0, q_1, q_2 \geq 0$ with $q_0 + q_1 + q_2 = 1$ such that $V \leq_{SL} G$ and moreover V and G have equal mean.

21. Compare two compound Poisson random variables S_1 and S_2 in the three stochastic orders $\leq_e$, $\leq_{st}$, and $\leq_{SL}$, if the parameters of S_1 and S_2 are given by

    1. $\lambda_1 = 5$, $p_1(x) = \frac{1}{5}$ for $x = 1, 2, 3, 4, 5$;
    2. $\lambda_2 = 4$, $p_1(x) = \frac{1}{4}$ for $x = 2, 3, 4, 5$.

22. Investigate the order relations $\leq_e$, $\leq_{st}$, and $\leq_{SL}$ for risks X and Y with $Y \equiv CX$, where C and X are independent and $\Pr[C = 0.5] = \Pr[C = 1.5] = 0.5$.

23. Let $N \sim$ binomial$(2, \frac{1}{2})$ and $M \sim$ Poisson(λ). For which λ do $N \geq_{st} M$, $N \leq_{st} M$ and $N \leq_{SL} M$ hold?

24. In the proof of Theorem 10.3.5, sketch the functions $\pi_i(d)$ for the case that $Y \sim$ uniform$(0, 3)$ and Z integer-valued with $\pi_Z(0) = 2$ and $\pi_Z(k) = \pi_Y(k)$ for $k = 1, 2, 3$. Describe the transitions $\pi_Y(d) \rightarrow \pi_2(d) \rightarrow \cdots \rightarrow \pi_Z(d)$ in terms of dispersion.

25. Let $A_j \sim$ Bernoulli(p_j), $j = 1, 2, \ldots, n$ be independent random variables, and let $\overline{p} = \frac{1}{n}\sum_j p_j$. Show that $\sum_j A_j \leq_{SL}$ binomial$(n, \overline{p})$.
    [This exercise proves the following statement: Among all sums of n independent Bernoulli

random variables with equal mean total μ, the binomial$(n, \frac{\mu}{n})$ is the stop-loss largest. Note that in this case by replacing all probabilities of success by their average, thus eliminating variation from the underlying model, we get a more spread result.]

26. Let $\Pr[X = i] = \frac{1}{6}$, $i = 0, 1, \ldots, 5$, and $Y \sim$ binomial$(5, p)$. For which p do $X \leq_{st} Y$, $Y \leq_{st} X$, $X \leq_{SL} Y$ and $Y \leq_{SL} X$ hold?

Section 10.4

1. Consider the family of distributions $F(\cdot; p, \mu)$, defined as $F(x; p, \mu) = 1 - pe^{-x/\mu}$ for some $p \in (0, 1)$ and $\mu > 0$. Investigate for which parameter values p and μ the cdf $F(\cdot; p, \mu)$ is stochastically or stop-loss larger or smaller than $F(\cdot; p_0, \mu_0)$, and when it is neither stop-loss larger, nor stop-loss smaller.
2. Investigate the order relations $\leq_{SL}$ and $\leq_{st}$ in the class of binomial(n, p) distributions, $n = 0, 1, \ldots, 0 \leq p \leq 1$.
3. Show that exponential order is preserved under compounding: if $X \leq_e Y$ and $M \leq_e N$, then $X_1 + X_2 + \cdots + X_M \leq_e Y_1 + Y_2 + \cdots + Y_N$.
4. What can be said about two individual claim amount random variables X and Y if for two risk processes with the same claim number process and the same premium c per unit of time, and individual claims such as X and Y respectively, it proves that for each c, the adjustment coefficient with the second ruin process is at most the one with the first?
5. Let S have a compound Poisson distribution with individual claim sizes $\sim X$, and let t_1, t_2 and α be such that $\mathrm{E}[(S - t_1)_+] = \lambda \mathrm{E}[(X - t_2)_+] = \alpha \mathrm{E}[S]$. For an arbitrary $d > 0$, compare $\mathrm{E}[(\min\{S, t_1\} - d)_+]$, $\mathrm{E}[(S - \sum_1^N (X_i - t_2)_+ - d)_+]$ and $\mathrm{E}[((1 - \alpha)S - d)_+]$.
6. If two risks have the same mean μ and variance σ^2, but the skewness of the first risk is larger, what can be said about the stop-loss premiums?
7. Compare the risks S and T in Exercise 3.7.6 as regards exponential, stochastic and stop-loss order.
8. In Example 10.4.3, show that, in areas where the separation argument does not lead to the conclusion that one is stop-loss larger than the other, the stop-loss premiums are sometimes larger, sometimes smaller.
9. Prove that indeed $\overline{X}_{n+1} \leq_{SL} \overline{X}_n$ in Remark 10.4.10.
10. Show that the random variables X and Y at the end of Example 10.4.2 are exponentially ordered, but not stop-loss ordered.

Section 10.5

1. Let $0 < d < b$ hold. Risk X has $\Pr[X \in \{0, d, b\}] = 1$, risk Y has $\Pr[0 \leq Y \leq b] = 1$. If the means and variances of X and Y are equal, show that $\mathrm{E}[(X - d)_+] \leq \mathrm{E}[(Y - d)_+]$.
2. Show that $X \leq_{SL} Y \leq_{SL} Z$ holds in Example 10.5.7. Use the fact that a unimodal continuous density with mode 0 is the same as a concave cdf on $[0, \infty)$. Consider the case that Y is not continuous separately.

3. Compute the minimal and the maximal stop-loss premium at retention $d = 0.5$ and $d = 3$ for risks with $\mu = \sigma^2 = 1$ and a support contained in $[0, 4]$.
4. Give expressions for the minimal and the maximal possible values of the stop-loss premium in case of mean μ, variance σ^2 and a support contained in $[0, b]$, cf. Figure 10.5. In this figure, sketch the stop-loss transform of the feasible risk which has the minimal stop-loss premium at retention $d = 2$.
5. Which two-point risk with mean μ, variance σ^2 and support contained in $[0, b]$ has the largest skewness? Which one has the smallest?
6. Show that the solutions of the previous exercise also have the extremal skewnesses in the class of arbitrary risks with mean μ, variance σ^2 and support contained in $[0, b]$.
7. Let $T = Y_1 + \cdots + Y_N$ with $N \sim$ Poisson(λ), $\Pr[0 \leq Y \leq b] = 1$ and $E[Y] = \mu$. Show that $\mu N \leq_{SL} T \leq_{SL} bM$, if $M \sim$ Poisson($\lambda\mu/b$). What are the means and variances of these three random variables?
8. Verify the assertions in the middle paragraph of Example 10.5.5.

Section 10.6

1. Prove that the first set of inequalities of (10.38) together with equal means implies the second set, by using $E[(X - d)_+] - E[(d - X)_+] = E[X] - d$.
2. Show that equality (3.82) can be generalized from risks to arbitrary random variables X with mean μ, leading to $\int_{-\infty}^{\infty} \{E[(X - t)_+] - (\mu - t)_+\} dt = \frac{1}{2}\text{Var}[X]$.
3. The function $f(x) = (d - x)_+$ is convex decreasing. Give an example with $X \leq_{SL} Y$ but not $E[(d - X)_+] \leq E[(d - Y)_+]$.
4. Consider n married couples with one-year life insurances, all having probability of death 1% for her and 2% for him. The amounts insured are unity for both sexes. Assume that the mortality between different couples is independent. Determine the distribution of the individual model for the total claims, as well as for the collective model approximating this, a) assuming that the mortality risks are also independent within each couple, and b) that they follow a comonotonic distribution. Compare the stop-loss premiums for the collective model in case of a retention of at least $0.03n$.
5. In Example 10.6.7, sketch the stop-loss transform of $X_1 + X_2$ for various values of x. In this way, show that $X_1 + X_2$ increases with x in stop-loss order.
6. Show that $X \leq_{st} Y$ holds if and only if their comonotonic joint density has the property $h(x, y) = 0$ for $x > y$.
7. Describe a comonotonic joint density for the case of a 2-dimensional random vector (X, Y) with values $x_1 < x_2 < \cdots < x_n$ and $y_1 < y_2 < \cdots < y_m$ for the components.
8. Prove Bonferroni's inequality: $\Pr[A \cap B] \geq \Pr[A] + \Pr[B] - 1$. Use it to derive the lower bound (10.57). Check that the right hand side of (10.57) has the right marginal distributions. Prove that $(F^{-1}(U), G^{-1}(1 - U))$ has this lower bound as its cdf.
9. Let X_1 and X_2 be the length of two random persons. Suppose that these lengths are iid random variables with $\Pr[X_i = 160, 170, 180] = \frac{1}{4}, \frac{1}{2}, \frac{1}{4}$. What is the distribution of the comonotonic upper bound S_u? Determine the distribution of the lower bound if we take as a conditioning

variable Z = the gender of person 1, of which we know it is independent of the length of person 2, while $\Pr[Z=0] = \Pr[Z=1] = \frac{1}{2}$ as well as $\Pr[X_1 = 160, 170|Z=0] = \Pr[X_1 = 170, 180|Z=1] = \frac{1}{2}$. What is the distribution of the improved upper bond S_u'? Compare the variances of the various convex upper and lower bounds derived.

10. Let X and Y be independent N(0,1) random variables, and let $S = X + Y$. Assume $Z = X + aY$ for some real a. What is the conditional distribution of X, given $Z = z$? Determine the distribution of the convex lower bound $\mathrm{E}[S|Z]$. Also determine the distribution of the comonotonic upper bound and the improved convex upper bound. Compare the variances of these bounds for various values of a. Consider especially the cases $Z \equiv S$, $Z \perp S$, $Z \equiv X$ and $Z \propto Y$, i.e., $|a| \to \infty$.

11. In Example 10.6.9, compute the variance of the lower bound in case we take $aY_1 + Y_2$ instead of $Y_1 + Y_2$ as the conditioning random variable. [♠] For which a is this variance maximal?

12. In case the event $Z = z$ occurs, the improved upper bound of Example 10.6.9 can be written as $F^{-1}_{X_1|Z=z}(U) + \cdots + F^{-1}_{X_n|Z=z}(U)$. Write the terms of this sum as $g_i(U, z)$, then $g_i(U, Z)$ is the unconditional contribution of component i to the improved upper bound $S_u' = \sum_i g_i(U, Z)$. In general, these random variables will not be comonotonic. Show that $g_i(U, Z)$ has the same marginal distribution as X_i. Conclude that the improved upper bound is indeed an improvement over the comonotonic upper bound.

13. If (X, Y) are PQD, what can be said of $\Pr[X \le x | Y \le y]$?

14. Show that the random pairs (X, X), $(X, X+Z)$ and $(X+Y, X+Z)$ are all PQD if X, Y and Z are independent random variables.

15. Let the joint cdf of X and Y be $F(x, y) = C(F(x), G(y))$, where $F(x) = F(x, \infty)$ and $G(y) = F(\infty, y)$ are the marginal cdf's, and where $C(\cdot, \cdot)$ is defined by $C(u, v) = uv[1 + \alpha(1-u)(1-v)]$. Which values of α are permitted? What is the Spearman rank correlation of X and Y? What is Kendall's τ (see Exercise 10.6.17 below)?

16. For (X, Y) continuous with cdf $F(x, y)$, prove that there exists a two-dimensional cdf $C(\cdot, \cdot)$ with uniform(0,1) marginals (copula function) such that $F(x, y) = C(F(x), G(y))$, where again $F(x)$ and $G(y)$ denote the marginal cdf's. [This result is known as Sklar's theorem.]

17. Next to the customary correlation and Spearman's ρ, there is another association measure which is useful in mathematical statistics. It is called Kendall's τ. For (X, Y) continuous, it is defined as the following quantity: $\tau(X, Y) = 2 \times \Pr[(X - X')(Y - Y') > 0] - 1$, where (X', Y') is independent of (X, Y) and has the same joint cdf. Prove that both Spearman's ρ and Kendall's τ can be computed from the copula function, see the previous exercise. Prove that if (X, Y) is more related than (X', Y'), then $\tau(X, Y) \ge \tau(X', Y')$.

18. For continuous random variables, compute ρ and τ for the comonotonic random variables. Prove that $\rho = 1$ or $\tau = 1$ imply comonotonicity.

19. Determine the correlation $r(X, Y)$, as a function of σ, if $X \sim$ lognormal$(0, 1)$ and $Y \sim$ lognormal$(0, \sigma^2)$, and $r(\log X, \log Y) = 1$. Verify that it equals 1 for $\sigma = 1$, and tends to zero for $\sigma \to \infty$. Also compute ρ and τ.

20. Prove that if random variables X and Y are comonotonic, then $\mathrm{Cov}[X, Y] \ge 0$. Can X and Y be at the same time comonotonic and independent?

21. Let $(X,Y) \sim$ bivariate normal, and let (X^c, Y^c) be comonotonic with the same marginals. Show that the cdf's of $X+Y$ and X^c+Y^c cross only once, and determine where.

22. Prove that for a pair of random variables (X,Y), the distributions of $S_u' = F_{X|Z}^{-1}(U)+F_{Y|Z}^{-1}(U)$ and $S = X+Y$ coincide when one conditions on $Z \equiv X$.

23. For $X \sim \mathrm{N}(0,1)$, determine $r(X^2, (X+b)^2)$.

24. In Example 10.6.8, assume that the interest term structure has i.i.d. increments $Y_j \sim \mathrm{N}(\mu, \sigma^2)$. If $X_1^c, X_2^c, \ldots$ denote comonotonic versions of $X_1, X_2, \ldots$, determine the distribution of the random variables $\log X_{k+1}^c - \log X_k^c$. Prove that $r(\log X_k, \log X_l) = \sqrt{k/l}$ for $k < l$.

Hints for the exercises

CHAPTER 1

Section 1.2

1. Take $x_0 = \mathrm{E}[X]$. If $v(x) = x^2$, we get $\mathrm{Var}[X] \geq 0$.
2. Consider especially the rv's X with $\Pr[X = a \pm \varepsilon] = 0.5$.
3. Use the previous exercise.
4. Examine the inequalities $\mathrm{E}[u(X)] > \mathrm{E}[u(Y)]$ and $\mathrm{E}[u(X)] > u(w)$. X is preferred over w for $w < 625$.
5. Apply Jensen's inequality to (1.11).
6. $P^+ = 20$; $P^+ \approx 19.98$.
7. $W = 161.5$.
8. Taking $w = 0$, $u(0) = 0$ and $u(1) = 1$ gives $u(2) > 2$, $u(4) = 2u(2)$ and $u(8) < 2u(4)$. There are x with $u''(x) > 0$ and with $u''(x) < 0$.

Section 1.3

4. Use $\lim_{\alpha\downarrow 0} \frac{\log(m_X(\alpha))-\log(m_X(0))}{\alpha} = \frac{d\log(m_X(\alpha))}{d\alpha}\Big|_{\alpha=0}$ or use a Taylor series argument.
5. See Table A at the end for the mgf of X.

6. $P_X = 412.5 < P_Y$; $\alpha > 0.008$.
7. Logarithmic.
8. $\alpha \geq 0.5$. Dimension of α is (unit of money)$^{-1}$.
9. Normal
10. Logarithmic utility. Use l'Hopital.

Section 1.4

1. Linear on $(-\infty, 2]$ with $\pi(0) = 2.5$, $\pi(2) = 0.5$; $\pi(x) = 1 - (4-x)^2/8$ on $[2,4]$, and $\pi(x) = 0$ on $[4, \infty)$. In your sketch it should be visible that $\pi'(2+0) \neq \pi'(2-0)$.
2. (1.37) gives $f_S(d) = 2(1-d)$ on $(0,1)$, 0 elsewhere.
3. Use partial integration.
4. Use that when the variance is fixed, stop-loss is optimal; next apply the previous exercise.
5. Use (1.38).
6. $\mathrm{E}[XI(X)] = \mathrm{E}[(X-d)_+] + d\mathrm{E}[I(X)]$.

CHAPTER 2

Section 2.2

1. a) $\mathrm{E}[X] = 1/2$; $\mathrm{Var}[X] = 9/4$; b) $\mathrm{E}[X] = 1/2$; $\mathrm{Var}[X] = 37/12$.
2. $\mathrm{E}[Y] = 7/4$, $\mathrm{Var}[Y] = 77/48$.
3. $P^+ = 5.996$. Not quite perfectly.
4. $\mathrm{E}[X] = 60$; $m_X(t) = 0.9e^0 + 0.02e^{1000t} + \int_0^{1000} 0.00008e^{tx}dx = \cdots$
5. Condition on $I = 1$ and $I = 0$.
6. $IX + (1-I)Y$ for $I \sim$ Bernoulli(0.5), $X \equiv 2$ and $Y \sim$ uniform$(2,4)$, independent.
7. $c = 1/3$, $dG(1) = dG(2) = 1/2$, $dH(x) = dx/2$ on $(0,1) \cup (2,3)$.
8. $\mathrm{E}[T] = \mathrm{E}[Z]$, $\mathrm{E}[T^2] \neq \mathrm{E}[Z^2]$.
9. $\mathrm{N}(0, q^2 + (1-q)^2)$ and $\mathrm{N}(0,1)$.

Section 2.3

1. Cf. Table 2.1.
2. Total number of multiplications is quadratic: $6n^2 - 15n + 12,\ n \geq 3$.
3. Write (2.29) as $\phi(s; \mu_1 + \mu_2, \sigma_1^2 + \sigma_2^2) \times \int \phi(x; \mu_3, \sigma_3^2)dx$.
4. For the second part, use induction, the convolution formula, and the relation $\binom{n}{h} + \binom{n}{h-1} = \binom{n+1}{h}$ for all n and h.

Section 2.4

1. $f_S(s) = 2(e^{-s} - e^{-2s})$; $m_S(t) = \frac{2}{1-t} - \frac{2}{2-t}$.
3. $\kappa_4 = \mathrm{E}[(X - \mu_1)^4] - 3\sigma^4$.
4. See Tables A and B at the end of the book for the mgf's.
5. $\kappa_3 = 0$, $\kappa_4 = -0.1$.
6. Use (2.48) and Tables A and B.
8. X is symmetrical around μ if $X - \mu \sim \mu - X$. Computer: $p = 0.4264056$.
9. $(1-2q)/\sqrt{q(1-q)}$ (see Table B at the end). If X is symmetrical, then the third central moment equals 0, therefore $q \in \{0, 0.5, 1\}$ must hold. Symmetry holds for all three of these q-values.
10. Use (2.49) and the tables at the end of the book.
11. The cumulants are the coefficients of $t^j/j!$ in the cgf.
12. Their pgf's are polynomials of degree n, that are identical only if all their coefficients are the same.
13. Show that X/δ and Y/δ have the same pgf.
14. Where is the mgf defined, where the characteristic function? Sometimes this function can be extended to all complex numbers, like $(1-t)^{-1}$ for the exponential distribution. $\mathrm{E}[e^{itX}] = \mathrm{E}[e^{-itX}]$ implies that the imaginary part of the functions must be equal to zero.
15. Use Exercise 11. For symmetry, $\Pr[Z = 0] = \Pr[Z = 10]$ is necessary. Prove that Z is symmetric whenever this is the case.
16. $\delta = \sqrt[3]{2}$.
17. Show that $g_X^{(n)}(1) = \mathrm{E}[X(X-1)\cdots(X-n+1)]$, and argue that the raw moments can be computed from these so-called factorial moments. See (2.49).

Section 2.5

1. You should get the following results:

Argument:	$3-0$	$3+0$	3.5	$4-0$	$4+0$
Exact:	.080		.019		.004
NP:	.045		.023		.011
Gamma:	.042		.021		.010
CLS:	.023		.006		.001

2. Solve $x = s + \gamma(s^2 - 1)/6$ for s. Verify if this inversion is allowed!
4. Use the rule of l'Hopital to prove that $\lim_{\gamma \downarrow 0} \left[\sqrt{9/\gamma^2 + 6x/\gamma + 1} - 3/\gamma\right] = x$. Take $X^* = (X - \mu)/\sigma$, then approximate $\Pr[X^* \leq z]$ by $\Pr[Z^* \leq z]$, where $Z^* = (Z - \alpha/\beta)\beta/\sqrt{\alpha}$, and $Z \sim$ gamma(α, β) with skewness γ, therefore $\alpha = 1/\gamma^2$. Then for $\alpha \to \infty$, we have $\Pr[Z^* \leq z] \to \Phi(z)$ because of the CLT.
5. Using (2.62), we see that the critical value at $1 - \varepsilon$ is $18 + 6(y + (y^2 - 1)/9)$ if $\Phi(y) = 1 - \varepsilon$. See further a χ^2-table.

6. $G(4.5; 4, 2) \approx 0.983$. Using $2\beta\cdot\text{gamma}(\alpha, \beta) \sim \chi^2(2\alpha)$ and interpolation in a χ^2-table one finds 0.978. Exact value: 0.9788.
7. If α is integer, Poisson-probabilities can be used to find gamma-cdf's.
8. For instance for $\varepsilon = 0.95$: table gives 28.9, (2.25) gives 28.59. The NP approximation from Exercise 5 gives 28.63.
9. Loading = 21.14%.
10. Loading = 21.60%.
11. For $x = -1$ we find $(3/\gamma - 1)^2 \geq 0$ under the square-root sign.
12. Using Table A one finds $\gamma = 4, 6, 14, \infty$.
13. Let X_1 be a claim of type 1, then $\Pr[X_1 = 0] = 1 - q_1$, $\Pr[X_1 = j] = q_1 p_1(j)$, $j = 1, 3$. $E[S_1] = 200$, $Var[S_1] = 460$, capital is $E[S] + 1.645\sqrt{Var[S]}$.
14. $E[\sqrt{U}] = \Gamma(\alpha + 0.5)/\Gamma(\alpha)\sqrt{\beta}$. $(\alpha - 0.5)\Gamma(\alpha - 0.5) = \Gamma(\alpha + 0.5)$, $\alpha\Gamma(\alpha) = \Gamma(\alpha + 1)$, therefore $\Gamma(\alpha + 0.5) \approx \Gamma(\alpha)\sqrt{\alpha - 0.25}$. $E[T^3] \approx E[Y^3] = (4\alpha + 2)\sqrt{4\alpha - 1}$; $E[T^4] = 16(\alpha^2 + \alpha) = E[Y^4] + 2$.

Section 2.6

1. $1 - \Phi(g(d))$ with $g^2(d) = \frac{\{B-380+10d\}^2}{297+49.5d^2}$, $d \in [2, 3]$.
2. Maximize $g^2(d)$.
3. $1 - \Phi(1.984) = .0235$.

CHAPTER 3

Section 3.2

1. For Poisson(λ): $E[S] = \lambda\mu_1$, $Var[S] = \lambda\mu_2$, $m_S(t) = e^{\lambda(m_X(t)-1)}$.
2. Use (2.49).
3. Let N' denote the number of females, then we have $N' = B_1 + \cdots + B_N$, if N is the number of eggs and $B_i = 1$ if from the ith egg, a female hatches. Now use (3.5) to prove that $N' \sim$ Poisson(λp).
4. $\Pr[S = 0, 1, 2, 3, 4] = e^{-2}, 0.2e^{-2}, 0.42e^{-2}, 0.681333e^{-2}, 1.0080667e^{-2}$.
5. $f(4, 5, 6) = 0.2232, 0.1728, 0.0864$; $E[S] = 3.2$, $Var[S] = 3.04$.
6. $E[S] = 3.2$ (cf. Exercise 5), $Var[S] = 5.6$.
7. Use mathematical induction. Or: prove that lhs=rhs by inspecting the derivatives as well as one value, e.g. at $x = 0$.

Section 3.3

1. Examine the mgf's; fill in $p = 1 - \lambda/r$ in the negative binomial mgf and let $r \to \infty$. Use that $\lim_{r\to\infty}(1 - \lambda/r)^r = e^{-\lambda}$.
2. In 3.3.1 if Λ is degenerate; in 3.3.2 if $c \downarrow 0$.
3. Compare the claim numbers and the claim sizes.

Section 3.4

1. See Example 3.4.3.
2. If $x_1 = x_2$, the frequency of this claim amount is $N_1 + N_2$.
3. $p(0) = p(1) = p(2)/2 = p(3) = p(4)$.
4. Show that $\Pr[N' = n, N - N' = m] = \Pr[N' = n]\Pr[N - N' = m]$ for all n and m. Or: apply Theorem 3.4.2 with $x_1 = 0$ and $x_2 = 1$.
5. Show that $\Pr[N_1 = 1]\Pr[N_2 = 1] = 0.3968 \times 0.3792 \neq \Pr[N_1 = 1, N_2 = 1] = 0.144$. (Note that Theorem 3.4.2 was proven for the Poisson-case only.)
6. $S = x_1N_1 + x_2N_2 + \cdots$ and $S_0 = 0N_0' + x_1N_1' + x_2N_2' + \cdots$ with $N_j, N_j' \sim \cdots$

Section 3.5

1. $f(s) = \frac{1}{s}[0.2f(s-1) + 0.8f(s-2) + 1.8f(s-3) + 3.2f(s-4)]$; $f(0) = e^{-2}$
2. Verify $s = 0$ separately; for $s > 0$, use (3.15) and induction.
3. Check if every point in the (a, b) plane has been dealt with. Make a sketch.
4. There are $2t$ multiplications $\lambda h p(h)$ for $h = 1, \ldots, t$. For $m > t$: $t(t+1)/2$, for $m \leq t$: $m(m+1)/2 + m(t-m)$. Asymptotically the number of operations increases linearly with t if the maximal claim size is finite, and quadratically otherwise.
5. $\mathrm{E}[N] = \sum_n nq_n = \sum_{n\geq 1} n(a + b/n)q_{n-1} = a\sum_{n\geq 1}(n-1)q_{n-1} + a + b$, and so on.
6. Interpolate between $\pi(2)$ and $\pi(3)$. $d = 2.548$. [The stop-loss premiums are linear because the cdf is constant.]
7. Use Panjer and interpolation.
8. $S_2 \sim N_1 + 3N_3$ with $N_1 \sim$ Poisson(2) and $N_3 \sim$ Poisson(1). Should you interpolate to determine the cdf?
9. $\lambda p(1) = \alpha$, $2\lambda p(2) = 2\alpha$ and $p(1) + p(2) = 1 - p(0)$.
10. $\pi(2.5) = 1.4014$.
11. Subtract (3.34) from $\mathrm{E}[(S - 0)_+]$.
12. Start with $\mathrm{E}[(S - (d-1))_+^2] - \mathrm{E}[(S - d)_+^2] = \cdots$. If $p(d)$ is the expression to be computed, then $p(d-1) - p(d) = 2\pi(d-1) - 1 + F(d-1)$.

Section 3.6

1. CLT: 0.977, gamma: 0.968, NP: 0.968.
2. $\alpha = 15$, $\beta = 0.25$, $x_0 = -20$. NP: $F_S(67.76) \approx 0.95$, and $F_S(\mathrm{E}[S] + 3\sqrt{\mathrm{Var}[S]}) \approx 0.994$ (Note: $\Phi(3) = 0.999$).

Section 3.7

1. If S^* is the collective model approximation with $\lambda_j = -\log(1 - q_j)$, prove that $\lambda_j > q_j$, hence $\mathrm{E}[S^*] = \sum_j \lambda_j b_j > \mathrm{E}[S]$; analogously for the variance.
2. $\widetilde{S}$: $E = 2.25$, $V = 3.6875$, $\gamma = 6.41655\sigma^{-3} = 0.906$. $S \sim$ compound Poisson with $\lambda = 1.5$, $p(1) = p(2) = 0.5$, therefore $E = 2.25$, $V = 3.75$, $\gamma = 6.75\sigma^{-3} = 0.930$. $\widetilde{S}$: $\alpha = 4.871$, $\beta = 1.149$, $x_0 = -1.988$. S: $\alpha = 4.630$, $\beta = 1.111$ and $x_0 = -1.917$.
4. The second. The ratio of the resulting variances is approximately 80%.
5. Use the fact that the first factor of the terms in the sum decreases with x.
6. $\mathrm{Max}[S] = 3000$, $\mathrm{Max}[T] = 4000$; $\mathrm{E}[S] = \mathrm{E}[T] = 30$; $\mathrm{Var}[S] = 49.5$, $\mathrm{Var}[T] = 49.55$; the claim number distribution is binomial$(2000, 0.01)$ for both; $S \sim$ weighted sum of binomial random variables, $T \sim$ compound binomial. If $B_i \sim$ Poisson, then $S \equiv T \sim$ compound Poisson.
7. Compound Poisson$(10\Pr[X > \beta])$, with claims $\sim$ uniform$(0, 2000 - \beta)$. Or: compound Poisson(10) with claims $\sim (X - \beta)_+$.
8. P1: $z_1^2 n_1 q_1(1 - q_1) + \cdots$; P2: larger. 'The' collective model: equal. The 'open' collective model: different.
9. Replacing the claims on a contract of type 1 by a compound Poisson(1) number of such claims leads to a random variable $\sim N_1 + 3N_3$ with $N_k \sim$ Poisson$(q_1 p_1(k))$, $k = 1, 3$. So $T \sim M_1 + 2M_2 + 3M_3$ with $M_1 \sim$ Poisson(25), $M_2 \sim$ Poisson(20), $M_3 \sim$ Poisson(5). Panjer: $f(s) = \frac{1}{s}\sum_h h\lambda p(h) f(s-h) = \frac{1}{s}[25f(s-1) + 40f(s-2) + 15f(s-3)]$. Apply NP or gamma.
10. Binomial(n, q), Poisson(nq), Poisson$(-n\log(1-q))$, no.

Section 3.8

1. Additionally use that $\mathrm{E}[Y^j] = m_{\log Y}(j)$, where the mgf's can be found in Table A.
2. $\beta X \sim$ gamma$(\alpha, 1)$ if $X \sim$ gamma(α, β); $X/x_0 \sim$ Pareto$(\alpha, 1)$ if $X \sim$ Pareto(α, x_0); $e^{-\mu}X \sim$ Lognormal$(0, \sigma^2)$ if $X \sim$ Lognormal(μ, σ^2); $\beta X \sim$ IG$(\alpha, 1)$ if $X \sim$ IG(α, β).
4. A vital step is that $p(x) \geq p(0)e^{-\beta x}$ for all $x \geq 0$.
5. $\Pr[Z - z > y | Z > z] = 1 - q(z)e^{-\alpha y} - (1 - q(z))e^{-\beta y}$ if $q(z) = \frac{qe^{-\alpha z}}{qe^{-\alpha z} + (1-q)e^{-\beta z}}$. $q(\cdot)$ is monotonous with $q(0) = q$, $q(\infty) = 1$.
6. The median of the lognormal distribution is e^{μ}. Mode: $f'(x) = 0$ holds for $x = e^{\mu - \sigma^2}$.

Section 3.9

1. 1000×0.004; $1000 \times .0070$ (NP) or $1000 \times .0068$ (Translated gamma).
2. Subtract from $E[(S-0)_+] = E[S]$.
3. Work with $(X-\mu)/\sigma$ rather than with X. $E[(X-\mu)_+] = \sigma\phi(0) = \cdots$
4. To compute $E[(S-(S-d)_+)^2]$, approximate $E[(S-d)^2]$ just as in (3.29).
5. $\lambda x_0^\alpha d^{1-\alpha}/(\alpha-1)$.
6. Write $X = e^Y$, so $Y \sim N(\mu, \sigma^2)$, and determine $E[(e^Y - d)_+]$.
7. $\pi(d)$ is convex.
8. Determine the left and right hand derivatives of $E[(N-d)_+]$ at $d=1$ from difference ratios. $\Pr[N=1] = 0.2408$.
9. Use the fact that U is symmetric.
10. Use Exercises 3.2.1 and 3.9.9.

Section 3.10

1. Use partial integration and $\int_0^\infty (\mu - t)_+ dt = 0.5\mu^2$. The function $(\mu - t)_+$ consists of two tangent lines to the stop-loss transform.
4. Use and prove that $(x-t)_+ + (y-d)_+ \geq (x+y-(t+d))_+$, and apply induction. Further, use the given rule of thumb to show that the premiums are about equal.
5. $\mathrm{Var}[T]/\mathrm{Var}[S] = 1.081$; $E[(T-d)_+]/E[(S-d)_+] = 1.022, 1.176, 1.221$ for $d = 0.5, 1, 1.5$. Note that $d = 0.5 \approx \mu + \sigma/6$, $d = 1 \approx \mu + \sigma$, $d = 1.5 \approx \mu + 2\sigma$.
6. Take $f(x) = E[(U-x)_+] - E[(W-x)_+]$ and $\delta = 1$; we have $f(x) = 0, x \leq 0$.

CHAPTER 4

Section 4.2

1. $\frac{f(t-s)dt}{1-F(t-s)}$.
2. $p_n(t+dt) = p_n(t) + p_n'(t)dt = (1-\lambda dt)p_n(t) + \lambda dt\, p_{n-1}(t)$. Both sides denote the probability of $n+1$ claims in $(0, t+dt)$.

Section 4.3

1. See further the remarks after (4.11).
2. Use (4.10).
3. $m_X(t) < \infty$ for $t < 3$, and $R = 1$.
4. $\theta = 2.03$.
5. $c = \log m_S(R)/R$ with $R = |\log \varepsilon|/u$.

6. Using e.g. 'goal seek' in Excel, one finds $R = 0.316$.
7. $R = 1$; $\theta = 1.52 > 0.4$ (or use $dR/d\theta > 0$).
8. Solve θ and R from $1 + (1+\theta)\mu_1 R = m_X(R) = (1-R)^{-2}$ for $0 < R < 1$; this produces $R = [3 + 4\theta - \sqrt{9+8\theta}]/[4(1+\theta)]$. No: $R < 1$ must hold.
9. $m_Y(r)$ is finite for $r \leq 0$ and $r \leq \beta/2$, respectively, and infinite otherwise.
10. Consider $\frac{dR}{dc}$. Then use $\frac{dc}{dR} \geq 0$.

Section 4.4

1. Compare the surpluses for $\theta < 0$ and $\theta = 0$, using the same sizes and times of occurrence of claims.
2. See (4.23): $(1+\theta)^{-1} = 0.5$, therefore $\theta = 1$, $\theta/\{(1+\theta)\mu_1\} = 1$ gives $\mu_1 = 0.5$, hence $X \sim$ exponential(β) with $\beta = 2$; λ is arbitrary. Or: claims $\sim IX$ with $I \sim$ Bernoulli(q).
3. Because of Corollary 4.4.2 we have $R = 1$; no; $(\alpha + \beta e^{-u})^{-1}$.
4. $1 - \psi(0) > \Pr\left[\text{no claim before } \varepsilon/c \text{ \& no ruin starting from } \varepsilon\right] > 0$. Or: $\psi(\varepsilon) < 1$, therefore $R > 0$, therefore $\psi(0) < 1$ by (4.17).
5. $R = 6$ is ruled out since $m_X(6) = \infty$; $R = 0$ is also not feasible. Then, look at $\psi(0)$ and the previous exercise, and at $\psi(u)$ for large u.
6. $R = 0.5$; $c = \frac{2}{5}$.

Section 4.5

1. $U(\widetilde{T}) = -1$; $\widetilde{\psi}(u) = e^{-\widetilde{R}(u+1)}$ with $\widetilde{R} = \log(p/q)$.
2. Processes with adjustment coefficient $\widetilde{R}$ apparently are only profitable (as regards expected utility) for decision makers that are not too risk averse.
3. It is conceivable that ruin occurs in the continuous model, but not in the discrete model; the reverse is impossible; $\Pr[T \leq \widetilde{T}] = 1$ implies that $\widetilde{\psi}(u) \leq \psi(u)$ for all u.
4. Use (4.23). $\widetilde{\psi}(u) \leq e^{-\widetilde{R}u} = e^{-Ru}$ with $R = 1$. But a better bound is $\widetilde{\psi}(u) \leq \psi(u)$.

Section 4.6

1. $R_h = \{\theta - \alpha\xi\}/\{(1-\alpha)(1+\theta-\alpha(1+\xi))\}$; relative safety loading after reinsurance: $\{\theta - \alpha\xi\}/\{1-\alpha\}$. α must satisfy $0 \leq \alpha \leq 1$ and $\alpha < \theta/\xi$.
2. Safety loading after reinsurance: $\{\theta - \xi e^{-\beta}\}/\{1 - e^{-\beta}\}$.
3. $\widetilde{R} = \{5 - 8\alpha\}/\{2(1-\alpha)^2\}$ is maximal for $\alpha = 0.25$.
4. $R = (1-2\alpha)/\{(1-\alpha)(3-4\alpha)\}$, so $0 \leq \alpha < 0.5$.

Section 4.7

1. $L_1 \sim$ uniform$(0, b)$; $L_1 \sim$ exponential with the same parameter as the claims.

2. $L = 0$ means that one never gets below the initial level.
3. $\psi(0) = \cdots$ as well as $\cdots$, and hence $\cdots$

Section 4.8

1. $\gamma = 1 + \theta$.
3. $R = 2, \theta = -1 + 1/(0.5 + \alpha)$. $\theta > 0 \Rightarrow \cdots$. Use that $\psi(u)$ decreases if $\psi'(0) < 0$.
4. $\psi(u) = \frac{4}{9}e^{-2u} + \frac{1}{9}e^{-4u}$.
5. e^{-2u}; $I \sim$ Bernoulli$(\frac{1}{9})$.
6. $\psi(u) = \frac{2}{5}e^{-0.3u} - \frac{1}{15}e^{-0.8u}$.
7. $\psi(u) = \frac{5}{8}e^{-u} - \frac{1}{24}e^{-5u}$.
8. One gets a non-increasing step function, see (4.28). A density like this is the one of a mixture of uniform$(0, x)$ distributions; it is unimodal with mode 0.
10. $p(x) = 2(e^{-x} - e^{-2x})$; take care when $R = 2.5$.
11. $c = c_1 + c_2, \lambda = \lambda_1 + \lambda_2 = 9, p(x) = \frac{1}{9}p_1(x) + \frac{8}{9}p_2(x) = \cdots$, and so on.

Section 4.9

1. $\beta = \mathrm{E}[L]/\{\mathrm{E}[L^2] - (1+\theta)\mathrm{E}^2[L]\}$; $\alpha = (1+\theta)\beta\mathrm{E}[L]$.

CHAPTER 5

Section 5.2

1. Take the derivative of (5.6) and set zero.
2. Portfolio premium = 49.17; optimal $u = 104.21$; optimal $R = 0.0287$; premiums for A and B are 5.72 and 1.0287 (variance premium) and 5.90 and 1.0299 (exponential premium).

Section 5.3

1. (a) 1 (b),(c),(d) $1 + \alpha$ (e) $-\log(1-\alpha)/\alpha$ (h) $-\log\varepsilon$ (i) ∞ (j) $(1-h)^{-1}$.
2. Show that $(\alpha^2\pi'[X;\alpha])' = \alpha\mathrm{Var}[X_\alpha]$, with X_α the Esscher transform of X with parameter $\alpha > 0$.
3. If $N \sim$ Poisson(λ) and $X \sim$ gamma(α, β), then the premium is $1.1\lambda\alpha/\beta$.
4. $\frac{\lambda}{\gamma}[m_X(\gamma) - 1]$.
5. $\frac{\lambda\alpha}{\beta}[1 + \frac{\gamma}{\beta}(1+\alpha)]$.
6. $\kappa_X(h) = \log \mathrm{E}[e^{hX}]$, and so on.
7. Members of the same family with different parameters result.
8. Show: derivative of the Esscher premium = variance of the Esscher transform.

9. $\lambda \mathrm{E}[Xe^{hX}]$.
10. Use Exercise 5.3.6 and a Taylor expansion.
11. Use $\mathrm{E}[e^{\alpha X}] \geq e^{\alpha(b-\varepsilon)} \Pr[X \geq b - \varepsilon]$.

Section 5.4

3. Such a mixture is additive.
4. X and Y not positively correlated; use $|r(X,Y)| \leq 1$.

Section 5.5

2. Cauchy-Schwarz; check this in any text on mathematical statistics.

CHAPTER 6

Section 6.2

1. 45%; 760% vs. 900%

Section 6.3

1. See the text before (6.8).
2. All rows of P^2 are (p, pq, q^2).
3. $l(\infty) = (p, q)$, $e(\lambda) = \lambda e^{-\lambda}(c-a)/[c(1-e^{-\lambda}) + ae^{-\lambda}]$.
4. Use $b(\lambda) > (c-b)(1-e^{-2\lambda})$, and $ue^{-u}/(1-e^{-u}) = u/(e^u - 1) \leq 1$ for $u \geq 0$. $e(\lambda) \approx 1$ for $b \ll c$ and λ small.
7. $\alpha = 0.3$.
8. $e(0.050) \approx 0.50$
9. $s/(1-t) = p/(1-p)$.

CHAPTER 7

Section 7.2

1. The basis for all these covariance relations is that $\mathrm{Cov}[\Xi_i + \Xi_{it}, \Xi_j + \Xi_{ju}] = 0$ if $i \neq j$; $= a$ if $i = j, t \neq u$; $= a + s^2$ if $i = j, t = u$.
4. a) Minimize $\mathrm{Var}[\{X_{j,T+1} - m - \Xi_j\} + \{m + \Xi_j - z\overline{X}_j - (1-z)\overline{X}\}]$. b) $z(\overline{X}_j - \overline{X})$.
5. $az + a(1-z^2)/(Jz)$; $s^2 + a(1-z)\{1 + (1-z)/(Jz)\}$; $a(1-z)\{1 + (1-z)/(Jz)\}$.
6. $z\overline{X}_j + (1-z)\overline{X}/[1 + a/(Jzm^2)] \leq$ (7.9), hence biased downwards.

7. Sum of premiums paid is $J\overline{X}$.
8. Use $\mathrm{E}[(\overline{X}_j - \overline{X})^2] = (a + s^2/T)(1 - 1/J)$ and $\mathrm{E}[(X_{jt} - \overline{X}_j)^2] = s^2(1 - 1/T)$.
9. Set $\frac{d}{dp}\mathrm{E}[(Y - p)^2] = 0$, or start from $\mathrm{E}[\{(Y - \mu) + (\mu - p)\}^2] = \cdots$
10. Block-diagonal with blocks $aJ + s^2 I$, with I the identity matrix and J a matrix of ones.

Section 7.3

1. Take expectations in $\mathrm{Cov}[X, Y|Z] = \mathrm{E}[XY|Z] - \mathrm{E}[X|Z]\mathrm{E}[Y|Z]$.

Section 7.4

1. The Lagrangian for this constrained minimization problem is $\sum_t \alpha_t^2 s^2/w_t - 2\lambda(\alpha_\Sigma - 1)$. Setting the derivatives with respect to α_i equal to zero gives $\alpha_i/w_i = \lambda/s^2$ for all i. Or: $\sum_t \alpha_t^2/w_t = \sum_t(\{\alpha_t - w_t/w_\Sigma\} + w_t/w_\Sigma)^2/w_t = \cdots$
2. See the remarks at the end of this section.
3. Follow the proof of Theorem 7.4.1, starting from the MSE of a linear predictor of m instead of $m + \Xi_j$.
4. Analogous to Theorem 7.2.4; apply Exercise 7.2.9.
9. See Remark 7.4.3.
10. $\widetilde{s^2} = 8, \widetilde{a} = 11/3 \Rightarrow \widetilde{z} = \cdots \Rightarrow \widetilde{m + \Xi_j} = 12.14, 13.88, 10.98$

Section 7.5

1. Write down the likelihood, take the logarithm, differentiate and set zero.
2. Use Bayes' rule.
3. Use Exercise 7.3.1 to determine $\mathrm{Cov}[K_1, K_2]$.
4. Take the derivative of the density and set zero.
5. $\widetilde{\alpha} = 1.6049$; $\widetilde{\tau} = 15.8778$; $\chi^2 = 0.21$.
6. Use that $\Lambda \equiv \mathrm{E}[N|\Lambda]$.

CHAPTER 8

Section 8.2

1. $\mu_i, \psi_i; \mu_i, \mu_i; \mu_i, \psi_i\mu_i; \mu_i, \psi_i\mu_i^2; \mu_i, \psi_i\mu_i(1 - \mu_i)$. Cf. Table E.
2. Coefficient of variation: s.d./mean $= \cdots = \sqrt{\phi}$; skewness $= 2\sqrt{\phi}$.

Section 8.3

4. Constant coefficient of variation.
6. The same values result for $x_i y_j$, but 0.1 times the χ^2 value.
8. Negative with BS, 0 with marginal totals method.

Section 8.4

1. $\hat{L}$ and $\widetilde{L}$ can be found by filling in $\mu_i = \hat{\mu}_i$ and $\mu_i = y_i$ in (8.22).
3. Take the sum in (8.11) over both i and j.

Section 8.5

3. For instance: IX⊂VIII⊂VII⊂IV⊂I.
4. There are the constant term, 4 extra parameters for age class, 2 for region and 1 for gender.

Section 8.6

1. Start from $e^{l(y)} \frac{\partial l}{\partial \theta} = \frac{\partial e^{l(y)}}{\partial \theta}$, and exchange the order of integration and differentiation.
2. See also Example 8.6.3.
3. Use $\frac{\partial l}{\partial \beta_j} = \frac{\partial l}{\partial \theta} \frac{d\theta}{d\mu} \frac{d\mu}{d\eta} \frac{\partial \eta}{\partial \beta_j} = \cdots$, cf. (8.47).
5. Use $\frac{\partial l}{\partial \theta} = 0$ for $y = b'(\theta) = \cdots$
6. Fill in $\widetilde{\theta}_i$ and $\hat{\theta}_i$ in $\log f_Y(y; \theta, \psi)$, see (8.29), and cf. (8.21), (8.23) and (8.26).
7. Derive $b(\theta(\mu))$ from $b(\theta)$ and $\theta(\mu)$.
8. Compute the densities, or look at the mgf's.

CHAPTER 9

Section 9.1

1. 24.

Section 9.2

2. The mode of the lognormal(μ, σ^2) distribution is $e^{\mu - \sigma^2}$, see Exercise 3.8.6.
5. See the previous chapter.

Section 9.3

1. Replace the α_i in the first model by $\alpha_i \gamma^{i-1}$.

2. $3(t-1) < t(t+1)/2$ if $t \geq 4$.
4. (9.13) implies $\hat{X}_{11} = 102.3 \times 1.00 \times 1 \times 0.42^0 = 102.3$; (9.14) implies $\hat{X}_{11} = 101.1$.
5. Use that $\sum_{j=1}^{\infty} \beta^{j-1} = (1-\beta)^{-1}$.

CHAPTER 10

Section 10.2

1. Use Theorem 10.2.3.
2. Use the previous exercise, or the additivity/multiplicativity properties of gamma random variables.
3. Compare B_i to $A_i B_i$ for suitable Bernoulli variables.
6. Verify that $F_N(i) \geq F_M(i)$ for $i = 0, 1, 2, 3$. Why is that sufficient for $N \leq_{st} M$?
7. Take $Y = X + I$ with $I = I(X) = 0$ if $X \in \{0, 2\}$, and $I = 1$ otherwise. Alternatively, fill a table with probabilities $\Pr[X = i, Y = j]$ such that the marginals are correct and $\Pr[X = i, Y = j] = 0$ for $i > j$.

Section 10.3

1. Look at the ratio of the densities. To avoid convergence problems, write the stop-loss premiums as finite sums: $\sum_d^{\infty} = \sum_0^{\infty} - \sum_0^{d-1}$.
2. Use the previous exercise and Exercise 10.2.3.
3. Use that $(x + y - d)_+ \leq (x - \frac{1}{2}d)_+ + (y - \frac{1}{2}d)_+$ for all non-negative x, y and d. From this, it follows that $\mathrm{E}[(X_1 + X_2 - d)_+] \leq 2\mathrm{E}[(X_1 - 0.5d)_+] = \mathrm{E}[(2X_1 - d)_+]$; independence is not necessary.
4. $\mathrm{E}[(X-a_1)_+] = \mathrm{E}[(Y-a_1)_+]$; $\mathrm{E}[(X-a_3)_+] = \mathrm{E}[(Y-a_3)_+]$; so $\mathrm{E}[(X-d)_+]$ and $\mathrm{E}[(Y-d)_+]$ cannot cross. Or: the cdf's cross once, the densities twice. For such a counterexample, see, e.g., Example 10.4.2.
5. Let $G(x) = p$ on (a, b) and let $F(x_0 + 0) \geq p$, $F(x_0 - 0) < p$. Then $F \leq G$ on $(-\infty, x_0)$, $F \geq G$ on (x_0, ∞). Note that unless $F \equiv G$, $F \geq G$ everywhere nor $F \leq G$ everywhere can hold, otherwise unequal means result.
7. If H is the uniform$(0, 3)$ cdf, consider G with $G = F$ on $(-\infty, 1.5)$, $G = H$ on $[1.5, \infty)$.
8. See Exercise 4.
9. a) Consider the ratio of the densities; b) use a) for Poisson($\mathrm{E}[M]$).
10. $X \leq_e Y$.
14. Consider a series expansion for $m_Y(t) - m_X(t)$.
15. No, no, no. [Why is it sufficient to prove only the last case?]
16. If $d \geq 0.5$ then $V \leq_{SL} W$. If $d < 0.5$, we never have $V \leq_{SL} W$. If $\mathrm{E}[W] \leq \mathrm{E}[V]$, hence $d \leq 1 - \sqrt{1/2}$, then $W \leq_{SL} V$, since the cdf's cross once.

17. See Theorem 10.6.2.
18. $X_1 \leq_{SL} X_2 \leq_{SL} X_3 \leq_{SL} X_4$ because of earlier exercises. $X_2 \leq_{SL} X_5$ by dispersion. $X_3 \leq_{SL} X_5$ nor $X_5 \leq_{SL} X_3$ since Var$[X_5] >$ Var$[X_3]$ but $\Pr[X_3 > 15] > 0$, and the same for X_4. To show that exponential order doesn't hold, consider $e^{5(e^t-1)}/\{2/3 + 1/3e^{5t}\}$ as $t \to \infty$, or use a similar argument as above.
19. No: $\mathrm{E}[X_p] \equiv 1$. The mgf of X_p is $\{1-t+t^2p(1-p)\}^{-1}$. Use $(p(Y-d)+(1-p)(Z-d))_+ \leq p(Y-d)_+ + (1-p)(Z-d)_+$, as well as $\mathrm{E}[X_p|X_{1/2}] \equiv X_{1/2}$ and Corollary 10.3.13.
20. G and V are cdf's of compound distributions with claim size $\sim F(\cdot)$. So determine q_i such that $(q_0, q_1, q_2) \leq_{SL} (1/4, 1/4, 1/4, 1/4)$.
21. By gathering terms, write $S_2 = 2N_2 + \cdots + 5N_5$ and $S_1 = N_1 + S_2$. Or: $S_3 \sim S_2$ if $\lambda_3 = 5$, $p_3(x) = 1/5$ for $x = 0, 2, 3, 4, 5$. Note: only compare compound Poisson distributions with the same λ.
22. $\mathrm{E}[X] = \mathrm{E}[Y]$ rules out stochastic order.
$\mathrm{E}[(Y-d)_+] = \frac{1}{2}\{\mathrm{E}[(\frac{3}{2}X-d)_+] + \mathrm{E}[(\frac{1}{2}X-d)_+]\} = \frac{3}{4}\mathrm{E}[(X-2d/3)_+] + \frac{1}{4}\mathrm{E}[(X-2d)_+] \geq \mathrm{E}[(X-d)_+]$ because of convexity.
23. $\lambda = 0$; λ such that $e^{-\lambda} \leq 1/4$ and $(1+\lambda)e^{-\lambda} \leq 3/4$, hence $\cdots$; $\lambda \geq 1$.
25. If $p_j < \overline{p} < p_k$, replace A_j and A_k by $B_j \sim$ Bernoulli($\overline{p}$) and $B_k \sim$ Bernoulli($p_j + p_k - \overline{p}$), and use Exercise 10.3.8. Proceed by induction.
26. Examine when the densities cross once, when twice. There is stochastic order when $p^5 \geq \frac{1}{6}$ or $(1-p)^5 \geq \frac{1}{6}$, stop-loss order when $p^5 \geq \frac{1}{6}$, hence $p \geq 0.699$, and stop-loss order the other way when $p \leq 0.5$. Verify that for $p \in (\frac{1}{2}, \sqrt[5]{1/6})$, neither $X \leq_{SL} Y$ nor $Y \leq_{SL} X$ holds.

Section 10.4

1. The cdf is monotonous in p as well as μ. The stop-loss premiums are $p\mu e^{-d/\mu}$. In case of equal means $p\mu$, there is stop-loss monotony in μ.
2. Use earlier results found on order between binomial random variables.
3. $m_M(\log m_X(t)) \leq m_M(\log m_Y(t)) \leq m_N(\log m_Y(t)),\ t \geq 0$.
4. $X \leq_e Y$.
5. One recognizes the stop-loss premiums at d of the retained claims after reinsurance of type stop-loss, excess of loss and proportional, all with equal expected value.
6. The reasoning that larger skewness implies fatter tails implies larger stop-loss premiums breaks down because of (3.82).
7. First show that $S \leq_{SL} T$ if instead of 1000 policies, there is only one policy in class $i = 1, 2$.
8. Compare the means, i.e., the stop-loss premiums at $d = 0$, and also the stop-loss premiums for large d.
9. See the final sentence of this section.
10. $m_X(t) - m_Y(t) = \cdots$

Section 10.5

1. If $\mathrm{E}[(X-d)_+] > \mathrm{E}[(Y-d)_+]$, then $\mathrm{E}[(X-t)_+] > \mathrm{E}[(Y-t)_+]$ for all t because of the form of the stop-loss transform of X. This is impossible in view of (3.82).
3. If (10.36) applies, it is the maximum, otherwise it is the best of $\{0, \bar{0}\}$ and $\{b, \bar{b}\}$.
5. $\{b, \bar{b}\}$ resp. $\{0, \bar{0}\}$. Express the third raw moment in $t = (d-\mu)/\sigma$.
6. Consider $\mathrm{E}[(X-d)(X-\bar{d})^2]$ for $d = 0$ and $d = b$.
7. Use concentration and dispersion. Variances: $\lambda \mathrm{E}^2[Y]$, $\lambda \mathrm{E}[Y^2]$, $\lambda b \mathrm{E}[Y]$.

Section 10.6

3. $X \sim \text{Bernoulli}(0.5)$, $Y \equiv 1$.
4. By the Rule of thumb 3.10.1, the ratio of the stop-loss premiums is about $5:3$.
6. For point (x, y) with $x > y$ to be in the support of the comonotonic joint cdf $H(x, y) = \min\{F_X(x), F_Y(y)\}$, we must have $H(x, y) > H(y, y)$. This is impossible because of $F_X(y) \geq F_Y(y)$.
7. In a table of probabilities, every row and every column has only one positive entry. The positive entries follow a diagonal pattern.
10. The conditional distribution of X, given $Z = z$ is again normal, with as parameters $\mathrm{E}[X|Z=z] = \mathrm{E}[X] + \rho\frac{\sigma_X}{\sigma_Z}(z - \mathrm{E}[Z])$ and $\mathrm{Var}[X|Z=z] = \sigma_X^2(1-\rho^2)$ for $\rho = r(X, Z)$.
12. $\Pr[g_i(U, Z) \leq x] = \int \Pr[F^{-1}_{X_i|Z=z}(U) \leq x] dF_Z(z) = \cdots$.
13. $\Pr[X \leq x | Y \leq y] = \Pr[X \leq x, Y \leq y] / \Pr[Y \leq y] \geq \cdots$, hence $\cdots$
14. Use $\Pr[X \leq x_1, X \leq x_2] \geq \Pr[X \leq x_1]\Pr[X \leq x_2]$, and condition on $Y = y$ and $Z = z$.
15. Prove that $C(1,1) = 1$ and $c(u,v) \geq 0$ if $|\alpha| \leq 1$, and that the marginal cdf's are uniform(0, 1). To determine the Spearman rank correlation of X and Y, compute $\iint uv\, c(u,v)\, du dv$ to show that this correlation is $\alpha/3$. $\tau = 2\alpha/9$.
16. $\Pr[X \leq x, Y \leq y] = \Pr[F_X(X) \leq F_X(x), F_Y(Y) \leq F_Y(y)]$.
17. $\Pr[(X - X')(Y - Y') > 0] = 2\int \Pr[X < x, Y < y | X' = x, Y' = y] dF(x, y)$. To prove the final assertion, let C and D be the respective copulas. Then for the ranks, we have $\mathrm{E}[D(U,V)] \geq \mathrm{E}[C(U,V)] \geq \mathrm{E}[C(U',V')]$, where the latter inequality is proven by writing, in the difference of the expectations, $C(u,v)$ as a double integral and invoking Fubini.
18. Both $\rho = 1$ and $\tau = 1$.
19. $r(X,Y) = \{e^\sigma - 1\}/\sqrt{(e^{\sigma^2}-1)(e-1)}$. Since $\sigma \to \infty$ implies $r(X,Y) \downarrow 0$, there exist perfectly dependent random variables with correlation arbitrarily close to zero. But $\rho = \tau = 1$ for any value of σ, hence Kendall's and Spearman's association measures are more well-behaved than Pearson's.
20. What does it mean that $\Pr[X \leq x]\Pr[Y \leq y] = \min\{\Pr[X \leq x], \Pr[Y \leq y]\}$ for all x, y?
21. Determine the distributions of $X + Y$ and $X^c + Y^c$.
22. Conditionally on $X = x$, the first term of S_u' equals x with probability one, the second has the conditional distribution of Y, given $X = x$.

Notes and references

CHAPTER 1

Basic material in the actuarial field on utility theory and insurance goes back to the work of Borch (1968, 1974). The origin of the utility concept dates back to Von Neumann and Morgenstern (1944). The Allais paradox is described in Allais (1953). Results on the stability of an insurance portfolio, see also Chapter 5, can be found in Bühlmann (1970). Recently an alternative ordering of risks concept based on Yaari's (1987) dual theory of risk has made its entrance in the actuarial literature. References are Wang & Young (1998) and Denuit *et al.* (1999). Both utility theory and Yaari's dual theory can be used to construct risk measures that are important in the framework of solvency, both in finance and in insurance, see e.g. Wason *et al.* (2001).

CHAPTER 2

A good reference for the individual model is Gerber (1979), as well as Bowers *et al.* (1986, 1997). Since the seminal article of Panjer (1981), many recursion relations for calculating the distribution of the individual model were given, based on the known recursion relations or involving manipulating power series, see e.g. Sundt & Jewell (1981). We refer to De Pril (1986) and Dhaene and De Pril (1994) for an overview of different methods.

CHAPTER 3

The chapter on collective models draws upon the textbook Bowers *et al.* (1986, 1997) already mentioned. An early reference is Beard *et al.* (1977, 1984), which contains a lot of material about the NP approximation. Other books covering this topic are Seal (1969), Bühlmann (1970), Gerber (1979), Goovaerts *et al.* (1990), Heilmann (1988) and Sundt (1999), as well as the recent work by Rolski *et al.* (1998). While collective risk models assume independence of the claim severities, a new trend is to study the sum of dependent risks, see e.g. Dhaene *et al.* (2002a,b). A text on statistical aspects of loss distributions is Hogg and Klugman (1984). Some references propagating the actuarial use of the inverse Gaussian distributions are Ter Berg (1980a, 1980b, 1994).

CHAPTER 4

Ruin theory started with F. Lundberg (1909), Cramér (1930, 1955) as well as O. Lundberg (1940). An interesting approach based on martingales can be found in Gerber (1979). The ruin probability as a stability criterion is described in Bühlmann (1970). The book by Beekman (1964) gives an early connection of Poisson processes and Wiener processes and is definitely worth reading in the context of financial insurance modelling. A recent book is Embrechts *et al.* (1997). Many papers have been published concerning the numerical calculation of ruin probabilities, starting with Goovaerts and De Vijlder (1984). The derivation of the algorithm (4.70) to compute ruin probabilities for discrete distributions can be found in Gerber (1989).

CHAPTER 5

The section connecting premium principles to the discrete ruin model is based on Bühlmann (1985); the section about insurance risk reduction by pooling is based on Gerber (1979). In the 1970's premium principles were a hot topic in actuarial research. The basics were introduced in Bühlmann (1970). See also Gerber (1979, 1983) and Goovaerts *et al.* (1984). The results in that period were mainly derived in the classical risk models with independent claims. Several sets of desirable properties for premium principles were derived, resulting in different outcomes. It emerged that general properties could not be applied to all insurance situations. While for independent risks the economic principle of subadditivity is desirable, it is clear that in some cases, superadditivity is desirable. Two unrelated earthquake risks may be insured for the total of the individual premiums, or somewhat less, but if they are related, the premium should be higher than that from an insurance point of view. Premium principles provide absolute quantities in some way, namely the price one has to pay for transferring the risk. Risk measures as they appear in finance, on the other hand, are relative, and serve only to rank risks. The desirable properties of premium principles are also used in deriving appropriate risk measures in finance, but quite often, the dependence structure is overlooked. Some recent results about premium principles can be found in Wang (1996). For a characterization of Wang's class of premium principles, see e.g. Goovaerts & Dhaene (1998).

CHAPTER 6

Pioneering work in the theoretical and practical aspects of bonus-malus systems can be found in Bichsel (1964), as well as in Loimaranta (1972). Lemaire (1985) gives a comprehensive description of the insurance aspects of bonus-malus systems. A paper trying to introduce penalization based both on claim intensity and claim severity is Frangos & Vrontos (2001). The study that led to the Dutch bonus-malus system described in this chapter was described fully in De Wit *et al.* (1982). Bonus-malus systems with non-symmetric loss functions are considered in Denuit & Dhaene (2001).

CHAPTER 7

The general idea of credibility theory can be traced back to the papers by Mowbray (1914) and Whitney (1918). A sound theoretical foundation was given by Bühlmann (1967, 1969). There are several approaches possible for introducing the ideas of credibility theory. The original idea was to introduce a risk parameter Θ, considered to be a random variable characterizing some hidden risk quality, and using a least squares error criterion. A more mathematical approach applies projections in Hilbert spaces, as in De Vijlder (1996). Of course these approaches are equivalent descriptions of the same phenomena. The educational approach taken in the text is based on the variance components model such as often encountered in econometrics. The advantage of this approach, apart of course from its simplicity and elegance, consists in the explicit relationship with ANOVA, in case of normality. A textbook on variance components models is Searle *et al.* (1992). We have limited ourselves to the basic credibility models of Bühlmann, because with these, all the relevant ideas of credibility theory can be illustrated, including the types of heterogeneity as well as the parameter estimation. For a more complete treatment of credibility, the reader is referred to Dannenburg *et al.* (1996), which was the basis for our Chapter 7, or to the Ph.D. thesis of Dannenburg (1996). The interpretation of a bonus-malus system by means of credibility theory was initiated by Norberg (1976); for the negative binomial model, we refer to Lemaire (1985).

CHAPTER 8

The paper by Nelder and Wedderburn (1972) introduces the generalized linear models. It gives a unified description of a broad class of statistical models, all with a stochastic regressand of exponential family type, of which the mean is related to a linear form in the regressors by some rather arbitrary link function. The textbook McCullagh and Nelder (1989) contains some applications in insurance rate making. Much more readable introductions in GLM application are provided by the manuals of, e.g., SAS and GLIM, see Francis *et al.* (1993). The heuristic methods we gave are treated more fully in Van Eeghen *et al.* (1983). Alting von Geusau (1989) attempts to fit a combined additive/multiplicative model to health insurance data.

CHAPTER 9

The first statistical approach to the IBNR problem goes back to Verbeek (1972). Another early reference is De Vijlder and Goovaerts (1979), in which the three dimensions of the problem are introduced. An encyclopedic treatment of the various methods is given in Taylor (1986). The relation with generalized additive and multiplicative linear models is explored in Verrall (1996, 2000). *The* model behind the chain ladder method is defended in Mack (1993). Doray (1996) gives UMVUEs of the mean and variance of IBNR claims for a model with lognormal claim figures, explained by row and column factors. While all of the above mentioned literature is concerned with the statistical approach to the estimation of the claims run-off, the present research goes in the direction of determining the economic value of run-off claims, taking into account discounting. The statistical framework gives the extrapolated claim figures as a cash flow, and the calendar year becomes definitely of another nature than the development year and the year of origin because it includes inflation and discounting. A reference dealing with this different approach is Goovaerts and Redant (1999).

CHAPTER 10

The notion of stop-loss order entered into the actuarial literature through the paper by Bühlmann *et al.* (1977). In the statistical literature many results generalizing stop-loss order are available in the context of convex order. See, e.g., Karlin and Studden (1966). A standard work for stochastic orders is Shaked & Shanthikumar (1994). Applications of ordering principles in operations research and reliability can be found in Stoyan (1983). Recently, the concept of convex order has been applied in the financial approach to insurance where the insurance risk and the financial risk are integrated. Object of study are sums of dependent risks. Some very interesting properties have been found recently and they will be published in a subsequent book by the same authors. Comonotonic risks play an important role in these dependency models. A review paper about this topic is Dhaene *et al.* (2002a,b).

Chapter 10 has some forerunners. The monograph by Kaas *et al.* (1994) was based on the Ph.D. thesis by Van Heerwaarden (1991), see also the corresponding chapters of Goovaerts *et al.* (1990).

REFERENCES

Allais M. (1953). "Le comportement de l'homme rationnel devant le risque: critique des postulats et axiomes de l'Ecole Americaine", *Econometrica*, 21, 503–546.

Alting von Geusau B.J.J. (1989). "The application of additive and multiplicative General Linear Interactive Models (GLIM) in health insurance", XXI ASTIN Colloquium, New York.

Beard R.E., Pentikäinen T. & Pesonen E. (1977, 1984). "Risk theory", Chapman and Hall, London.

Beekman J.A. (1964). "Two stochastic processes", Halsted Press, New York.

Bichsel F. (1964). "Erfahrungs-Tarifierung in der Motorfahrzeughaftplicht-Versicherung", *Mitteilungen der Vereinigung Schweizerischer Versicherungsmathematiker*, 64, 119–130.

Borch K. (1968). "The economics of uncertainty", Princeton University Press, Princeton.

Borch K. (1974). "The mathematical theory of insurance", Lexington Books, Toronto.

Bowers N.L., Gerber H.U., Hickman J.C., Jones D.A. & Nesbitt C.J. (1986, 1997). "Actuarial mathematics", Society of Actuaries, Itasca, Illinois.

Bühlmann H. (1967). "Experience rating and credibility I", *ASTIN Bulletin*, 4, 199–207.

Bühlmann H. (1969). "Experience rating and credibility II", *ASTIN Bulletin*, 5, 157–165.

Bühlmann H. (1970). "Mathematical methods in risk theory", Springer Verlag, Berlin.

Bühlmann H., Gagliardi B., Gerber H.U. & Straub E. (1977). "Some inequalities for stop-loss premiums", *ASTIN Bulletin*, 9, 169–177.

Bühlmann H. (1985). "Premium calculation from top down", *ASTIN Bulletin*, 15, 89–101.

Cramér H. (1930). "On the mathematical theory of risk", Skandia Jubilee Volume, Stockholm.

Cramér H. (1955). "Collective risk theory, a survey of the theory from the point of view of stochastic processes", Skandia Jubilee Volume, Stockholm.

Dannenburg D.R., Kaas R. & Goovaerts M.J. (1996). "Practical actuarial credibility models", Institute of Actuarial Science, Amsterdam.

Dannenburg D.R. (1996). "Basic actuarial credibility models — Evaluations and extensions", Ph.D. Thesis, Thesis/Tinbergen Institute, Amsterdam.

De Pril N. (1986). "On the exact computation of the aggregate claims distribution in the individual life model", *ASTIN Bulletin*, 16, 109–112.

De Vijlder F. (1996). "Advanced risk theory, a self-contained introduction", Editions de l'Université de Bruxelles, Brussels.

De Vijlder F. & Goovaerts M.J. (eds.) (1979). "Proceedings of the first meeting of the contact group Actuarial Sciences", Wettelijk Depot D/1979/2376/5, Leuven.

Denuit M., Dhaene J. & Van Wouwe M. (1999). "The economics of insurance: a review and some recent developments", *Mitteilungen der Vereinigung Schweizerischer Versicherungsmathematiker*, 99, 137–175.

Denuit M. & Dhaene J. (2001). "Bonus-malus scales using exponential loss functions", *Blätter der Deutsche Gesellschaft für Versicherungsmathematik*, 25, 13–27.

De Wit G.W. *et al.* (1982). "New motor rating structure in the Netherlands", ASTIN-groep Nederland.

Dhaene J. & De Pril N. (1994). "On a class of approximative computation methods in the individual risk model", *Insurance : Mathematics and Economics*, 14, 181–196.

Dhaene J., Denuit M., Goovaerts M.J., Kaas R. & Vyncke D. (2002a). "The concept of comonotonicity in actuarial science and finance: Theory", *Insurance: Mathematics & Economics*, forthcoming.

Dhaene J., Denuit M., Goovaerts M.J., Kaas R. & Vyncke D. (2002b). "The concept of comonotonicity in actuarial science and finance: Applications", *Insurance: Mathematics & Economics*, forthcoming.

Doray L.G. (1996). "UMVUE of the IBNR Reserve in a lognormal linear regression model", *Insurance: Mathematics & Economics*, 18, 43–58.

Embrechts P., Klüppelberg C. & Mikosch T. (1997). "Modelling extremal events for insurance and finance", Springer-Verlag, Berlin.

Francis P., Green M. & Payne C. (eds.) (1993). "The GLIM System: Generalized Linear Interactive Modelling", Oxford University Press, Oxford.

Frangos N. & Vrontos S. (2001). "Design of optimal bonus-malus systems with a frequency and a severity component on an individual basis in automobile insurance", *ASTIN Bulletin*, 31, 5–26.

Gerber H.U. (1979). "An introduction to mathematical risk theory", Huebner Foundation Monograph 8, distributed by Richard D. Irwin, Homewood Illinois.

Gerber H.U. (1985). "On additive principles of zero utility", *Insurance: Mathematics & Economics*, 4, 249–252.

Gerber H.U. (1989). "From the convolution of uniform distributions to the probability of ruin", *Mitteilungen der Vereinigung Schweizerischer Versicherungsmathematiker*, 89, 249–252.

Goovaerts M.J. & De Vijlder F. (1984). "A stable recursive algorithm for evaluation of ultimate ruin probabilities", *ASTIN Bulletin*, 14, 53–60.

Goovaerts M.J., De Vijlder F. & Haezendonck J. (1984). "Insurance premiums", North-Holland, Amsterdam.

Goovaerts M.J. & Dhaene J. (1998). "On the characterization of Wang's class of premium principles", *Transactions of the 26th International Congress of Actuaries*, 4, 121–134.

Goovaerts M.J., Kaas R., Van Heerwaarden A.E. & Bauwelinckx T. (1990). "Effective actuarial methods", North-Holland, Amsterdam.

Goovaerts M.J. & Redant R. (1999). "On the distribution of IBNR reserves", *Insurance: Mathematics & Economics*, 25, 1–9.

Heilmann W.-R. (1988). "Fundamentals of risk theory", Verlag Versicherungswirtschaft e.V., Karlsruhe.

Hogg R.V. & Klugman S.A. (1984). "Loss distributions", Wiley, New York.

Kaas R., Van Heerwaarden A.E., Goovaerts M.J. (1994). "Ordering of actuarial risks", Caire Education Series, Amsterdam.

Karlin S. & Studden W.J. (1966). "Tchebycheff systems with applications in analysis and statistics", Interscience Publishers, Wiley, New York.

Lemaire J. (1985). "Automobile insurance: actuarial models", Kluwer, Dordrecht.

Loimaranta K. (1972). "Some asymptotic properties of bonus systems", *ASTIN Bulletin*, 6, 233–245.

Lundberg F. (1909). "Über die Theorie der Rückversicherung", *Transactions of the first International Congress of Actuaries*, 2, 877–955.

Lundberg O. (1940). "On random processes and their applications to sickness and accidents statistics", Inaugural Dissertation, Uppsala.

Mack T. (1993). "Distribution-free calculation of the standard error of chain ladder reserve estimates", *ASTIN Bulletin*, 23, 213–225.

McCullagh P. & Nelder J.A. (1989). "Generalized Linear Models", Chapman and Hall, Londen.

Mowbray A.H. (1914). "How extensive a payroll exposure is necessary to give a dependable pure premium", *Proceedings of the Casualty Actuarial Society*, 1, 24–30.

Nelder J.A. & Wedderburn, R.W.M. (1972). "Generalized Linear Models", Journal of the Royal Statistical Society, A, 135, 370–384.

Norberg R. (1976). "A credibility theory for automobile bonus systems", *Scandinavian Actuarial Journal*, 92–107.

Panjer H.H. (1981). "Recursive evaluation of a family of compound distributions", *ASTIN Bulletin*, 12, 22–26.

Rolski T., Schmidli H., Schmidt V. & Teugels J. (1998). "Stochastic Processes for Insurance and Finance", Wiley, Chichester.

Searle S.R., Casella G. & McCulloch C.E. (1992). "Variance components", Wiley, New York.

Seal H.L. (1969). "Stochastic theory of a risk business", Wiley, New York.

Shaked M. & Shanthikumar J.G. (1994). "Stochastic orders and their applications", Academic Press, New York.

Stoyan (1983). "Comparison methods for queues and other stochastic models", Wiley, New York.

Sundt B. (1999). "An introduction to non-life insurance mathematics", 4th edition, Verlag Versicherungswirtschaft GmbH, Karlsruhe.

Sundt B. & Jewell W.S. (1981). "Further results of recursive evaluation of compound distributions", *ASTIN Bulletin*, 12, 27–39.

Taylor G.C. (1986). "Claims reserving in non-life insurance", North-Holland, Amsterdam.

Ter Berg P. (1980a), "On the loglinear Poisson and Gamma model", *ASTIN-Bulletin*, 11, 35–40.

Ter Berg P. (1980b), "Two pragmatic approaches to loglinear claim cost analysis", *ASTIN-Bulletin*, 11, 77–90.

Ter Berg P. (1994), "Deductibles and the Inverse Gaussian distribution", *ASTIN-Bulletin*, 24, 319–323.

Van Eeghen J., Greup E.K., Nijssen J.A. (1983). "Rate making", Nationale-Nederlanden N.V., Rotterdam.

Van Heerwaarden A.E. (1991). "Ordering of risks — Theory and actuarial applications", Thesis Publishers, Amsterdam.

Verbeek H.G. (1972). "An approach to the analysis of claims experience in motor liability excess of loss reinsurance", *ASTIN Bulletin*, 6, 195–202.

Verrall R. (1996). "Claims reserving and generalized additive models", *Insurance: Mathematics & Economics*, 19, 31–43.

Verrall R. (2000). "An investigation into stochastic claims reserving models and the chain-ladder technique", *Insurance: Mathematics & Economics*, 26, 91–99.

Von Neumann J. & Morgenstern O. (1944). "Theory of games and economic behavior", Princeton University Press, Princeton.

Wang S. (1996). "Premium calculation by transforming the layer premium density", *ASTIN Bulletin*, 26, 71–92.

Wang S. & Young V. (1998). "Ordering risks: expected utility theory versus Yaari's dual theory of risk", *Insurance: Mathematics & Economics*, 22, 145–161.

Wason S. *et al.* (2001). "Draft report of solvency working party, prepared for IAA Insurance Regulation Committee", unpublished.

Whitney A.W. (1918). "The theory of experience rating", *Proceedings of the Casualty Actuarial Society*, 4, 274–292.

Yaari M.E. (1987). "The dual theory of choice under risk", *Econometrica*, 55, 95–115.

Distribution	Density	Parameters, range	Moments, cumulants	Mgf
Uniform(a,b)	$\dfrac{1}{b-a}$	$a < x < b$	$\mathrm{E} = (a+b)/2$, $\mathrm{Var} = (b-a)^2/12$, $\gamma = 0$	$\dfrac{e^{bt} - e^{at}}{(b-a)t}$
Normal(μ,σ^2)	$\dfrac{1}{\sigma\sqrt{2\pi}} \exp \dfrac{-(x-\mu)^2}{2\sigma^2}$	$\sigma > 0$	$\mathrm{E} = \mu$, $\mathrm{Var} = \sigma^2$, $\gamma = 0\ (\kappa_j = 0, j \geq 3)$	$\exp(\mu t + \frac{1}{2}\sigma^2 t^2)$
Gamma(α,β)	$\dfrac{\beta^\alpha}{\Gamma(\alpha)} x^{\alpha-1} e^{-\beta x}$	$\alpha > 0, \beta > 0$ $x > 0$	$\mathrm{E} = \alpha/\beta$, $\mathrm{Var} = \alpha/\beta^2$, $\gamma = 2\alpha^{-1/2}$	$\left(\dfrac{\beta}{\beta - t}\right)^\alpha \ (t < \beta)$
Exponential(β)	$\equiv$ Gamma(1,β)			
$\chi^2(k)$	$\equiv$ Gamma($k/2$,1/2)			
Inverse Gaussian(α,β)	$\dfrac{\alpha x^{-3/2}}{\sqrt{2\pi\beta}} \exp\left(\dfrac{-(\alpha - \beta x)^2}{2\beta x}\right)$	$\alpha > 0, \beta > 0$ $x > 0$	$\mathrm{E} = \alpha/\beta$, $\mathrm{Var} = \alpha/\beta^2$, $\gamma = 3\alpha^{-1/2}$	$e^{\alpha(1-\sqrt{1-2t/\beta})}$ $(t \leq \beta/2)$
	$F(x) = \Phi\left(\dfrac{-\alpha}{\sqrt{\beta x}} + \sqrt{\beta x}\right) - e^{2\alpha}\Phi\left(\dfrac{-\alpha}{\sqrt{\beta x}} - \sqrt{\beta x}\right)$			
Beta(a,b)	$\dfrac{1}{B(a,b)} x^{a-1}(1-x)^{b-1}$	$a > 0, b > 0$ $0 < x < 1$	$\mathrm{E} = \dfrac{a}{a+b}$, $\mathrm{Var} = \dfrac{ab}{(a+b+1)(a+b)^2}$	
Lognormal(μ,σ^2)	$\dfrac{1}{x\sigma\sqrt{2\pi}} e^{\frac{-(\log x - \mu)^2}{2\sigma^2}}$	$\sigma > 0$ $x > 0$	$\mathrm{E} = e^{\mu + \sigma^2/2}$, $\mathrm{Var} = e^{2\mu + 2\sigma^2} - e^{2\mu + \sigma^2}$, $\gamma = c^3 + 3c$ with $c^2 = \mathrm{Var}/\mathrm{E}^2$	
Pareto(α,x_0)	$\dfrac{\alpha x_0^\alpha}{x^{\alpha+1}}$	$\alpha > 0$, $x > x_0 > 0$	$\mathrm{E} = \dfrac{\alpha x_0}{\alpha - 1}$, $\mathrm{Var} = \dfrac{\alpha x_0^2}{(\alpha-1)^2(\alpha-2)}$	

Table A Continuous distributions

Distribution	Density	Parameters, range	Moments, cumulants	Mgf
Binomial(n,p)	$\binom{n}{x} p^x (1-p)^{n-x}$	$0 \leq p \leq 1$, $n = 1, 2, \ldots$, $x = 0, 1, \ldots, n$	$\mathrm{E} = np$, $\mathrm{Var} = np(1-p)$, $\gamma = np(1-p)(1-2p)/\sigma^3$	$(1 - p + pe^t)^n$
Bernoulli(p)	$\equiv$ Binomial(1,p)			
Poisson(λ)	$e^{-\lambda} \frac{\lambda^x}{x!}$	$\lambda \geq 0$, $x = 0, 1, 2, \ldots$	$\mathrm{E} = \mathrm{Var} = \lambda$, $\gamma = \lambda^{-1/2}$, $\kappa_j = \lambda$, $j = 1, 2, \ldots$	$\exp[\lambda(e^t - 1)]$
Negative binomial(r,p)	$\binom{r+x-1}{x} p^r (1-p)^x$	$r > 0$, $0 < p \leq 1$, $x = 0, 1, 2, \ldots$	$\mathrm{E} = r(1-p)/p$, $\mathrm{Var} = r(1-p)/p^2$, $\gamma = r(1-p)(2-p)/p^3/\sigma^3$	$\left(\frac{p}{1-(1-p)e^t}\right)^r$
Geometric(p)	$\equiv$ Negative binomial(1,p)			

Table B Discrete distributions

	+0.00		+0.05		+0.10		+0.15		+0.20	
x	$\Phi(x)$	$\pi(x)$	$\Phi(x)$	$\pi(x)$	$\Phi(x)$	$\pi(x)$	$\Phi(x)$	$\pi(x)$	$\Phi(x)$	$\pi(x)$
0.00	0.500	0.3989	0.520	0.3744	0.540	0.3509	0.560	0.3284	0.579	0.3069
0.25	0.599	0.2863	0.618	0.2668	0.637	0.2481	0.655	0.2304	0.674	0.2137
0.50	0.691	0.1978	0.709	0.1828	0.726	0.1687	0.742	0.1554	0.758	0.1429
0.75	0.773	0.1312	0.788	0.1202	0.802	0.1100	0.816	0.1004	0.829	0.0916
1.00	0.841	0.0833	0.853	0.0757	0.864	0.0686	0.875	0.0621	0.885	0.0561
1.25	0.894	0.0506	0.903	0.0455	0.911	0.0409	0.919	0.0367	0.926	0.0328
1.50	0.933	0.0293	0.939	0.0261	0.945	0.0232	0.951	0.0206	0.955	0.0183
1.75	0.960	0.0162	0.964	0.0143	0.968	0.0126	0.971	0.0111	0.974	0.0097
2.00	0.977	0.0085	0.980	0.0074	0.982	0.0065	0.984	0.0056	0.986	0.0049
2.25	0.988	0.0042	0.989	0.0037	0.991	0.0032	0.992	0.0027	0.993	0.0023
2.50	0.994	0.0020	0.995	0.0017	0.995	0.0015	0.996	0.0012	0.997	0.0011
2.75	0.997	0.0009	0.997	0.0008	0.998	0.0006	0.998	0.0005	0.998	0.0005
3.00	0.999	0.0004	0.999	0.0003	0.999	0.0003	0.999	0.0002	0.999	0.0002
3.25	0.999	0.0002	1.000	0.0001	1.000	0.0001	1.000	0.0001	1.000	0.0001
3.50	1.000	0.0001	1.000	0.0000	1.000	0.0000	1.000	0.0000	1.000	0.0000

Table C Standard normal distribution; cdf $\Phi(x)$ and stop-loss premiums $\pi(x)$

x	1.282	1.645	1.960	2.326	2.576	3.090	3.291	3.891	4.417
$\Phi(x)$	0.900	0.950	0.975	0.990	0.995	0.999	0.9995	0.99995	0.999995

Table D Selected quantiles of the standard normal distribution

Examples of use: $\Phi(1.17) \approx 0.6\Phi(1+0.15) + 0.4\Phi(1+0.20) \approx 0.879$; $\Phi^{-1}(0.1) = -1.282$; $\Phi(-x) = 1 - \Phi(x)$; $\pi(-x) = x + \pi(x)$.

NP approximation: If S has mean μ, variance σ^2 and skewness γ, then

$$\Pr\left[\frac{S-\mu}{\sigma} \leq x\right] \approx \Phi\left(\sqrt{\frac{9}{\gamma^2} + \frac{6x}{\gamma} + 1} - \frac{3}{\gamma}\right)$$

$$\text{and} \quad \Pr\left[\frac{S-\mu}{\sigma} \leq s + \frac{\gamma}{6}(s^2-1)\right] \approx \Phi(s)$$

Translated gamma approximation: If $G(\cdot;\alpha,\beta)$ is the gamma cdf, then

$$\Pr[S \leq x] \approx G(x - x_0; \alpha, \beta) \quad \text{with} \quad \alpha = \frac{4}{\gamma^2}; \beta = \frac{2}{\gamma\sigma}; x_0 = \mu - \frac{2\sigma}{\gamma}.$$

Distribution	Density, domain	Reparametrizations $\phi = \cdots;\ \mu = \cdots$ Canonical link $\theta(\mu) =$	Cumulant function $b(\theta)$ $\mathrm{E}[Y;\theta] = \mu(\theta) = b'(\theta)$ $V(\mu) = b''(\theta(\mu))$
$\mathrm{N}(\mu, \sigma^2)$	$\frac{1}{\sigma\sqrt{2\pi}} e^{-\frac{(y-\mu)^2}{2\sigma^2}}$	$\phi = \sigma^2$ $\theta(\mu) = \mu$	$\frac{\theta^2}{2}$ θ 1
$\mathrm{Poisson}(\mu)$	$e^{-\mu}\frac{\mu^y}{y!}$ $y = 0, 1, 2, \ldots$	$\phi = 1$ $\theta(\mu) = \log\mu$	e^θ e^θ μ
$\mathrm{Poisson}(\mu, \phi)$	$e^{-\mu/\phi}\frac{(\mu/\phi)^{(y/\phi)}}{(y/\phi)!}$ $y = 0, \phi, 2\phi, \ldots$	$\theta(\mu) = \log\mu$	e^θ e^θ μ
$\mathrm{Binomial}(m, p)$	$\binom{m}{y} p^y (1-p)^{m-y}$ $y = 0, \ldots, m$	$\phi = 1;\ \mu = mp$ $\theta(\mu) = \log\frac{\mu}{m-\mu}$	$m\log(1 + e^\theta)$ $\frac{m\,e^\theta}{1+e^\theta}$ $\mu(1 - \frac{\mu}{m})$
$\mathrm{Negbin}(r, p)$	$\binom{r+y-1}{y} p^r (1-p)^y$ $y = 0, 1, \ldots$	$\phi = 1;\ \mu = \frac{r(1-p)}{p}$ $\theta(\mu) = \log\frac{\mu}{r+\mu}$	$-r\log(1 - e^\theta)$ $\frac{r\,e^\theta}{1-e^\theta}$ $\mu(1 + \frac{\mu}{r})$
$\mathrm{Gamma}(\alpha, \beta)$	$\frac{1}{\Gamma(\alpha)}\beta^\alpha y^{\alpha-1} e^{-\beta y}$ $y > 0$	$\phi = \frac{1}{\alpha};\ \mu = \frac{\alpha}{\beta}$ $\theta(\mu) = -\frac{1}{\mu}$	$-\log(-\theta)$ $-\frac{1}{\theta}$ μ^2
$\mathrm{IG}(\alpha, \beta)$	$\frac{\alpha y^{-3/2}}{\sqrt{2\pi\beta}} \exp\frac{-(\alpha-\beta y)^2}{2\beta y}$ $y > 0$	$\phi = \frac{\beta}{\alpha^2};\ \mu = \frac{\alpha}{\beta}$ $\theta(\mu) = -\frac{1}{2\mu^2}$	$-\sqrt{-2\theta}$ $\frac{1}{\sqrt{-2\theta}}$ μ^3

Table E The main classes of distributions in the GLM exponential dispersion family, parametrized in the customary way and with μ, ϕ and θ, ϕ reparametrizations, and some more properties

Index